Programming the Raspberry Pi Pico/W in MicroPython

Third Edition

Harry Fairhead & Mike James

I/O Press
I Programmer Library

Harry Fairhead & Mike James,
Programming the Raspberry Pi Pico in MicroPython
3rd Edition
ISBN Paperback: 9781871962970
ISBN Hardback: 9781871962376
First Printing, 2025
Revision 0

Published by IO Press   www.iopress.info
In association with I Programmer   www.i-programmer.info
and with I o T Programmer   www.iot-programmer.com

The publisher recognizes and respects all marks used by companies and manufacturers as a means to distinguish their products. All brand names and product names mentioned in this book are trade marks or service marks of their respective companies and our omission of trade marks is not an attempt to infringe on the property of others.

In particular we acknowledge that Raspberry Pi and Pico are registered trademarks of the Raspberry Pi Foundation.

For updates, errata, links to resources and the source code for the programs in this book, visit its dedicated page on the IO Press website: iopress.info.

Preface

The Raspberry Pi Pico is a remarkable microcontroller. Originally based on the RP2040 processor chip, designed by Raspberry Pi specially for this small form factor, it was launched in 2020. The Pico W with WiFi and Bluetooth followed in 2022. At the end of 2024 the Pico 2 was announced, followed shortly by the Pico 2W, the WiFi version which is identical to it in every other respect. The Pico 2 has double the memory of the Pico and uses a newly introduced chip, the RP2350, which has some significant improvements. The differences between the two generations are set out in Chapter 1 and specific differences are highlighted in the following chapters. Otherwise, throughout the book, references to "the Pico" encompass all four variants.

The MicroPython language is a good choice for programming the Pico. It isn't the fastest way, but in most cases it is fast enough to interface with the Pico's hardware and its big advantage is that it is easy to use. As a high-level language, MicroPython is based on Python 3 and is fully object-oriented. This means that you can create classes to encapsulate hardware and make your code easier to use and understand. It is also easier to implement complex algorithms and so make your data processing easier. In general, you can take an existing Python 3 program and simply run it under MicroPython, usually with no changes. If there are any changes then they are generally minor.

Another good thing about MicroPython on the Pico is that it is very easy to get started. After a simple installation procedure you have a working MicroPython machine which you can program almost at once using the Thonny IDE. While Thonny is a useful and capable IDE, our preference of IDE is VS Code not only because it has more extensive syntax checking and input prompting, but also because of the Pico VS Code extension. .

The Pico has so many resources that a comprehensive account would fill a book twice this size. In order to make things fit in the space available we have concentrated on things that are accessible from MicroPython and that are basic to getting started. We have avoided "advanced" topics which generally lead the beginner into deep water far too quickly. However, this edition covers the use of the second core, uasyncio and asynchronous programming in general. Another "advanced" topic that is covered is the use of the PIO (Programmable I/O) because it is one of the key advantages of using the Pico, allowing you to delegate interaction with external hardware to a peripheral. Using this facility you can avoid any problems that you might have with MicroPython's lack of speed as you can write a PIO program which runs at the full speed of the Pico. The PIO isn't the solution to every problem, but although challenging it is very useful and a lot of fun.

This book is about understanding concepts and the acquisition of skills. It doesn't teach you Python or MicroPython in the sense of basic programming, but a knowledge of how to program in almost any language is all you really need. All examples are written in a very simple style that avoids the use of some features of Python that are very "neat" but tend to obscure the meaning of the code from a beginner. You can easily refactor any of the examples into classes that suit your particular purpose and programming style.

While it is not a projects book, there isn't much left for you to do to round out the embryonic projects that are used as examples. All the programs in the book are included in its GitHub repo using the names assigned to them. The hope is that by the end of the book you will know how to tackle your own projects and get them safely to completion without wasting time in trial and error.

Thanks to our tireless editors Sue Gee and Kay Ewbank. Programming is the art of great precision, but English doesn't come with a built-in linter. Errors that remain, and we hope they are few, are ours.

For any updates or errata, links to its GitHub repo and to resources including recommendations for obtaining electronic components, visit its dedicated page on the IO Press website: iopress.info.

You can also contact us at harry.fairhead@i-programmer.info or mike.james@i-programmer.info

Harry Fairhead
Mike James
July, 2025

Table of Contents

Chapter 5
Some Electronics   **49**

Chapter 6
Simple Input   **75**

Chapter 7
Advanced Input – Events and Interrupts   **91**

Chapter 8
Pulse Width Modulation   **109**

Chapter 12
Using The I2C Bus   **183**

Chapter 13
Using The PIO   **203**

Chapter 14
The DHT22 Sensor Implementing A Custom Protocol   **227**

Chapter 15
The 1-Wire Bus And The DS1820   **245**

Chapter 16
The Serial Port   **277**

Chapter 1

The Raspberry Pi Pico – Before We Begin

The Raspberry Pi Pico is a bold step for the Raspberry Pi world. It isn't a full System On a Chip (SoC), but a microcontroller - a small system with a minimal operating system designed to be used to control and connect to other devices. Its uses range from controlling washing machines to making games that use buttons and lights. Unlike the Raspberry Pi Zero, which is often used as a microcontroller, you can program it without having to struggle with Linux drivers and system commands. Perhaps more importantly, you don't have to fight against the multi-tasking behavior of Linux which makes getting timing right difficult.

Programming the Pico means you know exactly what is happening and when, so timing becomes so much easier. It doesn't mean it's a solved problem, but it is easier. However, not having an operating system also brings its own problems and if you are used to working with the Pi Zero, say, you might well find that there are times when you would like to make a Linux call to solve a problem. Our opinion, and I hope yours too once you have read on, is that overall for the type of task the Pico is suited to, not having an operating system is a big plus point.

Some Advantages of the Pico

As to comparing the Pico to alternative microcontrollers, its big advantage is that it is powerful. It has a fast processor with enough memory to get most jobs done. It also has a great many built-in peripherals and can talk to devices such as the PWM, I2C, SPI, UART and ADC without much trouble and, with the help of the innovative PIO (Programmable I/O), just about anything else, including custom interfaces and the 1-Wire bus.

The PIO is a special feature of the Pico that is worth knowing about sooner rather than later. It is a processor in its own right and while it is restricted to only a handful of instructions it is targeted at the very specific job of working with pulsed input and output. This means that you can often write a fairly simple program to enable the PIO to code and decode any protocol that is or isn't already supported. For example, in Chapter 14 we implement a 1-Wire bus protocol and so extend the Pico to working with this popular class of device. It doesn't just stop at new protocols. For example, if you find an I2C or SPI device that doesn't quite fit into the very loose specifications of these two protocols, or goes beyond them in some way, then you can implement custom versions. Going beyond the very practical, it is worth saying that programming the PIO is great fun and very educational. It gives you an insight into how assembly language works in general.

Pico Variants

There are four flavors of Pico, the Pico and the improved Pico 2 and the W versions of these two with WiFi and Bluetooth. The big feature of the Pico 2 is its security features that make it suitable for industrial applications, but at the moment these features are not available via MicroPython and are not well supported by the C SDK. What this means is that from the point of view of the Python programmer, and even most C programmers, the Pico 2 is best regarded as a faster Pico.

The Pico 2 has double the memory of the Pico and uses a newly introduced chip, the RP2350, which has some significant improvements over the RP2040 used in the original Pico. The first is that is uses dual ARM Cortex M33 processors clocked at 150MHz compared to the 130MHz for the RP2040. This makes the processor faster. The RP2350 also has additional I/O – more GPIO lines, more PWM generators and ADC channels, but these are only available if you purchase the chip separately to build a custom Pico-like device. The Pico 2 is restricted to the same number of GPIO lines, PWM generators and ADCs as the Pico due to limitations on the overall design and the need for backward compatibility.

The Pico 2 introduces the possibility of using something other than an ARM processor at the heart of the board. The RP2350 has both a Dual Cortex-M33 and a Hazard3 RISC V processor. There is very little advantage in using the RISC V processor and it is currently not supported by MicroPython and so it can be ignored.

The key points about the Pico and Pico 2 hardware are:

Pico	Pico 2
RP2040	RP2350
Dual-core Arm Cortex M0+ processor, flexible clock running up to 133 MHz	Dual Cortex-M33 or Hazard3 processors at up to 150MHz
264KB of SRAM	520KB of SRAM
2MB of onboard Flash memory	4MB of on-board flash memory
USB 1.1 with device and host support	USB 1.1 with device and host support
Low-power sleep and dormant modes	
Drag-and-drop programming using mass storage over USB	
26 × multi-function GPIO pins	
2 × SPI, 2 × I2C, 2 × UART, 3 × 12-bit ADC,	2× SPI, 2× I2C, 2× UART, 3× 12-bit ADC,
16 × controllable PWM channels	24× controllable PWM channels but only 16 available for use
1x RTC, 1× Timer with 4 alarms	1× AON Timer, 2× Timer with 4 alarms
Temperature sensor	
Accelerated floating-point libraries on-chip	
2 × Programmable IO (PIO) blocks	3 × Programmable IO (PIO) blocks
Synchronous Serial Interface (SSI)	QSPI Memory Interface (QMI)
	high-speed serial transmit (HSTX)
	True Random Number Generator block
	SHA-256 Accelerator
	8 kB of one-time programmable storage (OTP)
	Glitch Detector

The good news is that the Pico and Pico 2 have identical pinouts:

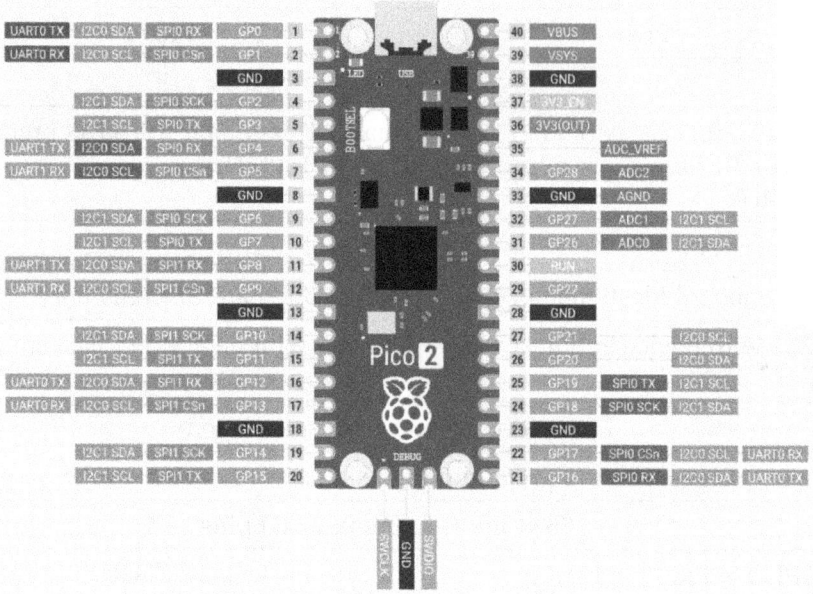

The WiFi version of both the Pico and Pico 2 is slightly different in the positioning of the debug connections but otherwise identical:

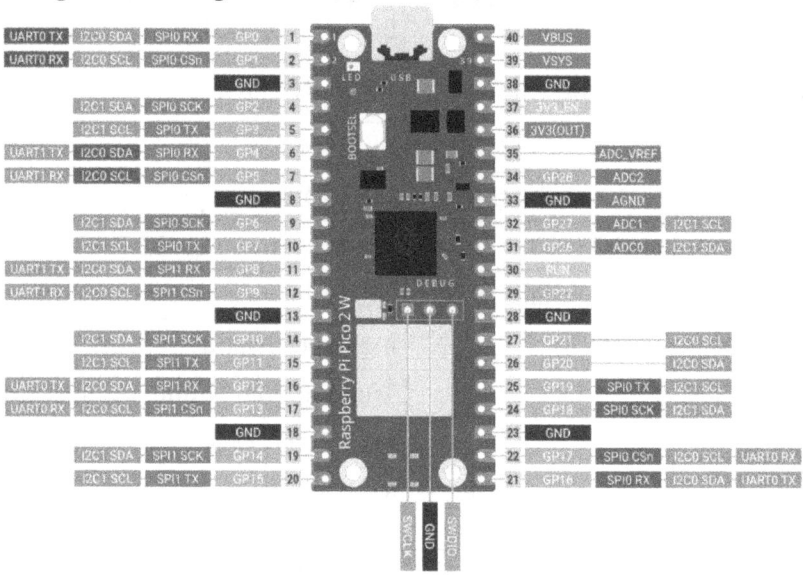

What all this means is that you can mostly treat the electrical connections for the Pico, Pico 2, Pico W and Pico 2W as being exactly the same. You can see larger color versions of these diagrams on the book's web page.

Alternative Pico Implementations

Both the RP2040 and the RP2350 can be bought as standalone chips and used to make alternatives to the Pico implementations. Some are very small and some have extras on board:

In particular, the Arduino family includes an RP2040-based board. In this case you have a choice of using the Arduino SDK or the Pico SDK.

These alternatives to the Pico are easy to use because they operate just like the Pico. You can program them using MicroPython and the same environment. The only differences might be that the smaller form factors expose fewer hardware lines so you might not be able to use everything you can use on the full Pico. In the remainder of this book the programs target the Raspberry Pi Pico, but they should just work or be easily modifiable for any device that used the RP2040.

There is also the problem of how to connect to the Pico. As it comes, the Pico has no pins soldered to its PCB. For development you either need to buy a slightly upgraded Pico or Pico 2, the Pico H/2H or HW/2HW with pins already soldered, or you need to solder your own.

What To Expect

There are no complete projects in this book – although some examples come very close and it is clear that some of them could be used together to create finished projects. The reason for this is that the focus is on learning how things work so that you can move on and do things that are non-standard.

What matters is that you can reason about what the processor is doing and how it interacts with the real world in real time. This is the big difference between desktop and embedded programming. In the desktop world you don't really care much about when something happens, but when you are programming a physical system you care very much.

This is a book about understanding general principles and making things work at the lowest possible level. This knowledge isn't always necessary when you are working on a relatively slow system in MicroPython, but it is always helpful for understanding what is going on when things go wrong. When you are working directly with the hardware knowing what is happening matters.

All of the examples are as basic as possible and the code is designed to be as easy to understand as possible. In most cases this means avoiding the use of constants that appear to come from nowhere and functions that make it difficult to see the basic steps. Also error handling is reduced to a bare minimum – simple programs look complicated if you add error handling code. Of course, there is no reason not to refactor these examples into something that looks more like production code and the effort in doing this is much less than getting the basic programs working in the first place.

Rather than go through multiple possible configurations for a development environment, this book uses Thonny and VS Code from the start. If you want to work in a different way then the documentation has instructions.

What Do You Need?
Well – a Pico at least and to make the most of this book a Pico 2W! In fact you would be well advised to buy at least two Picos – accidents happen. The Pico is small and lacks an operating system, so running all of the software you need to create programs on it needs another machine – the development machine. The good news is that you can use almost any desktop machine – PC, Mac or Linux system. If you want to use a Raspberry Pi then a Pi 4/5 or Pi 400/500 is recommended as running development software needs a reasonably powerful machine.

As to additional hardware over and above the Picos, you will need a solderless prototype board and some hookup wires – known as Dupont wires. You will also need some LEDs, a selection of resistors, some 2N2222 or other general purpose transistors and any of the sensors used in later chapters. See the Resources page for this book on the I/O Press website for links. It is probably better to buy what you need as you choose to implement one of the projects, but an alternative is to buy one of the many "getting started" kits. You will probably still need to buy some extra components, however.

While you don't need to know how to solder, you will need to be able to hook up a circuit on a prototyping board. A multimeter (less than $10) is useful, but if you are serious about electronic projects, investing in a logic analyzer (less than $100) will repay itself in no time at all.

A solderless prototype board and some Dupont wires

You can get small analyzers that plug in via a USB port and use an application to show you what is happening. It is only with a multichannel logic analyzer that you have any hope of understanding what is happening. Without one and the slight skill involved in using it, you are essentially flying blind and left to just guess what might be wrong.

A Low Cost Logic Analyzer

Finally, if you are even more serious, then a pocket oscilloscope is also worth investing in to check out the analog nature of the supposedly digital signals that microcontrollers put out. However, if you have to choose between these two instruments, the logic analyzer should be your first acquisition.

It is worth noting that the Pico can generate signals that are too fast to be reliably detected by low-cost oscilloscopes and logic analyzers, which work at between 1MHz and 25MHz. This can mean that working with pulses much faster than $1\mu s$ can be difficult as you cannot rely on your instruments. There are reasonably priced 200MHz and 500MHz logic analyzers and one of these is certainly worthwhile if you are serious about hardware. It is worth knowing that both instruments can mislead you if you try to work with signals outside of the range that they can work with.

It is also assumed that you are able to program in Python. While there are some differences between it and MicroPython, the programs are easy enough to follow and any out-of-the-ordinary coding is explained.

Community

If you get stuck the best place to ask for help is in the Pico forums or, second best, Stack Overflow. The quality of answers varies from misleading to excellent. Always make sure you evaluate what you are being advised in the light of what you know. Be kind and supportive of anyone offering an answer that indicates that they misunderstand your question.

You also need to keep in mind that the advice is also usually offered from a biased point of view. Experts in other languages will often give you a solution that abandons MicroPython. Electronics beginners will offer you solutions that are based on "off-the-shelf" modules, when a simple alternative solution is available, based on a few cheap components. Even when the advice you get is 100% correct, it still isn't necessarily the right advice for you. As a rule never follow any advice that you don't understand.

Summary

- The Pico is a remarkably powerful device given its low cost and is ideal for building prototypes, one-offs and production devices.

- The RP2040 and RP2350 chips that are the heart of the original Pico and the Pico 2 respectively are also used in a number of similar devices, all of which can be treated as variations on the basic Pico.

- You need to decide on a development machine to use in conjunction with your Pico. A PC, Mac or a Linux system are all suitable, including a Pi 4/5 or a Pi 400/500.

- Thonny or VS Code provide an easy-to-use and efficient development environment, irrespective of the type of development machine you choose.

- To work with electronics, you need a solderless prototyping board, some hookup wires and some components. You also need a multimeter and preferably a logic analyzer. After these basic instruments you can add what you can afford.

- There is an active Pico community forum and if you get stuck it's the place to ask for advice. However, always evaluate any advice proffered and, in general, don't accept it unless you understand it.

Chapter 2
Getting Started

The easiest language to use to program the Pico is MicroPython. This is a reasonably full implementation of Python 3 plus special modules to work with the Pico's hardware. If you know the Python language you will have no problem working in MicroPython. However, getting used to the ideas involved in working with hardware is another matter – you have to think a little differently. To put it simply, time matters. What this means will become clear in the rest of the book, but exactly when and in what order things happen are fundamental concerns to this sort of hardware programming, and this usually means needing the most efficient programming language possible. Sometimes, however, you don't need speed, even in an IoT application. For example, if you just want to flash a few LEDs or read a temperature sensor in a human timescale, then you can write in almost any language and MicroPython is ideal. You can also often avoid having to react at the highest possible speed by using the range of peripheral devices that the Pico has. In other words, you can offload time critical operations to specialized hardware.

Speed, or rather lack of speed, can be a problem with coding in Python, but it is worth explaining that while Python may not be fast, it is sophisticated. There are ways of writing code in MicroPython that would require a lot of work to implement in lower-level languages. You may not have raw speed, but you do have mature sophistication.

So MicroPython is worth learning and the Pico provides low-cost hardware to experiment with. How do we get started?

Installing MicroPython

The key to understanding how everything works is to realize that what we are about to do is convert a Pico into a MicroPython machine. That is, we are going to download the MicroPython system onto a Pico and from this moment on the Pico behaves quite differently because every time you switch it on it is running the MicroPython system.

We get the MicroPython program onto the Pico using the basic way of getting any program onto the Pico. The difference is that we are only going to do this once. If nothing goes wrong after we have installed MicroPython we can use it to download and run any MicroPython programs we write in future. You only have to repeat the installation if something damages the MicroPython system or you load some other program onto the Pico.

The basic Pico way of installing programs is to simply drag-and-drop a `.uf2` format file to a folder on the Pico. First you need to download the correct MicroPython uf2 file from the Raspberry Pi website. There is a version of MicroPython for the original Pico and one for the Pico 2 and downloads for the W versions of each which have additional WiFi modules.

At the time of writing the files are called:

- `RPI_PICO-20250415-v1.25.0.uf2`
- `RPI_PICO2-20250415-v1.25.0.uf2`
- `RPI_PICO_W-20250415-v1.25.0.uf2`
- `RPI_PICO2_W-20250415-v1.25.0.uf2`

but these names are likely to change.

To run the program the simplest thing to do is connect a Pico to the development machine, a PC, Mac or a Raspberry Pi, via USB. The USB connection will also power the Pico, and to get the Pico to present a USB drive to the development machine you have to hold down the `BootSel` button which is to the left of the USB connector as the power is applied. If you have done this correctly you will see a new drive added to the development machine and you will have to supply a password to mount it. Under Linux, for example, you will see something like:

If you don't see this dialog box then you haven't held down the `BootSel` button while the power is being applied. Now you can drag-and-drop the MicroPython `.uf2` file and you should see the on-board LED start to flash slowly. Notice that some operating systems will mount the Pico silently. Also note this procedure doesn't work if you are using remote desktop to a Pi with any user other than `pi` due to permissions.

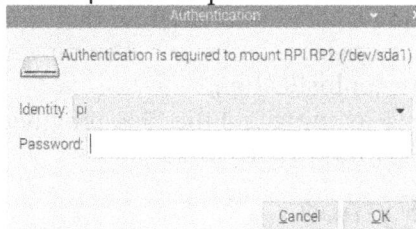

When the transfer is complete the Pico USB drive will automatically disconnect and you can remove the power from the Pico or start using it at once. The point is that now, whenever you power on that particular Pico, it will run as a MicroPython machine. If you don't want it to do this, you need to download another program using the same method.

There are various ways of checking that the program has been successfully loaded into the Pico, but the process is so simple that it rarely goes wrong and it is worth moving on to a more sensible way of working with the MicroPython Pico. Here we are going to look at using Thonny as a simple way to get started and then move on to using VS Code which is the IDE used in the rest of this book.

Hello World Using Thonny

As we have downloaded the MicroPython code into the Pico, we are ready to try out a first program which by tradition is "Blinky", i.e. a program to flash an LED. We could do this via the command prompt, but it is much more efficient to use an IDE. You may already be familiar with Thonny, which you will find already installed on most Raspberry Pis although not on the Pico. If you already have it installed you need to check that it is up to date. Visit the Thonny website:

```
https://thonny.org/
```

and download the latest version.

Thonny can be installed under Windows, Mac or Linux.

If you are working with Linux or a Pi you can use:

```
sudo apt install thonny
```

Once installed, start it running and make sure that the Pico with MicroPython is connected via a USB cable as Thonny and other IDEs communicate with the Pico via the serial port provided by the USB cable. You can connect to the Pico via an on-board UART, but this is complicated and unnecessary when you are first getting started.

You need to use Thonny in "regular" mode which presents the full range of menu options. Select the regular mode link from the top right-hand corner and restart Thonny and you should see all of the menus.

As long as the Pico is connected, and no other program is making use of its serial connection, Thonny should be able to find it automatically. Select the Tools, Options menu item and then the Interpreter tab in the dialog box:

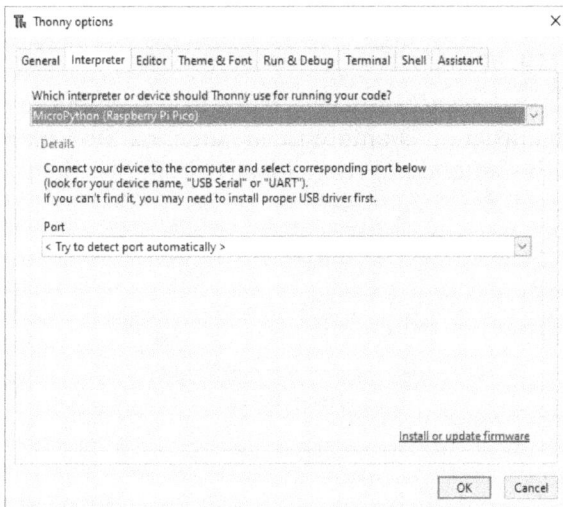

Select the MicroPython (Raspberry Pi Pico) option and choose the <Try to detect port automatically> option. If it fails try setting the port that you know the Pico is connected to.

As long as this works you will see an editing window and a Shell that you can type immediate MicroPython instructions into and see the commands that Thonny issues to the Pico.

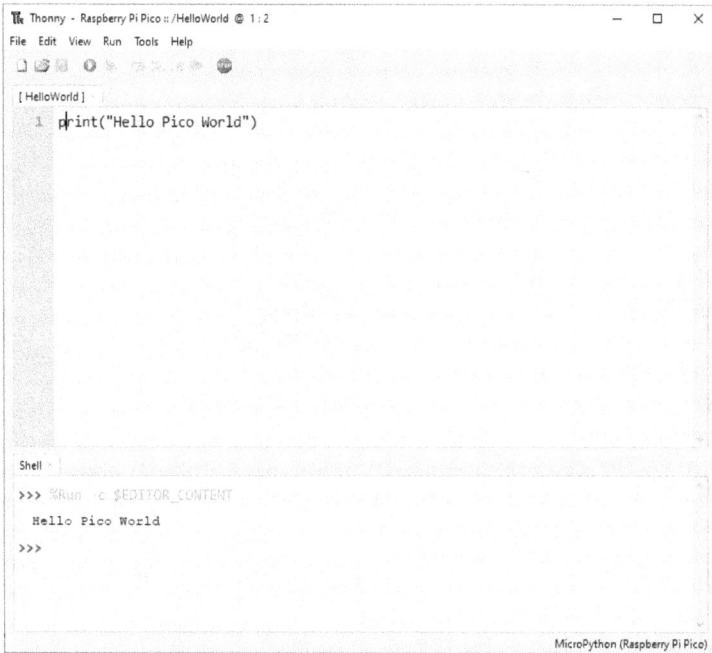

Enter the following program:

```
print("Hello Pico World")
```

This will print the message to the Pico console at the bottom of the Thonny window. Once the program is entered you can click the Run icon and select where you want the program to run – locally or on the Pico:

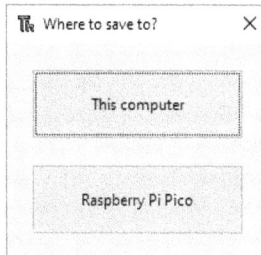

If you select the Pico, you will be asked to provide a name for the program. Use "helloworld" and it will be downloaded to the Pico and run. You should see the confirmation message appear.

MicroPython creates a small filing system on the Pico and you can save and open files stored there using Thonny.

Thonny is a good way to get started as it is simple and quick, but it lacks many of the facilities you may be used to in other IDEs. In particular it lacks any debug options and it has no Intellisense or syntax checking for MicroPython.

Hello World Using VS Code

There are some advantages to using VS Code to work with MicroPython on the Pico, but it is slightly more difficult to set up as you need to install a number of extensions. The main advantage is that you can make use of intelligent prompting when entering code and the Pylance linter to spot simple syntax problems. It also has a more comprehensive way of working with the Pico's filing system.

First you need to install VS Code. This is not difficult and instructions on how to do this on Windows, Mac and Linux are available on the VS Code website and there isn't any need to repeat them here. If you are using a Raspberry Pi as your development machine all you need to do is:

```
sudo apt update
sudo apt install code
```

Make sure you have VS Code installed and working before moving on to the next step.

You also need to install Python 3, and again there are good instructions on the website. Make sure that Python 3 is installed and working before you move on.

The final steps are installing the required VS Code extensions. You need to install the Microsoft Python Extension:

Python ms-python.python
Microsoft | ⟳ 34,394,495 | ★ ★ ★ ★ ☆ | Repository | License | v2021.3.680753044
Linting. Debugging (multi-threaded, remote). Intellisense. Jupyter Notebooks. code formatting. refactoring. unit tests. and more.
Disable ⌄ Uninstall ⌄ ⚙ This extension is enabled globally.
This extension is recommended by users of the current workspace.

Details Feature Contributions Changelog Dependencies

and Pylance:

Pylance ms-python.vscode-pylance `Preview`
Microsoft | ⊕ 1,507,789 | ★ ★ ★ ★ ☆ | Repository | License | v2021.4.1
A performant, feature-rich language server for Python in VS Code
[Disable ▾] [Uninstall ▾] ⚙ *This extension is enabled globally.*
This extension is recommended by users of the current workspace.

Details Feature Contributions Changelog Dependencies

Next you need to run VS Code and install the Raspberry Pi Pico extension.

This works on Windows, Linux and Mac OS. It also installs all of the other extensions you require. The extension installs and configures the editor so you can create Python projects.

To get started select the extension and then the New MicroPython Project. You need to give the project a name and specify the folder it is to be stored in. The Python Version box doesn't specify the version of Python used by the Pico but instead the version on the development machine used by the extension.

Raspberry Pi Pico

Raspberry Pi ⬤ raspberrypi.com | ⊕ 104,385 | ★ ★ ★ ★ ☆ (6)

The official VS Code extension for Raspberry Pi Pico development. It includes several features to sim...

[Disable ▾] [Uninstall ▾] [✓] Auto Update ⚙

DETAILS   FEATURES   CHANGELOG   DEPENDENCIES

Raspberry Pi Pico Visual Studio Code extension

| **Note: The extension is currently under development.**

This is the official Visual Studio Code extension for Raspberry Pi Pico development. This extension equips you with a suite of tools designed to streamline your Pico projects using Visual Studio Code and the official Pico SDK.

For comprehensive setup instructions, refer to the Getting Started guide PDF.

Installation

Identifier	raspberry-pi.raspberry-pi-pico
Version	0.17.5
Last Updated	2025-04-17, 14:17:52
Size	29.66MB

Create a project called `hello` in a suitable folder. Oddly this creates a file called `blinky.py` with code to to blink an LED. If you want to reuse this file you can, but it is probably better to create a new file called `hello.py` and enter:

```
print("Hello Pico World")
```

If you have the Pico extension correctly installed, you should see some useful icons in the bottom bar:

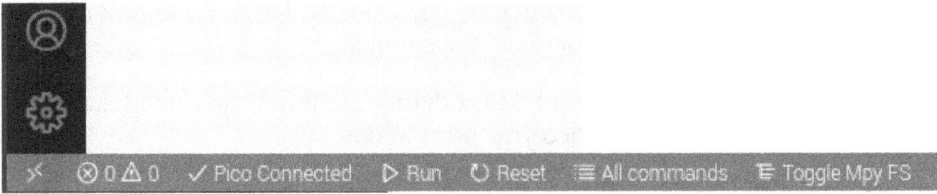

If you can see the tools in the status bar then, as long you can also see "Pico Connected", you are ready to run the program. To do this, simply click the Run command in the status bar. After a moment you should see the message appear in the Pico Console. The Run command always runs the program that is loaded into the current editor window i.e. it runs the current file.

You can see other commands in the status bar and the All Commands option at the end gives you access to even more:

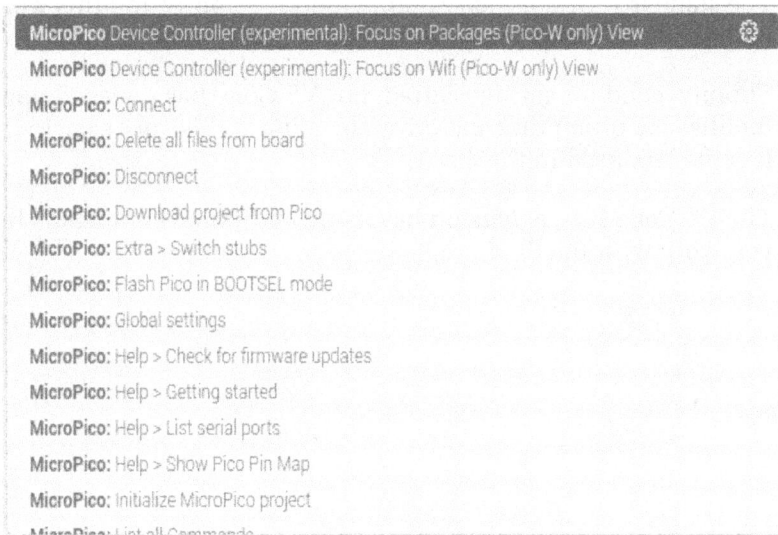

Summary

- MicroPython is a powerful and sophisticated language and, with the Pico's speed, you can achieve a great deal.

- Before you can start using MicroPython, you have to download it and install it on any Pico you want to use.

- Installing it onto a Pico is just a matter of connecting the Pico to the development machine, opening the Pico as a folder, and drag-and-dropping the appropriate .uf2 file onto it.

- Once MicroPython is installed on a Pico it is a MicroPython machine every time you switch it on.

- To program a MicroPython machine you can use the command prompt, but it is so much easier to use an IDE.

- The standard IDE for Pico MicroPython is Thonny and this works with the Pico without any additional configuration.

- Thonny good for getting started, but VS Code has the advantage of Intellisense prompting and error checking and is very easy to install. It is the IDE used in this book.

- The VS Code Pico extension has many additional commands that let you work with the Pico.

Chapter 3
Getting Started With The GPIO

In this chapter we take a look at the basic operations involved in using the Pico's General Purpose Input/Output (GPIO) lines with an emphasis on output. We'll consider questions such as how fast can you change a GPIO line, how do you generate pulses of a given duration and how can you change multiple lines in sync with each other?

Pico Pins

The first thing to make ourselves familiar with is the layout and range of GPIO pins available on a standard Pico. The RP2040 chip has 30 GPIO lines, GPIO 0 to GPIO 29, of which the Pico makes 26 available for general use on the edge of the board. The RP2050 chip has up to 54 GPIO lines, but the Pico 2 only makes the same 26 available at the board edge as the Pico.

The other four are used internally. In the case of the Pico they are:

GPIO29	Used in ADC mode (ADC3) to measure VSYS/3
GPIO25	Connected to user LED
GPIO24	VBUS sense - high if VBUS is present, otherwise low
GPIO23	Controls the onboard SMPS Power Save pin

The Pico W uses these four GPIO lines to interface with the WiFi chip, an Infineon CYW43439, via an SPI bus:

GPIO29	Used in wireless mode to measure VSYS/3
GPIO25	Wireless SPI CS - enables GPIO29 to read VSYS
GPIO24	Used for wireless SPI data/IRQ
GPIO23	Used for wireless power on signal

In addition, three of the WiFi chips's GPIO lines are used by the Pico W to make up for the loss of the original four lines:

WL_GPIO2	VBUS sense - high if VBUS is present, else low
WL_GPIO1	Controls the onboard SMPS power save pin
WL_GPIO0	Connected to user LED

Apart from the control of the onboard LED, none of these changes should make any difference to a typical Pico program.

Both Pico versions also have four additional GPIO lines, but these are dedicated for use as a quad SPI bus to interface to flash memory.

As is the case with most microprocessors, each GPIO line, with the exception of GPIO 22, has multiple uses as you can see in the diagram:

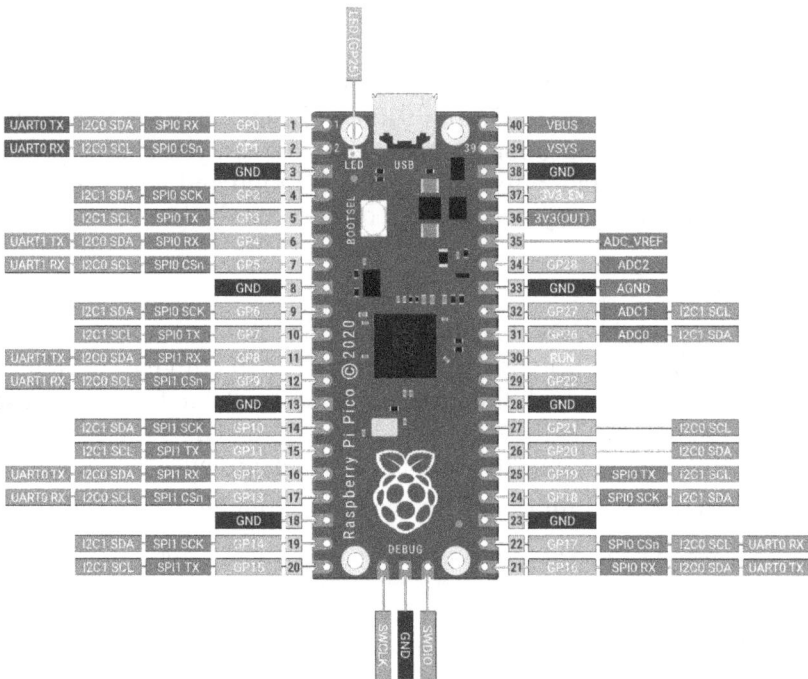

You can select what mode a pin is used in and in this chapter we concentrate on using pins in the simplest GPIO mode. Even so, which pins you select for general-purpose use should take into account what other uses you might put pins to. For example, using GPIO 26 as a general GPIO line when you need an additional ADC (Analog to Digital Converter) is sensible as one of its alternative functions. The only pin that has no alternative function is GPIO22 and this should be your first choice for any general-purpose duties.

Notice that, unlike when programming directly to the hardware, MicroPython doesn't use the idea of setting the GPIO pin into a particular mode. Instead it provides classes that make use of GPIO pins in particular ways. For example, if you were programming directly to the hardware you would first set the pins you wanted to use to the mode you wanted to use, e.g. PWM (Pulse Width Modulation) and then you would start working with PWM operations. In MicroPython you would simply create a PWM object using the pin in question and expect it to take care of setting the pin to the correct mode. Notice, however, that you are still restricted to using pins that support the mode you are using.

In most cases, to make use of the GPIO lines in a prototyping situation you need to solder pins onto the board so that it can be plugged into a prototype board. There is some argument about which side the pins should be soldered to. One side leaves the PCB legend visible, but the on-board LED is obscured, and the other leaves the LED visible, but obscures the legend.

Basic GPIO Functions

The MicroPython `Pin` class allows you to create an object which controls the way a single GPIO line works. The simplest form of the constructor is:

`Pin(id, mode=mode)`

where *id* is the number of the GPIO line you want to use and *mode* is one of:

`Pin.IN`

or

`Pin.OUT`

there are other possibilities and these are discussed later.

Notice that the id is the GPIO number and not the hardware pin number. For example, 22 means GPIO 22 and corresponds not to pin 22, but to pin 29. You can also use the string "LED" to refer to the GPIO line connected to the onboard LED which is actually connected to a different line on the Pico and Pico W.

There is also an `init` method which can be used to change the configuration of the pin. For example,

`pin.init(mode=Pin.IN)`

might be used to change a pin from output to input.

A number of methods are provided to work with the state of a Pin object:

Method	Description
`value(x)`	Sets the line to x, usually 0 or 1, but x can be anything that evaluates to true or false
`on()`	Sets the line to high
`off()`	Sets the line to low
`high()`	Sets the line high
`low()`	Sets the line low
`toggle()`	If the line is high set it low and vice versa

There are a number of other methods and properties, but these are the most basic.

Blinky

Note: The code for every program in this book is included in its GitHub repo listed on the book's web page. References are to Chapter number and program name.

The first IoT program you write is by tradition Blinky, i.e. flash an LED. The simplest Blinky program you can write on the Pico isn't really typical. The original Pico has its onboard LED connected to GPIO 25 but the Pico W has it connected to a GPIO line supplied by the additional WiFi hardware. As a result it isn't straightforward to write a Blinky that works on both versions of the Pico. MicroPython solves the problem by providing a string id "LED" which is interpreted differently depending on which version of the Pico it is running on. What this means is that the simplest Blinky program, blinky.py, is:

```
from machine import Pin
import time

pin = Pin("LED", Pin.OUT)

while True:
    pin.value(1)
    time.sleep(1)
    pin.value(0)
    time.sleep(1)
```

The Pin constructor selects the correct GPIO line depending on the version of the Pico it is running on. The while loop simply sets the line high and then low complete with a one-second delay.

A program to flash an LED uses a general I/O line and an external LED. With this in mind, let's flash an LED connected to GPIO 22.

Enter the program, blinky2.py:

```
from machine import Pin
import time

pin = Pin(22, Pin.OUT)
while True:
    pin.value(1)
    time.sleep(1)
    pin.value(0)
    time.sleep(1)
```

The program doesn't use any constants in order to make what is happening clearer. It first initializes GPIO 22 to be an output and sets it repeatedly high and low with a pause of one second between. If you try this program out on either version of the Pico you will see the onboard LED flash slowly.

If you want to connect an LED to see the "blinking" for real then this is easy enough, but you do need a current-limiting resistor to avoid the LED drawing more current than the Pico GPIO line can supply and possibly damaging the chip. A 200Ω resistor is a good choice, see Chapter 5. A better way to drive an LED is discussed more fully in Chapter 5.

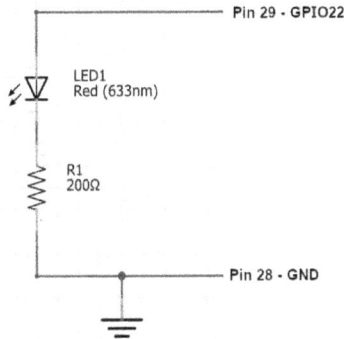

Notice that the diagram shows that GPIO 22 corresponds to pin 29 in the Pico board. How you build the circuit is up to you. You can use a prototyping board or just a pair of jumper wires. The short pin and/or the flat on the side of the case marks the negative connection on the LED – the one that goes to ground.

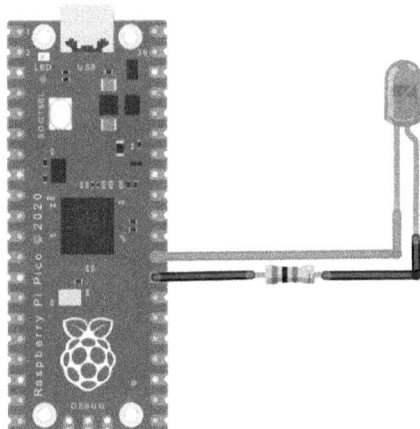

If you can't be bothered to go through the ritual of testing "Blinky" with a real LED, then just connect a logic analyzer to Pin 29 and you will see one-second pulses.

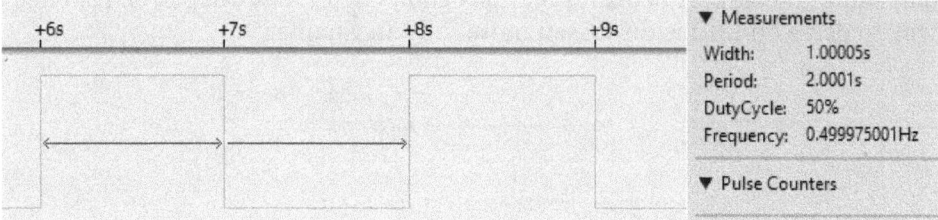

An even easier version of Blinky is to use the `toggle` function which changes the state of the GPIO line from 0→1 and 1→0, blinky3.py:

```
from machine import Pin
import time

pin = Pin(22,Pin.OUT)
while True:
    pin.toggle()
    time.sleep(1)
```

Which Hardware?

The difference in the way the onboard LED is connected can be used as an easy way to find out which version of the Pico a program is running on. If you use the `str` function on the pin instance you will discover that it returns the actual GPIO line used:

```
pin = Pin("LED", Pin.OUT)
print(str(pin))
```

On a Pico or Pico 2 it displays:

```
Pin(25, mode=OUT)
```

and on a Pico W or Pico 2W:

```
Pin(WL_GPIO0, mode=OUT)
```

So you can detect the difference between a non-WiFi Pico and a Pico W by testing for a "25" or a "WL" in the result of `str()`. This method has the advantage that you only have to import the Pin object.

The method given in the documentation is:

```
import network
print(hasattr(network, "WLAN"))
```

which displays True on a Pico W/2W, but fails with an exception on a Pico/2 as the network module cannot be found.

Summary

- The Pico has 34 GPIO lines in total. Four are used to interface to flash memory and of the remainder, GPIO 0 to GPIO 29, the Pico makes 26 available for general use on the edge of the board.

- Some of the GPIO lines have alternative functions and these are best avoided if all you need is a simple GPIO input/output line.

- The Pico uses GPIO 25 to control the onboard LED while the Pico W uses a GPIO line from the WiFi chip to do the same job.

- The only GPIO line that doesn't have another important function is GPIO 22 and this is your best first choice for a general-purpose GPIO line.

- MicroPython provides the Pin class to control a single GPIO line and its basic methods let you set the line high or low.

- A Blinky program to flash the on-board LED is complicated by the fact that the Pico and Pico W use different GPIO lines to control it. MicroPython irons out this difference by providing the "LED" GPIO identifier which it interprets correctly depending on the version of the Pico the program is running on.

- A general-purpose Blinky program can ignore the differences between Pico versions as all of the standard GPIO lines are identical.

- You can make use of the different implementation of the on-board LED to detect whether the Pico your program is running on has WiFi or not.

Chapter 4

Simple Output

A GPIO line is either configured to be an input or an output. The electronics of working with inputs and outputs are discussed in the next chapter, but first we focus on the software side of the task of using GPIO lines in output mode. While it isn't possible to ignore electronics entirely, keep in mind that more in details are provided in Chapter 5.

It is worth noting at this stage that output is easy. Your program chooses the time to change a line's state and you can use the system timer to work out exactly when things should happen. The real problems only start to become apparent when you are trying to change the state of lines very fast or when they need to be changed synchronously. This raises the question of how fast the Pico can change a GPIO line and this is something we consider at this early stage because it puts constraints on what we can easily do.

Basic GPIO Functions

We have already met the basic methods of the Pin object that let you work with a single GPIO line:

Method	Description
init(mode)	Set mode to input or output
value(x)	Sets the line to x, usually 0 or 1, but x can be anything that evaluates to true or false
on()	Sets the line to high
off()	Sets the line to low
high()	Sets the line high
low()	Sets the line low
toggle()	If the line is high set it low and vice versa

Using these methods is very straightforward, but notice that there is no way to set multiple lines in one operation. This can be a problem, something we'll come to later.

How Fast?

A fundamental question that you have to answer for any processor intended for use in embedded or IoT projects is, how fast can the GPIO lines work?

Sometimes the answer isn't of too much concern because what you want to do only works relatively slowly. Any application that is happy with response times in the tens of millisecond region will generally work with almost any processor. However, if you want to implement custom protocols or anything that needs microsecond, or even nanosecond, responses, the question is much more important.

It is fairly easy to find out how fast a single GPIO line can be used if you have a logic analyzer or oscilloscope. All you have to do is run the program speed.py:

```
from machine import  Pin
pin = Pin(22, Pin.OUT)
while True:
    pin.value(1)
    pin.value(0)
```

If you run this program you will discover that the pulses are about $7\mu s$ on the original Pico and $3.5\mu s$ on the Pico 2 and are not perfectly even:

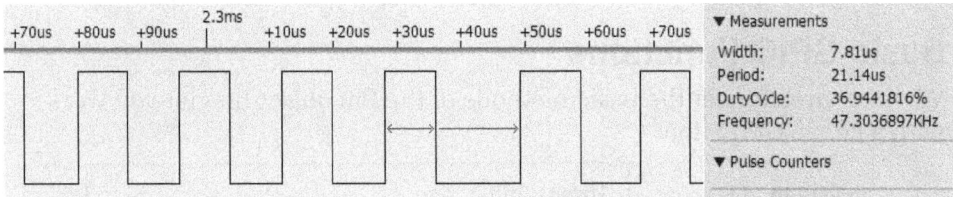

The unevenness is due to the internal workings of MicroPython. If you change the way that the code is specified, you are likely to see changes in timing. For example, if you try the equivalent code, flash.py:

```
from machine import Pin
def flash():
    pin = Pin(22, Pin.OUT)
    while True:
        pin.value(1)
        pin.value(0)
flash()
```

you will discover that the pulse width has dropped to around $5\mu s$ on the original Pico and $2.9\mu s$ on the Pico 2. This is not what you might expect given that a function call is an additional step!

There is a facility to compile functions to native code and this gives the largest speed increase without going to exceptional lengths. If you want a function to be compiled all you have to do is add the @micropython.native decorator, native.py:

```python
from machine import Pin

@micropython.native
def flash():
    pin = Pin(22, Pin.OUT)
    while True:
        pin.value(1)
        pin.value(0)
flash()
```

Don't worry if you see a warning message in VS Code for @micropython. This is just because pylance doesn't have a definition for this class.

If you run this program you will find that not only does the pulse time drop to 3.8μs on the original Pico and to 2.5μs on the Pico 2, but the pulses are very regular.

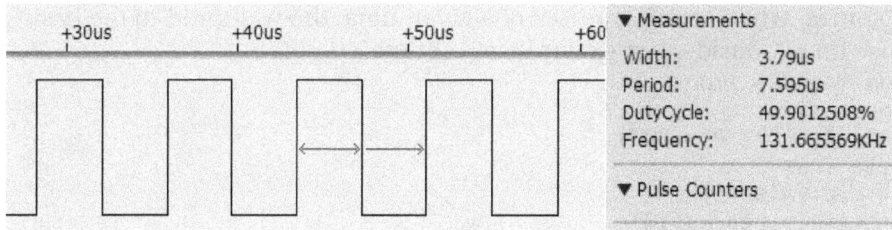

The reason the pulses are regular is that now the MicroPython system doesn't get involved in the while loop and it runs at the same speed all of the time. One problem with this approach is that, as the native function now doesn't give MicroPython a chance to run, you lose control of the Pico via the USB connection. You now have to reset to gain control of the Pico. You should restrict the use of native code as much as possible and only use it when speed is unattainable by other methods.

As frequently mentioned in this book, when speed is an important factor the programming language of choice is C and this provides a good example of why. If you compare the approximately 3μs pulses that can be produced using MicroPython on the Pico 2 to the 6ns pulses that can be produced using C, you can appreciate that MicroPython is about 500 times slower than C.

Including Pauses

To generate pulses of a known duration we need to pause the program between state changes. In the Blinky programs we used sleep to slow things down, but without properly introducing it.

Using sleep(*seconds*) gives a pause or "wait" for the specified number of seconds. As *seconds* is a floating-point number you can specify fractions of a second. So for half-second pulses you could use:

```
from machine import Pin
import time
pin = Pin(22, Pin.OUT)
while True:
    pin.value(1)
    time.sleep(0.5)
    pin.value(0)
    time.sleep(0.5)
```

As well as sleep, there are also sleep_ms and sleep_us which pause the program for the specified number of milliseconds and microseconds respectively. You can use utime or time to import the functions.

Of course, when creating pulses of a given time, the waits add to the basic pulse time. Consider, for example, pulsetime:

```
from machine import Pin
import time
pin = Pin(22, Pin.OUT)
while True:
    pin.value(1)
    time.sleep_us(10)
    pin.value(0)
    time.sleep_us(10)
```

This creates pulses that are $26\mu s$ wide in the case of the original Pico and $16\mu s$ wide using the Pico 2. In general, you have to add about $10\mu s$ to the wait time to get the pulse length for the Pico and $6\mu s$ for the Pico 2.

The traditional way of introducing a busy wait (also known as a spin wait) is to simply use a time-wasting for loop. A for loop busy wait can produce short wait times, wait.py:

```
from machine import Pin
import time
pin = Pin(22, Pin.OUT)
n = 10
while True:
    for i in range(n):
        pass
    pin.value(1)
    for i in range(n):
        pass
    pin.value(0)
```

which generates pulses according to the setting of n:

n	Time in μs Pico	Time in μs Pico 2
1	16	8
2	21	10
3	26	13
4	31	15
5	36	18
6	41	20
7	46	22
8	53	25
9	58	27
10	63	29

These figures are subject to change as MicroPython is optimized and the time for operations varies.

Fixed Time Delay

A common problem is making sure that something happens after a fixed time delay when you have a variable amount of work to do during that time interval. Consider the program snippet:

```
pin.value(1)
for i in range(n):
    pass
time.sleep_ms(1)
pin.value(1)
```

where the for loop is intended to stand in for doing some other work. The intention is that the GPIO line should be set high for 1ms, but clearly how long the line is set high depends on how long the loop takes, which is given by n plus 1ms of sleep time.

What is needed is a pause that takes into account the time that the loop uses up and simply delays the program for the remaining amount of time to make it up to 1ms. This is where the functions ticks_ms() and ticks_us() come in useful. They give the time since the machine was switched on in milliseconds or microseconds respectively. These both wrap around at some unspecified point and to take account of the wrap you need to use:

```
ticks_add(ticks,number)
ticks_diff(ticks1,ticks2)
```

to do arithmetic that takes account of the wrap.

We can now write the program snippet given earlier as:

```
while True:
    t=time.ticks_add(time.ticks_us(),1000)
    pin.value(1)
    for i in range(n):
        pass

    while time.ticks_us()<t:
        pass
    pin.value(0)
```

Now we obtain the ticks before setting the line high and add 1000 to it. No matter how long the for loop takes, the while loop will provide a delay of 1ms, as long as the loop takes less than this time.

This is a very general technique and one that can often make difficult timing problems very simple.

Phased Pulses

As a simple example of using the output functions, let's try to write a short program that pulses two lines, high and then low, out of phase.

The simplest program, phase1.py, to do this job is:

```
from machine import Pin

pin1 = Pin(21, Pin.OUT)
pin2 = Pin(22, Pin.OUT)
while True:
    pin1.value(1)
    pin2.value(0)
    pin1.value(0)
    pin2.value(1)
```

Notice that there is no delay in the loop so the pulses are produced at the fastest possible speed.

Using a logic analyzer reveals that the result isn't what you might expect:

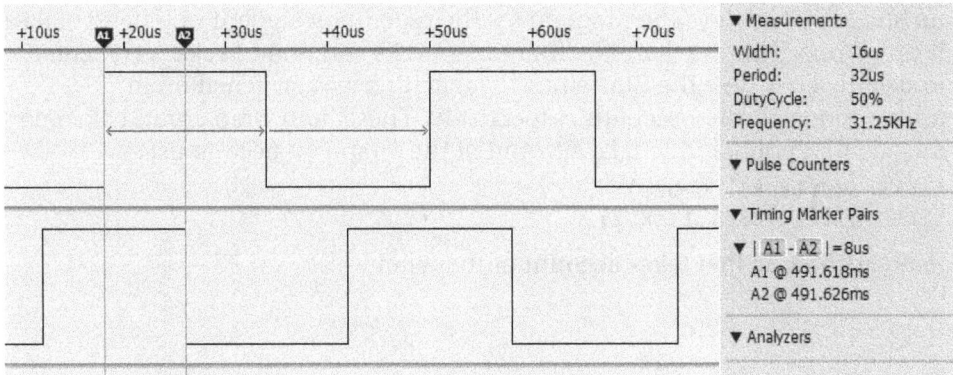

44

The top train switches on and the bottom train takes about half a pulse before it switches off, although the intent is for both actions to occur at the same time. The point is that it does take quite a long time to access and change the state of an output line.

Of course, if we include a delay to increase the pulse width then the delay caused by accessing the GPIO lines in two separate actions isn't so obvious, but it is still there. There are applications where the switching speed is so low that the delay between switching doesn't matter – flashing LEDs for instance. With a delay of around $8\mu s$ you could flash a line of around 2000 LEDs before the lag between the first and the last became apparent. On the other hand, if you use out-of-phase pulses to control a motor, then the overlap when both GPIO lines were on would burn out the drivers quite quickly. Of course, any sensible, cautious, engineer wouldn't feed a motor control bridge from two independently generated pulse trains unless they were guaranteed not to switch both sides of the bridge on at the same time.

Setting Multiple GPIO Lines

There is no way using MicroPython methods to change multiple GPIO lines at the same time, even though the hardware makes it possible. To do the job you need to write some code that accesses the hardware directly, see Chapter 21 for more details.

In this chapter we simply present and make use of the two functions explained there:

```
def gpio_get():
    return machine.mem32[0xd0000000+0x010]

def gpio_set(value,mask):
    machine.mem32[0xd0000000+0x010] =
        machine.mem32[0xd0000000+0x010] & ~mask | value & mask
```

Both functions work by directly accessing the GPIO registers.

The first, gpio_get, returns a 32-bit word that has a single bit for the current state of each of the GPIO lines. That is, it reads all of the GPIO lines in a single operation. The second, gpio_set, uses a mask to determine which lines will be set and a value that gives the states to set them to. As in the case of gpio_get, each line is represented by a single bit in the value and the mask. Any bits not set in the mask leave the corresponding GPIO line unchanged.

It is easy to create a mask for any GPIO lines. For example if you want to modify only lines GPn and GPm then the mask is:

```
mask = 1<<n | 1<<m
```

and so on if you have more lines to modify.

The value can be constructed in the same way. If you want to set the lines to a and b then the value is:

```
value = a<<n | b<<m
```

Notice that if the corresponding bit isn't set in mask then the bit in value has no effect.

Making use of this we can write phase2, a new version of the previous program without the lags:

```
from machine import Pin
import machine

def gpio_get():
    return machine.mem32[0xd0000000+0x010]

def gpio_set(value,mask):
    machine.mem32[0xd0000000+0x010] =
        machine.mem32[0xd0000000+0x010] & ~mask | value & mask

pin=Pin(22,Pin.OUT)
pin=Pin(21,Pin.OUT)
value1=1<<22 | 0<<21
value2=0<<22 | 1<<21
mask=1<<22 | 1<<21
while True:
    gpio_set(value1,mask)
    gpio_set(value2,mask)
```

As we are changing the same pins each time, we only need a single mask. The value, however, changes each time. If you run this program you will see an almost perfect pair of out-of-phase pulses, $44\mu s$ for the Pico and $14\mu s$ for the Pico 2:

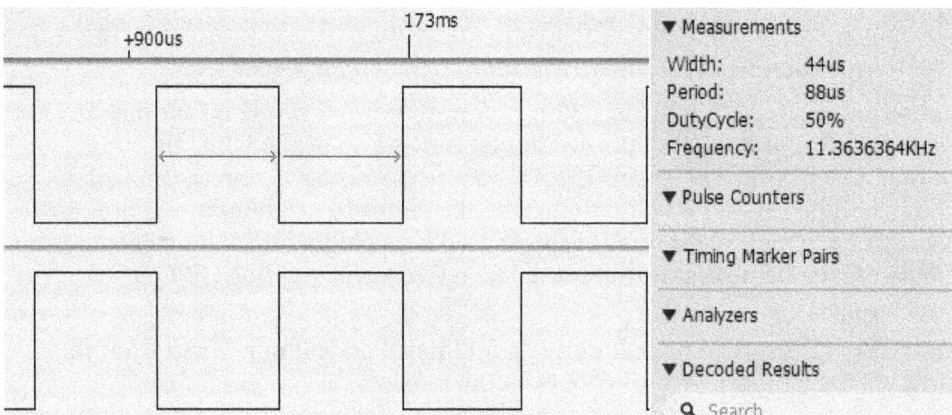

46

Summary

- Output is easy because the program decides when to change the state of a line. Input is hard because you never know when an input line will change state.

- GPIO lines can be set to act as inputs or outputs when you create a Pin object.

- If a line is set to output it can be set high or low using a number of Pin Methods function.

- You can generate pulses as short as 7μs with the Pico and 3.5μs with the Pico 2, but not reliably.

- If you compile a function that changes the GPIO lines you can generate reliable pulses, of 4μs with the Pico and 2.5μs with the Pico 2.

- A delay can be introduced into a program using the `sleep`, `sleep_ms` or `sleep_us` functions.

- An alternative is to use a busy wait loop which is simply a loop that keeps the CPU busy for an amount of time. It is easy to obtain an equation that gives the delay per loop repetition.

- By using the tick methods you can set an action to have an exact repeat time, even if what it does varies in time.

- Producing pulses which are in accurately in phase is not possible using Pin methods.

- If you access the hardware directly you can change multiple lines in one operation.

Chapter 5

Some Electronics

Now that we have looked at some simple I/O, it is worth spending a little time on the electronics of output and input. We cover the electronics of input before looking at how the software handles input because we need to understand some of the problems that the software has to deal with.

First some basic electronics – how transistors can be used as switches. The approach is very simple, but it is enough for the simple circuits that digital electronics makes use of. It isn't enough to design a high quality audio amplifier or similar analog device, but it might be all you need.

The basis of all electronics is Ohm's law, $V = IR$, and this prerequisite implies an understanding of voltage, current and resistance.

How to Think About Circuits

For a beginner electronics can seem very abstract, but that's not how old hands think about it. Most understand what is going on in terms of a hydraulic model, even if they don't admit it. The basic idea is that an electric current running in a wire is very much like a flow of water in a pipe. The source of the electricity plays the role of a pump and the wires, the pipe. The flow of electricity is measured in Amps and this is just the amount of electricity that flows per second. The flow is governed by how hard the pump is pumping, which is measured by voltage and how restrictive the pipe is, the resistance which is measured in Ohms.

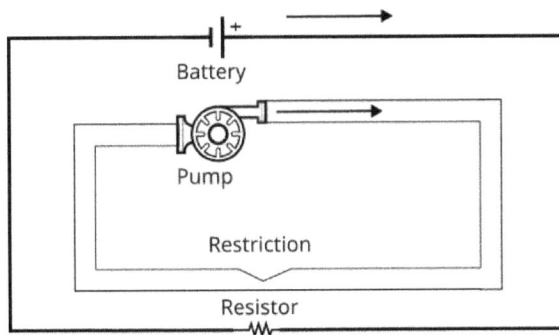

As an analogy, when you are doing electronics you are basically doing plumbing with a fluid that you generally can't see that flows in pipes called wires.

The only difficult idea here is that of a pumping force. We tend to think of a pump providing a flow at the location of the pump, but there is something, "a pumping force" that keeps the water flowing around every part of the circuit. In your imagination you have to think of the water being forced ever onward at every point in the pipe. In particular, when there is constriction in the pipe then you might need more pumping force to get the water through. In a sense the pump provides the total pressure available and this distributes itself around the circuit as needed to push the flow through each restriction.

In electric circuits the pumping force is called EMF or ElectroMotive Force or just voltage. We also assume that the force needed to push electricity through wires is negligible and resistors are the only place that a voltage is needed to make the current flow.

The relationship between these quantities is characterized by Ohm's law:

$$V = IR \text{ or } I = V/R \text{ or } R = V/I$$

where V is the voltage in Volts, I is the current in Amps and R is the resistance in Ohms.

It is worth pointing out that when using Ohm's law we generally work in Volts (V) and milliamps (mA), one thousandth of an amp and this automatically gives resistance in kilo-ohms (kΩ).

You can see that if you increase the voltage, the flow, then the current increases. If you increase the resistance then the current decreases. Slightly more difficult is the idea that for a given resistance you need particular pumping force to achieve a given flow. If you know the actual flow and the resistance then you can work out the pumping force needed to get that flow.

The following points should be obvious. The flow through a pipe has to be the same at each point in the pipe – otherwise water would backup or need to be introduced. The total pressure that the pump provides has to be distributed across each of the resistances in the pipe to ensure the same flow. These pressures have to add up to the total pressure that the pump provides.

Slightly less obvious, but still an idea you can understand in terms of water flow, is that pressures add, currents add and resistances to flow in the same pipe add.

One of the main reasons for understanding electrical flow is that you can use Ohm's law to avoid damaging things. As a current flows through a resistor, it gets hot. The rule here is that the energy produced is proportional to VI. If you double the current, you double the heating effect. Most electronic devices have current limits beyond which they are liable to fail. One of the basic tasks in designing any electronic circuit is to work out what the current is and, if it is too high, add a resistor or lower the voltage to reduce it. To do this you need a good understanding of the hydraulic model and be able to use Ohm's law. There are examples later in this chapter.

It is also worth pointing out that there are devices which do not obey Ohm's law – so-called non-Ohmic devices. These are the interesting elements in a circuit – LEDs, diodes, transistors and so on, but even these devices can be understood in terms of the flow of a fluid.

This is a lightning introduction to electronics, pun intended, and there is much to learn and many mistakes to make, most of which result in blue smoke.

Electrical Drive Characteristics

If you are not familiar with electronics, the important things to know are what voltages are being worked with and how much current can flow. The most important thing to know about the Pico is that it works with two voltage levels – 0V and 3.3V. The Pico's chip can work at a range of voltages from 1.8V to 3.3V, but the Pico has a power supply that converts whatever you supply it with to 3.3V – as a result the Pico is a 3.3V logic device.

If you have worked with other logic devices you might be more familiar with 0V and 5V as being the low and high levels. The Pico uses a lower output voltage to reduce its power consumption, which is good, but you need to keep in mind that you may have to use some electronics to change the 3.3V to other values. The same is true of inputs, which must not exceed 3.3V or you risk damaging the Pico.

An important question is how much current the GPIO lines can handle without damaging the chip. This isn't an easy question and at the time of writing the documentation isn't clear on the matter. According to the documentation, each GPIO line can be set to "drive" 12mA. However, this doesn't quite mean what you might think. This is not an upper limit on the supplied current, but a configuration that is needed to ensure that the output voltages of the GPIO line are within specification while it is working at 12mA, see Chapter 19 for more information.

What this means is that the designers intended the GPIO line to be used at 12mA, but this is not an upper limit on supply current. The only upper limit quoted is that the total current in the GPIO lines should be less than 50mA.

Given that there are 30 GPIO lines this gives an average of 1.6mA per GPIO line. In practice, you are most likely to be safe at around the 12mA maximum for a small number of lines.

In practice, if you are planning to use more than 1.6mA from multiple GPIO lines, consider using a transistor. If your circuits draw more than 50mA from the 3.3V supply rail, consider a separate power supply.

Notice that the 12mA limit means that you cannot safely drive a standard 20mA red LED without restricting the current to below 12mA. A better solution is to use a low-power 2mA LED or use a transistor driver.

Driving An LED

One of the first things you need to know how to do is compute the value of a current-limiting resistor. For example, if you just connect an LED between a GPIO line and ground then no current will flow when the line is low and the LED is off, but when the line is high, at 3.3V, it is highly likely that the current will exceed the safe limit. In most cases nothing terrible will happen as the Pico's GPIO lines are rated very conservatively, but if you keep doing it eventually something will fail. The correct thing to do is to use a current-limiting resistor. Although this is an essential part of using an LED, it is also something you need to keep in mind when connecting any output device. You need to discover the voltage that the device needs and the current it uses and calculate a current-limiting resistor to make sure that is indeed the current it draws from the GPIO line.

An LED is a non-linear electronic component – the voltage across it stays more or less the same irrespective of the current passing through the device. Compare this to a more normal linear, or "ohmic", device where the current and voltage vary together according to Ohm's law, $V = IR$, which means that if the current doubles, so does the voltage and vice versa.

This is not how an LED behaves. It has a fairly constant voltage drop, irrespective of the current. (If you are curious, the relationship between current and voltage for an LED is exponential, meaning that big changes in the current hardly change the voltage across the LED.) When you use an LED you need to look up its forward voltage drop, about 1.7V to 2V for a red LED and about 3V for a blue LED, and the maximum current, usually 20mA for small LEDs. You don't have to use the current specified, this is the maximum current and maximum brightness.

To work out the current-limiting resistor you simply calculate the voltage across the resistor and then use Ohm's law to give you the resistor you need for the current required. The LED determines the voltage and the resistor sets the current.

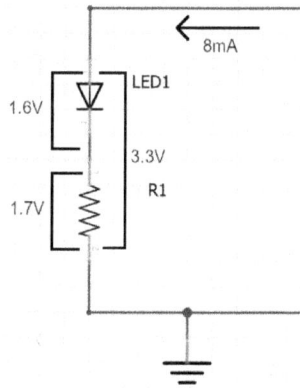

A GPIO line supplies 3.3V and if you assume 1.6V as the forward voltage, across the LED, that leaves 1.7V across the current-limiting resistor since voltage distributes itself across components connected in series. If we restrict the current to 8mA, which is very conservative, then the resistor we need is given by:

R = V/I = 1.7/8 = 0.212

The result is in kiloohms, kΩ, because the current is in milliamps, mA. So we need at least a 212Ω resistor. In practice, you can use a range of values as long as the resistor is around 200 ohms – the bigger the resistor the smaller the current, but the dimmer the LED. If you were using multiple GPIO lines then keeping the GPIO current down to 1 or 2mA would be better, but that would need a transistor.

You need to do this sort of calculation when driving other types of output device. The steps are always the same. The 3.3V distributes itself across the output device and the resistor in some proportion and we know the maximum current – from these values we can compute the resistor needed to keep the actual current below this value.

LED BJT Drive

Often you need to reduce the current drawn from a GPIO line. The Bipolar Junction Transistor (BJT) may be relatively old technology, but it is a current amplifier, low in cost and easy to use.

A BJT is a three-terminal device - base, emitter and collector - in which the current that flows through the emitter/collector is controlled by the current in the base:

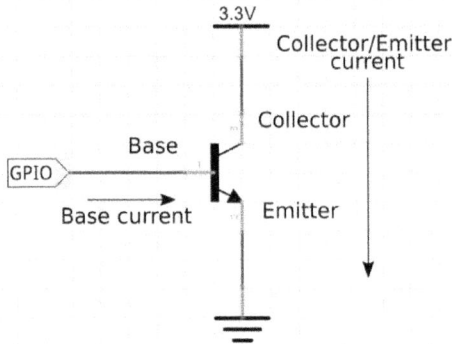

The diagram shows an NPN transistor, which is the most common. This diagram is a simplification in that, in reality, the current in the emitter is slightly larger than that in the collector because you have to add the current flowing in the base.

In most cases you need just two additional facts. Firstly, the voltage on the base is approximately 0.6V, no matter how much current flows since the base is a diode, a non-linear device just like the LED in the previous section. Secondly, the current in the collector/emitter is hfe or ß (beta) times the current in the base. That is, hfe or beta is the current gain of the transistor and you look it up for any transistor you want to use. While you are consulting the datasheets, you also need to check the maximum currents and voltages the device will tolerate. In most cases, the beta is between 100 and 200 and hence you can use a transistor to amplify the GPIO current by at least a factor of 100.

Notice that, for the emitter/collector current to be non-zero, the base has to have a current flowing into it. If the base is connected to ground then the transistor is "cut off", i.e. no current flows. What this means is that when the GPIO line is high the transistor is "on" and current is flowing and when the GPIO line is low the transistor is "off" and no current flows. This high-on/ low-off behavior is typical of an NPN transistor.

A PNP transistor works the other way round:

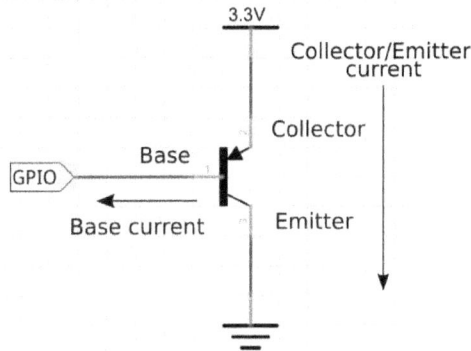

The 0.6V is between the base and the collector and the current flows out of the base. In this case to switch the transistor on you have to connect the base to ground. What this means is that the transistor is off when the GPIO line is high and on when it is low.

This complementary behavior of NPN and PNP BJTs is very useful and means that we can use such transistors in pairs. It is also worth knowing that the diagram given above is usually drawn with 0V at the top of the diagram, i.e. flipped vertically, to make it look the same as the NPN diagram. You always need to make sure you know where the +V line is.

A BJT Example

For a simple example we need to connect a standard LED to a GPIO line with a full 20mA drive. Given that all of the Pi's GPIO lines work at 3.3V and ideally only supply a few milliamps, we need a transistor to drive the LED which typically draws 20mA.

You could use a Field Effect Transistor (FET) of some sort, but for this sort of application an old-fashioned BJT (Bipolar Junction Transistor) works very well and is cheap and available in a thru-hole mount, i.e. it comes with wires. Almost any general purpose NPN transistor will work, but the 2N2222 is very common. From its datasheet you can discover that the max collector current is 800mA and beta is at least 50, which makes it suitable for driving a 20mA LED with a GPIO current of at most 20mA/50 = 0.4mA, where 50 is the HFE or beta .

The circuit is simple but we need two current-limiting resistors:

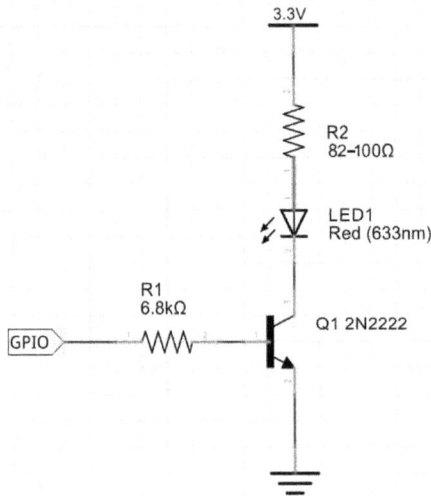

3.3V

R2
82–100Ω

LED1
Red (633nm)

R1
6.8kΩ

GPIO

Q1 2N2222

If you connected the base to the GPIO line directly then the current flowing in the base would be unrestricted – it would be similar to connecting the GPIO line to ground. R1 restricts the current to 0.39mA, which is very low and, assuming that the transistor has a minimum gain (hfe) of 50, this provides just short of 20mA to power it.

The calculation is that the GPIO supplies 3.3V and the base has 0.6V across it so the voltage across R1 is 3.3 - 0.6V = 2.7V. To limit the current to 0.4mA would need a resistor of 2.7V/0.4mA = 6.7kΩ. The closest preferred value is 6.8kΩ, which gives a slightly smaller current.

Without R2 the LED would draw a very large current and burn out. R2 limits the current to 20mA. Assuming a forward voltage drop of 1.6V and a current of 20mA the resistor is given by (3.3-1.6)V/20mA = 85Ω. In practice, we could use anything in the range 82Ω to 100Ω.

The calculation just given assumes that the voltage between the collector and emitter is zero, but of course in practice it isn't. Ignoring this results in a current less than 20mA, which is erring on the safe side. The datasheet indicates that the collector emitter voltage is less than 200mV.

The point is that you rarely make exact calculations for circuits such as this, you simply arrive at acceptable and safe operating conditions.

You can also use this design to drive something that needs a higher voltage. For example, to drive a 5V dip relay, which needs 10mA to activate it, you would use something like:

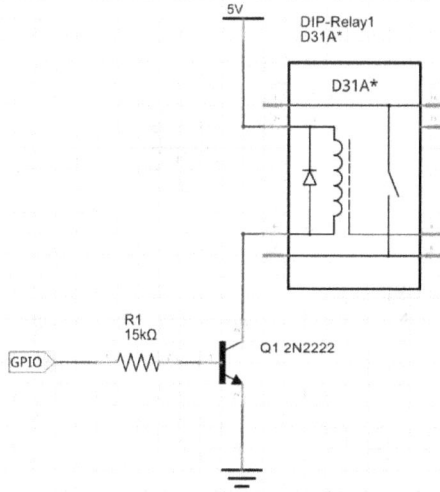

Notice that in this case the transistor isn't needed to increase the drive current – the GPIO line could provide the 10mA directly. Its purpose is to change the voltage from 3.3V to 5V. The same idea works with any larger voltage.

If you are using the 2N2222 then the pinouts are:

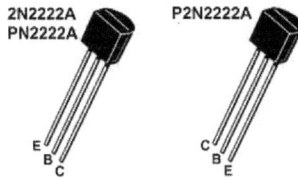

As always, the positive terminal on the LED is the long pin.

MOSFET Driver

There are many who think that the FET (Field Effect Transistor) or more precisely the MOSFET (Metal Oxide Semiconductor FET) is the perfect amplification device and we should ignore BJTs. They are simpler to understand and use, but it can be more difficult to find one with the characteristics you require.

Like the BJT, a MOSFET has three terminals called the gate, drain and source. The current that you want to control flows between the source and drain and it is controlled by the gate. This is analogous to the BJT's base, collector and emitter, but the difference is that it is the voltage on the gate that controls the current between the source and drain.

The gate is essentially a high resistance input and very little current flows in it. This makes it an ideal way to connect a GPIO line to a device that needs more current or a different voltage. When the gate voltage is low the source drain current is very small. When the gate voltage reaches the threshold voltage $V_{GS(th)}$, which is different for different MOSFETs, the source drain current starts to increase exponentially. Basically, when the gate is connected to 0V or below $V_{GS(th)}$ the MOSFET is off and when it is above $V_{GS(th)}$ the MOSFET starts to turn on. Don't think of $V_{GS(th)}$ as the gate voltage that the MOSFET turns on, but as the voltage below which it is turned off.

The problem is that the gate voltage to turn a typical MOSFET fully on is in the region of 10V. Special "logic" MOSFETs need a gate voltage around 5V to fully turn on and this makes the 3.3V at which the Pico's GPIO lines work a problem. The datasheets usually give the fully on resistance and the minimum gate voltage that produces it, usually listed as Drain-Source On-State Resistance. For digital work this is a more important parameter than the gate threshold voltage.

You can deal with this problem in one of two ways – ignore it or find a MOSFET with a very small $V_{GS(th)}$. In practice MOSFETs with thresholds low enough to work at 3.3V are hard to find and when you do find them they are generally only available as surface-mount. Ignoring the problem sometimes works if you can tolerate the MOSFET not being fully on. If the current is kept low then, even though the MOSFET might have a resistance of a few ohms, the power loss and voltage drop may be acceptable.

What MOSFETs are useful for is in connecting higher voltages to a GPIO line used as an input – see later.

Also notice that this discussion has been in terms of an N-channel MOSFET. A P-channel works in the same way, but with all polarities reversed. It is cut off when the gate is at the positive voltage and on when the gate is grounded. This is exactly the same as the NPN versus PNP behavior for the BJT.

MOSFET LED

A BJT is the easiest way to drive an LED, but as an example of using a common MOSFET we can arrange to drive one using a 2N7000, a low-cost, N-channel device available in a standard TO92 form factor suitable for experimentation:

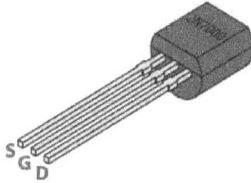

Its datasheet states that it has a $V_{GS(th)}$ typically 2V, but it could be as low as 0.8V or as high as 3V. Given we are trying to work with a gate voltage of 3.3V you can see that in the worst case this is hardly going to work – the device will only just turn on. The best you can do is to buy a batch of 2N7000 and measure their $V_{GS(th)}$ to weed out any that are too high. This said, in practice the circuit given below does generally work.

Assuming a $V_{GS(th)}$ of 2V and a current of 20mA for the LED the datasheet gives a rough value of 6Ω for the on resistance with a gate voltage of 3V. The calculation for the current-limiting resistor is the same as in the BJT case and the final circuit is:

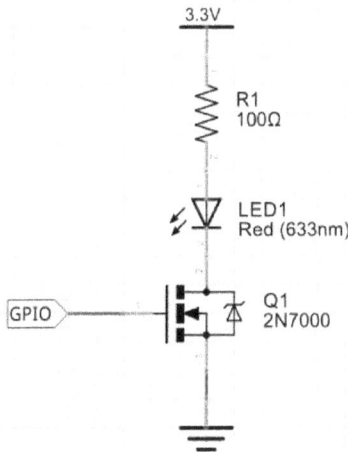

Notice that we don't need a current-limiting resistor for the GPIO line as the gate connection is high impedance and doesn't draw much current. In practice, it is usually a good idea to include a current-limiting resistor in the GPIO line if you plan to switch it on and off rapidly. The problem is that the gate looks like a capacitor and fast changes in voltage can produce high currents. Notice that there are likely to be devices labeled 2N7000 that will not work in this circuit due to the threshold gate voltage being too high, but encountering one is rare.

A logic-level MOSFET like the IRLZ44 has a resistance of 0.028Ω at 5V compared to the 2N2222's of 6Ω. It also has a $V_{GS(th)}$ guaranteed to be between 1V and 2V. It would therefore be a better candidate for this circuit.

Setting Drive Type

The GPIO output can be configured into one of a number of modes, but the most important is pull-up/down. Before we get to the code to do the job it is worth spending a moment explaining the three basic output modes, push-pull, pull-up and pull-down.

Push-Pull Mode

In push-pull mode two transistors of opposite polarity, one PNP and one NPN, are used:

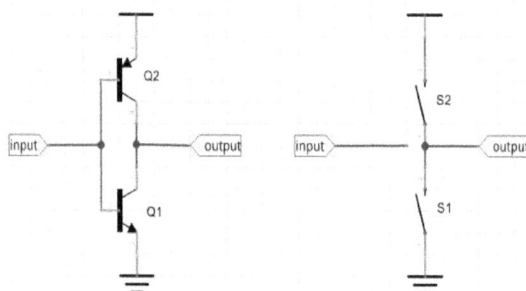

The circuit behaves like the two-switch equivalent shown on the right. Only one of the transistors, or switches, is "closed" at any time. If the input is high then Q1 is saturated and the output is connected to ground - exactly as if S1 was closed. If the input is low then Q2 is saturated and it is as if S2 was closed and the output is connected to 3.3V. You can see that this pushes the output line high with the same "force" as it pulls it low. This is the standard configuration for a GPIO output.

Pull-Up Mode

In pull-up mode one of the transistors is replaced by a resistor:

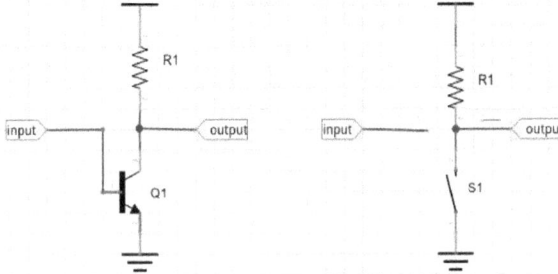

In this case the circuit is equivalent to having a single switch. When the switch is closed, the output line is connected to ground and hence driven low. When the switch is open, the output line is pulled high by the resistor. You can see that in this case the degree of pull-down is greater than the pull-up, where the current is limited by the resistor. The advantage of this mode is that it can be used in an AND configuration. If multiple GPIO or other lines are connected to the output, then any one of them being low will pull the output line low. Only when all of them are off does the resistor succeed in pulling the line high. This is used, for example, in a serial bus configuration like the I2C bus.

Pull-Down Mode

Finally the pull-down mode, which is the best mode for driving general loads, motors, LEDs, etc, is exactly the same as the pull-up only now the resistor is used to pull the output line low.

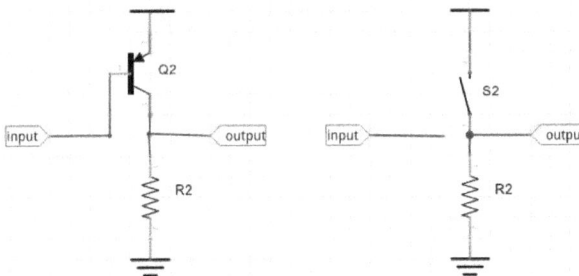

The line is held high by the transistor and pulled low by the resistor only when all the switches are open. Putting this the other way round, the line is high if any one switch is closed. This is the OR version of the shared bus idea.

Open Collector

There is one final output configuration – open collector or, when referring to a MOSFET, open drain. The idea is simple, you don't connect the collector or the drain to anything at all – you simply use it as the output:

There is no pull-up resistor, but you can supply one as an external pull-up if needed. You can also drive a device that needs a current flow through it rather than just a voltage – a coil is the standard example. However, a GPIO line usually cannot supply enough current for such devices.

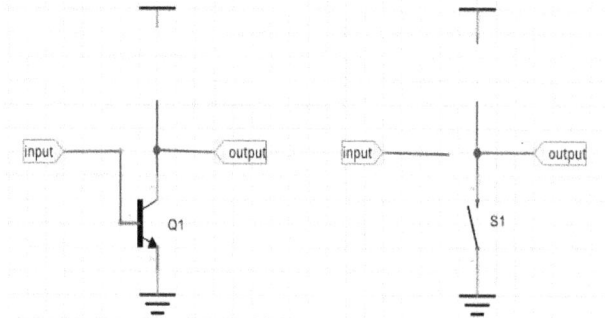

The real use of the open collector arrangement is to implement a shared data line:

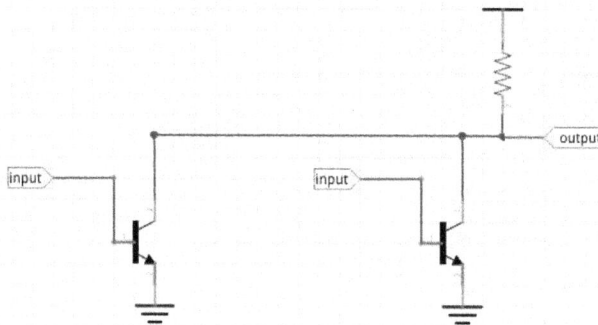

In this case two inputs control one output. If the first transistor is on then the output is low, irrespective of the state of the second transistor. The same is true if the second transistor is on. If you work through the possible combinations we have:

Input 1	Input 2	Output
Off	Off	High
Off	On	Low
On	Off	Low
On	On	Low

You might recognize this as the truth table for an OR gate. This is exactly what an open collector output used in this way implements. Early integrated circuits referred to as Resistor Transistor Logic or RTL implemented logic in this way. This was soon replaced by Transistor Transistor Logic or TTL because transistors are easier to implement in an integrated circuit.

In IoT applications, open collector connections are used to allow any number of devices to share a line. If all of the devices are configured to be open collectors then any one of them can pull the line low. In most cases only one device will be active and sending data at any one time.

Setting Output Mode

MicroPython's `Pin` class has some additional parameters in the constructor to set the mode for a GPIO line:

`machine.Pin(id, mode, pull, value)`

We have already met `id` and `mode` and the `pull` parameter can be any of:

`None` - No pull-up/down resistor

`Pin.PULL_UP = 1`   - Pull-up resistor enabled.

`Pin.PULL_DOWN = 2`   - Pull-down resistor enabled.

In addition to these you can also set `mode` to `Pin.OPEN_DRAIN = 2`, which gives you an active low and a high impedance for the 1 state. As the Pico doesn't support open drain in hardware it is simulated using a simple method.

When the GPIO line is in input mode it has high impedance and the line state is controlled by the pull-up/pull-down resistors and any other devices connected to the line. That is, it behaves like a standard open collector:

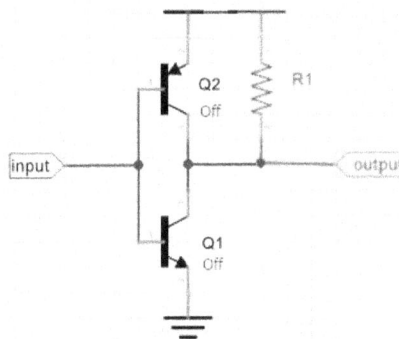

In input mode the Pico can read the bus and collect any data that another device sends it. If the Pico wants to take over the bus and send some data, it can change to output mode.

If it drives the line low then only the "bottom" transistor is on and we have the standard configuration of an open collector bus being driven to a zero:

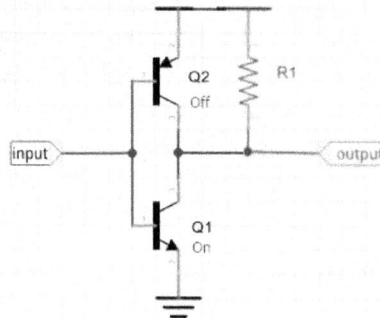

If the Pico wants to send a one on the bus it can simply switch back to input mode when the bus will be pulled up by the resistor. Of course, if anything else on the bus drives it low then the data will be incorrect but this is true of a correctly implemented open collector bus.

To summarize:

- Set things with the pin in input mode or output mode set to high
- To receive data set input mode and read the line
- To send a zero switch to output mode and pull the line low.
- To send a one switch to input mode.

This is exactly what MicroPython does if you select OPEN_DRAIN. If you set the line to output, i.e. OUT or OPEN_DRAIN then you can set an initial state using value.

If you set:

```
Pin.init(OPEN_DRAIN, PULL_UP, value)
```

then if value is 1 the pin is set to input, if the value is 0 the pin is set to output. After this setting the line high with Pin.on() sets the line to output and high, setting the line low, i.e. sets it to input, but it doesn't read the value of the line. Reading the line sets it to input and simply reads the line. Note: At the time of writing this does not work with PULL_DOWN because it fails to reverse the role of zero and one.

For example, using the internal pull up you can simulate open collector using the basic approach, openpullup.py:

```
from machine import Pin
from utime import sleep_us
pin =Pin(22,Pin.IN,Pin.PULL_UP)
while True:
    pin.init(Pin.OUT,Pin.PULL_UP,value=0)
    sleep_us(100)
    pin.init(Pin.IN,Pin.PULL_UP)
    sleep_us(100)
```

This generates a 100μs pulse train in open collector mode.

An equivalent program using OPEN_DRAIN with PULL_UP is, openpullup2.py:

```
from machine import Pin
from utime import sleep_us

pin =Pin(22,Pin.OPEN_DRAIN,Pin.PULL_UP)

while True:
    pin.low()
    sleep_us(100)
    pin.high()
    sleep_us(100)
```

After you have created a Pin object you can change its configuration using the init method which takes the same parameters:

```
Pin.init(mode, pull, value)
```

Only the parameters specified are changed.

The init method is particularly useful for changing a line from input to output and vice versa.

Pull Down Problems Erratum E9

There is a design fault in the RP2350 chip which causes problems with GPIO use in pull-down mode. In fact, the problem is independent of the pull mode selected, but it shows itself more clearly with pull-down enabled. This section describes the fault in detail, but you don't need to understand it to appreciate its effects. Put simply the problem is:

- All of the user GPIO lines have additional leakage current in input mode.
- If you are using a pull-down resistor of more than around 10k then the pull-down may not return to 0V but latch into a stable state at around 2.2V.
- This is true for the internal pull-down resistors – don't use them.
- The latched state is read as a 1 and hence makes working with an open emitter bus impossible.
- Pull-up configurations are not affected but there is still additional leakage current.
- If you have to use pull-down mode use an external resistor of at most 8k.

The problem is the input stage itself. In principle, the input stage of the PAD should draw only a tiny current that we can usually regard as zero. Unfortunately, the design fault means that, when in input mode, the PAD

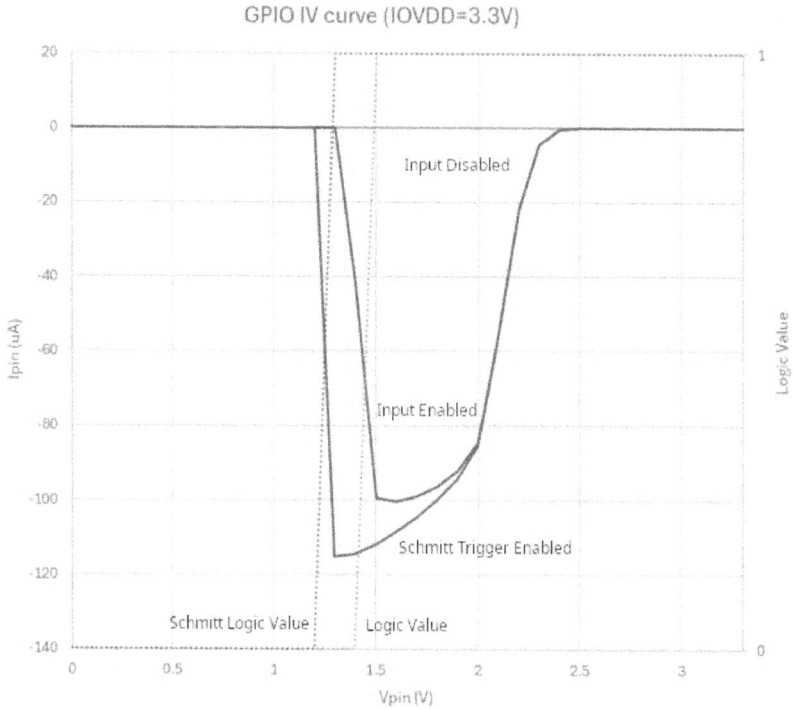

GPIO IV curve (IOVDD=3.3V)

draws a current that depends on the voltage applied:

In principle the leakage current should be less than 1 μA.

What this means is that any of the GPIO lines in input mode will distort an input signal if the source cannot supply sufficient current to overcome the leakage. This isn't usually a problem for digital inputs with active outputs. However, for passive pull up/down it can be a big problem.

Analyzing what happens in this non-linear circuit is difficult and uses techniques that are not usually encountered in digital electronics – load line, differential resistance and equilibrium points.

For a moment consider using the internal pull-down resistor which has a value of 80 to 50kΩ. The driver is nonlinear as represented by the graph, but the resistor is linear. To analyze what happens we can draw a line on the current voltage chart that shows the behavior of the pull-down resistor.

The system can only operate in equilibrium where the line and the curve intersect – the current in the resistor has to be the same as the leakage current.

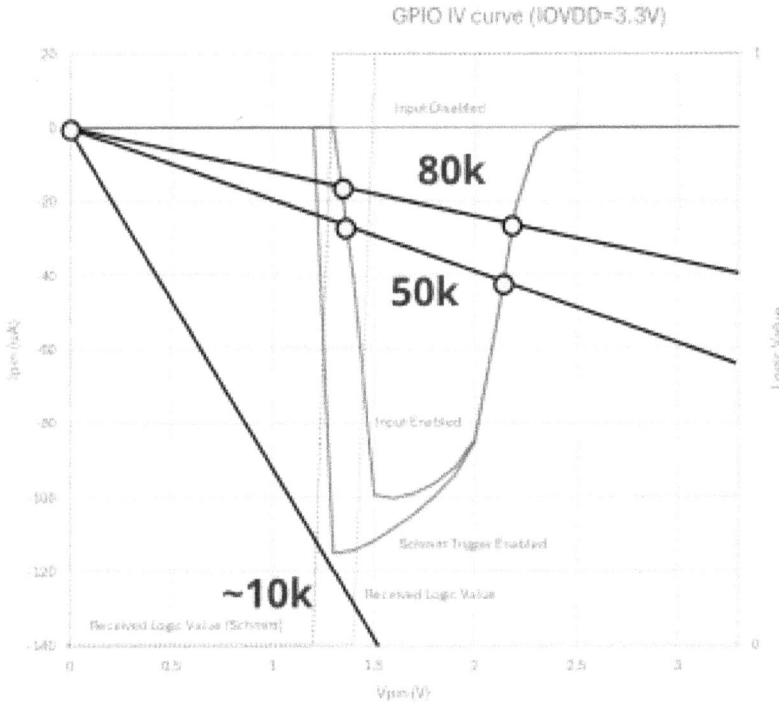

GPIO IV curve (IOVDD=3.3V)

The resistors "load line" intersects in three places as shown in the diagram:

The equilibrium point corresponding to zero current is stable. The one at around 1.5V is unstable as the differential resistance of the leakage source is positive, but the one at around 2V is stable as the differential resistance is negative.

Now consider what happens when you ground the line. In this case the stable state is 0V and 0μA and this is where the line stays until you release it.

Now consider what happens when you pull the line high, i.e. to 3.3V, and then release it. What should happen is that the line returns to 0V because of the pull down resistor. What actually happens is that the voltage starts to fall but it stops falling at around 2V when it reaches the first stable state. What this means is that the line does not return to 0V and, as 2V is still in the region that represents 1, this means that once the line has been driven to 1 it stays set to 1 even after the device releases the line.

In other words, the first time the line is pulled high and released it remains high when it should be pulled low by the pull-down resistor. This stops many programs working – in particular the open collector program given earlier doesn't work in a pull-down configuration, openpulldown.py:

```
from machine import Pin
from utime import sleep

pin =Pin(22,Pin.IN,Pin.PULL_DOWN)

while True:
    pin.init(Pin.OUT,Pin.PULL_DOWN,value=1)
    sleep(.001)
    pin.init(Pin.IN)
    sleep(.001)
```

This should generate a pulse train similar to that produced by the pull-up version, but if you view it on a logic analyzer the output remains high. If you view it on an oscilloscope then what you see is:

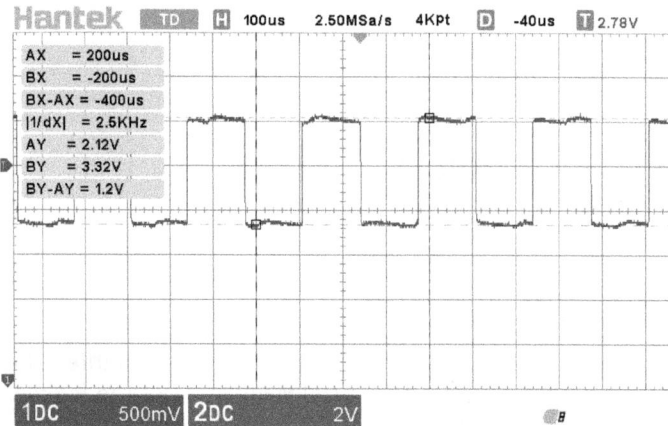

The output is changing, but between 3.3V and 2.12V rather than 3.3V and 0V, and 2.12V is regarded as a logic 1 hence the logic analyzer doesn't see it.

What is the solution?

The best solution would be for Raspberry Pi to fix the flaw in the input stage of the PAD, but until that happens you can either change your software or the hardware.

The software solution is to turn off the input buffer and re-enable input before reading the line, but while this can be done using MicroPython it results in a very slow program.

A much better solution is to not use the internal pull-down resistor. If you look back at the diagram with the load lines drawn on it you can see that a 10k resistor has a load line that just misses the negative differential resistance part of the curve. This means that for this value and lower of pull-down resistor there is only one stable equilibrium, i.e. 0V. The documentation suggests using 8k or smaller. This gives a pull-down current of 412μA, which is small enough for most applications. Notice that the problem isn't with the pull-down resistor, but with the input buffer stage and if you use an external resistance of around 80k then you will get the same behavior.

The documentation also states that the problem does not occur with a pull-up resistor as the input buffer sources leakage current rather than sinking it and so the pull-up succeeds in setting the line to 3.3V. Notice that if you use a potential divider with two resistors, the lower resistor acts like a pull-down and this might trigger the same behavior.

The problem extends to all of the available user GPIO lines, but not to the QSPI pads or the USB pins. It does however affect the GPIO line in all of the usual modes, including PIO. In this case the simplest and most robust solution is to use an external pull-down resistor of, at most, 8k.

Basic Input Circuit - The Switch

Now it is time to turn our attention to the electrical characteristics of GPIO lines as inputs. One of the most common input circuits is the switch or button.

Many beginners make the mistake of wiring a GPIO line to a switch something like:

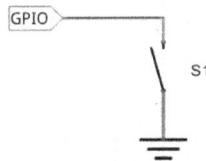

The problem with this is that, if the switch is pressed, the GPIO line is connected to ground and will read as zero. The question is, what does it read when the switch is open? A GPIO line configured as an input without pull up or pull down enabled has a very high resistance. It isn't connected to any particular voltage and the voltage on it varies due to the static it picks up. The jargon is that the unconnected line is "floating". When the switch is open the line is floating and if you read it the result, zero or one, depends on whatever noise it has picked up.

The correct way to do the job is to tie the input line either high or low when the switch is open using a resistor. A pull-up arrangement would be something like:

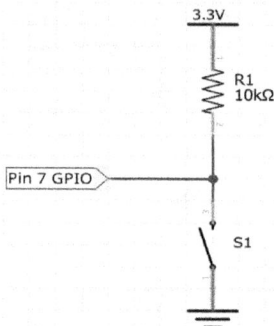

3.3V

R1
10kΩ

Pin 7 GPIO

S1

The value of the resistor used isn't critical. It simply pulls the GPIO line high when the switch isn't pressed. When it is pressed a current of a little more than 0.3mA flows in the resistor. If this is too much, increase the resistance to 100kΩ or even more - but notice that the higher the resistor value the noisier the input to the GPIO and the more it is susceptible to RF interference.   Notice that this gives a zero when the switch is pressed.

If you want a switch that pulls the line high instead of low, reverse the logic by swapping the positions of the resistor and the switch in the diagram to create a pull-down:

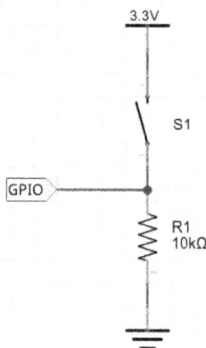

3.3V

S1

GPIO

R1
10kΩ

Notice that this gives a one when the switch is pressed.

The good news is that the Pico defaults to an input configuration with a pull-up resistor of around 50kΩ which means you can connect a switch directly to a default GPIO line and it will give a zero when the switch is pressed.

Debounce

Although the switch is the simplest input device, it is very difficult to get right. When a user clicks a switch of any sort, the action isn't clean - the switch bounces. What this means is that the logic level on the GPIO line goes high then low and high again and bounces between the two until it settles down. There are electronic ways of debouncing switches, but software does the job much better. All you have to do is insert a delay of a millisecond or so after detecting a switch press and read the line again - if it is still low then record a switch press. Similarly, when the switch is released, read the state twice with a delay. You can vary the delay to modify the perceived characteristics of the switch.

A more sophisticated algorithm is based on the idea of integration to debounce a switch. All you have to do is read the state multiple times, every few milliseconds say, and keep a running sum of values. If you sum say ten values each time then a total of between 6 and 10 can be taken as an indication that the switch is high. A total less than this indicates that the switch is low. You can think of this as a majority vote in the time period for the switch being high or low.

The Potential Divider

If you have an input that is outside of the range of 0V to 3.3V then you can reduce it using a simple potential divider. In the diagram V is the input from the external logic and Vout is the connection to the GPIO input line:

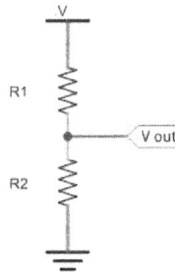

```
Vout = V*R2/(R1+R2)
```

You can spend a lot of time working out good values of R1 and R2. For loads that take a lot of current you need R1+R2 to be small and divided in the same ratio as the voltages. For example, for a 5V device, R1 = 18KΩ or 20KΩ and R2 = 33KΩ work well to drop the voltage to 3.3V.

A simpler approach that works for a 5V signal is to notice that the ratio R1:R2 has to be the same as (5-3.3):3.3, i.e. the voltage divides itself across the resistors in proportion to their value, which is roughly 1:2. What this means is that you can take any resistor and use it for R1 and use two of the same value in series for R2 and the Vout will be 3.3V.

The problem with a resistive divider is that it can round off fast pulses due to the small capacitive effects. This usually isn't a problem, but if it is then the solution is to use a FET or a BJT as an active buffer:

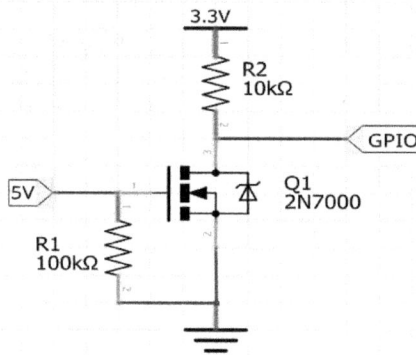

Notice that this is an inverting buffer, the output is low when the input is high, but you can usually ignore this and simply correct it in software, i.e. read a 1 as a low state and a 0 as a high state. The role of R1 is to make sure the FET is off when the 5V signal is absent and R2 limits the current in the FET to about 0.3mA. In most cases you should try the simple voltage divider and only move to an active buffer if it doesn't work.

This very basic look at electronics isn't all that you need to know, but it is enough for you to see some of the problems and find some answers. In general, this sort of electronics is all about making sure that voltages and currents are within limits. As switching speeds increase you have additional problems, which are mainly concerned with making sure that your circuits aren't slowing things down. This is where things get more subtle.

Summary

- You can get a long way with only a small understanding of electronics, but you do need to know enough to protect the Pico and things you connect to it.
- The maximum current from any GPIO line should be less than 12mA and the total current should be less than 30mA.
- All of the GPIO lines work at 3.3V and you should avoid directly connecting any other voltage.
- You can drive an LED directly from a GPIO line, but only at 16mA rather than the nominal 20mA needed for full brightness.
- Calculating a current-limiting resistor always follows the same steps – find out the current in the device, find out the voltage across the device and work out the resistor that supplies that current when the remainder of the voltage is applied to it.
- For any load you connect to a GPIO output, you generally need a current-limiting resistor.
- In many cases you need a transistor, a BJT, to increase the current supplied by the GPIO line.
- To use a BJT you need a current-limiting resistor in the base and generally one in the collector.
- MOSFETs are popular alternatives to BJTs, but it is difficult to find a MOSFET that works reliably at 3.3V.
- GPIO output lines can be set to active push-pull mode, where a transistor is used to pull the line high or low, or passive pull-up or pull-down mode, where one transistor is used and a resistor pulls the line high or low when the transistor is inactive.
- GPIO lines have built-in pull-up and pull-down resistors which can be selected or disabled under software control.
- When used as inputs, GPIO lines have a very high resistance and in most cases you need pull-up or pull-down resistors to stop the line floating.
- The built-in pull-up or pull-down resistors can be used in input mode.
- The Pico 2 has a fault that causes the GPIO lines to leak more current than they should, making using the internal pull-down difficult.
- Mechanical input devices have to be debounced to stop spurious input.
- If you need to connect an input to something bigger than 3.3V then you need a potential divider to reduce the voltage back to 3.3V. You can also use a transistor.

Chapter 6
Simple Input

There is no doubt that input is more difficult than output. When you need to drive a line high or low you are in command of when it happens, but input is in the hands of the outside world. If your program isn't ready to read the input, or if it reads it at the wrong time, then things just don't work. What is worse, you have no idea what your program is doing relative to the event you are trying to capture. Welcome to the world of input.

In this chapter we look at the simplest approach to input – the polling loop. This may be simple, but it is a good way to approach many tasks. In Chapter 7 we look at more sophisticated alternatives – events and interrupts.

GPIO Input

GPIO input is a much more difficult problem than output from the point of view of measurement and verification. For output at least you can see the change in the signal on a logic analyzer and know the exact time that it occurred. This makes it possible to track down timing problems and fine tune things with good accuracy.

Input on the other hand is "silent" and unobservable. When did you read in the status of the line? Usually the timing of the read is with respect to some other action that the device has taken. For example, you read the input line $20\mu s$ after setting the output line high. But how do you know when the input line changed state during that 20 microseconds? The simple answer is in most cases you don't.

In some applications the times are long and/or unimportant but in some they are critical and so we need some strategies for monitoring and controlling read events. The usual rule of thumb is to assume that it takes as long to read a GPIO line as it does to set it. This means we can use the delay mechanisms that we looked at with regard to output for input as well.

One common and very useful trick when you are trying to get the timing of input correct is to substitute an output command to a spare GPIO line and monitor it with a logic analyzer. Place the output instruction just before the input instruction and where you see the line change on the logic analyzer should be close to the time that the input would be read in the unmodified program. You can use this to debug and fine tune and then remove the output statement.

Basic Input Functions

The `Pin` object can be set to input mode using the constructor:

```
pin = Pin(22, Pin.IN)
```

You can also set the direction to input using the `init` method:

```
pin.init(mode=Pin.IN)
```

Once set to input, the GPIO line is high impedance so it won't take very much current, no matter what you connect it to. However, notice that the Pico uses 3.3V logic and you should not exceed this value on an input line. For a full discussion of how to work with input see the previous chapter.

You can read the line's input state using the `value` method:

```
result=pin.value()
```

Notice that this is an "overloaded" method. If you supply a value as a parameter then it attempts to set the value as output. If you don't specify a value then it gets the GPIO level as a zero or a one.

This is all there is to using a GPIO line as an input, apart from the details of the electronics and the small matter of interrupts.

As introduced in the previous chapter you can also set the internal pull-up or pull-down resistors using one of:

```
None                     No pull-up
Pin.PULL_UP = 1          Pull-up resistor enabled
Pin.PULL_DOWN = 2        Pull-down resistor enabled
```

in the constructor or the `init` method.

The pull-up/down resistors are between 50 and 80kΩ but recall the the Pico 2 has a problem with its input stage that makes using the pull-down resistor a bad idea.

The Simple Button

One of the most common input circuits is the switch or button. If you want another external button you can use any GPIO line and the circuit explained in the previous chapter. That is, the switch has to have either a pull-up or pull-down resistor either provided by you or a built-in one enabled using software.

The simplest switch input program using an internal pull-up is, button1.py:

```
from machine import Pin
import time
pinIn = Pin(22, Pin.IN,Pin.PULL_UP)
pinLED = Pin("LED", Pin.OUT)

while True:
    if pinIn.value():
        pinLED.on()
    else:
        pinLED.off()
    time.sleep(0.5)
```

As the internal pull-up resistor is used, the switch can be connected to the line and ground without any external resistors:

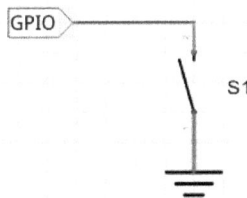

The program simply tests for the line to be pulled high by the switch not being closed and then sets the LED pin high. The on-board LED it will light up while S1 is not pressed. Notice GPIO 22 goes low to when the switch is pressed.

If you change PULL_UP to PULL_DOWN, the way the switch is connected becomes:

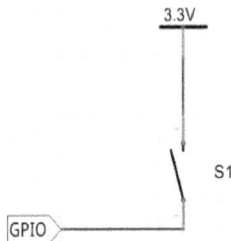

The program still works, but now GPIO 22 is high when the switch is pressed and hence the LED is on when the switch is pressed.

Should you use an internal or external resistor? The answer is that it mostly doesn't matter as long as there is a resistor included in your circuit. So if you use None make sure there is an external resistor. The only problem with using an internal resistor is the possibility that the software fails to set the pull-up/down mode and leaves the input floating.

Also notice that this switch input is not debounced. The simplest way to do this is include a time delay in the loop before the line is sampled again.

If you want to respond to a button press, that is a press and a release event, then you have to test for a double transition, button2.py:

```
from machine import Pin
import time
pinIn = Pin(22, Pin.IN,Pin.PULL_UP)
pinLED = Pin("LED", Pin.OUT)

while True:
    while pinIn.value()==1:
        pass
    while pinIn.value()==0:
        pass
    pinLED.on()
    time.sleep(1)
    pinLED.off()
```

In this case you really do need the debounce delays if you want to avoid responding twice to what the user perceives as a single press.

A 1-millisecond delay is probably the smallest delay that produces a button that feels as if it works. In practice, you would have to tune the delay to suit the button mechanism in use and the number of times you can allow the button to be pressed in one second.

Press Or Hold

You can carry on elaborating on how to respond to a button. For example, most users have grown accustomed to the idea that holding a button down for a longer time than a press makes something different happen.

To distinguish between a press and a hold all you need to do is time the difference between line down and line up, button3.py:

```
from machine import Pin
import time
pinIn = Pin(22, Pin.IN,Pin.PULL_UP)
pinLED = Pin("LED", Pin.OUT)

while True:
    while pinIn.value()==1:
        pass
    t=time.ticks_ms()
    time.sleep_ms(1)
    while pinIn.value()==0:
        pass
    t=time.ticks_diff(time.ticks_ms(),t)
    if t<2000:
        pinLED.on()
        time.sleep(1)
        pinLED.off()
    else:
        for i in range(10):
            pinLED.on()
            time.sleep_ms(100)
            pinLED.off()
            time.sleep_ms(100)
```

In this case holding the button for 2s registers a "held" – the LED flashes 10 times and anything less is a "push" – the LED flashes just once. Notice the 1ms debounce pause between the test for no-press and press.

One of the problems with all of these sample programs is that they wait for the button to be pressed or held and this makes it difficult for them to do anything else. You have to include whatever else your program needs to do within the loop that waits for the button – the polling loop. You can do this in an ad hoc way, but the best approach is to implement a finite state machine, see later.

How Fast Can We Measure?

Buttons are one form of input, but often we want to read data from a GPIO line driven by an electronic device and decode the data. This usually means measuring the width of the pulses and this raises the question of how fast can we accept input?

The simplest way to find out how quickly we can take a measurement is to perform a pulse width measurement. Applying a square wave to GPIO 22 we can measure the time that the pulse is high using timer.py:

```
from machine import Pin
import time
pinIn = Pin(22, Pin.IN)

while True:
    while pinIn.value()==1:
        pass
    while pinIn.value()==0:
        pass

    t = time.ticks_us()
    while pinIn.value()==1:
        pass
    t = time.ticks_diff(time.ticks_us(),t)
    print(t)
    time.sleep(1)
```

This might look a little strange at first. The inner while loops are responsible for getting us to the right point in the waveform. First we loop until the line goes low, then we loop until it goes high again and finally measure how long before it goes low. You might think that we simply have to wait for it to go high and then measure how long till it goes low, but this misses the possibility that the signal might be part way through a high period when we first measure it. This can be measured down to around $25\mu s$.

Notice that in either case if you try measuring pulse widths much shorter than the lower limit that works, you will get results that look like longer pulses are being applied. The reason is simply that the Pico will miss the first transition to zero but will detect a second or third or later transition. This is the digital equivalent of the aliasing effect found in the Fourier Transform or general signal processing.

MicroPython also provides a special method that implements the algorithm used in the above program. The method:

```
machine.time_pulse_us(pin, level, timeout)
```

will block until the pin specified changes to the level specified or the timeout occurs. Once the pin attains the level specified it times how long it takes for it to change and returns the result in microseconds. The only problem is that, if the pin is already at the specified level, the timing begins at once.

Using this method the program above can be written more simply as:

```
import time
import machine

pinIn = machine.Pin(22, machine.Pin.IN)

while True:
    t = machine.time_pulse_us(pinIn, 1)
    print(t)
    time.sleep(1)
```

Notice that you will get some fractional measurements using this method. To get accurate results you would have to be sure that the line was at zero just before the method is used. For example:

```
import machine
import time

import machine
pinIn = machine.Pin(22, machine.Pin.IN)

while True:
    while pinIn.value() == 1:
        pass
    t = machine.time_pulse_us(pinIn, 1)
    print(t)
    time.sleep(1)
```

The time_pulse_us method is not a big improvement on the more basic way of doing the job, but it is more accurate for lengthier intervals. It is also very useful when implementing protocols that use different length pulses to represent a zero or a one, see Chapter 14.

The Finite State Machine

If your project requires a complex set of input and output lines then you need an organizing principle to save you from the complexity. When you first start writing IoT programs that respond to the outside world you quickly discover that all of your programs take a similar form:

```
while(True):
    wait for some input lines
    process the input data
    write some output lines
    wait for some input lines
    read some more input lines
    write some output lines
```

For most programmers this is a slightly disturbing discovery because programs are not supposed to consist of infinite loops, but IoT programs nearly always, in principle if not in practice, take the form of an apparently infinite polling loop. A second, and more important, aspect is that the way in which reading and writing GPIO lines is related can be so complex that it can be difficult to see exactly when any particular line is read and when it is written.

It is natural to try to find implementations that make this simpler. In most cases, programmers discover or invent the idea of the event or, better, the interrupt. In this case when something happens in the outside world a function is automatically called to deal with it and the relation between the external state and the system's response is seemingly well-defined. Of course, in practice it isn't, as you have to deal with what happens when multiple events or interrupts occur at the same, or very nearly the same, time.

Often more sophisticated approaches are used to try and handle more external changes of state in a given time. Somehow the infinite polling loop is seen as wasteful. What is the CPU doing if it spends all its time looping round waiting for something to happen? Of course, if it has nothing better to do then it isn't a waste. In fact IoT devices are often dedicated to just getting one job done so the "polling is wasteful" meme, so prevalent in the rest of computing, is completely unjustified.

What is more, the polling loop is usually the way to get the greatest throughput. If a processor can handle X external state changes per second and respond to these with Y external state changes per second, then moving to an event- or interrupt-based implementation reduces both X and Y. In short, if a processor cannot do the job using a polling loop then it cannot do the job. This is not to say that there aren't advantages to events and interrupts – there are, but they don't increase throughput.

So how should you organize a polling loop so that what it does is self-evident by looking at the code?

There are many answers to this according to the system being implemented and there are no "pure" theoretical answers that solve all problems, but the finite state machine, or FSM, is a model every IoT programmer should know.

A finite state machine is very simple. At any given time the machine/program has a record of the current state S. At a regular interval the external world provides an input I which changes the state from S to S' and produces an output O. That's all there is to a finite state machine. There are variations on the definition of the FSM but this one, a Mealy machine because its outputs depend on both its state and the input, is most suitable for IoT programming.

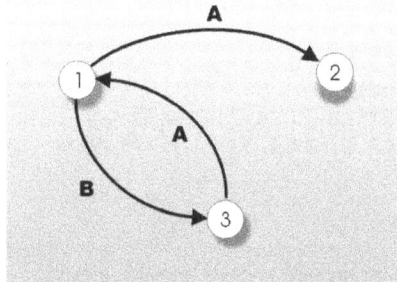

You can design an FSM with the help of a diagram. In the FSM shown we have three states 1, 2 and 3 and if you are in state 1 an input of A moves the system to state 2 and an input of B moves it into state 3.

Your program simply needs to take the form of a polling loop that implements a finite state machine. It reads the input lines as I and uses this and the current state S to determine the new state S' and the output O. There is some overhead in using this organization, but it is usually worth it. Notice that this organization implies that you read input once, make changes once and set outputs once in the loop. If you fix the time that the polling loop takes then you know the characteristic time for any changes to the system.

FSM Button

As an example, let's implement the simple button given earlier in the chapter. The first version used multiple loops to wait for changes in the state of the input line. The finite state version uses only a single polling loop, fsmbutton.py:

```
from machine import Pin
import time
pinIn = Pin(22, Pin.IN)

s=0
count=0
while True:
    i=pinIn.value()
    t=time.ticks_add(time.ticks_us(),1000*100)
    if s==0:    #button not pushed
        if i:
            s=1
            count=count+1
            print("Button Push ",count)
    elif s==1: #button pushed
        if not i:
            s=0
    else:
        s=0
    while time.ticks_us()<t:
        pass
```

This looks more complicated than the original, and there are more lines of code, but it is much easier to extend to more complex situations. In this case we have only two states – s = 0 for button not pushed and s = 1 for button pushed. Ideally the states that we use shouldn't refer to inputs or outputs, but to the overall state of the system. For example, if you were using a Pico to control a nuclear reactor you might use a state "CoreMeltdown" in preference to "TempSensorOverLimit". States should be about the consequence of the inputs and the outputs should be the consequence of the current state. In the example above the inputs and output are too simple to give rise to an abstract concept of "state". Even if you were to change the state labels to "LEDOn" or "LEDOff" they are directly related to the state of a single output line.

The key idea, however, is that the states indicate the state of the system at the time of the input. That is, s = 0 (button not pushed) is the state when the system reads in a low on the GPIO line (recall the line is pulled low so pushing the button makes it go high). You can see at the start of the polling loop we read the input line and store its value in the variable i. Next, a case statement is used to process the input depending on the current state. You

84

can see that if s = 0, i.e. button not pushed, then the state moves to s = 1, i.e. button pushed, and a message is printed giving the number of times the button has been pressed as a simple action. In general, the action could be setting a GPIO line high or doing anything that is appropriate for the new state. Notice that actions occur on state changes.

If the state is in s = 1, i.e. button pushed, then the input has to be 0 for anything to happen. In this case the state changes to s = 0 and any actions that are needed to take the system from state 1 to state 0 are performed – none in this case. Finally, if the state is anything other than 0 or 1, we set it to 0 as something is wrong.

Notice that the polling loop is set up so that the whole thing repeats every 100ms. The time is taken at the start of the loop and after everything has been processed we wait for 100ms to be up. What this means is that, no matter how long the processing in the loop takes, as long as it takes less than 100ms the loop will repeat every 100ms.

This is a very simple finite state machine polling loop. In practice, there is usually a set of ifs that deals with each current state, but there is often another set of if statements within each state case to deal with what happens according to different inputs. An alternative way of designing a finite state machine loop is to use a lookup table, indexed by state and input, which gives you the new state and the actions.

FSM Hold Button

As a slightly more complicated example of using the FSM approach, let's implement the button with hold. You might think that button with hold has three states – button not pushed, button pushed and button held. You can implement it in this way, but there is an argument that there are still only two states – not pushed and pushed. The held state is better implemented as extra input data to the state, i.e. the time the button has been in the pressed state.

Remember, the output of a FSM depends on the state and the input and in this case the input is the line level and the time pressed, `fsmholdbutton.py`:

```
from machine import Pin
import time
pinIn = Pin(22, Pin.IN)

s=0
while True:
    i=pinIn.value()
    t=time.ticks_add(time.ticks_us(),1000*100)
    if s==0:            #button not pushed
        if i:
            s=1
        tpush=t
    elif s==1:          #button pushed
        if not i:
            s=0
            if time.ticks_diff(t, tpush) > 2000000:
                print("Button held \n\r")
            else:
                print("Button pushed \n\r")
    else:
        s=0
    while time.ticks_us()<t:
        pass
```

It is clear that you can't know the time the button has been pressed until it is released so the actions are now all in the button-pushed state. While the button is in the pushed state it can be released and we can compute the time it has been pressed and modify the action accordingly.

FSM Ring Counter

Another very common input configuration is the ring counter. A ring counter moves on to a new output each time it receives an input and repeats when it reaches the last output of the set. For example, if you have three output lines connected to three LEDs then initially LED 0 is on, when the user presses the button LED 1 is on and the rest off, the next user press moves on to LED 2 on and another press turns LED 0 on. You can see that as the user keeps pressing the button the LEDs go on and off in a repeating sequence.

A common implementation of a ring counter has a state for each button press and release for each LED being on. For three LEDs this means six states and this has a number of disadvantages. A better idea is to have just two states, button pressed and button released and use a press counter as an additional input value. This means that what happens when you enter the button pressed state depends on the value in the counter.

We also change from using the measurement of the button as pressed or released and move to considering an "edge" signal. Generally we need inputs that indicate an event localized in time. Button "pressed" and button "released" are events that are extended in time but "press" and "release" are localized to small time intervals that can be thought of as single time measurements. In general we prefer "edge" signals because these indicate when something has changed.

Implementing this is fairly easy, fsmring.py:

```
from machine import Pin
import time
pinIn = Pin(22, Pin.IN)
pinLED1 = Pin(21, Pin.OUT)
pinLED2 = Pin(20, Pin.OUT)
pinLED3 = Pin(19, Pin.OUT)
pinLED1.on()
pinLED2.off()
pinLED3.off()
s = 0
buttonState = pinIn.value()
while True:
    buttonNow = pinIn.value()
    edge = buttonState-buttonNow
    buttonState = buttonNow
    t = time.ticks_add(time.ticks_us(), 1000*100)
    if s == 0:
        if edge == 1:
            s = 1
            pinLED1.off()
            pinLED2.on()
            pinLED3.off()

    elif s == 1:
        if edge == 1:
            s = 2
            pinLED1.off()
            pinLED2.off()
            pinLED3.on()
    elif s == 2:
        if edge == 1:
            s = 0
            pinLED1.on()
            pinLED2.off()
            pinLED3.off()
    else:
        s = 0
    while time.ticks_us() < t:
        pass
```

First we set up the GPIO lines for input and output and set the outputs so that LED 0 is on, i.e. s = 0. Next we start the polling loop. Inside the loop there is a `switch` statement that manages three states. At the start of the loop the difference between the current button value and its previous value are used to calculate `edge` which is 1 only when the button has changed from pressed, 1, to released, 0. That is, `edge=1` only on a down-going edge. If the button has just been pressed then the state is moved on to the next state, 0→1, 1→2 and 2→0, and the LEDs are set to the appropriate values.

You might wonder why all three LEDs are set and not just the two that are changing? There are a number of reasons including it's easier to see what is happening from the code and it makes sure that all of the LEDs are in the state you intend. Notice that the polling loop is set up to repeat every 100ms so providing debouncing and a predictable service time. If you try this out you will find that the LEDs light up sequentially on each button press.

Like many more advanced methods the FSM approach can make things seem more complicated in simple examples, but it repays the effort as soon as things get more complicated. A polling loop with tens of states and lots of input and outline lines to manage becomes impossible to maintain without some organizing principle.

Summary

- Input is hard because things happen at any time, irrespective of what your program might be doing.

- You can call the `value` method at any time to discover the state of a GPIO line – the problem is when and how often to call it.

- You can choose between external or internal pull-up/down resistors.

- Mechanical input devices such as buttons have to be debounced.

- The power of software is that it can enhance a simple device. A simple button is either pushed or released, but you can use this to generate a third "held" state.

- Using a polling loop you can handle inputs as short as a few tens of microseconds.

- Most IoT programs are best written as a polling loop.

- The Finite State Machine (FSM) is one way of organizing a complex polling loop so that inputs are tested and outputs are set once for each time through the loop.

- Ideally the states of a FSM should not be simple statements of the inputs of outputs that determine the state, but for simple systems this can be difficult to achieve.

- It can be difficult to work out what constitutes the events of a FSM. Ideally they should be localized in time so that they indicate the moment that something happens.

Chapter 7
Advanced Input – Events and Interrupts

When you start to work with multiple inputs that mean a range of different things, input really becomes a challenge. You can control much of the complexity using finite state machines and similar organizational principles, but sooner or later you are going to have to deal with the problem of input when your program isn't ready for it. There are two general and closely related ways to deal with this problem – events and interrupts. The Pico SDK and MicroPython don't really support events, preferring interrupts, but its hardware certainly is event-capable and it isn't difficult to add some software to make it work. In this chapter we look first at events and then at interrupts.

Events

An event is like a latch or a memory that something happened. Imagine that there is a flag that will be automatically set when an input line changes state. The flag is set without the involvement of software, or at least any software that you have control over. It is useful to imagine an entirely hardware-based setting of the flag, even if this is not always the case. With the help of an event you can avoid missing an input because the polling loop was busy doing something else. Now the polling loop reads the flag rather than the actual state of the input line and hence it can detect if the line has changed since it last polled. The polling loop resets the event flag and processes the event. Of course, it can't always know exactly when the event happened, but at least it hasn't missed it altogether.

A simple event can avoid the loss of a single input, but what if there is more than one input while the polling loop is unavailable? The most common solution is to create an event queue – that is, a FIFO (first in, first out) queue of events as they occur. The polling loop now reads the event at the front of the queue, processes it and reads the next. It continues like this until the queue is empty, when it simply waits for an event. As long as the queue is big enough, an event queue means you don't miss any input, but input events are not necessarily processed close to the time that they occurred. They should be processed in order, but unless the events are timestamped the program has no idea when they happened.

An event queue is a common architecture, but to work or have any advantages, it needs either multiple cores so that events can always be added to the queue before another occurs or it needs the help of hardware, usually in the form of interrupts. Notice that an event, or an event queue, cannot increase the program's throughput or decrease its latency – the time to react to an input. In fact, an event queue decreases throughput and increases latency due to overheads of implementation. All an event system does is to ensure that you do not miss any input and that all input gets processed eventually.

Interrupts Considered Harmful?

Interrupts are often confused with events, but they are very different. An interrupt is a hardware mechanism that stops the computer doing whatever it is currently doing and makes it transfer its attention to running an interrupt handler. You can think of an interrupt as an event flag that, when set, interrupts the current program to run the assigned interrupt handler.

Using interrupts means the outside world decides when the computer should pay attention to input and there is no need for a polling loop. Most hardware people think that interrupts are the solution to everything and polling is inelegant and only to be used when you can't use an interrupt. This is far from the reality. There is a general feeling that real-time programming and interrupts go together and if you are not using an interrupt you are probably doing something wrong. In fact, the truth is that if you are using an interrupt you are probably doing something wrong. So much so that some organizations are convinced that interrupts are so dangerous that they are banned from being used at all.

Interrupts are only really useful when you have a low-frequency condition that needs to be dealt with on a high-priority basis. Interrupts can simplify the logic of your program, but rarely does using an interrupt speed things up because the overhead involved in interrupt handling is usually quite high.

If you have a polling loop that takes 100ms to poll all inputs and there is an input that demands attention in under 60ms then clearly the polling loop is not going to be good enough. Using an interrupt allows the high-priority event to interrupt the polling loop and be processed in less than 100ms. However, if this happens very often the polling loop will cease to work as intended. An alternative is to simply make the polling loop check the input twice per loop.

For a more real-world example, suppose you want to react to a doorbell push button. You could write a polling loop that simply checks the button status repeatedly and forever or you could write an interrupt service routine (ISR) to respond to the doorbell. The processor would be free to get on with other things until the doorbell was pushed when it would stop what it was doing and transfer its attention to the ISR.

How good a design this is depends on how much the doorbell has to interact with the rest of the program and how many doorbell pushes you are expecting. It takes time to respond to the doorbell push and then the ISR has to run to completion - what is going to happen if another doorbell push happens while the first push is still being processed? Some processors have provision for forming a queue of interrupts, but that doesn't help with the fact that the process can only handle one interrupt at a time. Of course, the same is true of a polling loop, but if you can't handle the throughput of events with a polling loop, you can't handle it using an interrupt either, because interrupts add the time to transfer to the ISR and back again.

Finally, before you dismiss the idea of having a processor do nothing but ask repeatedly "is the doorbell pressed", consider what else it has to do. If the answer is "not much" then a polling loop might well be your simplest option. Also, if the processor has multiple cores, then the fastest way of dealing with any external event is to use one of the cores in a fast polling loop. This can be considered to be a software emulation of a hardware interrupt – not to be confused with a software interrupt or trap, which is a hardware interrupt triggered by software.

If you are going to use interrupts to service input then a good design is to use the interrupt handler to feed an event queue. This at least lowers the chance that input will be missed.

Despite their attraction, interrupts are usually a poor choice for anything other than low-frequency events that need to be dealt with quickly.

Hardware Events

MicroPython doesn't support events, but the hardware does as part of its implementation of GPIO interrupts. Each GPIO line records four events:

```
GPIO_IRQ_LEVEL_LOW
GPIO_IRQ_LEVEL_HIGH
GPIO_IRQ_EDGE_FALL
GPIO_IRQ_EDGE_RISE
```

The level events are not latched and simply reflect the current state of the GPIO line. The edge events are latched and stay set until you clear them. In practice, the edge events are far more useful.

Each of these events can also be set to cause an interrupt and this is something we look at later in this chapter. For the moment, all we are concerned with is using these events as "memories" that something happened.

Currently MicroPython doesn't have any methods that support events, but it is fairly easy to add a pair of functions that do the job:

```
def gpio_get_events(pinNo):
    IO_BANK0_BASE=0x40028000   #Pico 2
    INTR0=0x230 #Pico 2
  # IO_BANK0_BASE=0x40014000 #Pico
  # INTR0=0xF0 #Pico

    mask = 0xF << 4 * (pinNo % 8)
    intrAddr = IO_BANK0_BASE + INTR0 + (pinNo // 8)*4
    return (machine.mem32[intrAddr] & mask) >> (4 * (pinNo % 8))

def gpio_clear_events(pinNo, events):
    IO_BANK0_BASE=0x40028000   #Pico 2
    INTR0=0x230 #Pico 2
  # IO_BANK0_BASE=0x40014000 #Pico
  # INTR0=0xF0 #Pico

    intrAddr = IO_BANK0_BASE + INTR0 + (pinNo // 8)*4
    machine.mem32[intrAddr] = events << (4 * (pinNo % 8))
```

Notice that you need to set the address and offset, IO_BANK0_BASE and INTR0, different for the Pico and Pico 2 as the memory map is different see Chapter 21 for a full explanation. For the moment all you really need to know is that gpio_get_events will return four bits that reflect the status of the events corresponding to pinNo. Similarly, gpio_clear_events is used to clear the latched events on pinNo. The latched events correspond to the constants:

```
Pin.IRQ_FALLING
Pin.IRQ_RISING
```

You can define more suitably named constants if you want to.

For example:

```
event = gpio_get_events(22)
if event & Pin.IRQ_RISING:
```

tests to see if a rising edge event has occurred on GPIO 22.

Putting all this together, the steps in using events are:

1. Set the line to be an input:

```
pin=Pin(22,Pin.IN,Pin.PULL_UP)
```

2. Clear the event:

```
gpio_clear_events(22, Pin.IRQ_RISING)
```

3. After this you can do something else and eventually read the status bit to see if the event occurred in the intervening time, clearing the event to allow it to record another:

```
event = gpio_get_events(22)
gpio_clear_events(22, Pin.IRQ_RISING)
```

For example, to print which sort of latched event has occurred on GPIO 22 you could use event.py:

```
from utime import sleep
from machine import Pin
import machine

def gpio_get_events(pinNo):
    IO_BANK0_BASE=0x40028000  #Pico 2
    INTR0=0x230 #Pico 2
  # IO_BANK0_BASE=0x40014000 #Pico
  # INTR0=0xF0 #Pico
    mask = 0xF << 4 * (pinNo % 8)
    intrAddr = IO_BANK0_BASE + INTR0 + (pinNo // 8)*4
    return (machine.mem32[intrAddr] & mask) >> (4 * (pinNo % 8))

def gpio_clear_events(pinNo, events):
    IO_BANK0_BASE=0x40028000  #Pico 2
    INTR0=0x230 #Pico 2
  # IO_BANK0_BASE=0x40014000 #Pico
  # INTR0=0xF0 #Pico
    intrAddr = IO_BANK0_BASE + INTR0 + (pinNo // 8)*4
    machine.mem32[intrAddr] = events << (4 * (pinNo % 8))

pin=Pin(22,Pin.IN,Pin.PULL_UP)
while True:
    event=gpio_get_events(22)
    if(event & Pin.IRQ_FALLING):
        print("falling")
    if(event & Pin.IRQ_RISING):
        print("rising")
    gpio_clear_events(22, Pin.IRQ_FALLING | Pin.IRQ_RISING)
    sleep(0.5)
```

An Edgy Button

To make the difference between reading the line to detect a change of state and using the events, let's consider another version of event.py, our button program given earlier. In this case the GPIO line is set up for input and a message to press the button is printed. Then the program waits for 10 seconds and finally tests the state of the line.

Even if the user has pressed the button lots of times during the pause, all that matters is the final state of the line as read when the sleep(10) ends:

```
from utime import sleep
from machine import Pin

pin=Pin(22,Pin.IN,Pin.PULL_UP)

print("Press Button")
sleep(10)
if pin.value()==0:
    print("Button Pressed")
else:
    print("Button Not Pressed")
```

In other words, this program misses any button presses during the 10-second pause. This is a silly program, but now compare it to a version using edge events, edgy.py:

```
from utime import sleep
from machine import Pin
import machine

def gpio_get_events(pinNo):
    IO_BANK0_BASE=0x40028000  #Pico 2
    INTR0=0x230 #Pico 2
  # IO_BANK0_BASE=0x40014000 #Pico
  # INTR0=0xF0 #Pico
    mask = 0xF << 4 * (pinNo % 8)
    intrAddr = IO_BANK0_BASE + INTR0 + (pinNo // 8)*4
    return (machine.mem32[intrAddr] & mask) >> (4 * (pinNo % 8))

def gpio_clear_events(pinNo, events):
    IO_BANK0_BASE=0x40028000  #Pico 2
    INTR0=0x230 #Pico 2
  # IO_BANK0_BASE=0x40014000 #Pico
  # INTR0=0xF0 #Pico
    intrAddr = IO_BANK0_BASE + INTR0 + (pinNo // 8)*4
    machine.mem32[intrAddr] = events << (4 * (pinNo % 8))

pin=Pin(22,Pin.IN,Pin.PULL_UP)

print("Press Button")
gpio_clear_events(22, Pin.IRQ_FALLING)
sleep(10)
event = gpio_get_events(22)
gpio_clear_events(22, Pin.IRQ_FALLING)
if event & Pin.IRQ_FALLING:
    print("Button Pressed")
else:
    print("Button Not Pressed")
```

In this case the GPIO line is set up as an input with a pull-up and we test for a falling edge event rather than the line state. The difference is that if the user presses the button at any time during the 10-second sleep, the flag is set and the program registers the button press. The flag is set no matter what the program is doing, so instead of sleeping it could be getting on with some work, confident that it won't miss a button press. However, it cannot know exactly when the button was pressed and it cannot know how many times the button was pressed.

Events allow you to avoid missing a single input while polling, but cannot handle multiple inputs – if the user presses the button multiple times you still only detect a single press. You could implement a full queue-based event handling system, but this probably isn't worth the effort. A more reasonable alternative is to use the interrupt abilities of the GPIO lines, see later.

Measuring Pulses With Events

Now we have all of the functions we need to implement a pulse measurement program using events. In this case we can measure the width of any pulse as the distance between a rising and a falling edge or a falling and a rising edge.   The main difference between this and the previous program that measured the width of a pulse is that now we are using the hardware to detect the state transitions, i.e. the "edges" of the signal.

To do this we need to detect the rising and falling edge for the pin.

The complete program, measure.py, is:

```
import time
from utime import import sleep
from machine import Pin
import machine

def gpio_get_events(pinNo):
    mask = 0xF << 4 * (pinNo % 8)
    intrAddr = 0x40014000 + 0x0f0 + (pinNo // 8)*4
    return (machine.mem32[intrAddr] & mask) >> (4 * (pinNo % 8))


def gpio_clear_events(pinNo, events):
    intrAddr = 0x40014000 + 0x0f0 + (pinNo // 8)*4
    machine.mem32[intrAddr] = events << (4 * (pinNo % 8))
```

```
pin=Pin(22,Pin.IN,Pin.PULL_DOWN)
while True:
    gpio_clear_events(22, Pin.IRQ_FALLING | Pin.IRQ_RISING)
    while  not(gpio_get_events(22) & Pin.IRQ_RISING):
        pass
    t=time.ticks_us()
    while  not(gpio_get_events(22) & Pin.IRQ_FALLING):
        pass
    t=time.ticks_diff(time.ticks_us(),t)
    print(t)
    sleep(1)
```

After clearing both events we wait for a rising edge, clear it and then wait for a falling edge and take the time difference between the two.

measure.py produces very similar results to those of the previous program that simply read the inputs on the GPIO line. In this case there is no real advantage in using the events approach to polling as we are reading data as fast as we can anyway. However, if you had multiple GPIO lines and perhaps multiple conditions to test, you could set all the events you were interested in and then check to see if any of them had happened.

Interrupts

The Pico supports 32 distinct interrupts, but only 26 are actually used whereas the Pico 2 has 52 interrupts and all are used. . All of the user GPIO lines act together to create a single IO interrupt. A subtle point is that each of the Pico's two processors can respond at the same time to an IO interrupt caused by a different GPIO line – that is, the IO interrupts are not shared between cores. In all other cases interrupts can only be enabled on one core at a time.

The fact that there is only a single interrupt for all of the GPIO lines means it is up to the interrupt handler to work out which line caused the interrupt and to reset it after dealing with it. Which GPIO line can generate an interrupt is specified by the same bits in the same register that we have been using as event indicators in the earlier sections. If an interrupt is enabled for a given line and a given event then the interrupt will occur if that bit is set to one.

The events that you can use are the same as before:
```
GPIO_IRQ_LEVEL_LOW
GPIO_IRQ_LEVEL_HIGH
GPIO_IRQ_EDGE_FALL
GPIO_IRQ_EDGE_RISE
```

MicroPython provides a simple method for working with the edge GPIO interrupts, level interrupts are not implemented:

```
pin.irq(ISR, edge)
```

This sets `ISR` as the Interrupt Service Routine for the edge event. This is a very simplified version of what happens at a lower level. The `ISR` function has to accept a single parameter, which is a Pin object associated with the GPIO line that caused the event.

Notice that the `ISR` will still be called even if your MicroPython program has come to an end:

```
def HelloIRQ(pin):
    print("IRQ")

pin=Pin(22,Pin.IN,Pin.PULL_UP)
pin.irq(HelloIRQ,Pin.IRQ_RISING)
while(True):
    pass
```

You will see `IRQ` printed whenever GPIO 22 has a rising edge, even after the program has finished.

Although the hardware only supports a single ISR for all of the GPIO lines, MicroPython implements a system that lets you associate a different ISR for each GPIO line. For example, `irq.py`:

```
def HelloIRQ1(pin):
    print("IRQ1")

def HelloIRQ2(pin):
    print("IRQ2")

pin1=Pin(21,Pin.IN,Pin.PULL_UP)
pin2=Pin(22,Pin.IN,Pin.PULL_UP)

pin1.irq(HelloIRQ1,Pin.IRQ_RISING)
pin2.irq(HelloIRQ2,Pin.IRQ_RISING)
while(True):
    pass
```

You will see `IRQ1` or `IRQ2` printed depending on which pin the interrupt occurred on. Also notice that the implementation automatically clears the interrupt and disables interrupts while in the ISR. This makes using MicroPython interrupts much easier, but it also slows down the basic IRQ handling from what is possible using the raw hardware.

The Interrupt Queue

The interrupt as implemented in MicroPython isn't like the raw hardware interrupt produced by the Pico. Instead of immediately causing an ISR to run it places the ISR into the MicroPython dispatch queue. This queue is used by MicroPython to run asynchronous code. The disadvantage of this method is that there is no guarantee when the ISR will run – other functions in the queue can be run first. Its advantage is that it allows the ISR to be treated as a standard MicroPython function and it solves the problem of what to do if an interrupt occurs before the ISR has completed. Interrupts simply cause the system to add ISRs to the queue and they are processed in the order that they occurred but not necessarily at the time they occurred. The only problem is that the time that an interrupt occurred is often very important in an application.

To see how all this works and what effect it has, consider this simple example. An interrupt signal is applied to GPIO 22 that provides a rising edge every second, i.e. it is a 1Hz square wave. The interrupt handler records the time of the interrupt and prints the difference between this time and the previous interrupt time. If no interrupts are missed this should always be a little more than 1 second. However, there is a sleep for 1.5 seconds at the end of the interrupt routine and so it should miss the next rising edge but get the following one. This means that the time should be reported as 2 seconds, tick.py:

```
import time
from machine import Pin
t = 0
def myHandler(pin):
    global t
    temp = time.ticks_us()
    print(time.ticks_diff(temp,t))
    t = temp
    time.sleep(1.5)
    return

pin = Pin(, Pin.IN, Pin.PULL_UP)
pin.irq(myHandler, Pin.IRQ_FALLING)
```

If you try this program you will find that it prints around 1.5 seconds. The reason is that the supposedly missed interrupt event is added to a queue and as soon as the interrupt handler is finished it is called again – hence the supposed 1.5 seconds between interrupts.

You can clear the queue of interrupts waiting to be handled by disabling interrupts within the interrupt handler and then turning them back on again, `tick.py` with comments:

```python
import time
from machine import Pin
t = 0
def myHandler(pin):
    global t
    pin.irq(None, Pin.IRQ_FALLING)
    temp = time.ticks_us()
    print(time.ticks_diff(temp,t))
    t = temp
    time.sleep(1.5)
    pin.irq(myHandler, Pin.IRQ_FALLING)
    return
pin = Pin(4, Pin.IN, Pin.PULL_UP)
pin.irq(myHandler, Pin.IRQ_FALLING)
```

With this change the interrupt handler does miss the very next edge and the time displayed is slightly more than 2 seconds.

Notice the use of None as an interrupt handler to turn interrupts off. How to deal with missing interrupts is a matter of what is most important – responding to all interrupts or responding at the time that the interrupt occurred.

Hard Interrupts

If you want to deal with interrupts as close to the hardware as possible i.e. without using the MicroPython execution queue you can add hard=True to the irq function. In this case the ISR is run as soon as possible after the interrupt – i.e. it is not added to the execution queue. This means that the IRQ can result in the ISR running at any point in the execution of the MicroPython program and as a result the ISR cannot interact with other functions or the system in any significant way. This is a problem but a bigger problem is that interrupts are not turned off and there is no queue to deal with interrupts that occur while the ISR is running. If an interrupt does occur while the ISR is running then the results are generally difficult to predict but the observed behavior varies from complete system lock to long unexpected delays.

Interrupt Service Routine Restrictions

There are restrictions on writing an ISR. Firstly, it should only run for a short time because while the ISR is running the main Python thread is suspended and cannot service any other peripheral. A long-running ISR not only blocks the main thread, but also other interrupts. In most cases the best design is to allow the ISR to set status indicators and then to hand off and allow the main thread to react to the new status.

For example, if an ISR is called to collect data from a sensor it should simply acquire the data and store it in a shared variable. It should avoid trying to process the data. Instead it should set a flag that signals to the main thread that new data is available and that it should process it.

Another problem is that ISRs shouldn't allocate memory, i.e. create or extend objects. The reason is that an ISR can interrupt the Python main thread at a point that is part way though an operation. This means that the Python heap might well be locked when the ISR runs and so cannot create anything new without risking an exception. There are a number of possible solutions. The simplest is to create all objects that the ISR needs to use before it runs and, if you need to add to an object, find a representation that allows you to allocate the space needed before using it.

For example, prefer an Array.array object to a List or Dictionary object as an Array.array object is pre-allocated at its initialized size. To know more about this and about how appending data to a List or adding to a Dictionary causes memory to be allocated see *Programmer's Python: Everything Is Data*, ISBN:9781871962598.

Things are actually more subtle as there are actions which create objects on the heap that you might not expect to do so. For example, creating a reference to a method causes an object to be created on the heap. Equally using floats in an ISR is a problem as these are allocated on the heap.

Another consequence of not being able to allocate memory is that an ISR can't raise an exception as this requires memory allocation. The solution is to add:

```
micropython.alloc_emergency_exception_buf(100)
```

to the main program.

An alternative to having to avoid allocating memory in general is to hand it off to a non-interrupt routine using the micropython.schedule function:

```
schedule(function, arg)
```

This will call function(arg) at the first possible moment after the ISR terminates. The "first possible moment" is determined by when the main thread is between complete Python instructions. That is, an ISR can be called in the middle of a Python instruction, but the schedule function is always called between Python instructions and so it can always access the heap. The exception to this is if the function passed to schedule is an object method – this requires the ISR to allocate memory and so it fails. Notice that you can use an object method as an ISR because the reference is created before the ISR is called. As long as you only pass a standard unbound function to schedule it all should work. A schedule function will also run to completion without being interrupted by another schedule function, but it can be suspended by an interrupt.

This is all there is to using GPIO to generate an interrupt and handling it. In practice, things are more difficult to get right than you might expect. In particular, access to shared resources presents a problem. A Python program can share data with an ISR by declaring a variable to be global.

Race Conditions and Starvation

Implementing an ISR is a step into the complex world of asynchronous programs and if this is something of interest see ***Programmer's Python: Async***, ISBN:978-1871962765. The biggest new problem that asynchronicity introduces is the possibility of race conditions. A race condition occurs when two sections of code modify a shared resource in such an uncontrolled way that the final outcome depends on the timing of the code execution. Race conditions are particularly difficult to debug because they look random and the tendency is to think that they are due to faulty hardware and, worse, an intermittent fault.

It is difficult to provide a clear and simple example of a race condition for the Pico because real time programming is inherently difficult to test. In addition, the implementation of interrupt handling in the Pico is at a higher level than raw interrupts in the sense that an ISR, once started, runs to completion. That is, ISRs are not interrupted. This means that it is the code in the main thread of execution which is interrupted and is the source of any race conditions. So while race conditions happen, they are difficult to demonstrate.

Consider the problem of setting a byte array to either all ones or all zeros. In an ideal world this data structure would always be in either one of the two states – the setting would be atomic and not interruptible. However, the main thread can be interrupted both within and between MicroPython instructions. The following program, race.py, uses an interrupt on GPIO 22 to set a byte array to zero and a while loop in the main program to set it to all ones:

```
import time
from machine import Pin

data = bytearray(b'\xf0\xf1\xf2')

def myHandler(pin):
    global data
    for i in range(3):
        data[i]=0

pin = Pin(4, Pin.IN, Pin.PULL_UP)
pin.irq(myHandler, Pin.IRQ_RISING)
```

```
while True:
    for i in range(3):
        data[i] = 255
    if data[0]!=data[1] or data[1]!=data[2] or data[2]!=data[0]:
        print(data)
```

If you run race.py you will discover that the byte array is often in a state that is a mix of the two:

```
bytearray(b'\x00\x00\xff')
bytearray(b'\x00\xff\xff')
bytearray(b'\x00\xff\xff')
bytearray(b'\x00\xff\xff')
bytearray(b'\x00\xff\xff')
bytearray(b'\x00\x00\xff')
```

This occurs frequently even with interrupts occurring at ten per second. What happens is that the for loop starts to set the byte array to all ones a byte at a time. If an interrupt occurs during this process then the bytes are set to zero and when the loop restarts only the remaining bytes are set to all ones.

If you don't want the byte array to be in an inconsistent state then you need to disable the ISR while the main thread is using it:

```
from machine import Pin
data=bytearray(b'\xf0\xf1\xf2')
def myHandler(pin):
    global data
    for i in range(3):
        data[i] = 0
    print(data)

pin = Pin(22, Pin.IN, Pin.PULL_UP)
pin.irq(myHandler, Pin.IRQ_RISING)
while True:
    pin.irq(None, Pin.IRQ_RISING)
    for i in range(3):
        data[i] = 255
    if data[0]!=data[1] or data[1]!=data[2] or data[2]!=data[0]:
        print(data)
    pin.irq(myHandler, Pin.IRQ_RISING)
```

This now works and you never see an inconsistent state for the byte array but now the ISR hardly ever gets to run. It only gets called once per while loop iteration and this severely limits its responsiveness. This is an example of "starvation" where one process hogs the CPU for so much of the time other processes fail to make much progress. In this case it is the ISR that is slowed down, but a CPU-hogging ISR can slow the main program in exactly the same way. Notice the way that we set None as an ISR to disable the interrupt.

In theory you can use:

```
s=machine.disable_irq()
print("doing something useful")
machine.enable_irq(s)
```

to create sections of code where interrupts cannot occur, but notice that this disables all interrupts, including timer ticks and this generally causes the Pico to crash.

Measuring Pulse Width

In Chapter 6 we saw how to use polling to measure pulse widths. You can do the same job with interrupts – simply detect a rising edge followed by another rising edge. At this point it is tempting to get the ISRs to do all of the task of measuring the temperature, but again a state machine approach is much better. In general, it is nearly always a good idea to get the ISRs to set the value of a state variable and then return as soon as possible. This approach reduces the ISRs to their minimum and makes the program work faster and more reliably. For example, in `fast.py`:

```
import time
from time import sleep
from machine import Pin

pin=Pin(22,Pin.IN,Pin.PULL_UP)
event=0
def rise(pin):
    global event
    event=1

def fall(pin):
    global event
    event=2

while True:
    pin.irq(rise, Pin.IRQ_RISING)
    while  not(event==1):
        pass
    t=time.ticks_us()
    pin.irq(fall, Pin.IRQ_RISING)
    while  not(event==2):
        pass
    t=time.ticks_diff(time.ticks_us(),t)
    print(t)
    sleep(1)
```

the main program simply tests the state variable, event, and reacts accordingly. The only global variable needed is event and the ISRs do nothing but set its value and return – what could be simpler.

If you try this out, you will find that the pulse measurements are reasonably accurate down to 50μs, after which the next rising edge is missed and the second rising edge is detected. There is no obvious speedup from using a hard interrupt.

Timers

A very common use of interrupts is to run a function after a delay or run one regularly every so often. The Pico has software timers that can be used to do just this.

To create a `Timer` object use its constructor:

```
timer=Timer(n)
```

where n is the number of the hardware timer you want to use. You can create timers up to the limit of memory.

Once you have a `Timer` object you can use its `init` method to set up either a periodic callback or a one-off callback, a one-shot:

```
Timer.init(mode = mode, period = - 1, callback = None)
```

Mode can be either of:

- `Timer.ONE_SHOT`   The timer runs once and the callback is called when the period is up
- `Timer.PERIODIC`   The timer runs repeatedly calling the callback each time the period is up.

When you are finished with a timer you can use `Timer.deinit()` to free the hardware and stop any periodic callback.

Notice that the callback function is a soft interrupt handler and therefore it is run as a standard function, but it has to wait its turn in the queue.

Responding To Input

This look at methods of dealing with the problems of input isn't exhaustive – there are always new ways of doing things, but it does cover the most general ways of implementing input. As already mentioned, the problem with input is that you don't know when it is going to happen. What generally matters is speed of response.

For low-frequency inputs, interrupts are worthwhile. They can leave your program free to get on with other tasks and simplify its overall structure. For high-frequency inputs that need to be serviced regularly, a polling loop is still the best option for maximum throughput. How quickly you can respond to an input depends on how long the polling loop is and how many times you test for it per loop.

Summary

- Events are a stored indication that something happened.

- Interrupts are events that cause something to happen.

- You can use an event with a polling loop to protect against missing input because the program is busy doing something else.

- If an event occurs before the current event has been cleared then it might be missed. To avoid missing events, you can use an event queue which stores events in the order they happened until they are processed.

- MicroPython doesn't support events, but it is easy to add a function to make use of them. You can enable a bit to be set if a GPIO line goes high, low or is high or low. Edge-triggered events are the easiest to work with.

- Using events in a polling loop hardly slows things down at all.

- You can use events to generate an interrupt and call an interrupt handler.

- MicroPython has two interrupt implementations. The default, hard=False allows interrupts to occur during the interrupt handler and a queue of interrupts is formed. The alternative, hard=True allows interrupts while in the interrupt handler and doesn't keep a queue.

- Both interrupt implementations have a latency of at least 20μs and usually more. Only hard=True interrupt handling has any chance of responding to an interrupt close to the time it occurred.

- Whenever possible, avoid using interrupts and only use them for low frequency events that have to be handled promptly.

Chapter 8

Pulse Width Modulation

One way around the problem of getting a fast response from a microcontroller is to move the problem away from the processor. In the case of the Pico there are some built-in devices that can use GPIO lines to implement protocols without the CPU being involved. In this chapter we take a close look at the use of Pulse Width Modulation (PWM) including generating sound, driving LEDs and servos.

When performing their most basic function, i.e. output, the GPIO lines can be set high or low by the processor. How fast they can be set high or low depends on the speed of the processor.

Using the GPIO line in its Pulse Width Modulation (PWM) mode you can generate pulse trains up to 60MHz. The reason for the increase in speed is that the GPIO is connected to a pulse generator and, once set to generate pulses of a specific type, the pulse generator just gets on with it, without needing any intervention from the GPIO line or the processor. In fact, the pulse output will continue after your program has ended. Of course, even though the PWM line can generate very fast pulses, usually what you want to do is change the nature of the pulses and this is a slower process involving the processor.

Some Basic Pico PWM Facts

There are some facts worth getting clear right from the start, although some of their significance will only become clear as we progress.

First, what is PWM? The simple answer is that a pulse width modulated signal has pulses that repeat at a fixed rate, say one pulse every millisecond, but the width of the pulse can be changed.

There are two basic things to specify about the pulse train that is generated, its repetition rate and the width of each pulse. Usually the repetition rate is set as a simple repeat period and the width of each pulse is specified as a percentage of the repeat period, referred to as the duty cycle.

So, for example, a 1ms repeat and a 50% duty cycle specifies a 1ms period, which is high for 50% of the time, i.e. a pulse width of 0.5ms. The two extremes are 100% duty cycle, i.e. the line is always high, and 0% duty cycle, i.e. the line is always low.

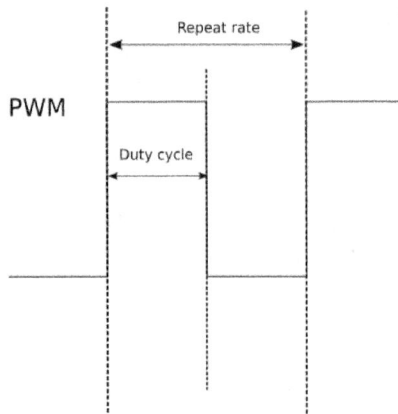

Notice it is the duty cycle that carries the information in PWM and not the frequency. What this means is that, in general, you select a repeat rate and stick to it and what you change as the program runs is the duty cycle.

In many cases PWM is implemented using special PWM-generator hardware that is either built into the processor chip or provided by an external chip. The processor simply sets the repeat rate by writing to a register and then changing the duty cycle by writing to another register. This ideally provides the best sort of PWM with no load on the processor and glitch-free operation. You can even buy add-on boards that will provide additional channels of PWM without adding to the load on the processor.

The alternative to dedicated PWM hardware is to implement it in software. You can work out how to do this quite easily. All you need is a timing loop to set the line high at the repetition rate and then set it low again according to the duty cycle. You can implement this using either interrupts or a polling loop and in more advanced ways, such as using a DMA (Direct Memory Access) channel.

Pico PWM

In the case of both generation of the Pico, the PWM lines are implemented using special PWM hardware. The Pico has eight PWM generators and the Pico 2 has 12, each capable of two PWM outputs. Any of the GPIO lines can be used as PWM lines and this means you can have up to 16 or 24 PWM lines in operation at any given time. The only snag is that the extra four PWM generators are only available via GPIOs 32 to 47 which are not exposed on the external pins and only available for custom designs using the QFN-80 package.

What this means is that in most cases using PWM on the Pico 2 is exactly the same as using it on the original Pico. The one difference is that the PWM clock is different for the Pico, 125MHz, and Pico 2, 150MHz, but MicroPython automatically adjusts for this difference.

Things are a little more complicated in that each pair of outputs has the same frequency, which means you have eight, independently set, pairs of outputs. In addition, one of the outputs can be used as an input and this reduces the number of outputs available.

The PWM generators are assigned to GPIO pins in a fixed order:

GPIO	0	1	2	3	4	5	6	7	8	9	10	11	12	13	14	15
PWM Channel	0A	0B	1A	1B	2A	2B	3A	3B	4A	4B	5A	5B	6A	6B	7A	7B

GPIO	16	17	18	19	20	21	22	23	24	25	26	27	28	29		
PWM Channel	0A	0B	1A	1B	2A	2B	3A	3B	4A	4B	5A	5B	6A	6B		

You don't have to know about how the PWM hardware works, but it helps with understanding some of the restrictions.

To create a `PWM Pin` object you have to pass its constructor a `Pin` object. For example:

```
pwm16 = PWM(Pin(16))
```

creates a `PWM` object associated with GPIO 16. You can set the frequency using:

```
pwm16.freq(500)
```

which sets the frequency in Hz. The PWM hardware isn't enabled at this point. To start it generating a signal you have to set the duty cycle. This is done using:

```
pwm16.duty_u16((duty)
```

where `duty` is a value in the range 0 to 65,535 corresponding to 0 to 100%.

There is also:

```
pwm16.duty_ns(ns)
```

which sets the time the line is high in nanoseconds. This isn't as useful for general use and if you specify a time that is greater than the set period you will generate an exception.

You can easily create your own duty cycle methods that work in terms of percentages or whatever way you want to specify the duty cycle. For example, you can create a new class which has a duty cycle set as a percentage:

```
class myPWM(PWM):
    def __init__(self, pin: Pin):
        super().__init__(pin)
    def duty(self,d):
        print(65535*d//1000)
        super().duty_u16(65535*d//1000)
```

In this case the percentage is specified multiplied by 10. For example, to set a 50% duty cycle you would use:

```
pwm16 = myPWM(Pin(16))
pwm16.freq(250)
pwm16.duty(500)
```

Once you have set the duty cycle the PWM generator starts to output the specified PWM signal on the pin. Notice that this works even after your program has completed. To stop the PWM signal use:

```
pwm16.deinit()
```

You can change the frequency or duty cycle at any time.

Although you don't need to know anything about the PWM hardware, there is one limitation you need to be aware of. Each PWM generator supports two outputs which work at the same frequency and optionally different duty cycles. For example, if you look back to the table of PWM pin assignments you can see that PWM 0 has outputs on GPIO 16 and GPIO 17. This means that these two pins can only work at the same frequency.
For example, pwm1.py:

```
from machine import Pin, PWM
pwm16 = PWM(Pin(16))
pwm17 = PWM(Pin(17))

pwm16.freq(250)

pwm16.duty_u16(65535//2)
pwm17.duty_u16(65535//4)
while(True):
    pass
```

produces a PWM signal on GPIO 16 and GPIO 17 with the same frequency of 250Hz and duty cycles of 50% and 25% respectively. If you change the frequency on either pin, both change frequency.

You can see the result in this logic analyzer display:

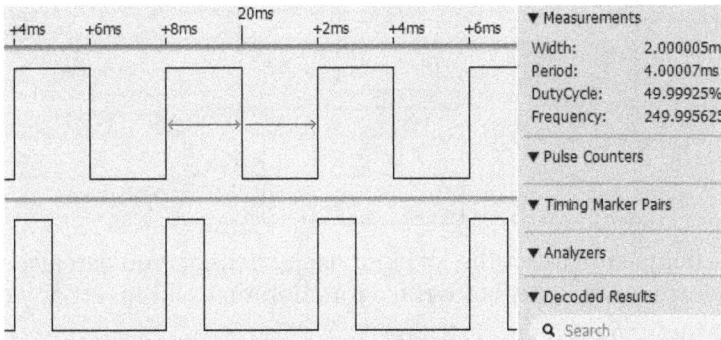

You can see from the logic analyzer trace that the pulses on each line start their duty cycle at exactly the same time. The PWM hardware can create phase-correct pulses where the pulses are aligned about their center point, but MicroPython doesn't support this mode. However, it is fairly easy to write a function, pwm2.py, that sets or unsets phase-correct mode:

```
from machine import Pin, PWM, mem32
def pwm_set_phase(sliceNo,phase):
    PWM_BASE=0x400a8000 # 0x40050000 pico
    CH1_CSR=0x14
    Addr = PWM_BASE +CH1_CSR*sliceNo
    if phase:
        mem32[Addr]=mem32[Addr] | 0x2
    else:
        mem32[Addr]=mem32[Addr] & 0xFFFFFFFD
```

Using this function we can generate phase-correct pulses:

```
pwm16 = PWM(Pin(16))
pwm17 = PWM(Pin(17))
pwm16.freq(250)
pwm_set_phase(0,True)
pwm16.duty_u16(65535//2)
pwm17.duty_u16(65535//4)
while(True):
    pass
```

Now you can see that the pulses don't start at the same time, but they are centered around the same time:

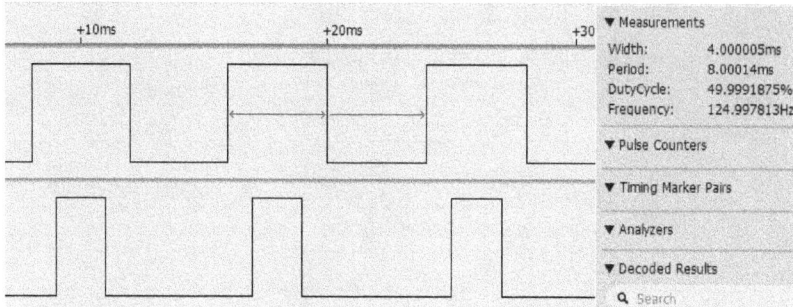

As well as being able to set the level for each channel, you can also set the polarity. However, it is easy to write a function that will invert any channel:

```
from machine import Pin, PWM,mem32

def pwm_set_polarity(sliceNo,channel,invert):
    PWM_BASE=0x400a8000 # 0x40050000 pico
    CH1_CSR=0x14
    Addr = PWM_BASE +CH1_CSR*sliceNo
    if invert:
        mem32[Addr]=mem32[Addr] | 0x1 << (2+channel)
    else:
        mem32[Addr]=mem32[Addr] & ~(0x1<<(2+channel))
```

For example, if you use this in pwm3.py:

```
pwm16 = PWM(Pin(16))
pwm17 = PWM(Pin(17))

pwm16.freq(250)

pwm16.duty_u16(65535//4)
pwm17.duty_u16(65535//4)
pwm_set_polarity(0,1,True)
```

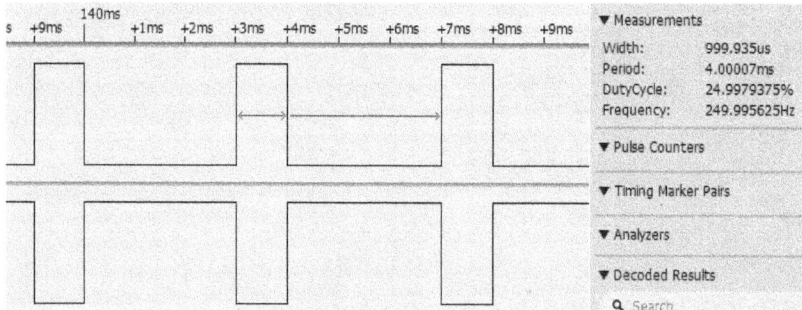

you can see that the output of channel B is inverted. Notice that duty resets the polarity.

Changing The Duty Cycle

For reasons that will be discussed later, in most cases the whole point is to vary the duty cycle or the period of the pulse train. This means that the next question is, how fast can you change the characteristics of a PWM line? In other words, how fast can you change the duty cycle? There is no easy way to give an exact answer and, in most applications, an exact answer isn't of much value. The reason is that for a PWM signal to convey information it generally has to deliver a number of complete cycles with a given duty cycle. This is because of the way pulses are often averaged in applications.

We also have another problem – synchronization. This is more subtle than it first seems. The hardware won't change the duty cycle until the current pulse is complete. You might think that the following program, sync.py, works to switch between two duty cycles on a per pulse basis:

```
pwm16 = PWM(Pin(16))

pwm16.freq(50)

pwm16.duty_u16(65535//2)
while True:
    pwm16.duty_u16(65535//2)
    pwm16.duty_u16(65535//4)
```

but if you try this out the result isn't what you might expect on a first analysis:

You don't get one 25% followed by one 50% pulse, but a varying number of each in turn. The reason is, of course, that the duty cycle is being set asynchronously.

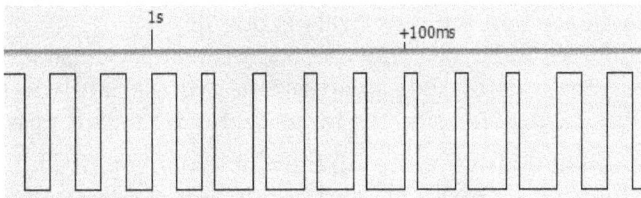

Duty Cycle Resolution

It seems as if you can set the duty cycle to a 16-bit value giving you 65535 different settings, however, this is only true in a few cases. The PWM hardware implements the following algorithm:

```
set GPIO line high
for count in range(wrap):
    wait one clock cycle
    if count>level:
        set GPIO line low
```

In other words, the frequency of the PWM signal depends on the value of wrap and the clock frequency and duty cycle depend on level. When you set the frequency of the PWM signal that you want, the software works out the best value for the clock frequency and wrap value. In an ideal world the wrap would always be the maximum 16-bit value, 65535, but to achieve the desired frequency it often has to be less. Clearly you can only set the duty cycle between 0 and wrap and this can limit the precision that you can set. For example, if wrap is 4 then you can only set duty cycles of 0, 25%, 75% and 100%, i.e. level = 0, 1, 2, 3, and such low values of wrap do occur.

In other words, the frequency you select affects the accuracy of the setting of the duty cycle. In most cases the wrap value is large enough to ignore the problem, but sometimes it is important. MicroPython doesn't provide any way to explicitly set or get the wrap value, but it is easy to add a function to get it:

```
def pwm_get_wrap(sliceNo):
    Addr = 0x40050000 +0x10+0x14*sliceNo
    return (machine.mem32[Addr])
```

Problems with small wrap values usually occur at high frequencies. The reason is that the clock runs at 125MHz and so if you want a PWM frequency of say 30MHz then the wrap value has to be 4 and hence the duty cycle can only be 0,1,2,3. You can see that this is the case in the following example, wrap.py:

```
pwm16 = PWM(Pin(16))
pwm16.freq(125000000//4)
print(pwm_get_wrap(0))
pwm16.duty_u16(65535//2)
```

You will see the wrap is 2 and if you examine the output using a logic analyzer you will see that the duty cycle is not 50%.

At lower frequencies the duty cycle precision is usually close to 16-bits. Also notice that the duty cycle is always set as if it was a full 16-bit value and MicroPython scales this into the range that wrap makes possible.

There is an additional effect related to the clock that you need to consider. The clock divider can be fractional and in this case the fractional division is achieved by varying the division between two integer dividers so that the average frequency is as requested. This can lead to jitter in the pulse positions.

Uses Of PWM – Digital To Analog

What sorts of things do you use PWM for? There are lots of very clever uses for PWM. However, there are two use cases which account for most PWM applications - voltage or power modulation and signaling to servos.

The amount of power delivered to a device by a pulse train is proportional to the duty cycle. A pulse train that has a 50% duty cycle is delivering current to the load only 50% of the time and this is irrespective of the pulse repetition rate. So the duty cycle controls the power, but the period still matters in many situations because you want to avoid any flashing or other effects. A higher frequency smooths out the power flow at any duty cycle.

If you add a low-pass filter to the output of a PWM signal then what you get is a voltage that is proportional to the duty cycle. This can be looked at in many different ways, but again it is the result of the amount of power delivered by a PWM signal. You can also think of it as using the filter to remove the high-frequency components of the signal, leaving only the slower components due to the modulation of the duty cycle.

How fast you can work depends on the duty cycle resolution. If you work with 8-bit resolution your D-to-A conversion will have 256 steps, which at 3.3V gives a potential resolution of 3.3/256 or about 13mV. This is often good enough. If you understand the previous section on duty cycle resolution this means that the PWM frequency has to be 125000000//256 to give a wrap of 256. The PWM output in this configuration mimics the workings of an 8-bit D-to-A converter.

To demonstrate the sort of approach that you can take to D-to-A conversion, the following program creates a sine wave. To do this we need to compute the duty cycle for 256 points in a complete cycle. We could do this each time a value is needed, but to make the program fast enough we have to compute the entire 256 points and store them in an array.

While there are fixed-point arithmetic ways of computing the sine or the cos of an angle, it is simpler to use the Pico's built-in floating-point software. Notice that the Pico doesn't have floating-point arithmetic implemented in hardware and it is best to avoid it if possible as demonstrated in sin.py:

```
from machine import Pin, PWM, mem32
import array
import math

def pwm_get_wrap(sliceNo):
    PWM_BASE=0x400a8000 # 0x40050000 pico
    CH1_CSR=0x14
    Addr = PWM_BASE +0x10+CH1_CSR*sliceNo
    return (mem32[Addr])
```

```
wave = array.array('H', [0]*256)
for i in range(256):
    wave[i] = int(65535//2 +
            (math.sin(i * 2.0 * 3.14159 / 255.0) * 65535//2))

pwm16 = PWM(Pin(16))
pwm16.freq(125000000//256)

print(pwm_get_wrap(0))
while(True):
    for i in range(256):
        pwm16.duty_u16(wave[i])
```

The 16-bit duty cycle values needed are computed and stored in the wave array. Then the PWM is set up with the highest frequency that will provide 256 levels of duty cycle. Finally, a for loop is used to set the duty cycle from the array. Notice that there is no attempt at synchronizing when the duty cycle update will occur – it happens as fast as possible.

The waveform repeats after around 8.8ms on the Pico and around 2.8ms on the Pico 2, which makes the frequency around 113Hz and 350Hz respectively.

To see the analog waveform, we need to put the digital output into a low-pass filter. A simple resistor and capacitor work reasonably well:

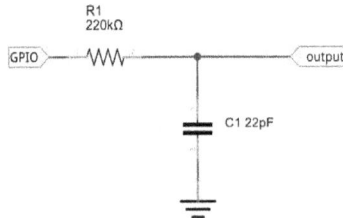

The filter's cutoff is around 33kHz and might be a little on the high side for this low-frequency, 200Hz, output, but it produces a reasonable waveform:

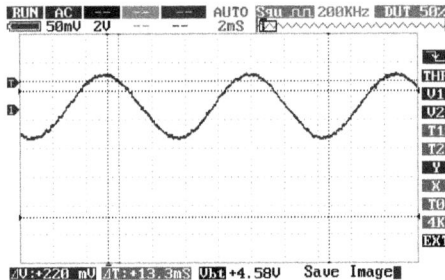

You can use this technique to create a sine wave, or any other waveform you need, but for high-quality audio you need a higher sampling rate.

Frequency Modulation

Using PWM to create musical tones, and sound effects in general, is a well-explored area which is too wide to cover in this book. In most cases we choose to vary the duty cycle at a fixed sample rate, but an alternative is to leave the duty cycle fixed at, say, 50% and modulate the frequency. You can use this approach to create simple musical tones and scales.

As the frequency of middle C is 281.6Hz, to generate middle C you could use:

```
pwm16 = PWM(Pin(16))
pwm16.freq(282)
pwm16.duty_u16(65535//2)
```

The resulting output is a square wave with a measured frequency of 282.1Hz which isn't particularly nice to listen to. You can improve it by feeding it through a simple low-pass filter like the one used above for waveform synthesis. You can look up the frequencies for other notes and use a table to generate them.

Controlling An LED

You can also use PWM to generate physical quantities such as the brightness of an LED or the rotation rate of a DC motor. The only differences required by these applications are to do with the voltage and current you need and the way the duty cycle relates to whatever the physical effect is. In other words, if you want to change some effect by 50%, how much do you need to change the duty cycle? For example, how do we "dim" an LED?

The simplest example is to drive the on-board LED using a PWM signal as in led1.py:

```
from machine import Pin, PWM
from time import sleep_ms
pwm17 = PWM(Pin(17))
pwm17.freq(2000)

while True:
    for d in range(0,65535,655):
        pwm17.duty_u16(d)
        sleep_ms(50)
```

If you try this out you will see the LED slowly increase in brightness, but it seems to be a longer time at maximum brightness than at any other value. This is a consequence of the non-linear relationship between duty cycle and perceived brightness.

By changing the duty cycle of the PWM pulse train you can set the amount of power delivered to an LED, or any other device, and hence change its brightness. If you use a 50% duty cycle, the LED is on 50% of the time and it has been determined that this makes it look as if it is half as bright. However, this is not the end of the story as humans don't respond to physical brightness in a linear way. The Weber-Fechner law gives the general relationship between perceived intensity and physical stimulus as logarithmic.

In the case of an LED, the connection between duty cycle and brightness is a complicated matter, but the simplest approach uses the fact that the perceived brightness is roughly proportional to the cube root of the physical brightness. The exact equations, published as CIE 1931, are:

$L= 903.3 \cdot (Y / Y_n)$ $\qquad$ $(Y/ Y_n) \leq 0.008856$

$L= 116 \cdot (Y / Y_n)^{1/3} - 16$ $\qquad$ $(Y/ Y_n) > 0.008856$

where L is the perceived brightness and Y / Y_n is a measure of physical brightness.

The exact relationship is complicated, but in most cases a roughly cubic law, obtained by inverting the CIE relationship, can be used:

$d=kb^3$

where b is the perceived brightness and d is the duty cycle. The constant k depends on the LED. The graph below shows the general characteristic of the relationship for a duty cycle of 0 to 100% on the y-axis and arbitrary, 0 to 100, perceived brightness units on the x-axis.

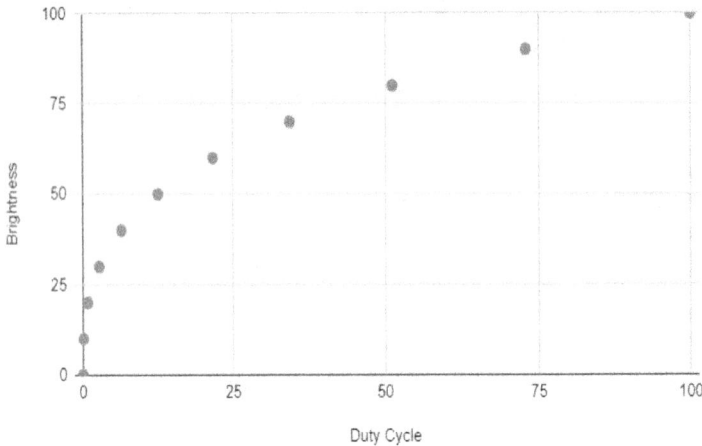

Notice that, as the LED when powered by a PWM signal is either full on or full off, there is no change in LED light output with current - the LED is always run at the same current.

What all of this means is that if you want an LED to fade in a linear fashion you need to change the duty cycle in a non-linear fashion. Intuitively it means that changes when the duty cycle is small produce bigger changes in brightness than when the duty cycle is large.

A program, led2.py, to implement cubic dimming is:

```
from utime import sleep_ms
from machine import Pin, PWM

pwm25 = PWM(Pin(17))
pwm25.freq(2000)

while True:
    for b in range(0,100):
        pwm25.duty_u16(int(65535*b*b*b/1000000))
        sleep_ms(50)
```

If you try this out you should notice that the LED changes brightness more evenly across its range. The only problem is that now 100 steps are insufficient to mask the steps in brightness at the lower level. The solution is to work with a more precise specification of duty cycle.

In most cases it is irrelevant exactly how linear the response of the LED is - a rough approximation looks as smooth to the human eye. You can even get away with using a square law to dim the LED. The only exception is when you are trying to drive LEDs to create a gray-level or color display when color calibration is another level of accuracy.

There is also the question of what frequency we should use. Clearly it has to be fast enough not to be seen as flickering and this generally means it has to be greater than 80Hz, the upper limit for human flicker fusion, but, because of the strobe effect, flickering becomes more visible with moving objects. The faster the LED switches on and off, the less flicker should be visible, but before you select frequencies in the high kHz range it is worth knowing that an LED has a minimum time to turn on and so frequencies at low kHz work best.

What Else Can You Use PWM For?

PWM lines are incredibly versatile and it is always worth asking the question "could I use PWM?" when you are considering almost any problem. The Pico's PWM generator is particularly versatile. For example, it has an input option which can be used to determine the duty cycle of an input wave form. However, MicroPython doesn't support this and many of its more advanced features are hidden from you for the sake of simplicity. For most of the time this tradeoff is worth it.

The LED example suggests how you can use PWM as a power controller. You can extend this idea to a computer-controlled switch-mode power supply. All you need is a capacitor to smooth out the voltage and perhaps a transformer to change the voltage. You can also use PWM to control the speed of a DC motor and, by adding a simple bridge circuit, you can control its direction and speed. Finally, you can use a PWM signal as a modulated carrier for data communications. For example, most infrared controllers make use of a 38kHz carrier, which is roughly a 26μs pulse. This is switched on and off for 1ms and this is well within the range that the PWM can manage. So all you have to do is replace the red LED in the previous circuit with an infrared LED and you have the start of a remote control, or data transmission, link.

One big area of use is in controlling motors, and servo motors in particular, and this is the subject of the next chapter.

Summary

- PWM, Pulse Width Modulation, has a fixed repetition rate but a variable duty cycle, i.e. the amount of time the signal is high or low changes.

- PWM can be generated by software simply by changing the state of a GPIO line correctly, but it can also be generated in hardware so relieving the processor of some work.

- As well as being a way of signaling, PWM can also be used to vary the amount of power or voltage transferred. The higher the duty cycle, the more power/voltage.

- The Pico has eight hardware PWM generators and these are capable of a range of operational modes.

- The PWM lines are controlled by a counter and two values wrap which gives the frequency and level which gives the duty cycle. This is mostly hidden from the MicroPython programmer and you can specify frequency and duty cycle without worrying too much about how they are generated.

- You can generate phase-correct PWM or allow the phase to vary with the duty cycle.

- The higher the wrap value, the higher the resolution of the duty cycle. It is possible to work out the best value for the clock frequency for any PWM frequency to maximize the duty cycle resolution.

- PWM can be used to implement digital to analog conversion simply by varying the duty cycle. In the same way, by varying the duty cycle, you can dim an LED.

Chapter 9

Controlling Motors And Servos

Controlling motors is an obvious use for the low cost Pico, but it is important to understand the different types of motor that you can use and exactly how to control them using PWM. In addition to PWM control, we also look at the very useful stepper motor which doesn't make use of PWM.

The simplest division among types of motor is AC and DC. AC motors are generally large and powerful and run from mains voltage. As they are more difficult to work with, and they work at mains voltages, these aren't used much in IoT applications. DC motors generally work on lower voltage and are much more suitable for the IoT. In this chapter we will only look at DC motors and how they work thanks to pulse width modulation. The parts used are listed in the Resources section of the book's webpage at www.iopress.info.

DC Motor

There are two big classes of DC motor – brushed and brushless. All motors work by using a set of fixed magnets, the stator, and a set of rotating magnets, the rotor. The important idea is that a motor generates a "push" that rotates the shaft by the forces between the magnet that makes up the stator and the magnet that makes up the rotor. The stronger these magnets are, the stronger the push and the more torque (turning force) the motor can produce. To keep the motor turning, one of the two magnetic fields has to change to keep the rotor being attracted to a new position.

DC motors differ in how they create the magnetism in each component, either using a permanent magnet or an electromagnet.

This means there are four possible arrangements:

	1	2	3	4
Stator	Permanent	Permanent	Electromagnet	Electromagnet
Rotor	Permanent	Electromagnet	Permanent	Electromagnet
Type	Can't work	Brushed DC	Brushless DC	Series or shunt

Arrangement 1 can't produce a motor because there is no easy way of changing the magnetic field. Arrangement 4 produces the biggest and most powerful DC motors used in trains, cars and so on. Arrangement 2, Brushed DC, is the most commonly encountered form of "small" DC motor. However, arrangement 3, brushless DC, is becoming increasingly popular.

Different arrangements produce motors which have different torque characteristics, i.e. how hard they are to stop at any given speed. Some types of motor are typically low torque at any speed, i.e. they spin fast but are easy to stop.

Low torque motors are often used with gearboxes, which reduce the speed and increase the torque. The big problem with gearboxes, apart from extra cost, is backlash. The gears don't mesh perfectly and this looseness means that you can turn the input shaft and at first the output shaft won't move. Only when the slack in the gears has been taken up will the output shaft move. This makes a geared motor less useful for precise positioning, although there are ways to improve on this using feedback and clever programming.

Brushed Motors

To energize the electromagnets, a brushed motor supplies current to the armature via a split ring or commutator and brushes. As the rotor rotates, the current in the coil is reversed and it is always attracted to the other pole of the magnet.

The only problem with this arrangement is that, as the brushes rub on the slip ring as the armature rotates, they wear out and cause sparks and hence RF interference. The quality of a brushed motor depends very much on the design of the brushes and the commutator.

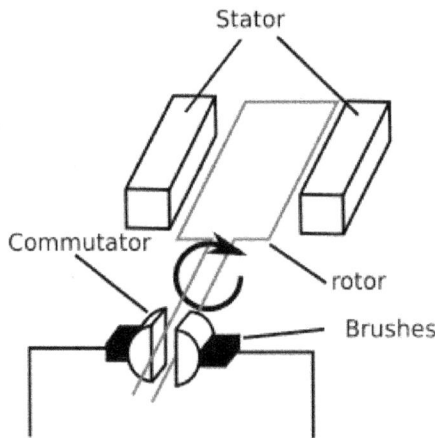

Very small, cheap, brushed DC motors, of the sort in the picture below, tend to not have brushes that can be changed and when they wear out the motor has to be replaced. They also tend to have very low torque and high speed. This usually means that they have to be used with a gearbox. If you overload a brushed motor then the tendency is to demagnetize the stator magnets. The cheapest devices are basically toys.

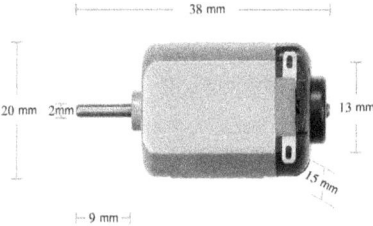

Higher quality brushed motors are available and they also come in a variety of form factors. For example, the 775 motor is 66.7 by 42mm with a 5mm shaft:

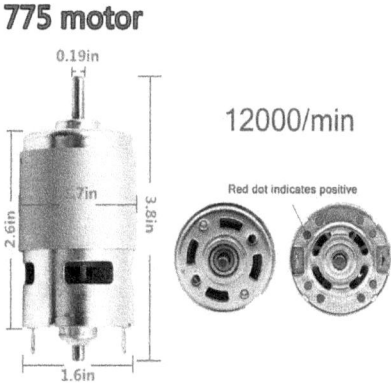

Even these motors tend not to have user-serviceable brushes, but they tend to last a long time due to better construction.

Unidirectional Brushed Motor

A brushed motor can be powered by simply connecting it to a DC supply. Reversing the DC supply reverses the direction of the motor. The speed is simply proportional to the applied voltage. If all you want is a unidirectional control then all you need is a PWM driver that can supply the necessary current and voltage.

A single transistor solution is workable as long as you include a diode to allow the energy stored in the windings to discharge when the motor is rotating, but not under power:

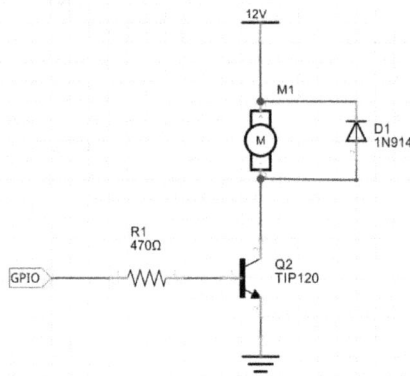

This circuit is simple and will work with motor voltages up to 40V and motor currents up to 5A continuous, 8A peak. The only small point to note is that the TIP120 is a Darlington pair, i.e. it is two transistors in the same case, and as such the base voltage drop is twice the usual 0.6V, i.e. 1.2V, and this has to be taken into account when calculating the current-limiting resistor.

It is sometimes said that the TIP120 and similar are inefficient power controllers because, comprising two transistors, they have twice the emitter-collector voltage you would expect, which means they dissipate more power than necessary.

If you are running a motor from a battery you might want to use a MOSFET, but, as described earlier, 3.3V is low to switch a MOSFET on and off. One solution is to use a BJT to increase the voltage applied to the gate:

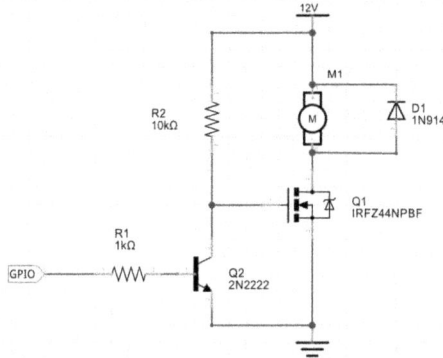

The BJT connects the gate to 12V. As the IRFZ44NPBF has a threshold voltage between 2V and 4V, devices should work at 5V and sometimes at 3.3V without the help of the BJT, but providing 12V ensures that the MOSFET is fully on. One problem with the circuit is that the use of the BJT inverts the signal. When the GPIO line is high the BJT is on and the MOSFET is off and vice versa. In other words, GPIO line high switches the motor off and low switches it on. This MOSFET can work with voltages up to 50V and currents of 40A. The 2N2222 can only work at 30V, or 40V in the case of the 2N2222A.

A third approach to controlling a unidirectional motor is to use half an H-bridge. Why this is so-called, and why you might want to do it, will become apparent in the next section on bidirectional motors. Half an H-bridge makes use of two complementary devices, either an NPN and a PNP BJT or an N- and P-type MOSFET.

For example:

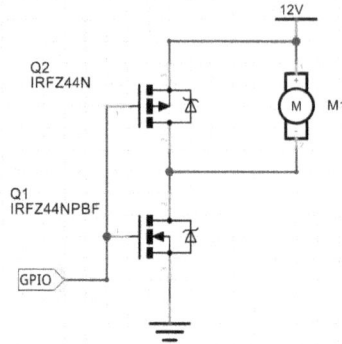

If the GPIO line is high then Q1 is on and Q2 off and the motor runs. If the GPIO line is low then Q1 is off and Q2 is on and the motor is braked – it has a resistance to rotating because of the back electromotive force (EMF) generated when the rotor turns. You probably need a BJT to feed the MOSFETs as selected.

Unidirectional PWM Motor Controller

A function to control the speed of a unidirectional motor is very simple. The speed is set by the duty cycle – the only parameter you have to choose in addition is the frequency. If you want an optimal controller then setting the frequency is a difficult task. Higher speeds make the motor run faster and quieter – but too high a frequency and the motor loses power and the driving transistor or MOSFET becomes hot and less efficient. The determining factor is the inductance of the motor's coil and any other components connected to it such as capacitors. In practice, PWM frequencies from 100Hz to 20kHz are commonly used, but in most cases 1kHz to 2kHz is a good choice.

How should we implement code to make motor control easy? A good pattern is to create an object which has fields that represent the state of the entity and methods to control it. For example, to implement a unidirectional motor we can create a Motor class:

```
class Motor:
    def __init__(self, pinNo):
        self.gpio = pinNo
        self._on = False
        self.speed=0

        self.pwm1=PWM(Pin(pinNo))
        self.pwm1.freq(2000)
        self.pwm1.duty_u16(0)
```

130

You can see that this has all of the information needed to define the current state of a motor. All we need now are some functions to modify the fields and implement the changes to the state.

First we need a function to set the speed:

```
def setSpeed(self,s):
    self._on=True
    self.speed=s
    self.pwm1.duty_u16(int(65535*s/100))
```

and two functions to turn the motor on and off:

```
def off(self):
    self._on=False
    self.pwm1.duty_u16(0)
def on(self):
    self._on=True
    self.pwm1.duty_u16(int(65535*self.speed/100))
```

After this we can create and use a motor very easily. A full program, unimotor.py, complete with a demonstration is:

```
from machine import Pin, PWM
from time import sleep
class Motor:
    def __init__(self, pinNo):
        self.gpio = pinNo
        self._on = False
        self.speed=0
        self.pwm1=PWM(Pin(pinNo))
        self.pwm1.freq(2000)
        self.pwm1.duty_u16(0)
    def setSpeed(self,s):
        self._on=True
        self.speed=s
        self.pwm1.duty_u16(int(65535*s/100))
    def off(self):
        self._on=False
        self.pwm1.duty_u16(0)
    def on(self):
        self._on=True
        self.pwm1.duty_u16(int(65535*self.speed/100))
motor=Motor(16)
motor.setSpeed(50)
sleep(1)
motor.off()
sleep(1)
motor.setSpeed(90)
sleep(1)
motor.off()
```

This sets up a motor connected to GPIO 16, sets it to 50% speed, pauses, turns it off, then on again at 90% and finally off.

Bidirectional Brushed Motor

If you want bidirectional control then you need to use an H-bridge:

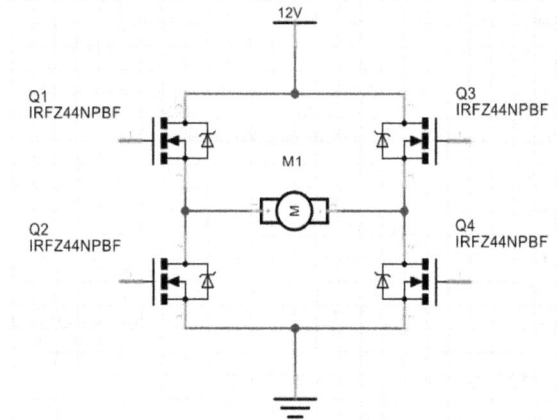

It is easy to see how this works. If Q1 and Q4 are the only MOSFETs on the motor, + is connected to 12V and − to ground. The motor runs in the forward direction. If Q2 and Q3 are the only MOSFETs on the motor, + is connected to ground and − is connected to 12V. The motor runs in the reverse direction. Of course, if none or any single one is on the motor is off. If Q1 and Q3, or Q2 and Q4, are on then the motor is braked as its windings are shorted out and the back EMF acts as a brake.

You can arrange to drive the four MOSFETs using four GPIO lines - just make sure that they switch on and off in the correct order. To make the bridge easier to drive, you can add a NOT gate to each pair so that you switch Q1/Q2 and Q3/Q4 to opposite states.

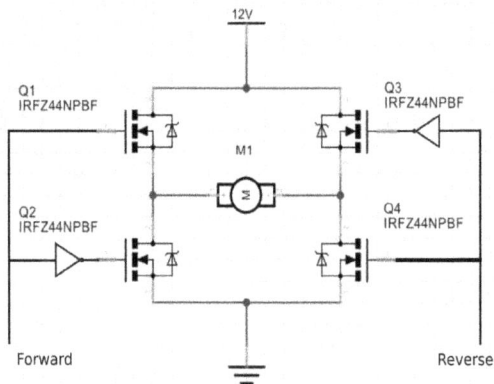

An alternative design is to use complementary MOSFETs:

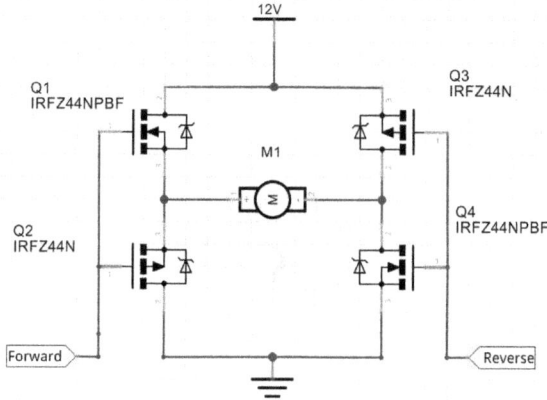

12V

Q1
IRFZ44NPBF

Q3
IRFZ44N

M1

Q2
IRFZ44N

Q4
IRFZ44NPBF

Forward

Reverse

In this configuration, the first GPIO line drives the motor forward and the second drives it in reverse. The effect of setting the two lines is:

Forward	Reverse	Motor
Low	Low	Off
Low	High	Reverse
High	Low	Forward
High	High	Braked

You can also drive the GPIO lines for Forward/Reverse with a PWM signal and control the motor's speed as well as direction. If you use the MOSFETs shown in the diagram then you would also need a BJT to increase the drive voltage to each MOSFET, as in the unidirectional case. You also need to include diodes to deal with potential reverse voltage on each of the MOSFETs. The most important thing about an H-bridge is that Q1/Q2 and Q3/Q4 should never be on together – this would short circuit the power supply.

If working with four power BJTs or MOSFETs is more than you want to tackle, the good news is that there are chips that implement two H-bridges per device. You can also buy low-cost ready-made modules with one or more H-bridges. One of the most used devices is the L298 Dual H-bridge which works up to 46V and total DC current of 4A.

The block diagram of one of the two H-bridges shows exactly how it works:

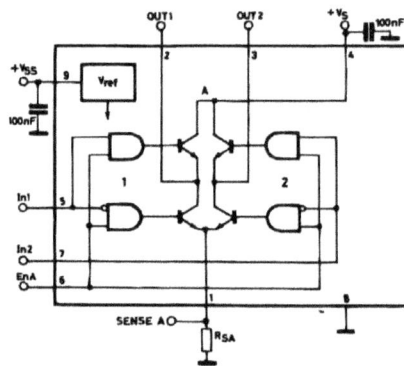

You can see that the bridge is made up of four BJTs and there are logic gates to allow IN1 and IN2 to select the appropriate pairs of devices. The only extras are AND gates and that the ENA (enable) line is used to switch all of the transistors off. The line shown as SENSE A can be used to detect the speed or load of the motor, but is rarely used.

A typical module based on the L298 can be seen below.

It is easier to describe how to use this sort of module with a single motor. The motor is connected to OUT1 and OUT2. Three GPIO lines are connected to ENA, IN1 and IN2. ENA is an enable line, which has to be high for the motor to run at all. IN1 and IN2 play the role of direction control lines – which one is forward and which is reverse depends on which way round you connect the motor. Putting a PWM signal onto ENA controls the speed of the motor and this allows IN1 and IN2 to be simple digital outputs.

Notice that the power connector shows 5V and 12V supplies, but most of these modules have a voltage regulator which will reduce the 12V to 5V. In this case you don't have to supply a 5V connection. If you want to use more than 12V then the regulator has to be disconnected and you need to arrange for a separate 5V supply – check with the module's documentation. Notice that the transistors in the H-bridge have around a 2V drop, so using 12V results in just 10V being applied to the motor.

Another very popular H-bridge device is the SN754410 driver. This is suitable for smaller, lower-powered, motors and has two complete H-bridges. It can supply up to 1A per driver and work from 4.5 to 36V. It has the same set of control lines as the L298, i.e. each motor has a forward/reverse control line and an enable line. You don't have use the enable line - it can be connected to +5V to allow PWM to be applied on the forward/reverse lines.

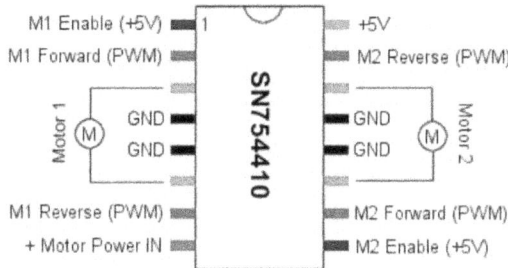

Bidirectional Motor Software

We can easily extend the `Motor` class and its methods to work with a bidirectional motor. The only real difference is that now we have to use two GPIO lines and these are most easily used if they are the A and B channels of the same slice – note for simplicity the code doesn't check this condition and you specify the GPIO line for channel A in the constructor. To go forward we activate the first GPIO line and for reverse we activate the second as shown in `bimotor.py`:

```
class BiMotor(Motor):
    def __init__(self, pinNo):
        super().__init__(pinNo)
        self.forward=True
        self.pwm2=PWM(Pin(pinNo+1))
        self.pwm2.duty_u16(0)

    def setForward(self,forward):
        if self.forward==forward:
            return
        self.pwm1.duty_u16(0)
        self.pwm1,self.pwm2=self.pwm2,self.pwm1
        self.forward=forward
        self.pwm1.duty_u16(int(65535*self.speed/100))
```

```
motor=BiMotor(16)
motor.setSpeed(50)
sleep(1)
motor.setForward(False)
sleep(1)
motor.setSpeed(90)
sleep(1)
motor.setForward(True)
motor.off()
```

Notice that changing direction is just a matter of swapping `pwm1` and `pwm2` – only `pwm1` is active and driving the motor.

This is a very basic set of functions, you can add others to improve motor control according to how sophisticated you want it to be. For example, a `brake` function would set both lines high for brake mode, or you could introduce limits on how fast the speed can be changed.

There are H-bridges that use two lines to control Phase and Enable (PWM). These map to the usual Forward, Reverse and Enable as shown below:

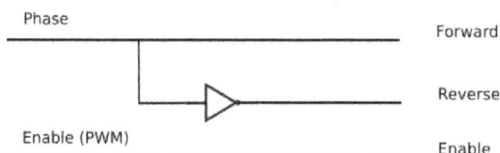

The disadvantage of this arrangement is that you cannot set Forward and Reverse to put the motor into brake mode. If you do have this sort of controller, anything based on the MAX14870/2 for example, then you can modify the functions to use a single PWM line and one standard GPIO line for speed and direction.

Using A Single Full H-Bridge As Two Half H-Bridges

It is easy to think of an H-bridge as being only for bidirectional control, but each full bridge is composed of two half bridges and this means a typical dual full H-bridge can control four unidirectional motors:

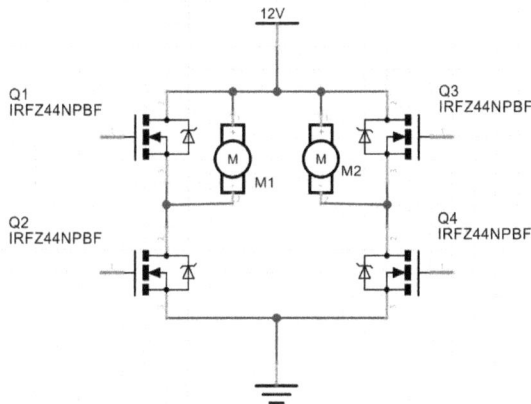

In this case Forward is now MotorM1 speed control and Reverse is now MotorM2 speed control. Any enable line has to be set high to allow the two motors to be controlled. You can make use of this arrangement with the unidirectional software given earlier.

Controlling a Servo

Hobby servos, of the sort used in radio control models, are very cheap and easy to use and they connect via a standard PWM protocol. Servos are not drive motors, but positioning motors. That is, they don't rotate at a set speed, they move to a specified angle or position.

A servo is a motor, usually a brushed DC motor, with a feedback sensor for position, usually a simple variable resistor (potentiometer) connected to the shaft. The output is usually via a set of gears which reduces the rotation rate and increases the torque. The motor turns the gears, and hence the shaft, until the potentiometer reaches the desired setting and hence the shaft has the required angle/position.

A basic servo has just three connections, ground, a power line and a signal line. The colors used vary, but the power line is usually red, ground is usually black or brown and the signal line is white, yellow or orange. If a standard J-connector is fitted then the wire nearest the notch, pin 3, is Signal, the middle wire, pin 2, is 5V and outer wire, pin 1, is Ground.

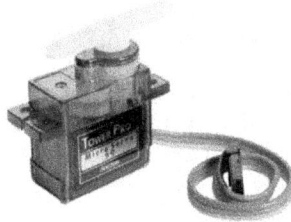

The power wire has to be connected to a 5V supply capable of providing enough current to run the motor - anything up to 500mA or more depending on the servo. The good news is that the servo's signal line generally needs very little current, although it does, in theory, need to be switched between 0V and 5V using a PWM signal.

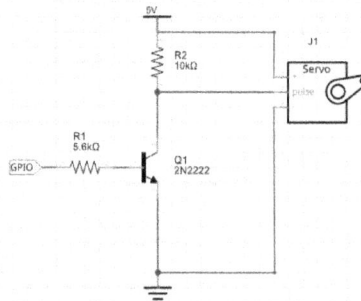

You can assume that the signal line needs to be driven as a voltage load and so the appropriate way to drive the servo is:

- The servo's + line needs to be connected to an external 5V power supply.
- The 10K resistor R1 can be a lot larger for most servos - 47K often works. The 5.6K resistor limits the base current to slightly less than 0.5mA.

Notice, however, that if you are using a single BJT driver, like the one shown above, the input is inverted.

This is the correct way to drive a servo, but in nearly all cases you can drive the servo signal line directly from the 3.3V GPIO line with a 1K resistor to limit the current if anything goes wrong with the servo. Some servos will even work with their motor connected to 3.3V, but at much reduced torque.

Now all we have to do is set the PWM line to produce 20ms pulses with pulse widths ranging from 0.5ms to 2.5ms – i.e. a duty cycle of 2.5 to 12.5%. Once again, in servo.py it is easier to use a class to represent the current state of a servo and create methods to change the state:

```
from machine import Pin, PWM
from time import sleep
class Servo:
    def __init__(self, pinNo):
        self.pwm = PWM(Pin(pinNo))
        self.pwm.freq(50)
        self.position = 65535*2.5/100
    def setPosition(self, p):
        self.position = p
        self.pwm.duty_u16(int(65535*p/1000 + 65535*2.5/100))
servo=Servo(16)
servo.setPosition(100.0)
sleep(1)
servo.setPosition(50.0)
sleep(1)
servo.setPosition(0)
sleep(1)
```

Notice that in servo.py we set the frequency to 50Hz. If you want to work with a non-standard servo you can change this or make it settable. The setPosition function sets the position in terms of percentages. That is, setPosition(50) sets the servo to the middle of its range. This assumes that the servo has a standard positioning range and most don't. In practice, to get the best out of a servo you need to calibrate each servo and discover what range of movement is supported. The main program creates a Servo object on GPIO 16 and then moves the servo to its maximum, middle and minimum positions.

If you run the program using the transistor circuit given earlier, you will discover that the servo does nothing at all, apart perhaps from vibrating. The reason is that the transistor voltage driver is an inverter. When the PWM line is high, the transistor is fully on and the servo's pulse line is effectively grounded. When the PWM line is low, the transistor is fully off and the servo's pulse line is pulled high by the resistor.

The solution is to use an inverted output from the GPIO line using the polarity inverting function given in the previous chapter. However, to make this easier to use we need to integrate it into the Servo class:

```
def setPolarity(self,invert):
    sliceNo=self.getSlice()
    channel=self.getChannel()
    PWM_BASE=0x400a8000 # 0x40050000 pico
    CH1_CSR=0x14
    Addr = PWM_BASE +CH1_CSR*sliceNo
    if invert:
        mem32[Addr]=mem32[Addr] | 0x1 << (2+channel)
    else:
        mem32[Addr]=mem32[Addr] & ~(0x1<<(2+channel))
```

We also need two helper functions that convert the GPIO number to the slice and channel number:

```
def getSlice(self
    return (self.pin>>1) & 0x07

def getChannel(self):
    return self.pin & 1
```

and we need a new attribute to record the pin number:

```
self.pin=pinNo
```

The complete class, and a main program to make use of it inverted, is in servo2.py:

```
from machine import Pin, PWM,mem32
from time import sleep

class Servo:
    def __init__(self, pinNo):
        self.pwm = PWM(Pin(pinNo))
        self.pin=pinNo
        self.pwm.freq(50)
        self.position = 65535*2.5/100

    def setPosition(self, p):
        self.position = p
        self.pwm.duty_u16(int(65535*p/1000 + 65535*2.5/100))

    def getSlice(self):
        return (self.pin>>1) & 0x07

    def getChannel(self):
        return self.pin & 1
```

```
    def setPolarity(self,invert):
        sliceNo=self.getSlice()
        channel=self.getChannel()
        PWM_BASE=0x400a8000 # 0x40050000 pico
        CH1_CSR=0x14
        Addr = PWM_BASE +CH1_CSR*sliceNo
        if invert:
            mem32[Addr]=mem32[Addr] | 0x1 << (2+channel)
        else:
            mem32[Addr]=mem32[Addr] & ~(0x1<<(2+channel))
servo=Servo(16)

servo.setPosition(100.0)
servo.setPolarity(True)
sleep(1)
servo.setPosition(50.0)
servo.setPolarity(True)
sleep(1)
servo.setPosition(0)
sleep(1)
```

Notice that we have to set the polarity after each setPosition as setting the duty cycle resets the polarity.

It is worth mentioning that servos make good low-cost DC motors, complete with gearboxes. All you have to do is open the servo, unsolder the motor from the control circuits and solder two wires to the motor. If you want to use the forward/reverse electronics you can remove the end stops on the gearbox, usually on the large gearwheel, and replace the potentiometer with a pair of equal value resistors, 2.2kΩ, say.

Brushless DC Motors

Brushless DC motors are more expensive than brushed DC motors, but they are superior in many ways. They don't fail because of commutator or brush wear and need no maintenance. They provide maximum rotational torque at all points of the rotation and generally provide more power for the same size and weight. They can also be controlled more precisely. The only negative points are higher cost and slightly more complex operation. In practice, it is usually better to use a brushed DC motor unless you really need something extra.

A brushless DC motor is basically a brushed motor turned inside out – the stator is a set of electromagnets and the rotor is a set of permanent magnets. In some designs the permanent magnets are inside the stator in the manner of a brushed motor, an inrunner, and sometimes the magnets are outside of the stator, an outrunner.

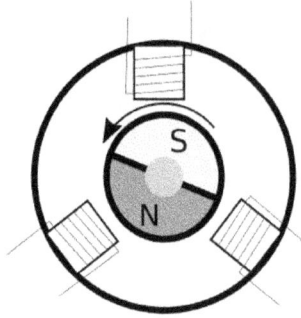

An inrunner – the permanent magnets form the rotor and the coils are switched to attract.

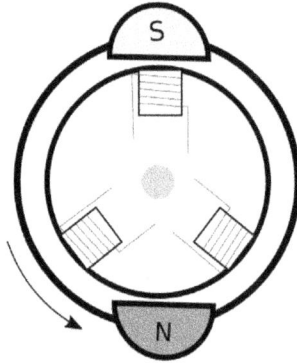

An outrunner – the permanent magnets are on the outside of the stator and the whole cover rotates.

A brushless motor works in exactly the same way as a brushed motor. As the coils are stationary there is no need for a mechanical commutator, but there is still need for commutation – the coils have to be switched on in sequence to create a rotating magnetic field which pulls the rotor around with it. This means that you have to implement an electronic commutator, which is another name for a brushless DC motor.

An electronic commutator has to sense the position of the rotor and change the magnetic field generated by the stator to keep the rotor moving. Brushless motors differ in the number of magnets they have and the number of phases. The most common is a three-phase motor as these are used in radio control modeling. Essentially you need at least a driver for each of the phases and a GPIO line to generate the signal. In practice, you need two drivers for each phase and they have to be driven from a dual supply so that the magnetic field can be positive, zero or negative.

This would be possible to do with software, but it isn't easy and a more reasonable alternative is to buy a ready-built controller. There are two types of brushless motor – with Hall sensors and without. The former are more expensive, but easier to control because the electronics always knows where the rotor is and can apply the correct drive. The ones without sensors are controlled by measuring the back EMF from the motor and this is much harder. Most of the lower-cost speed controllers need motors with Hall sensors.

The radio control community has taken to using three-phase brushless motors and this has resulted in a range of motors and controllers at reasonable prices intended as high-power, high-speed, unidirectional motors for use in quadcopters and model planes.

If you can live with their limitations they provide a good way to couple a Pico to a brushless motor. In this case all you need is a three-phase brushless motor of the sort used in RC modeling and an ESC (Electronic Speed Controller) of the sort shown below:

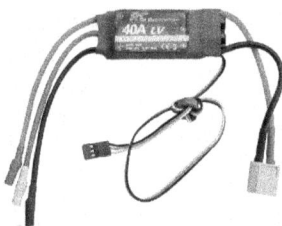

The three leads on the left go to the three phases of the motor and the red and black leads on the right go to a power supply – often a LiPo battery. The small three-wire connector in the middle is a standard servo connector and you can use it exactly as if the brushless motor was a servo, with a few exceptions. The first is that pin 2 supplies 5V rather than accepts it. Don't connect this to anything unless you want a 5V supply. The second problem is that ESCs are intelligent. When you first apply power they beep and can be programmed into different modes by changing the PWM signal from Max to Min. Also, to use an ESC you have to arm it. This is to avoid radio control modelers from being injured by motors that start unexpectedly when the power is applied. The most common arming sequence is for the ESC to beep when power is applied. You then have to set the PWM to Min, when the ESC will beep again. After a few moments you will have control of the motor.

The need for an arming procedure should alert you to the fact that these model motors are very powerful. Don't try working with one loose on the bench as it will move fast if switched on and at the very least make a twisted mess of your wires. Most importantly of all, don't run a motor with anything attached to it until you have everything under control.

Stepper Motors

There is one sort of brushless motor that is easy to use and low cost – the stepper motor. This differs from a standard brushless motor in that it isn't designed for continuous high-speed rotation. A stepper motor has an arrangement of magnets and coils such that powering some of the coils holds the rotor in a particular position. Changing which coils are activated makes the rotor turn until it is aligned with the coils and stops moving. Thus the stepper motor moves the rotor in discrete steps. This makes driving it much simpler, but note it doesn't use PWM for speed control. Stepper motors have no brushes and so don't wear out as fast as brushed motors. They also have roughly the same torque at any speed and can be used at low speeds without a gearbox. They can remain in a fixed position for a long time without burning out, as DC motors would. Unlike a servo, however, if a stepper motor is mechanically forced to a new position, it will not return to its original position when released.

The only disadvantage of a stepper motor is that the continuous rotation produced by repeated stepping can make the motor vibrate. Stepper motors vary in the size of step they use – typically 1.8 degrees giving 200 steps per rotation, although gearing can be used to reduce the step size. Another big difference is that the rotor is made up of either permanent magnets or soft iron. The first type is called a Permanent Magnet or PM stepper and the second is called a Variable Reluctance or VR and they differ in how you drive them with PM steppers being easier to understand. There are also hybrid steppers which share the good characteristics of both PM and VR stepper motors. These are more expensive and are generally only used where accuracy of positioning is important. They also differ in the number of phases, i.e. independent banks of coils, they have.

The diagram below shows a two-phase PM motor with Phase 1 activated:

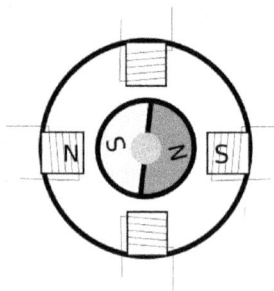

If Phase two is activated, the rotor turns through 90 degrees:

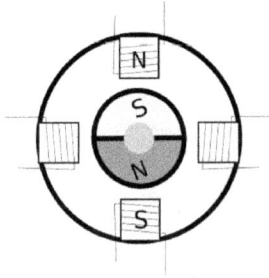

This is the simplest stepper motor you can make.

A typical stepper motor will have many more coils than four, but they are usually connected into two or three phases.

Another big difference is bipolar versus unipolar. A bipolar motor is like the one shown in the diagram. To generate a north pole the current has to flow in the opposite direction to when you want to create a south pole. This means you have to drive each bank of coils with a bidirectional driver, e.g. an H-bridge. A unipolar motor has two windings, one in each direction, and both windings can be driven by a unidirectional driver – one giving a north pole and the other a south pole. Notice that a unipolar motor has twice the number of coils to drive and the switching sequence is slightly different.

A two-phase bipolar motor with Phases A and B would switch on in the sequence:

A → B → A- → B- → A etc

where the minus sign means the current flows the other way.

A two-phase unipolar motor has two coils per phase, A1, A2 and B1, B2 with the 1 and 2 windings creating opposite magnetic fields for the same current flow. Now the sequence is:

A1 → B1 → A2 → B2 → A1 etc

and all driven in the same direction.

Switching single phases fully on and off in sequence makes the motor make repeated steps. You can also switch on more than one phase at a time to generate micro-steps.

For example, in our two-phase example, switching on two phases makes the rotor settle between the two, so producing a half micro-step:

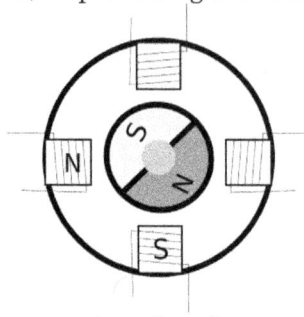

The driving sequence for a two-phase bipolar motor is:

A → AB →B → BA- → A- → A- B- → B- → AB- → A

with minus indicating that the coil is energized in the opposite direction, giving a total of eight, rather than four, steps.

You can even vary the current through the coils and move the rotor to intermediate positions. At the extreme limit you can vary the current sinusoidally and produce a smooth rotation. Micro-stepping is smoother and can eliminate buzzing. For high accuracy positioning, micro-stepping is a poor performer under load.

Stepper Motor Driver

How best to drive a stepper motor using a Pico? There are some specialized chips that work with unipolar and bipolar stepper motors. However, you can easily control a bipolar stepper motor using one the H-bridges described in the section on directional motor control.

For example, using complementary MOSFETS:

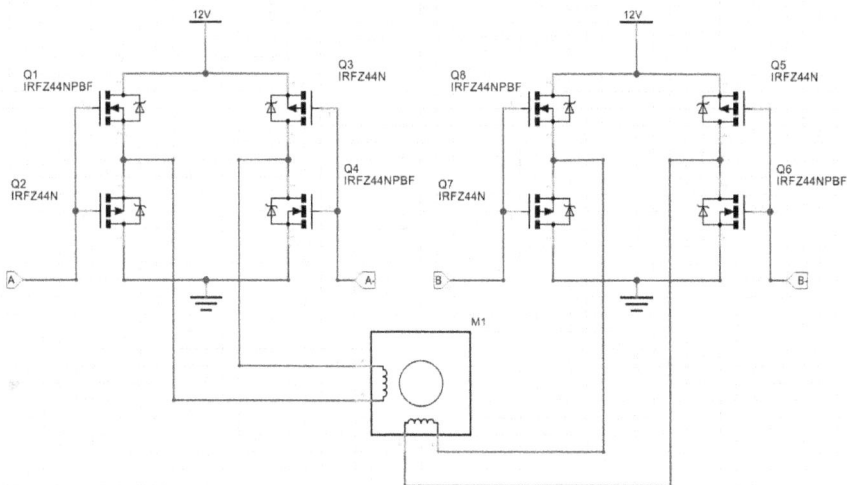

You can use a dual H-bridge module in the same way if you don't want to build it from scratch. The motor has to be a bipolar two-phase motor, often called a four-wire stepper motor. You can see that for this arrangement you need four GPIO lines, A, A-, B and B-.

What about driving the dual H-bridge using software? You need four GPIO lines and you need to pulse them in a specific phase to make the motor rotate. This could be done using the PIO, see Chapter 13, but it is easier to start with software-controlled GPIO lines. The first question to answer is how to specify the four GPIO lines to be used. As we will see, there is a big advantage and simplification in using a block of four consecutive lines. The reason is that we can easily set the bits corresponding to these lines in a mask and so set them in a single operation. In this case we simply record the number of the numerically lowest GPIO line GPIO n and assume that a block of four GPIO lines are allocated:

GPIO n → A, GPIO n+1 → B, GPIO n+2 → A- and GPIO n+3 → B-

As before, we use a class to record the current state of the motor and its methods:

```
class StepperBi4():
    def __init__(self, pinA):
        self.phase=0
        self.pinA=pinA
        self.gpios= tuple([Pin(pinA,Pin.OUT),Pin(pinA+1,Pin.OUT),
                    Pin(pinA+2,Pin.OUT),Pin(pinA+3,Pin.OUT)])
        self.gpios[0].high()
        self.gpioMask=0xF<<self.pinA
        self.halfstepSeq =[0x1, 0x3, 0x2, 0x6, 0x4, 0xC, 0x8, 0x9]
#    [
#                [0,0,0,1],
#                [0,0,1,1],
#                [0,0,1,0],
#                [0,1,1,0],
#                [0,1,0,0],
#                [1,1,0,0],
#                [1,0,0,0],
#                [1,0,0,1]
#    ]
    def _gpio_set(self,value,mask):
        # 0x01C for Pico 0x028 for Pico 2
        machine.mem32[0xd0000000+0x028]=
            (machine.mem32[0xd0000000+0x010])^value & mask

    def setPhase(self,phase):
        value=self.halfstepSeq[phase] << self.pinA
        self._gpio_set(value,self.gpioMask)
        self.phase=phase
```

```
    def stepForward(self):
        self.phase=(self.phase+1) % 8
        self.setPhase(self.phase)

    def stepReverse(self):
        self.phase=(self.phase-1) % 8
        self.setPhase(self.phase)

step=StepperBi4(16)
step.setPhase(0)

while True:
    step.stepForward()
    sleep_ms(1)
```

You can see that `halfstepSeq` is just the hex value corresponding to the binary representation of which line is high and which is low in each state. The bits correspond to the GPIO lines such that the low order bits control the lowest numbered GPIO line.

You can see that if GPIO 16 is A, GPIO 17 is B, GPIO 18 is A- and GPIO 19 is B- and stepping through the `stepTable` gives the sequence given earlier:

A → AB → B → BA- → A- → A-B- → B- → AB- → A

Now all we need are some methods to set and work with the phase:

The `setPhase` function uses the `_gpio_set` function given in Chapter 4 to change only the GPIO lines we are using to the bit pattern in the `stepTable` for the specified phase. The `stepForward` and `stepReverse` simply move down or up in the phase table, making sure to go back to the start when the end is reached. This is what the modulus operator, `%`, does for us and `phase` follows the sequence 0,1,2,3,4,5,6,7,0,1 and so on.

You can use a full step table if you want to, as long as you remember to work in mod 4 rather than 8:

```
self.stepSeq =[0x1,0x2,0x4,0x8]
# [
#              [0, 0, 0, 1],
#              [0, 0, 1, 0],
#              [0, 1, 0, 0],
#              [1, 0, 0, 0],
#          ]
```

Of course, these are identical to the even elements of the half step table so we can achieve the same result by using that table but increasing the increment by 2 instead of 1:

```
def stepForward(self):
    self.phase=(self.phase+2) % 8
    self.setPhase(self.phase)

def stepReverse(self):
    self.phase=(self.phase-2) % 8
    self.setPhase(self.phase)
```

To try either version of the program you need an H-bridge connected so that GPIO 16 is A, GPIO 17 is B, GPIO 18 is A- and GPIO 19 is B-. The maximum stepping speed, i.e. with no timer delay, is such that a 200-step motor, i.e. 400 half steps, will rotate in 400*0.1 ms= 0.04 s, i.e. 1500rpm, which is maximum most stepper motors can run at. In practice include delays to slow things down to a few hundred rpm.

If you are using one of the many dual H-bridge modules then the wiring is as shown below:

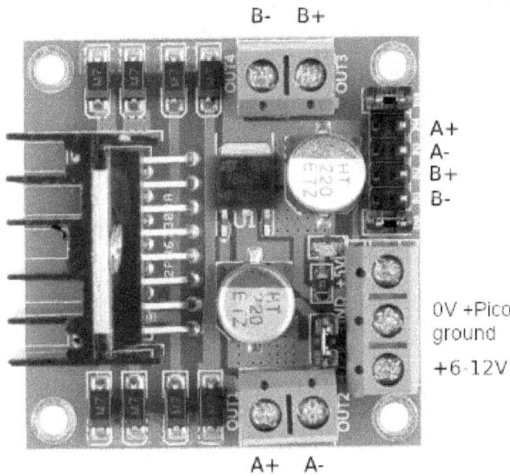

Notice that you have to connect the ground of the power supply and the Pico's ground together. It is also a good idea to use a power supply with a current trip when first trying things out.

The outputs are as you would expect for a half-stepping motor:

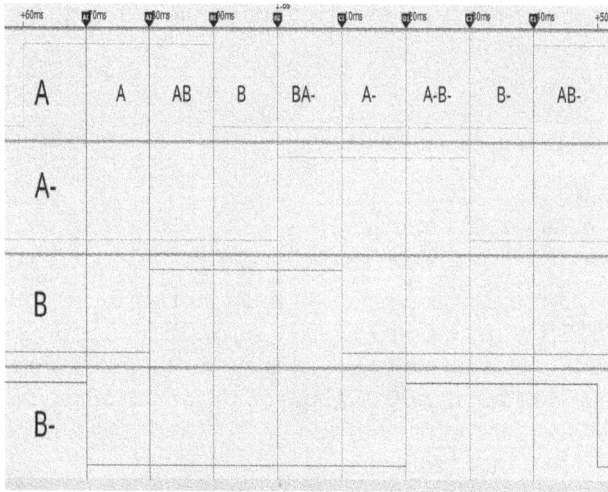

Stepper Motor Rotation – Using Timers

Most of the time you use a stepper motor to move to a given position by executing an exact number of steps. If you do want to make a stepper motor rotate then you need to arrange to step at a regular rate. The simplest way to do this with a Pico is to use a timer interrupt.

To create a Timer object use its constructor:

```
timer=Timer()
```

Once you have a Timer object you can use its `init` method to set up either a periodic callback or a one-off callback, a one-shot:

```
Timer.init(mode=mode, period=- 1, callback=None)
```

Mode can be either of:

`Timer.ONE_SHOT`	The timer runs once and the callback is called when the period is up.
`Timer.PERIODIC`	The timer runs repeatedly calling the callback each time the period is up.

When you are finished with a timer you can use:

```
Timer.deinit()
```

to free the hardware and stop any periodic callback.

Notice that the callback function is an interrupt handler and is subject to all of the restrictions and cautions that apply to a general interrupt handler. The callback accepts a single parameter which is the `Timer` object that called it. You can use a lambda function to define the callback. If you want to know how, see *Programmer's Python: Everything Is An Object, 2nd Ed*, ISBN:9781871962765. We use this technique in Chapter 17.

To make the motor rotate on its own we need a timer interrupt handler:

```
def _doRotate(self,timer):
    if self.forward:
        self.stepForward()
    else:
        self.stepReverse()
```

You can see that this function simply steps the motor forward or backward depending on the setting of the forward attribute.

To make this work we need a function to set up the timer interrupt:

```
def rotate(self,forward,speed):
    self.forward = forward
    self.speed = speed
    if speed==0:
        self.timer.deinit()
        self.timer = None
        return
    if self.timer==None:
        self.timer = machine.Timer()
    self.timer.init(freq=speed,mode =
                machine.Timer.PERIODIC,callback=self.doRotate)
```

The speed is specified in half steps per second. So setting speed to 200 gives a step rate of 200 half steps per second, i.e. 5ms per step or a rotation of 30rpm. Notice that we have to deal with a speed of zero differently by removing the timer. We also has to check that there isn't already a timer allocated – if there is we just use it. We also need some additional attributes:

```
        self.forward = True
        self.speed = 0
```

A main program to rotate the motor for 500ms at 10ms per step i.e. 0.25rpm and then stop it for another 500ms is:

```
step = StepperBi4(16)
step.setPhase(0)
while True:
    step.rotate(True,100)
    sleep_ms(500)
    step.rotate(True,0)
    sleep_ms(500)
```

151

Notice that when the motor is stopped the phase is still active and so the motor holds its position under power:

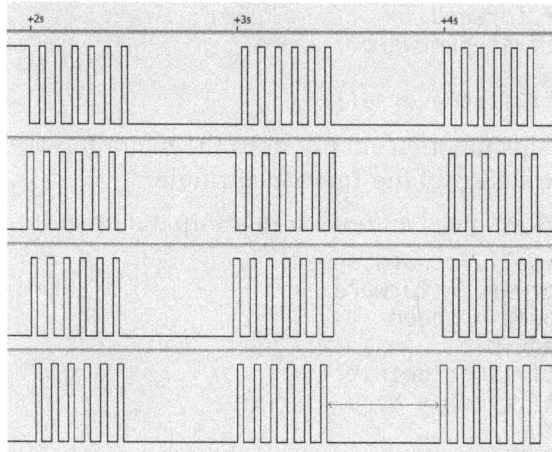

You can elaborate on this basic scheme to include more complex controls on the motor's behavior, including things like allowing it to freewheel and selecting full or half stepping.

The complete program, stepper.py, including the timer interrupt handling is:

```
from utime import sleep_ms
from machine import Pin
import machine
class StepperBi4():
    def __init__(self, pinA):
        self.phase=0
        self.pinA=pinA
        self.timer=None
        self.forward=True
        self.speed=0
        self.gpios= tuple([Pin(pinA,Pin.OUT),Pin(pinA+1,Pin.OUT),
Pin(pinA+2,Pin.OUT),Pin(pinA+3,Pin.OUT)])
        self.gpios[0].high()
        self.gpioMask=0xF<<self.pinA
        self.halfstepSeq =[0x1, 0x3, 0x2, 0x6, 0x4, 0xC, 0x8, 0x9]
#     [
#                 [0,0,0,1],
#                 [0,0,1,1],
#                 [0,0,1,0],
#                 [0,1,1,0],
#                 [0,1,0,0],
#                 [1,1,0,0],
#                 [1,0,0,0],
#                 [1,0,0,1]
#     ]
```

```python
    def _gpio_set(self,value,mask):
    # 0x01C for Pico 0x028 for Pico 2
        machine.mem32[0xd0000000+0x028]=
                    (machine.mem32[0xd0000000+0x010])^value & mask


    def setPhase(self,phase):
        value=self.halfstepSeq[phase] << self.pinA
        self._gpio_set(value,self.gpioMask)
        self.phase=phase

    def stepForward(self):
        self.phase=(self.phase+1) % 8
        self.setPhase(self.phase)

    def stepReverse(self):
        self.phase=(self.phase-1) % 8
        self.setPhase(self.phase)

    def doRotate(self,timer):
        if self.forward:
            self.stepForward()
        else:
            self.stepReverse()

    def rotate(self,forward,speed):
        self.forward=forward
        self.speed=speed
        if speed==0:
            self.timer.deinit()
            self.timer=None
            return
        if self.timer==None:
            self.timer=machine.Timer()
        self.timer.init(freq=speed,mode=
            machine.Timer.PERIODIC,callback=self.doRotate)


step=StepperBi4(16)
step.setPhase(0)
while True:
    step.rotate(True,100)
    sleep_ms(500)
    step.rotate(True,0)
    sleep_ms(500)
```

Summary

- There are a number of different types of electric motor, but DC brushed or brushless motors are the most used in the IoT.

- Brushed motors can be speed controlled using a single transistor driver and a PWM signal.

- For bidirectional control you need an H-bridge. In this case you need two PWM signals.

- Servo motors set their position in response to the duty cycle of a PWM signal.

- Brushless DC motors are very powerful and best controlled using off-the-shelf electronic modules. They are very powerful and thus dangerous if used incorrectly. They can be driven using a simple PWM signal.

- Stepper motors are a special case of a Brushless DC motor. They move in discrete steps in response to energizing different coils.

- A unipolar motor has coils that can be driven in the same direction for every step. A bipolar motor has coils that need to be driven in reverse for some steps.

- Bipolar motors need two H-bridges to operate and four GPIO lines.

- You can easily create a stepper motor driver using four GPIO lines.

Chapter 10

Getting Started With The SPI Bus

The Serial Peripheral Interface (SPI) bus can be something of a problem because it doesn't have a well-defined standard that every device conforms to. Even so, if you only want to work with one specific device it is usually easy to find a configuration that works - as long as you understand what the possibilities are.

SPI Bus Basics

The SPI bus is commonly encountered as it is used to connect all sorts of devices from LCD displays, through realtime clocks and A-to-D converters, but as different companies have implemented it in different ways, you have to work harder to implement it in any particular case. However, it does usually work, which is a surprise for a bus with no standard, or clear, specification.

The reason it can be made to work is that you can specify a range of different operating modes, frequencies and polarities. This makes the bus slightly more complicated to use, but generally it is a matter of looking up how the device you are trying to work with implements the SPI bus and then getting the Pico to work in the same way.

The SPI bus is odd in another way - it does not use bidirectional serial connections. There is a data line for the data to go from the master to the slave and a separate data line from the slave back to the master. That is, instead of a single data line that changes its transfer direction, there is one for data going out and one for data coming in. It is also worth knowing that the drive on the SPI bus is push-pull and not open-collector/drain. This provides higher speed and more noise protection as the bus is driven in both directions. There is a bidirectional mode, where a single wire is used for the data, and the Pico supports this.

In the configuration most used for the Pico, there is a single master and, at most, two slaves. The signal lines are:

- ◆ MOSI (Master Output Slave Input), i.e. data to the slave
- ◆ MISO (Master Input Slave Output), i.e. data to the master
- ◆ SCLK (Serial Clock), which is always generated by the master

155

In general, there can also be any number of SS (Slave Select), CE (Chip Enable) or CS (Chip Select) lines, which are usually set low to select which slave is being addressed. Notice that unlike other buses, I2C for example, there are no SPI commands or addresses, only bytes of data. However, slave devices do interpret some of the data as commands to do something or send some particular data.

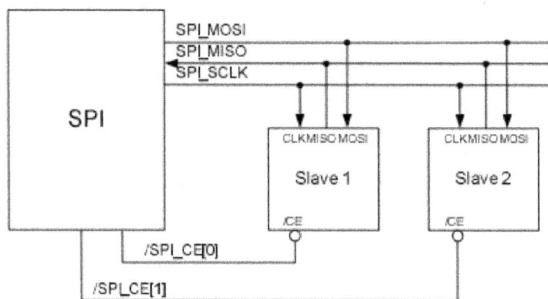

There are two other modes of operation of the SPI interface – bidirectional and LoSSI mode. The bidirectional mode simply uses a single data line, MIMO, for both input and output. The direction of the line is determined by writing a command to the slave. LoSSI mode is used to communicate with sophisticated peripherals such as LCD panels. Both of these are unsupported and beyond the scope of this chapter. However, once you know how standard mode works, the other two are simple variations.

The data transfer on the SPI bus is also slightly odd. What happens is that the master pulls one of the chip selects low, which activates a slave. Then the master toggles the clock SCLK and both the master and the slave send a single bit on their respective data lines. After eight clock pulses, a byte has been transferred from the master to the slave and from the slave to the master. You can think of this as being implemented as a circular buffer, although it doesn't have to be.

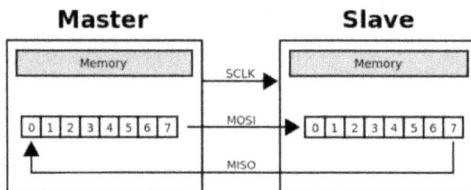

This full-duplex data transfer is often hidden by the software and the protocol used. For example, there is a read function that reads data from the slave and sends zeros or data that is ignored by the slave. Similarly, there is a write function that sends valid data, but ignores whatever the slave sends. The transfer is typically in groups of eight bits, usually most significant bit first, but this isn't always the case. In general, as long as the master supplies clock pulses, data is transferred.

Notice this circular buffer arrangement allows for slaves to be daisy-chained with the output of one going to the input of the next. This makes the entire chain one big circular shift register. This can make it possible to have multiple devices with only a single chip select, but it also means any commands sent to the slaves are received by each one in turn. For example, you could send a convert command to each A-to-D converter in turn and receive back results from each one.

The final odd thing about the SPI bus is that there are four modes which define the relationship between the data timing and the clock pulse. The clock can be either active high or low, which is referred to as clock polarity (CPOL), and data can be sampled on the rising or falling edge of the clock, which is clock phase (CPHA).

All combinations of these two possibilities gives the four modes:

SPI Mode*	Clock Polarity CPOL	Clock Phase CPHA	Characteristics
0	0	0	Clock active high data output on falling edge and sampled on rising
1	0	1	Clock active high data output on rising edge and sampled on falling
2	1	0	Clock active low data output on falling edge and sampled on rising
3	1	1	Clock active low data output on rising edge and sampled on falling

*The way that the SPI modes are labeled is common but not universal.

There is often a problem trying to work out what mode a slave device uses. The clock polarity is usually easy and the Clock phase can sometimes be worked out from the data transfer timing diagrams and:

- First clock transition in the middle of a data bit means CPHA=0
- First clock transition at the start of a data bit means CPHA=1

So to configure the SPI bus to work with a particular slave device:

1. Select the clock frequency - anything from 125MHz to 3.8kHz
2. Determine the CS polarity - active high or low
3. Set the clock mode Mode0 thru Mode3

Now we have to find out how to do this using MicroPython.

Pico SPI Interfaces

The Pico has two SPI controllers, SPI0 and SPI1, that can work as a master or a slave. The connections from both controllers can be routed to different pins:

SPI0	MISO	GPIO 0	GPIO 4	GPIO 16	GPIO 20
	CSn	GPIO 1	GPIO 5	GPIO 17	GPIO 21
	SCLK	GPIO 2	GPIO 6	GPIO 18	GPIO 22
	MOSI	GPIO 3	GPIO 7	GPIO 19	GPIO 23
SPI1	MISO	GPIO 8	GPIO 12	GPIO 24	GPIO 28
	CSn	GPIO 9	GPIO 13	GPIO 25	GPIO 29
	SCLK	GPIO 10	GPIO 14	GPIO 26	
	MOSI	GPIO 11	GPIO 15	GPIO 27	

For a full SPI interface you need to use one pin for MISO , one for MOSI and one for SCLK. The CSn lines are not really part of the SPI implementation. To make use of them you have to treat them like standard GPIO lines and set them high and low to select the device under program control. What this means is that you can use as many of the CSn lines with any SPI interface as you need.

You can make use of the hardware SPI implementation via the `machine.SPI` object.

There is also a software implementation of the SPI protocol in the form of the `machine.SoftSPI` object. This has all of the same methods as the hardware implemented SPI object. If possible make use of the hardware based SPI object as it minimizes CPU load, but if you run out of SPI controllers then you could make use of the software SPI object which works with any selection of pins. In the rest of the chapter the hardware SPI object is used, but the modification to use `SoftSPI` are minor.

The SPI Functions

Before you can make use of the SPI methods you have to import the SPI module:

```
from machine import SPI
```

and you have to create an SPI object:

```
spi=SPI(n)
```

where n is zero or one to select one of the two SPI controllers. You can also include parameters that are used in the initialization method to the constructor. If you don't the SPI controller keeps the last configuration it was used in.

The SPI methods can be grouped into initialization and data transfer. Let's look at each group in turn.

Initialization

There is an init method that can be used to set up the hardware:

```
SPI.init(baudrate=1000000, polarity=0, phase=0, bits=8,
         firstbit=SPI.MSB, sck=None, mosi=None, miso=None)
```

At the time of writing this doesn't seem to work as a way to specify the pins in use. Until this is changed you should use:

```
spi=SPI(0, sck=Pin1, mosi=Pin2, miso=Pin3)
spi.init(baudrate=1000000, polarity=0, phase=0, bits=8,
                                        firstbit=SPI.MSB)
```

This lets you set the number of data bits, and the SPI mode. Notice that, for the Pico the bit order can only be SPI_MSB. The mode is set by specifying polarity and phase using:

phase=0   Data latched on first clock transition
phase=1   Data latched on second clock transition
together with:

polarity=0   Clock active high
polarity=1   Clock active low
You have to specify the pins used for sck, mosi and miso in the constructor and these have to be Pin objects, not just GPIO numbers.

You can use the:

```
SPI.deinit()
```

function to turn off the SPI bus you have been using.

Data Transfer Functions

Because of the way the SPI bus uses a full-duplex transfer, things are a little different from other buses when it comes to implementing functions to transfer data. The most basic transfer function is:

```
SPI.write_readinto(write_buf, read_buf)
```

The buffers are byte arrays and they have to be of the same length. The write_buf is sent byte-by-byte as data is read into the read_buf at the same time. If you don't understand this idea of a send (source) and a receive (destination) byte array then see the discussion about how SPI works given earlier.

Notice that a call to any of the transfer functions is blocking, i.e. the function doesn't return until the transfer is complete. There is also no need for a timeout as all SPI transfers end after the number of clock pulses needed to transfer the specified data. Also all of the transfer functions return the number of elements read/written.

If you are only interesting in reading or writing data then you can use:

```
SPI.read(nbytes, write=0)

SPI.readinto(buf, write=0)
```

The read function returns a byte array with nbytes elements. The readinto function uses the specified buffer and reads data until it is full. Both send the byte specified by write as the data to the slave. Finally you can send data using:

```
SPI.write(buf)
```

In the case of the write function, the received data is simply discarded.

There is one final complication that you can mostly ignore. The SPI hardware is buffered. Both the MISO and MOSI connections have an 8-deep FIFO buffer and this means that you can send and receive data faster if the buffer isn't full or empty. Unfortunately, MicroPython doesn't provide any way to find the state of the buffer.

Using the Data Transfer Functions

When you first start using SPI it can be difficult to get used to the idea that you send and receive data both at the same time. Indeed, you cannot receive data unless you send the same number of data elements.

The most basic of the transfer functions is spi.write_readinto and it makes the bidirectional transfer obvious. For example:

```
read=bytearray(3)
write=bytearray('ABC','utf-8')
spi.write_readinto(write,read)
```

This sends the three elements in write and receives back three elements in read. Whether the three elements in read make any sense is a matter of what the slave sends back and they may be of no interest at all. If this is the case, you might as well use:

```
write=bytearray('ABC','utf-8')
spi.write(write)
```

Whatever three elements the slave sends back are simply ignored.

In the same way, if what you transmit to the slave isn't of any interest, you could use:

```
read=bytearray(3)
SPI.readinto(read, write=0)
```

This reads three bytes into read while sending three null bytes to the slave. Alternatively you could use:

```
read=spi.read(3, write=0)
```

which returns a three-element byte array while sending null bytes to the slave.

Now we come to a subtle point. What is the difference between transferring multiple bytes and simply sending the bytes individually using multiple transfer calls? The answer is that each time you make a transfer call the chip select line should be activated, the data transferred and then deactivated. Using the buffer transfers, the chip select can be left active for the entire transfer, i.e. it isn't necessary to deactivate it between each byte. Sometimes this difference isn't important and you can transfer three bytes using three calls, or just one, to a transfer function. However, some slaves will abort the current multibyte operation if the chip select line is deactivated in the middle of a multibyte transfer. As the Pico requires you to activate and deactivate the chip select line manually, it is up to you to make the distinction between single and multibyte transfers.

It is important to realize that the nature of the transfer is that the first element is sent at the same time that the first element is received. That is, unlike other protocols, the whole of the send buffer isn't sent before the received data comes back. The entire transfer works a data element at a time – the first element is sent while the first element is being received, then the second element is sent at the same time as the second element is being received and so on. Not fully understanding this idea can lead to some interesting bugs.

A Loopback Example

Because of the way that data is transferred on the SPI bus, it is very easy to test that everything is working without having to add any components. All you have to do is connect MOSI to MISO so that anything sent is also received in a loopback mode.

First we have to select which pins to use and, as this is fairly arbitrary at this stage, we might as well use:

```
SPI0   MISO    GPIO 4      pin 6
       SCLK    GPIO 6      pin 9
       MOSI    GPIO 7      pin 10
```

We can ignore the CS line at the moment as it isn't used in a loopback.

First, connect pin 6 to pin 10 using a jumper wire and start a new project.

The program, loopback.py, is very simple. First we initialize the SPI bus to use SPI0 and pins GPIO 6, GPIO 7 and GPIO 4.

```
spi=SPI(0,sck=Pin(6),miso=Pin(4),mosi=Pin(7) )
```

Next we configure the interface:

```
spi.init(baudrate=500_000,bits=8, polarity=0,
                                  phase=0,firstbit=SPI.MSB )
```

We are using 8-bit data and SPI mode 0.

Check that the received data matches the sent data:

```
read=bytearray(3)
write=bytearray([0xAA,0xAA,0xAA])
spi.write_readinto(write,read)

print(read,write)
```

The hex value AA is useful in testing because it generates the bit sequence 10101010 which is easy to see on a logic analyzer. Finally we close the bus:

```
spi.deinit()
```

Putting all of this together gives us the complete `loopback.py` program:

```
from machine import Pin, SPI

spi=SPI(0,sck=Pin(6),miso=Pin(4),mosi=Pin(7))
spi.init(baudrate=500_000,bits=8, polarity=0,
                        phase=0,firstbit=SPI.MSB )

read=bytearray(3)
write=bytearray([0xAA,0xAA,0xAA])
spi.write_readinto(write,read)

print(read,write)
spi.deinit()
```

If you run the program and don't receive any data then the most likely reason is that you have connected the wrong two pins or not connected them at all.

If you connect a logic analyzer to the three GPIO lines involved – 4, 6 and 7, you will see the data transfer:

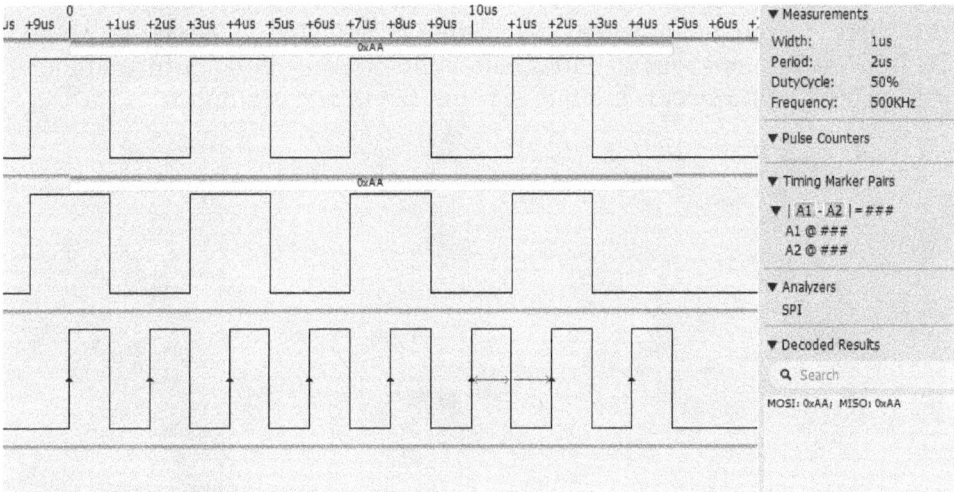

Using The CS Line

Of course there is no CS line activity on the logic analyzer because, unlike many SPI implementations, the Pico doesn't automatically control the CS line. It is up to you to initialize a CS line as a standard GPIO line and set it as appropriate during the data transfer.

For example, let's add GPIO 5:

```
SPI0    MSIO    GPIO 4      pin 6
        CSn     GPIO 5      pin 7
        SCLK    GPIO 6      pin 9
        MOSI    GPIO 7      pin 10
```

Notice that there is no real reason to use GPIO 5, any of the possible CSn pins would do.

Using CS active low we first have to initialize the GPIO line to output and set it high:

```
CS = Pin(5,Pin.OUT)
CS.high()
```

Now we can use the CS line to activate the slave by setting it low before starting the transfer and then setting it back high again afterwards:

```
CS.low()
spi.write_readinto(write,read)
CS.high()
```

If you try this out, remove comments from loopback.py, you might notice that there is a problem if you examine what is happening. The setting of the CS line low occurs about 20 - 40μs before the first data or clock bit and the setting back to low occurs around 8μs after the final clock pulse.

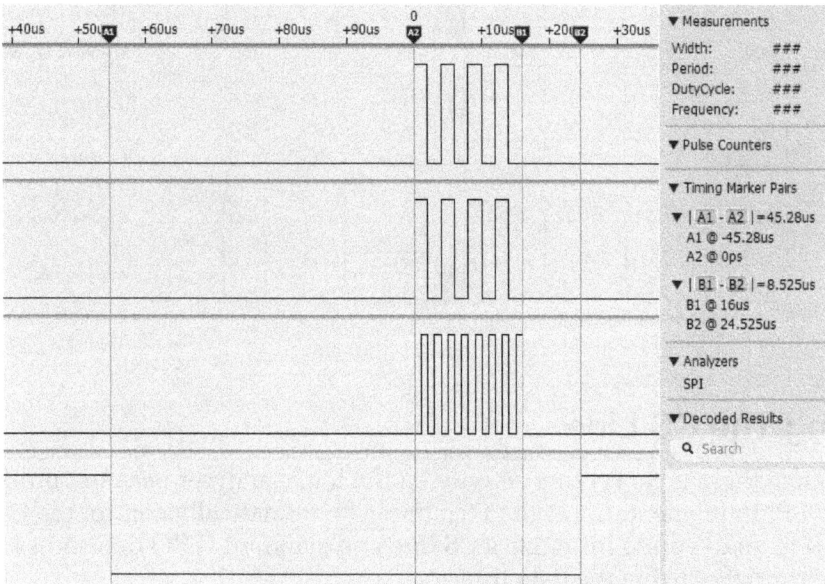

For many devices this over-long CS pulse doesn't make any difference, but it slows down how fast you can send data using the bus.

The BME280 Humidity, Pressure and Temperature Sensor

As an example of getting to grips with a real SPI device, we can write some code to get data from the commonly used BME280 sensor. You can also use the earlier BMP280, which is register-compatible but doesn't have a humidity sensor. Both work as an SPI and an I2C device and some of their operations as an SPI device are compromised relative to their performance as an I2C device. The BME280 is also the subject of a complete example in the Pico's SDK which implements a full interface, including the correction of raw data values. In this section we will simply implement a basic read of the raw data to show how it is done. If you want to use the device in a real application you will need the additional functions that you can find in the C SDK example they are not difficult to convert to MicroPython.

To make the SDK example easier to use we will connect the device using the same GPIO pins:

PICO	BME280
GPIO 16 (pin 21) MISO/spi0_rx	SDO/SDO
GPIO 17 (pin 22) Chip Select	CSB/!CS
GPIO 18 (pin 24) SCK/spi0_sclk	SCL/SCK
GPIO 19 (pin 25) MOSI/spi0_tx	SDA/SDI
3.3v (pin 36)	VCC
GND (pin 38)	GND

Notice that what the pins are called on a typical BME280 board varies, but you should be able to identify them.

Once you have the device connected what you need to know to send and receive data via the SPI bus varies according to the device and you have little choice but to find and read the datasheet. In this case the important table is the "memory map":

Register Name	Address	bit7	bit6	bit5	bit4	bit3	bit2	bit1	bit0	Reset state
hum_lsb	0xFE	hum_lsb<7:0>								0x00
hum_msb	0xFD	hum_msb<7:0>								0x80
temp_xlsb	0xFC	temp_xlsb<7:4>				0	0	0	0	0x00
temp_lsb	0xFB	temp_lsb<7:0>								0x00
temp_msb	0xFA	temp_msb<7:0>								0x80
press_xlsb	0xF9	press_xlsb<7:4>				0	0	0	0	0x00
press_lsb	0xF8	press_lsb<7:0>								0x00
press_msb	0xF7	press_msb<7:0>								0x80
config	0xF5	t_sb[2:0]			filter[2:0]				spi3w_en[0]	0x00
ctrl_meas	0xF4	osrs_t[2:0]			osrs_p[2:0]			mode[1:0]		0x00
status	0xF3					measuring[0]			im_update[0]	0x00
ctrl_hum	0xF2						osrs_h[2:0]			0x00
calib26..calib41	0xE1...0xF0	calibration data								individual
reset	0xE0	reset[7:0]								0x00
id	0xD0	chip_id[7:0]								0x60
calib00..calib25	0x88...0xA1	calibration data								individual

Registers:	Reserved registers	Calibration data	Control registers	Data registers	Status registers	Chip ID	Reset
Type:	do not change	read only	read / write	read only	read only	read only	write only

The important registers for our simple implementation are the first eight data registers, which give the raw values of humidity, temperature and pressure. These are all read-only registers and the way that these work on the SPI bus is that first you write the address of the register you want to read and then you read as many bytes as you need. The address is auto-incremented each time you read, so sending the first address followed by eight reads transfers the contents of all of the registers.

There is one other detail to note. The most significant bit of the address byte is used to indicate a read or write operation – it has to be set to one for a read. If it is zero then the bytes that you send following the address are stored in the registers – the data registers are read-only. Notice that all the registers already have bit 7 set in their usual addresses and there is no need to do anything extra for a read.

So a read operation is typically:

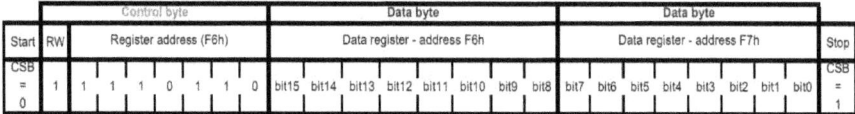

		Control byte	Data byte	Data byte	
Start	RW	Register address (F6h)	Data register - address F6h	Data register - address F7h	Stop
CSB = 0	1	1 1 1 0 1 1 0	bit15 bit14 bit13 bit12 bit11 bit10 bit9 bit8	bit7 bit6 bit5 bit4 bit3 bit2 bit1 bit0	CSB = 1

and a write operation is:

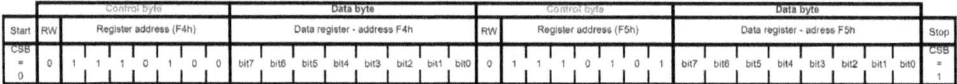

		Control byte	Data byte		Control byte	Data byte	
Start	RW	Register address (F4h)	Data register - address F4h	RW	Register address (F5h)	Data register - adress F5h	Stop
CSB = 0	0	1 1 1 0 1 0 0	bit7 bit6 bit5 bit4 bit3 bit2 bit1 bit0	0	1 1 1 0 1 0 1	bit7 bit6 bit5 bit4 bit3 bit2 bit1 bit0	CSB = 1

Notice that the operation is started by lowering the CS line and is stopped by raising the CS line. You can read or write as many values as you like and you can send another address to start the operation off at a different location.

If you look at the detailed specification of the SPI bus you will find that the CS line has to be low at least 20ns before the first clock pulse and has to remain low until at least 20ns after the final clock pulse. It also limits the clock to less than 10Mhz. It also uses mode zero by default.

This is enough information to start to create some functions that will read the BME280's raw data registers. First we need to set the SPI hardware and the GPIO lines correctly:

```
spi = SPI(0, sck=Pin(18), miso=Pin(16), mosi=Pin(19))
spi.init(baudrate=500_000, bits=8, polarity=0, phase=0,
                                    firstbit=SPI.MSB)
```

CS line has to be set high before we start:

```
CS = Pin(17, Pin.OUT)
CS.high()
sleep_ms(1)
```

As a proof that the SPI bus is working, the first thing to try is to read the ID register which is at address 0xD0 and which returns a single byte giving the id number which should be 0x60 for the BME280 and 0x58 for the BMP280.

```
write = bytearray([0xD0])
CS.low()
spi.write(write)
read = spi.read(1)
CS.high()

print("Chip ID is",hex(read[0]))
spi.deinit()
```

As long as this works we can move on to read the raw data. If it doesn't work then either you have connected the device incorrectly or the device is broken.

We first have to set up what measurements we want to make and exactly how. This is controlled by two registers - 0xF4 controls pressure and temperature and 0xF2 controls humidity. You can see how the different bits in these registers set the accuracy and rate of measurement in the datasheet, but for general use we can set both registers using:

```
CS.low()
write=bytearray([0xF2,0x01])
spi.write(write)
write=bytearray([0xF4,0x27])
spi.write(write)
CS.high()
```

This sets the humidity, temperature and pressure measurement to x1 over-sampling and normal mode sampling, which reads the sensors at a regular interval set by another register.

To read the raw data we can use the same technique of writing a register address, but this time we read eight items of data:

```
CS.low()
write=bytearray([0xF7])
spi.write(write)
sleep_ms(10)
rBuff = spi.read(8)
CS.high()
```

We can now put the bytes read from the device together to get the three readings:

```
pressure = (rBuff[0] << 12) |(rBuff[1] << 4) | (rBuff[2] >> 4)
temperature = (rBuff[3] << 12) | ( rBuff[4] << 4) | (rBuff[5] >> 4)
humidity = rBuff[6] << 8 | rBuff[7]
```

Putting all this together with some print statements to display the data gives the complete program, bme280.py:

```
from utime import sleep_ms
from machine import Pin, SPI
from time import sleep

spi = SPI(0, sck=Pin(18), miso=Pin(16), mosi=Pin(19))
spi.init(baudrate=500_000, bits=8, polarity=0, phase=0,
                                        firstbit=SPI.MSB)

CS = Pin(17, Pin.OUT)
CS.high()
sleep_ms(1)

write = bytearray([0xD0])
CS.low()
spi.write(write)
read = spi.read(1)
CS.high()
print("Chip ID is",hex(read[0]))

CS.low()
write=bytearray([0xF2,0x01])
spi.write(write)
write=bytearray([0xF4,0x27])
spi.write(write)
CS.high()

CS.low()
write=bytearray([0xF7])
spi.write(write)
sleep_ms(10)
rBuff = spi.read(8)
CS.high()

pressure = (rBuff[0] << 12) |(rBuff[1] << 4) | (rBuff[2] >> 4)
temperature = (rBuff[3] << 12) | ( rBuff[4] << 4) | (rBuff[5] >> 4)
humidity = rBuff[6] << 8 | rBuff[7]

print("Humidity = ", humidity)
print("Pressure = ", pressure)
print("Temp. = ", temperature)
```

If you try this out you will be disappointed to discover that the raw values aren't easy to interpret as real values. They are readings from the internal A-to-D converter and they have to be converted using the compensation formulas before they can be used.

Of course, it makes sense to factor out into functions the repetitive parts of the code to make it easier to extend the program. In particular, a read_registers function is sensible:

```
def read_registers(spi, CS, reg,n):
    CS.low()
    spi.write(bytearray([reg]))
    buf=spi.read(n)
    CS.high()
    return buf
```

If you want to make use of the BME280 for accurate measurements then it is essential that you read the compensation data and use it to compute corrected values. This isn't difficult, but the calculations are complicated and you can find them fully implemented in the example included in the C SDK examples. Now that you know the general logic of working with the device, the rest should be easier to understand as it is just a matter of implementing calculations.

Problems

The SPI bus is often a real headache because of the lack of a definitive standard, but in most cases you can make it work. The first problem is in discovering the characteristics of the slave device you want to work with. In general, this is solved by a careful reading of the datasheet or perhaps some trial and error, see the next chapter for an example.

If you are working with a single slave then generally things work once you have the SPI bus configuration set correctly. Things are more difficult when there are multiple devices on the same bus. The Pico has enough CS lines to handle eight devices, more if you only want to use a single SPI interface. Typically you will find SPI devices that don't switch off properly when they are not being addressed. In principle, all SPI devices should present high impedance outputs (i.e. tri-state buffers) when not being addressed, but some don't. If you encounter a problem you need to check that the selected slave is able to control the MISO line properly.

Summary

- The SPI bus is often problematic because there is no SPI standard.

- Unlike other serial buses, it makes use of unidirectional connections.

- The data lines are MOSI (master output slave input) and MISO (master input slave output).

- In addition, there is a clock line, output from master, and a number of select lines that you have to drive under program control.

- Timing for the select lines is a problem as you have to include a delay that makes sure that it remains low until the end of the final clock pulse.

- Data is transferred from the master to the slave and from the slave to the master on each clock pulse, arranged as a circular buffer.

- The Pico has two SPI devices which can work with almost any of the GPIO lines.

- MicroPython also provides a software SPI implementation which can be used to convert any GPIO lines into an SPI bus. It isn't as efficient as the hardware implementation.

- The MicroPython provides all the functions you need to set up the SPI bus and transfer data one byte or multiple bytes at a time.

- You can test the SPI bus using a simple loopback connection.

- Working with a single slave is usually fairly easy, working with multiple slaves can be more of a problem.

- The BME280 is included as a complete example as part of the C SDK, but serves as a good example of how the SPI bus works.

Chapter 11

A-To-D And The SPI Bus

The SPI bus can be difficult to make work at first, but once you know what to look for about how the slave claims to work it gets easier. To demonstrate how it is done, let's add eight channels of 12-bit A-to-D using the MCP3008.

The Pico has a single A-to-D Converter (ADC) with analog inputs, four of which can be used via external pins. The RP2350B has more ADC inputs but the Pico 2 is identical to the Pico as it uses the RP2350. Before moving on to look at the use of SPI to add more A-to-D converters, let's take a look at those the Pico already has. If you are only interested in the detail of using the SPI bus, skip to that section.

Pico ADC

The Pico has a single onboard ADC which has four multiplexed inputs. Three are available on the external pins and one is used for an internal temperature sensor.

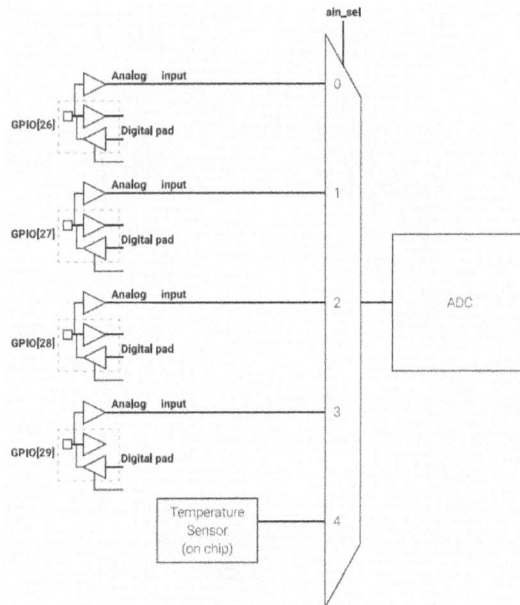

You can see from the diagram that pins GPIO 26, GPIO 27, GPIO 28 and GPIO 29 can be used as analog inputs. The ADC is a successive approximation converter. You don't need to know how it works to use it, but it isn't difficult to understand. The input voltage is compared to a standard voltage, V_{REF}. The idea is that first a voltage equal to $V_{REF}/2$ is generated and the input voltage is compared to this. If it is lower then the most significant bit is a 0 and if it is equal or greater then it is a 1. At the next step the voltage generated is $V_{REF}/2+V_{REF}/4$ and the comparison is repeated to generate the next bit. Successive approximation converters are easy to build, but they are slow. The ADC needs 96 clock cycles to create a 12-bit result, which gives a maximum sampling rate of 500kS/s with a default clock of 48MHz.

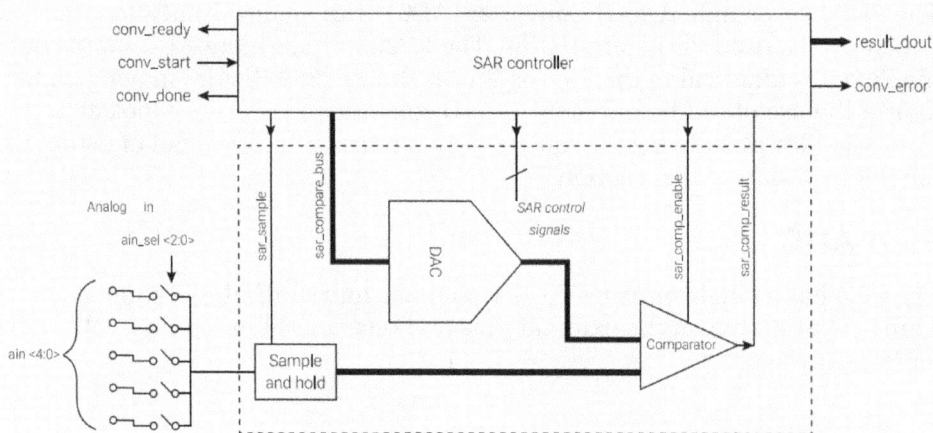

conv_ready
conv_start
conv_done

SAR controller

result_dout
conv_error

Analog in
ain_sel <2:0>

sar_sample
sar_compare_bus
SAR control signals
sar_comp_enable
sar_comp_result

DAC

Comparator

ain <4:0>

Sample and hold

The Pico's ADC is very useful, but it isn't as accurate as you might hope. Although it has 12 bits, the claimed effective accuracy is only 9 bits and most of this loss of precision is due to the way the reference voltage is supplied and to noise due to its integration with other digital devices. According to the documentation, you can improve the accuracy by modifying the reference voltage:

For much improved ADC performance, an external 3.0V shunt reference, such as LM4040, can be connected from the ADC_V_{REF} pin to ground. Note that if doing this the ADC range is limited to 0-3.0V signals (rather than 0-3.3V), and the shunt reference will draw continuous current through the 200R filter resistor (3.3V-3.0V)/200 = ~1.5mA.

The ADC can be set to do conversions continuously, reading each of the possible inputs in a round-robin fashion, storing the results in an 8-deep FIFO (the documentation says 4-deep) buffer. Alternatively, you can simply start a conversion on a given input when you need the data – this is the only mode that MicroPython supports.

The simplest way of using the ADC is to perform a single read of a single input under software control. Before making use of it, you have to create an ADC object associated with the channel:

```
adc = machine.ADC(channel)
```

Once you have selected the input you are going to read, you can start a conversion and get the result using:

```
ADC.read_u16()
```

The result is in the range 0-65535 and this has to be scaled to give a physically meaningful reading.

The simplest A-to-D program you can write is temp.py:

```
import machine
import utime
sensor_temp = machine.ADC(4)
conversion_factor = 3.3 / (65535)

while True:
    reading = sensor_temp.read_u16() * conversion_factor
    temperature = 27 - (reading - 0.706)/0.001721
    print(temperature)
    utime.sleep(2)
```

This reads the temperature sensor which has a temperature voltage relationship given by:

T = 27 – (V - 0.796)/0.001721

You can create individual ADC objects for each channel and read them in nay order.

If you want to use any of the more advanced features of the Pico's ADC you will need either to create the functions that directly access the hardware or move to C.

The MCP3008 SPI ADC

An alternative to using the Pico's built-in ADC with its noise and stability problems is to use an external chip. The MCP3000 family is a low-cost versatile SPI-based set of A-to-D converters. Although the MCP3008, with eight analog inputs at 10-bit precision, and the MCP3004, with four analog inputs at 10-bit precision, are the best known, there are other devices in the family, including ones with 12-bit and 13-bit precision and differential inputs, at around the same sort of cost - $1 to $2.

In this chapter the MCP3008 is used because it is readily available and provides a good performance at low cost, but the other devices in the family work in the same way and could be easily substituted.

The MCP3008 is available in a number of different packages but the standard 16-pin PDIP is the easiest to work with using a prototyping board. You can buy it from the usual sources including Amazon, see Resources on this book's webpage. Its pinouts are fairly self-explanatory:

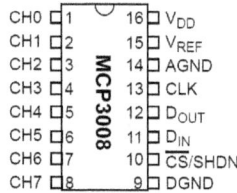

```
CH0  1        16  V_DD
CH1  2        15  V_REF
CH2  3   M    14  AGND
CH3  4   C    13  CLK
CH4  5   P    12  D_OUT
CH5  6   3    11  D_IN
CH6  7   0    10  CS/SHDN
CH7  8   0     9  DGND
         8
```

You can see that the analog inputs are on the left and the power and SPI bus connections are on the right. The conversion accuracy is claimed as 10 bits, but how many of these bits correspond to reality and how many are noise depends on how you design the layout of the circuit.

You need to take great care if you need high accuracy. For example, you will notice that there are two voltage inputs, VDD and VREF. VDD is the supply voltage that runs the chip and VREF is the reference voltage that is used to compare the input voltage. Obviously, if you want highest accuracy, VREF, which has to be lower than or equal to VDD, should be set by an accurate low-noise voltage source. However, in most applications VREF and VDD are simply connected together and the usual, low- quality, supply voltage is used as the reference. If this isn't good enough then you can use anything from a Zener diode to a precision voltage reference chip such as the TL431. At the very least, however, you should add a $1\mu F$ capacitor to ground connected to the VDD pin and the VREF pin.

The MC3000 family is based on the same type of ADC as the Pico's built-in device, a successive approximation converter.

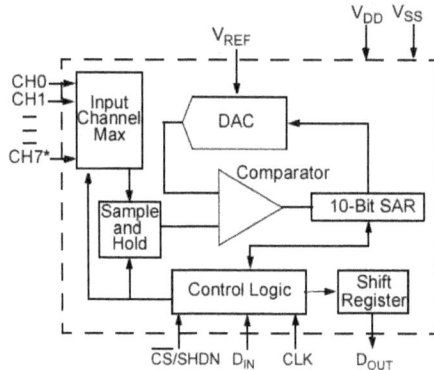

You can see that successive approximation fits in well with a serial bus as each bit can be obtained in the time needed to transmit the previous bit. However, the conversion is relatively slow and a sample-and-hold circuit has to be used to keep the input to the converter stage fixed. The sample-and-hold takes the form of a 20pF capacitor and a switch. The only reason you need to know about this is that the conversion has to be completed in a time that is short compared to the discharge time of the capacitor. So, for accuracy, there is a minimum SPI clock rate as well as a maximum.

Also, to charge the capacitor quickly enough for it to follow a changing voltage, it needs to be connected to a low-impedance source. In most cases this isn't a problem, but if it is you need to include an op amp. If you are using an op amp buffer then you might as well implement an anti-aliasing filter to remove frequencies from the signal that are too fast for the ADC to respond to. How all this works takes us into the realm of analog electronics and signal processing and well beyond the core subject matter of this book.

You can also use the A-to-D channels in pairs, i.e. in differential mode, to measure the voltage difference between them. For example, in differential mode you measure the difference between CH0 and CH1, i.e. what you measure is CH1-CH0. In most cases, you want to use all eight channels in single-ended mode. In principle, you can take 200k samples per second, but only at the upper limit of the supply voltage, i.e. VDD=5V, falling to 75k samples per second at its lower limit of VDD=2.7V.

The SPI clock limits are a maximum of 3.6MHz at 5V and 1.35MHz at 2.7V. The clock can go slower, but because of the problem with the sample-and-hold mentioned earlier, it shouldn't go below 10kHz. How fast we can take samples is discussed later in this chapter.

Connecting To The Pico

The connection from the MCP3008 to the Pico's SPI bus is very simple and can be seen in the diagram below.

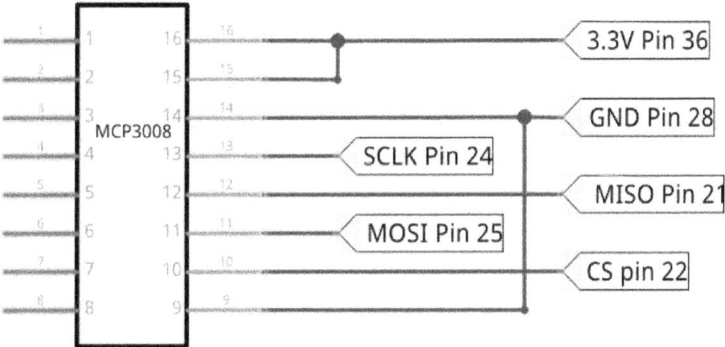

Pico	MCP3008
GPIO 16 (Pin 21) MISO	Pin 12
GPIO 17 (Pin 22) Chip Select	Pin 10
GPIO 18 (Pin 24) SCLK	Pin 13
GPIO 19 (Pin 25) MOSI	Pin 11
3.3v (Pin 36)	Pin 15 and Pin 16
GND (Pin 38)	Pin 14 and Pin 9

The only additional component that is recommended is a $1\mu F$ capacitor connected between pins 15 and 16 to ground, which is mounted as close to the chip as possible. As discussed in the previous section, you might want a separate voltage reference for pin 15 rather than just using the 3.3V supply.

Basic Configuration

Now we come to the configuration of the SPI bus. We have some rough figures for the SPI clock speed - around 10kHz to a little more than 1.35MHz. So a clock frequency of 500kHz seems a reasonable starting point.

From the datasheet, the chip select has to be active low and, by default, data is sent most significant bit first for both the master and the slave. The only puzzle is what mode to use? This is listed in the datasheet as mode 0 0 with clock active high or mode 1 1 with clock active low. For simplicity we will use mode 0 0.

We now have enough information to initialize the slave:

```
spi = SPI(0, sck=Pin(18), miso=Pin(16), mosi=Pin(19))
spi.init(baudrate=500_000, bits=8, polarity=0, phase=0,
firstbit=SPI.MSB)

CS = Pin(17, Pin.OUT)
CS.high()
sleep_ms(1)
```

The Protocol

Now we have the SPI initialized and ready to transfer data, but what data do we transfer? As already discussed in the previous chapter, the SPI bus doesn't have any standard commands or addressing structure. Each device responds to data sent in different ways and sends data back in different ways. You simply have to read the datasheet to find out what the commands and responses are.

Reading the datasheet might be initially confusing because it says that you have to send five bits to the slave - a start bit, a bit that selects its operating mode single or differential, and a 3-bit channel number. The operating mode is 1 for single-ended and 0 for differential.

So to read Channel 3, i.e. 011, in single-ended mode you would send the slave:

    11011xxx

where an x can take either value. In response, the slave holds its output in a high impedance state until the sixth clock pulse, then sends a zero bit on the seventh, followed by bit 9 of the data on the eighth clock pulse.

That is, the slave sends back:

    xxxxxx0b9

where x means indeterminate.

The remaining nine bits are sent back in response to the next nine clock pulses. This means you have to transfer three bytes to get all ten bits of data. This all makes reading the data in 8-bit chunks confusing.

The datasheet suggests a different way of doing the job that delivers the data more neatly packed into three bytes. What it suggests to send a single byte is:

    00000001

At the same time, the slave transfers random data, which is ignored. The final 1 is treated as the start bit. If you now transfer a second byte with the most significant bit indicating single or differential mode, then a 3-bit channel address and the remaining bits set to 0, the slave will respond with the null and the top two bits of the conversion. Now all you have to do to get the final eight bits of data is to read a third byte:

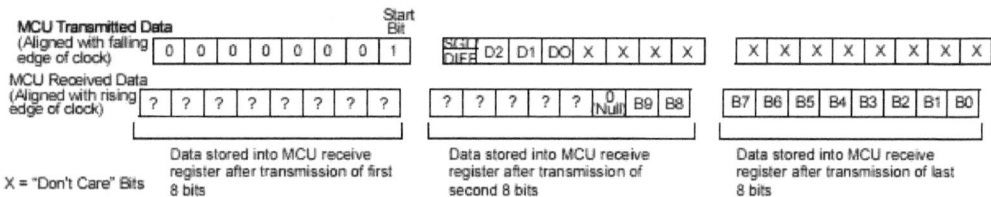

MCU Transmitted Data (Aligned with falling edge of clock) — Start Bit on final bit of first byte:

0	0	0	0	0	0	0	1		SGL/DIFF	D2	D1	D0	X	X	X	X		X	X	X	X	X	X	X	X

MCU Received Data (Aligned with rising edge of clock):

?	?	?	?	?	?	?	?		?	?	?	?	?	0 (Null)	B9	B8		B7	B6	B5	B4	B3	B2	B1	B0

X = "Don't Care" Bits

Data stored into MCU receive register after transmission of first 8 bits | Data stored into MCU receive register after transmission of second 8 bits | Data stored into MCU receive register after transmission of last 8 bits

This way you get two neat bytes containing the data with all the low-order bits in their correct positions.

Using this information we can now write some instructions that read a given channel. For example, to read Channel 0 we first send a byte set to 0x01 as the start bit and ignore the byte the slave transfers. Next we send 0x80 to select single-ended and Channel 0 and keep the byte the slave sends back as the two high-order bits. Finally, we send a zero byte (0x00) so that we get the low-order bits from the slave:

```
CS.low()
write=bytearray([0x01, 0x80, 0x00])
read=bytearray(3)
spi.write_readinto(write,read)
CS.high()
```

Notice you cannot send the three bytes one at a time using transfer because that results in the CS line being deactivated between the transfer of each byte.

To get the data out of rBuff we need to do some bit manipulation:

```
data =  (read[1] & 0x03) << 8 |  read[2]
```

The first part of the expression extracts the low three bits from the first byte the slave sent and, as these are the most significant bits, they are shifted up eight places. The rest of the bits are then ORed with them to give the full 10-bit result. To convert to volts we use:

```
volts =  data * 3.3 / 1023.0
```

assuming that VREF is 3.3V.

In a real application you would also need to convert the voltage to some other quantity, like temperature or light level.

If you connect a logic analyzer to the SPI bus you will see something like:

You can see the commands and the response, in this case a reading of 0.693V.

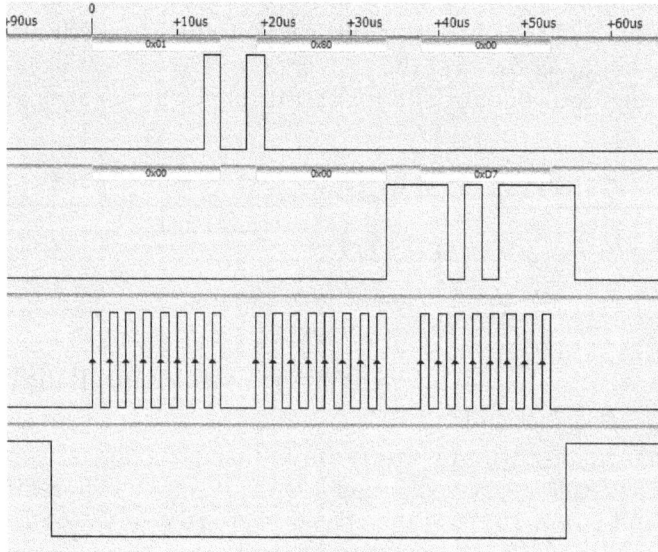

The complete program, adc1.py, is:

```
from utime import sleep_ms
from machine import Pin, SPI
from time import sleep

spi = SPI(0, sck=Pin(18), miso=Pin(16), mosi=Pin(19))
spi.init(baudrate=500_000, bits=8, polarity=0, phase=0,
firstbit=SPI.MSB)
CS = Pin(17, Pin.OUT)
CS.high()
sleep_ms(1)
CS.low()
write=bytearray([0x01, 0x80, 0x00])
read=bytearray(3)
spi.write_readinto(write,read)
CS.high()
data =  (read[1] & 0x03) << 8 |  read[2]
volts =  data * 3.3 / 1023.0
print(volts)
spi.deinit()
```

SPI ADC Class

This all works, but it would be good to have a class with a method that read
the ADC on a specified channel, adc2.py:

```
class spiADC:
    def __init__(self,spi,sckNo,misoNo,mosiNo,CSNo):
        self.spi = SPI(spi, sck=Pin(sckNo),
                            miso=Pin(misoNo), mosi=Pin(mosiNo))
        self.spi.init(baudrate=500_000, bits=8,
                            polarity=0, phase=0, firstbit=SPI.MSB)
        self.CS = Pin(CSNo, Pin.OUT)
        self.CS.high()
        sleep_ms(1)

    def read(self,chan):
        write=bytearray([0x01, (0x08 | chan) << 4 , 0x00])
        self.CS.low()
        read=bytearray(3)
        self.spi.write_readinto(write,read)
        self.CS.high()
        data =  (read[1] & 0x03) << 8 |  read[2]
        volts =  data * 3.3 / 1023.0
        return volts
```

With this class the revised main program, adc2.py, is very simple:

```
adc = spiADC(0,18,16,19,17)
volts = adc.read(1)
print(volts)
```

179

How Fast?

Once you have the basic facilities working, the next question is always how fast does something work. In this case we need to know what sort of data rates we can achieve using this ADC. The simplest way of finding this out is to use the fastest read loop for a channel:

```
adc = spiADC(0,18,16,19,17)
while True:
    volts = adc.read(1)
```

With the SPI clock set to 500kHz, the sampling rate is measured to be 4.5kHz on a Pico1 and 6.4kHz on a Pico2, which compares to the approximately 17kHz achievable with a basic C program.

Increasing the clock rate to 1MHz pushes the sampling rate to 6kHz. Also notice that as the clock rate goes up, you have to ensure that the voltage source is increasingly low-impedance to allow the sample-and-hold to charge in a short time.

Summary

- The Pico has a single ADC with four inputs. It is subject to a lot of noise from the power supply and the circuits around it which reduces its accuracy.

- You can read individual input lines using the ADC class.

- The ADC class doesn't support many of the more advanced features of the Pico's ADC hardware.

- Making SPI work with any particular device has four steps:

    1. Discover how to connect the device to the SPI pins. This is a matter of identifying pinouts and mostly what chip selects are supported.

    2. Find out how to configure the Pi's SPI bus to work with the device. This is mostly a matter of clock speed and mode.

    3. Identify the commands that you need to send to the device to get it to do something and what data it sends back as a response.

    4. Find, or work out, the relationship between the raw reading, the voltage and the quantity the voltage represents.

- The MCP3000 range of A-to-D converters is very easy to use via SPI.

- You can read data at rates as fast as 6kHz.

Chapter 12

Using The I2C Bus

The I2C, standing for I-Squared-C or Inter IC, bus is one of the most useful ways of connecting moderately sophisticated sensors and peripherals to any processor. The only problem is that it can seem like a nightmarish confusion of hardware, low-level interaction and high-level software. There are few general introductions to the subject because at first sight every I2C device is different, but there are shared principles that can help you work out how to connect and talk to a new device.

The I2C bus is a serial bus that can be used to connect multiple devices to a controller. It is a simple bus that uses two active wires: one for data and one for a clock. Despite there being lots of problems in using the I2C bus, because it isn't well standardized and devices can conflict and generally do things in their own way, it is still commonly used and too useful to ignore.

The big problem in getting started with the I2C bus is that you will find it described at many different levels of detail, from the physical bus characteristics and protocol to the details of individual devices. It can be difficult to relate all of this together and produce a working project. In fact, you only need to know the general workings of the I2C bus, some general features of the protocol, and know the addresses and commands used by any particular device.

To explain and illustrate these ideas we really do have to work with a particular device to make things concrete. However, the basic stages of getting things to work, the steps, the testing and verification, are more or less the same irrespective of the device.

I2C Hardware Basics

The I2C bus is very simple from the hardware point of view. It has just two signal lines, SDA and SCL, the data and clock lines respectively. Each of these lines is pulled up by a suitable resistor to the supply line at whatever voltage the devices are working - 3.3V and 5V are common choices. The size of the pull-up resistors isn't critical, but 4.7K is typical as shown in the circuit diagram.

You simply connect the SDA and SCL pins of each of the devices to the pull-up resistors. Of course, if any of the devices have built-in pull-up resistors you can omit the external resistors. More of a problem is if multiple devices each have pull-ups. In this case you need to disable all but one.

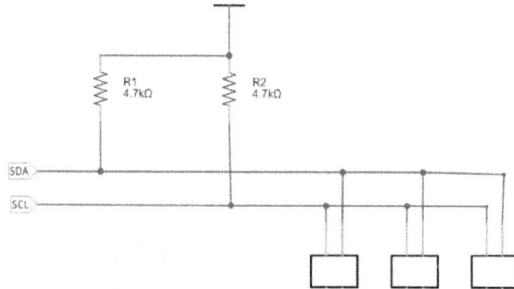

The I2C bus is an open collector bus. This means that it is actively pulled down by a transistor set to on. When the transistor is off, however, the bus returns to the high voltage state via the pull-up resistor. The advantage of this approach is that multiple devices can pull the bus low at the same time. That is, an open collector bus is low when one or more devices pull it low and high when none of the devices is active.

The SCL line provides a clock which is used to set the speed of data transfer, one data bit is presented on the SDA line for each pulse on the SCL line. In all cases, the master drives the clock line to control how fast bits are transferred. The slave can, however, hold the clock line low if it needs to slow down the data transfer. In most cases the I2C bus has a single master device, the Pico in our case, which drives the clock and invites the slaves to receive or transmit data. Multiple masters are possible, but this is advanced and usually not necessary.

All you really need to know is that all communication usually occurs in 8-bit packets. The master sends a packet, an address frame, which contains the address of the slave it wants to interact with. Every slave has to have a unique address, which is usually 7 bits, but it can be 10 bits, and the Pico does support this. In the rest of this chapter we will use 7-bit addressing because it is commonly supported.

One of the problems in using the I2C bus is that manufacturers often use the same address, or same set of selectable addresses, and this can make using particular combinations of devices on the same bus difficult or impossible.

The 7-bit address is set as the high-order 7 bits in the byte and this can be confusing as an address that is stated as 0x40 in the datasheet results in 0x80 being sent to the device. The low-order bit of the address signals a write or a read operation depending on whether it is a 0 or a 1 respectively. After sending an address frame it then sends or receives data frames back from the slave. There are also special signals used to mark the start and end of an exchange of packets, but the library functions take care of these.

This is really all you need to know about I2C in general to get started, but it is worth finding out more of the details as you need them. You almost certainly will need them as you debug I2C programs.

The clock SCL and data SDA lines rest high. The master signals a Start bit by pulling the SDA line down – S in the diagram below. The clock is then pulled low by the master, during which time the SDA line can change state. The bit is read in the middle of the following high period of the clock pulse B1, B2 and so on in the diagram. This continues until the last bit has been sent when the data line is allowed to rise while the clock is high, so sending a stoP bit – P in the diagram. Notice that when data is being transmitted the data line doesn't change while the clock is high. Any change in the data line when the clock is high sends a start or a stop bit, i.e. clock high and falling data line is a start bit and clock high and rising data line is a stop bit:

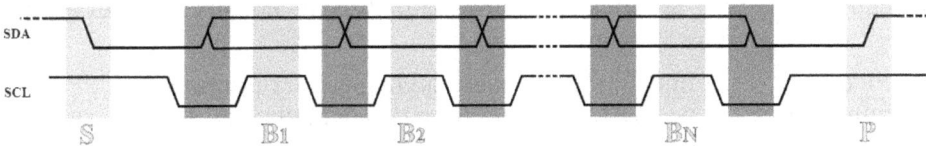

The clock speed was originally set at 100kHz, standard mode, but then increased to 400kHz in fast mode. In practice, devices usually specify a maximum clock speed that they will work with.

The Pico I2C

The Pico has two I2C controllers, I2C0 and I2C1, that can work as a master or a slave. The connections from both controllers can be routed to different pins:

I2C0	SDA	GPIO 0	GPIO 4	GPIO 8	GPIO 12	GPIO 16	GPIO 20		GPIO 28
	SCL	GPIO 1	GPIO 5	GPIO 9	GPIO 13	GPIO 17	GPIO 21		

I2C1	SDA	GPIO 2	GPIO 6	GPIO 10	GPIO 14	GPIO 18	GPIO 22	GPIO 26
	SCL	GPIO 3	GPIO 7	GPIO 11	GPIO 15	GPIO 19		GPIO 27

To use one of the controllers you have to select a pair of GPIO lines to act as SDA and SCL when you create an I2C object.

The `machine.I2C` object provides access to the hardware-implemented I2C bus, but there is also a software implementation in the form of `machine.SoftI2C` which has the advantage of working with any GPIO pins. The disadvantage is that it places a load on the CPU and so is less efficient. You should always use `machine.I2C` unless you need more than two I2C controllers. In the rest of this chapter `machine.I2C` is used, but the software implementation can be used with hardly any changes.

The I2C Functions

There are I2C functions for initialization, configuration and for writing and reading to the registers. Let's look at each group in turn.

Initialization

The constructor lets you set up a I2C object ready to use:

```
machine.I2C(id, scl=Pin, sda=Pin, freq=400000)
```

The `id` gives the I2C controller to use and the `scl` and `sda` parameters specify the `Pin` object to use for the I2C lines.

You can use the `init` method to set things up after the constructor, but at the time of writing it doesn't seem to work.

The Pico doesn't support the most recent high speed modes and the maximum clock rate is 1MHz. MicroPython doesn't support I2C in slave mode, although the Pico does.

There is also a `scan` method that will return a list of addresses that correspond to active I2C devices on the bus. Not all I2C devices respond well to `scan` and the method's use is best avoided if possible.

To stop using I2C hardware use the `deinit` method.

Write

There are a two similar write methods. The most basic is:

```
I2C.writeto(addr, buf, stop=True)
```

The first parameter is the address of the device and `buf` is a byte array containing the data you want to send.

The final parameter, `stop`, needs some explanation. When you use this method it first sends an address frame, a byte containing the address of the device you specified. Notice that the 7-bit address has to be shifted into the topmost bits and the first bit has to be zeroed for a write operation. So when you write to a device with an address of 0x40, you will see 0x80 on a logic analyzer, i.e. 0x40<<1. After the address frame as many data frames are sent as specified in `src` and `len`.

The final parameters control how the stop bit is sent or not. The usual write transaction is:

```
START|ADDR|ACK|DATA0|ACK|
              DATA1|ACK|
                 . . . .
              DATAn|ACK|STOP
```

Notice that it is the slave that sends the ACK bit and, if the data is not received correctly, it can send NAK instead. Also notice that there is a single STOP bit at the end of the transaction and this is what you get if you set stop to True. If you set stop to False then the final stop bit isn't sent and the next data transfer can continue as part of the same transaction.

Notice that multibyte transfer is quite different from sending single bytes one at a time:

```
START|  ADDR  |ACK|DATA0|ACK|STOP
START|  ADDR  |ACK|DATA1|ACK|STOP
       . . .
START|  ADDR  |ACK|DATAn|ACK|STOP
```

Notice that there are now multiple ADDR frames sent as well as multiple START and STOP bits. What this means in practice is that you have to look at a device's datasheet and send however many bytes it needs as a single operation. You cannot rely on being able to send the same number of bytes broken into chunks.

The other write function works in the same way, but with a slight variation.

```
I2C.writevto(addr, vector, stop=True)
```

This writes vector, which can be a List or a tuple of objects which support the Buffer Protocol. You can create custom objects for this or you can use bytes or a bytearray.

Writing To A Register

A very standard interaction between master and slave is writing data to a register. This isn't anything special and, as far as the I2C bus is concerned, you are simply writing raw data. However, datasheets and users tend to think in terms of reading and writing internal storage locations, i.e. registers in the device. In fact, many devices have lots of internal storage, indeed some I2C devices, for example I2C EPROMS, are nothing but internal storage.

In this case a standard transaction to write to a register is:

1. Send address frame
2. Send a data frame with the command to select the register
3. Send a data frame containing the byte, or word, to be written to the register

So, for example, you might use:

```
buf=bytearray([registerAddress,data])
i2c.writeto(addr,buf,stop= True)
```

Notice the command that has to be sent depends on the device and you have to look it up in its datasheet. Also notice that there is a single START and STOP bit at the beginning and end of the transaction.

To make working with memory devices easier, MicroPython provides some special methods:

```
I2C.writeto_mem(addr, memaddr, buf,  addrsize=8)
```

This writes to a device at addr and then access its memory location at memaddr writing the contents of buf. You don't need these methods as you can do the same job using more basic methods.

Read

The read functions are similar to the write functions. The most important is:

```
I2C.readfrom_into(addr, buf, stop=True)
```

and the parameters mean the same things as for the corresponding write function. This sends an address frame and then reads as many bytes from the slave as specified by the size of the buf bytearray. As in the case of write, the address supplied is shifted up one bit and the lower-order bit set to 1 to indicate a read operation. So, if the current slave is at address 0x40, the read sends a read address of 0x81 – this is important to remember if you are viewing the transaction on a logic analyzer.

A simple alternative read method is:

```
buf=I2C.readfrom(addr, nbytes, stop=True)
```

which reads nbytes into a byte array.

The read transaction is:

```
START|ADDR|ACK|DATA0|ACK|
          |DATA1|ACK|
          |DATA2|ACK|
     ...
          |DATAn|NAK|STOP
```

The master sends the address frame and the slave sends the ACK after the address to acknowledge that it has been received and it is ready to send data. Then, the slave sends bytes, one at a time, and the master sends ACK in response to each byte. Finally, the master sends a NAK to indicate that the last byte has been read and then a STOP bit. That is, the master controls how many bytes are transferred.

As in the case of the write functions, a block transfer of n bytes is different from transferring n bytes one at a time and you can suppress the final stop bit by setting nostop to true.

Reading A Register

As for writing to a register, reading from a register is a very standard operation, but it is slightly more complicated in that you need both a write and a read operation. That is, to read a register you need a write operation to send the address of the register to the device and then a read operation to get the data that the device sends as the contents of the register.

So, for example, you would use something like:

```
buf=bytearray([registerAddress])
i2c.writeto(addr,buf,stop= True)
buf=i2c.readfrom(addr,1,stop=True)
```

If the register sends multiple bytes then you can usually read these one after another as a block transfer without sending an address frame each time. Notice that we don't suppress the stop bit between the read and the write to make it a single transaction.

In theory, and mostly in practice, a register read of this sort can work with a stop-start separating the write and the read operation, which is what you get if you use separate write and read function calls without suppressing the stop bit. That is, the transfer sequence is:

```
START|ADDR|ACK|REGADDR|ACK|STOP|
START|ADDR|ACK|DATA1|ACK|
                |DATA2|ACK|
                   ...
             |DATAn|NAK|STOP
```

If you look at the end of the write and the start of the read using a logic analyzer, you will see that there is a STOP and START bit between them.

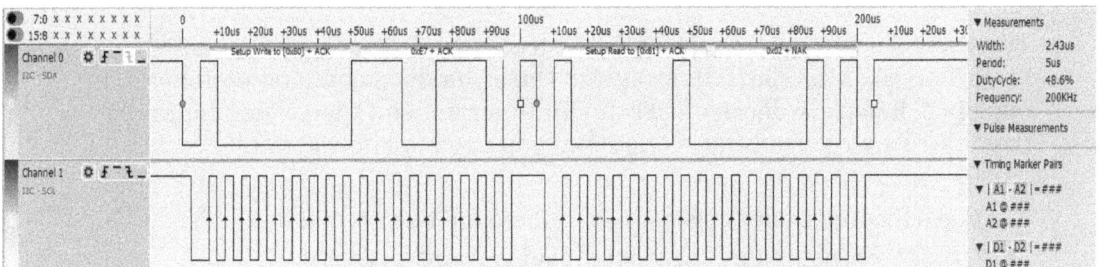

For some devices this is a problem. A STOP bit is a signal that another transaction can start and this might allow another master to take over the bus. To avoid this some devices demand a repeated START bit between the write and the read and no STOP bit. This is referred to as a "repeated start bit" or a "restart" transaction.

189

The sequence for a repeated start bit register read is:

```
START|ADDR|ACK|REGADDR|ACK|
START|ADDR|ACK|DATA0|ACK|
              |DATA1|ACK|

        . . .

              |DATAn|NAK|STOP
```

Notice that there is only one STOP bit.

In theory, either form of transaction should work, but in practice you will find that some slave devices state that they need a repeated start bit and no stop bits in continued transactions. In this case you need to be careful how you send and receive data. For example, to read a register from a device that requires repeated START bits but no STOP bit you would use:

```
buf=bytearray([registerAddress])
i2c.writeto(addr,buf,stop= False)
buf=i2c.readfrom(addr,1,stop=True)
```

You can see in the logic analyzer display that there is now just a single START bit between the write and the read.

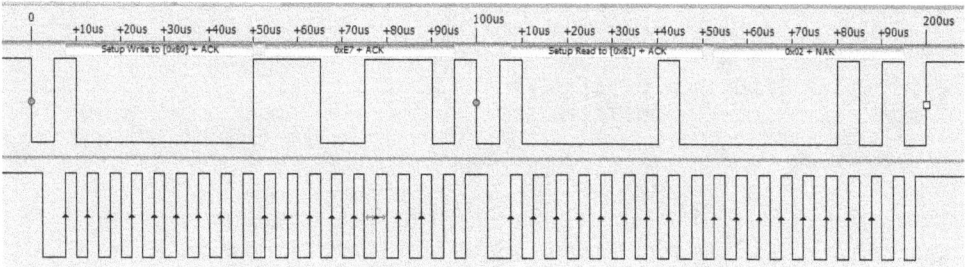

Very few devices need a repeated start transaction. The documentation mentions the MLX90620 IR array, but this is hardly a common peripheral. In practice, it usually doesn't make any difference if you send a stop bit in the middle of a write/read transaction, but you need to know about it just in case.

To make reading from a register easier there are two special methods:

```
I2C.readfrom_mem(addr, memaddr, nbytes, addrsize=8)
I2C.readfrom_mem_into(addr, memaddr, buf,  addrsize=8)
```

Both first write the memaddr to the device at addr and then perform a read of that device. They are equivalent to the write/reads given earlier.

Slow Read Protocols

The I2C clock is mostly controlled by the master and this raises the question of how we cope with the speed that a slave can or cannot respond to a request for data.

There are two broad approaches to waiting for data on the I2C bus. The first is simply to request the data and then perform reads in a polling loop. If the device isn't ready with the data, then it sends a data frame with a NAK bit set. In this case the read function throws an exception rather than return the number of bytes read. So all we have to do is test for an error response with a Try. Of course, the polling loop doesn't have to be "tight". The response time is often long enough to do other things and you can use the I2C bus to work with other slave devices while the one you activated gets on with trying to get the data you requested. All you have to do is to remember to read its data at some later time.

The second way is to allow the slave to hold the clock line low after the master has released it – so called "clock stretching". In most cases the master will simply wait before moving on to the next frame while the clock line is held low. This is very simple and it means you don't have to implement a polling loop, but also notice that your program is frozen until the slave releases the clock line.

Many devices implement both types of slow read protocol and you can use whichever suits your application.

A Real Device

Using an I2C device has two problems - the physical connection between master and slave and figuring out what the software has to do to make it work. Here we'll work with the HTU21D/Si7021 and the information in its datasheet to make a working temperature humidity sensor using the I2C functions we've just met.

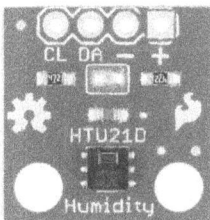

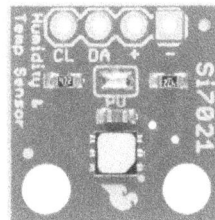

First the hardware. The HTU21D Humidity and Temperature sensor is one of the easiest of I2C devices to use. Its only problem is that it is only available as a surface-mount package. To overcome this you could solder some wires onto the pads or buy a general breakout board. However, it is much simpler to buy the HTU21D breakout board because this has easy connections and built-in pull-up resistors. The HTU21D has been replaced by the Si7021, which is more robust than the original and works in the same way, but the HTU21D is still available from many sources.

If you decide to work with some other I2C device you can still follow the steps given, modifying what you do to suit it. In particular, if you select a device that only works at 5V you might need a level converter.

Given that the HTU21D has pull-up resistors you don't need to enable the onboard pull-ups provided by the Pico. If you notice any irregularity in the signal at higher frequencies then adding some additional pull-ups might help.

You can use a prototype board to make the connections and this makes it easier to connect other instruments such as a logic analyzer. Given that the pinouts vary according to the exact make of the device, you need to compare the suggested wiring with the breakout board you are actually using.

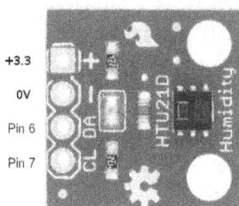

Pico	HTU21
SDA GPIO 4 pin 6	SDA/DA
SCK GPIO 5 pin 7	SCL/CL
3.3v pin 36	VCC/VIN/+
GND pin 38	GND/-

A First Program

After wiring up any I2C device, the first question that needs to be answered is, does it work? Unfortunately for most complex devices finding out if it works is a multi-step process. Our first program aims to read some data back from the HTU21D, any data will do.

If you look at the datasheet you will find that the device address is 0x40 and that it supports the following commands/registers:

Command	Code	Comment
Trigger Temperature Measurement	0xE3	Hold master
Trigger Humidity Measurement	0xE5	Hold master
Trigger Temperature Measurement	0xF3	No Hold master
Trigger Humidity Measurement	0xF5	No Hold master
Write user register	0xE6	
Read user register	0xE7	
Soft Reset	0xFE	

The easiest of these to get started with is the Read user register command. The user register gives the current setup of the device and can be used to set the resolution of the measurement.

Notice that the codes that you send to the device can be considered as addresses or commands. In this case you can think of sending 0xE7 as a command to read the register or the read address of the register, it makes no difference. In most cases, the term "command" is used when sending the code makes the device do something, and the term "address" is used when it simply makes the device read or write specific data.

To read the user register we have to write a byte containing 0xE7 and then read the byte the device sends back. This involves sending an address frame, a data frame, and then another address frame and reading a data frame. The device seems to be happy if you send a stop bit between each transaction or just a new start bit.

A program to read the user register is fairly easy to put together. The address of the device is 0x40, so its write address is 0x80 and its read address is 0x81. Recall that bus addresses are shifted one bit to the left and the base address is the write address and the read address is base address+1. As the I2C functions adjust the address as needed, we simply use 0x40 as the device's address, but it does affect what you see if you sample the data being exchanged, as in reg.py:

```
from machine import Pin,I2C

i2c0=I2C(0,scl=Pin(5),sda=Pin(4),freq=400000)

buf = bytearray([0xE7])
i2c0.writeto( 0x40, buf, True)
read= i2c0.readfrom(0x40, 1, True)
print("User Register =",read)
```

This sends the address frame 0x80 and then the data byte 0xE7 to select the user register. Next it sends an address frame 0x81 to read the data.

If you run `reg.py` you will see:

```
User Register = 2
```

This is the default value of the register and it corresponds to a resolution of 12 bits and 14 bits for the humidity and temperature respectively and a supply voltage greater than 2.25V.

You can use the read-from-a-register method to do the same job:

```
read=i2c0.readfrom_mem(0x40,0xE7,1)
```

This does exactly the same as the previous code – it writes `0xE7` to device `0x40` and then reads one byte.

The I2C Protocol In Action

If you have a logic analyzer that can interpret the I2C protocol connected, what you will see is:

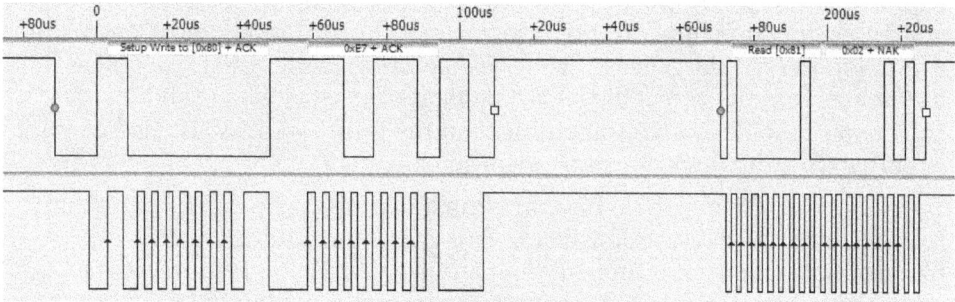

You can see that the `write_byte` function sends an address packet set to the device's 7-bit address `0x40` as the high-order bits with the low-order bit set to zero to indicate a write, i.e `0x80`. After this you get a data packet sent containing `0xE7`, the address of the register. After a few microseconds it sends the address frame again, only this time with the low-order bit set to one to indicate a read. It then receives back a single byte of data from the device, `0x02`. Also notice the start and stop bits at the end of each byte. The big gap between the write and the read is due to the time it takes MicroPython to process the method call. It is a limiting factor on how fast I2C can work.

This all demonstrates that the external device is working properly and we can move on to getting some data of interest.

Reading The Raw Temperature Data

Now we come to reading one of the two quantities that the device measures, temperature. If you look back at the command table you will see that there are two possible commands for reading the temperature:

Command	Code	Comment
Trigger Temperature Measurement	0xE3	Hold master
Trigger Temperature Measurement	0xF3	No Hold master

What is the difference between Hold master and No Hold master? This was discussed earlier in a general context under the section Slow Read Protocols. The device cannot read the temperature instantaneously and the master can either opt to be held waiting for the data, i.e. Hold master, or released to do something else and poll for the data until it is ready, i.e No Hold master.

The Hold master option works by allowing the device to stretch the clock pulse by holding the line low after the master has released it. In this mode the master will wait until the device releases the line. Not all masters support this mode, but the Pico does and this makes it the simpler option. To read the temperature using the Hold master mode you simply send 0xE3 and then read three bytes. The simplest program that will work is htu21.py:

```
from utime import sleep_ms
from machine import Pin,I2C
from time import sleep

i2c0=I2C(0,scl=Pin(5),sda=Pin(4),freq=400000)

buf = bytearray([0xE3])
i2c0.writeto( 0x40, buf, False)
read= i2c0.readfrom(0x40, 3, True)
msb = read[0]
lsb = read[1]
check = read[2]
print("msb lsb checksum =", msb, lsb, check)
```

The read bytearray is unpacked into three variables with more meaningful names:
msb - most significant byte, lsb - least significant byte, check - checksum

If you try this out you should find that it works and it prints something like:

```
msb lsb checksum = 110 194 29
```

with the temperature in the 20°C range.

You can also use the read-from-a-register method to do the same job:

```
read=i2c0.readfrom_mem(0x40, 0xE3, 3)
```

The logic analyzer reveals what is happening. First we send the usual address frame and write the 0xE3. Then, after a short pause, the read address frame is sent and the clock line is held low by the device (lower trace):
The clock line is held low by the device for over 42ms while it gets the data ready. It is released and the three data frames are sent:

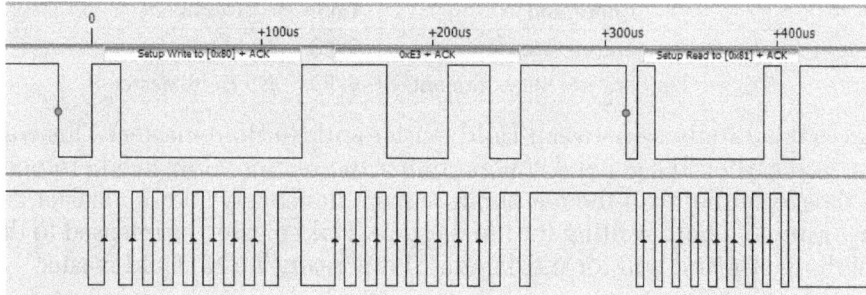

This response is a long way down the logic analyzer trace (40ms+) so keep scrolling until you find it.

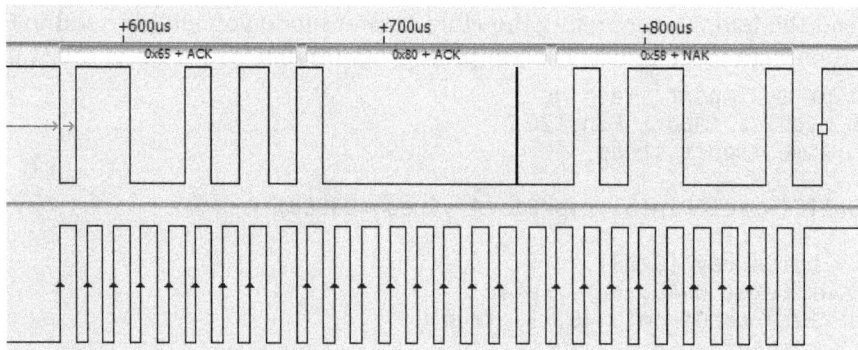

Notice that we suppress the stop bit between the write and the read to make it a single transaction.

Processing The Data

Our next task isn't really directly related to the problem of using the I2C bus, but it is a very typical next step. The device returns the data in three bytes, but the way that this data relates to the temperature isn't simple.

If you read the datasheet you will discover that the temperature data is the 14-bit value that results from putting together the most and least significant bytes and zeroing the bottom two bits. The bottom two bits are used as status bits, bit zero currently isn't used and bit one is a 1 if the data is a humidity measurement and a 0 if it is a temperature measurement.

To put the two bytes together we use:

```
data16= (msb << 8) |  (lsb & 0xFC)
```

This zeros the bottom two bits, shifts the `msb` up eight bits and ORs the two together. The result is a 16-bit temperature value with the bottom two bits zeroed. Now we have a raw temperature value but we have still have to convert it to standard units. The datasheet gives the formula:

```
Temperature in °C= -46.85 + 175.72 * data16 / 2¹⁶
```

The only problem in implementing this is working out 2^{16}. You can work out 2^x with the expression `1<<x`, i.e. shift `1` x places to the right.
This gives:

```
temp = (-46.85 +(175.72 * data16 /(1<<16)))
```

Now all we have to do is print the temperature:

```
print("Temperature C ", temp)
```

The full listing is at the end of this chapter.

Reading Humidity

The nice thing about using I2C devices is that it gets easier. Once you have seen how to do it with one device, the skill generalizes and, once you know how to deal with a particular part of a device, other aspects of the device are usually similar.
While clock stretching is simple it sometimes doesn't work with some slave and master combinations. It is worth knowing how the alternative method works. For this reason let's implement the humidity reading using polling. We also find out how to use the No Hold master mode of reading the data, which is sometimes useful.
We write the `0xF5` once to the slave and then repeatedly attempt to read the three-byte response. If the slave isn't ready it simply replies with a `NAK` which the read method signals throwing an exception. We need to keep reading until the data is ready and this means using try to deal with the exception :

```
while True:
    sleep_ms(1)
    try:
        i2c0.readfrom_into(0x40,read, True)
        break
    except:
        continue
```

This polls repeatedly until the slave device returns an `ACK`, when the data is loaded into the buffer.

Once we have the data, the formula to convert the 16-bit value to percentage humidity is:

```
RH= -6 + 125 * data16 / 216
```

Putting all this together, and reusing some variables from the previous parts of the program, we have:

```
buf = bytearray([0xF5])
i2c0.writeto( 0x40, buf, True)
read=bytearray(3)
while True:
    sleep_ms(1)
    try:
        i2c0.readfrom_into(0x40,read, True)
        break
    except:
        continue
msb = read[0]
lsb = read[1]
check = read[2]
print("msb lsb checksum =", msb, lsb, check)
data16 = (msb << 8) | (lsb & 0xFC)
hum = -6 + (125.0 * data16) / 65536
print("Humidity ", hum)
```

Checksum Calculation

Although computing a cyclic redundancy checksum, CRC, isn't specific to I2C, it is another common task. The datasheet explains that the polynomial used is:

$$X^8+X^5+X^4+1$$

Once you have this information you can work out the divisor by writing a binary number with a one in each location corresponding to a power of X in the polynomial. In this case the 8th, 5th, 4th and 1st bit. Hence the divisor is:

```
0x0131
```

What you do next is roughly the same for all CRCs. First you put the data that was used to compute the checksum together with the checksum value as the low-order bits:

```
data32 = (msb << 16)|(lsb <<8)| check
```

Now you have three bytes, i.e 24 bits, in a 32-bit variable. Next you adjust the divisor so that its most significant non-zero bit aligns with the most significant bit of the three bytes. As this divisor has a 1 at bit eight, it needs to be shifted 15 places to the right to move it to be the 24th bit:

```
divisor =  0x0131 <<15
```

or

```
divisor = 0x988000
```

Now that you have both the data and the divisor aligned, you step through the topmost 16 bits, i.e. you don't process the low-order eight bits which hold the received checksum. For each bit you check to see if it is a **1**. If it is you replace the data with the data XOR divisor. In either case you shift the divisor one place to the right:

```
for i in range(16):
      if data32 & 1<<(23 - i):
          data32 ^= divisor
      divisor>>= 1
```

When the loop ends, if there was no error, the `data32` should be zeroed and the received checksum is correct and as computed on the data received.

A complete function to compute the checksum, with some optimization, is:

```
def crcCheck(msb, lsb,check):
    data32 = (msb << 16)|(lsb <<8)| check
    divisor = 0x988000
    for i in range(16):
        if data32 & 1<<(23 - i):
            data32 ^= divisor
        divisor>>= 1
    return data32
```

It is rare to get a CRC error on an I2C bus unless it is overloaded or subject to a lot of noise.

Complete Listing

The complete program for reading temperature and humidity, including checksums, `temp.py` is:

```
from utime import sleep_ms
from machine import Pin,I2C
from time import sleep

def crcCheck(msb, lsb,check):
    data32 = (msb << 16)|(lsb <<8)| check
    divisor = 0x988000
    for i in range(16):
        if data32 & 1<<(23 - i):
            data32 ^= divisor
        divisor>>= 1
    return data32

i2c0=I2C(0,scl=Pin(5),sda=Pin(4),freq=400000)
buf = bytearray([0xE3])
i2c0.writeto( 0x40, buf, False)
read= i2c0.readfrom(0x40, 3, True)
msb = read[0]
lsb = read[1]
check = read[2]
print("msb lsb checksum =", msb, lsb, check)
```

```
data16= (msb << 8) |  (lsb & 0xFC)
temp = (-46.85 +(175.72 * data16 /(1<<16)))
print("Temperature C ", temp)
print("Checksum=",crcCheck(msb,lsb,check))

buf = bytearray([0xF5])
i2c0.writeto( 0x40, buf, True)
read=bytearray(3)
while True:
    sleep_ms(1)
    try:
        i2c0.readfrom_into(0x40,read, True)
        break
    except:
        continue
msb = read[0]
lsb = read[1]
check = read[2]
print("msb lsb checksum =", msb, lsb, check)
data16 = (msb << 8) | (lsb & 0xFC)
hum = -6 + (125.0 * data16) / 65536
print("Humidity ", hum)
print("Checksum=",crcCheck(msb,lsb,check))
```

Notice that we used clock stretching in reading the temperature and polling in reading the humidity. In practice, you would choose one method according to your needs.

Of course, this is just the start. Once you have the device working and supplying data, it is time to write your code in the form of functions that return the temperature and the humidity and generally make the whole thing more useful and easier to maintain. This is often how this sort of programming goes. First you write a lot of inline code so that it works as fast as it can, then you move blocks of code to functions to make the program more elegant and easy to maintain, checking at each refactoring that it all still works.

Not all devices used standard bus protocols. In Chapter 14 we'll look at a custom serial protocol that we have to implement for ourselves.

Summary

- The I2C bus is simple yet flexible and is one of the most commonly encountered ways of connecting devices.

- The I2C bus uses two wires – a data line and a clock.

- The Pico has two I2C interfaces.

- MicroPython provides a software implementation of the I2C bus which can be used with any GPIO lines, but it isn't as efficient as the hardware implementation.

- Each I2C interface can be connected to a pair of GPIO lines.

- The I2C protocol isn't standardized and you have to take account of variations in the way devices implement it.

- There are single byte transfer operations and multibyte transfers which differ in when a stop bit is sent.

- The low-level protocol can be made slightly more high-level by thinking of it as a single write or read a register operation.

- Sometimes a device cannot respond immediately and needs to keep the master waiting for data. There are two ways to do this, polling and clock stretching.

- The HTU21D is a simple I2C device, but getting it working involves using polling or stretching.

- Computing a checksum is an involved, but common, operation.

Chapter 13

Using The PIO

The most interesting and attractive feature of the Pico is arguably its PIO – Programmable I/O hardware. So far we have used direct access to the GPIO lines or to some built-in hardware that controls them such as PWM, I2C or SPI. If you want to connect to a device that these standards apply to then your problem is solved. If, on the other hand, you have a device that doesn't use one of these standards then you are faced with the task of constructing your own implementation of the interface. For example, the DHT22 temperature and humidity sensor uses its own protocol for delivering its data and the 1-Wire bus is commonly encountered, but not often supported, in hardware. You can even go beyond any standard and implement your own custom data transfer protocol.

The traditional way to approach any custom or unsupported protocol is to use "bit banging". This is simply the act of writing a program which controls GPIO lines to simulate the hardware that might be used to implement the protocol. Basically what you have to do is set GPIO lines high and low as dictated by the timing of the protocol and then read data at set times. This is easy in theory, but getting the timings right is harder that it appears and synchronization between state changes is particularly challenging. In addition there is the problem that bit banging ties up the processor. In many cases this doesn't matter. In other cases you can use one core to implement the protocol and another to process the data. However the Pico's PIOs provide a general-purpose solution to the problem that offers advantages that go well beyond the traditional solutions.

The Pico documentation on the PIO even suggests that if you find yourself working on a bit-banging solution then you should stop and start again using the PIO. I wouldn't go this far because the PIO solution is more complex and specialized and if a simple bit-banging solution works you need a motivation to transfer your attention to the PIO. This said, it is worth spending time learning about the PIO if you anticipate ever making use of it. With the right approach it isn't as difficult as it first appears.

PIO Basic Concepts

The problem with getting to grips with the PIO is that there are two distinct views of it – inside and outside. You can also add to this the extra complication of setting up a project that makes use of it, but that is a one-time problem. The best way to think about the PIO is as a black box that performs some transaction using GPIO lines and presents and accepts data from the processor – exactly like other I/O subsystems PWM, SPI, I2C etc. The only difference is that the transaction it performs is programmable.

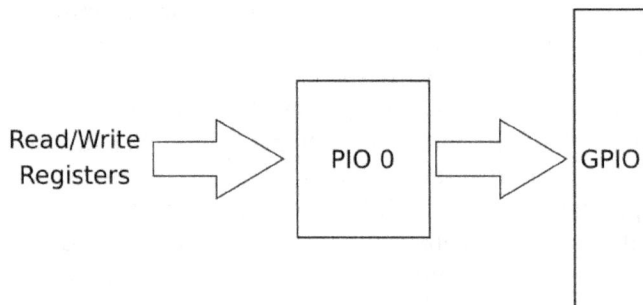

This is the same situation as for the I2C or SPI hardware – once set up, you communicate with the PIO by reading and writing registers and it is associated with a number of GPIO lines.

As you might guess from the illustration, there is more than one PIO. The original Pico has two, PIO0 and PIO1, and the Pico 2 has three, PIO0, PIO1 and PIO2, and each can be programmed independently of the other. To make things simple, we will use PIO0, but everything translates to PIO1 or PIO2 if you need to use an alternative.

You communicate with the PIO by reading and writing registers and, as with other hardware modules, MicroPython provides functions and methods to do this for you.

There are two independent PIOs and each one has four state machines. The state machines can be set to run a program stored in the PIO. It is the state machines that deal with the outside world while the PIO deals with your program. Each PIO only has storage for 32 instructions, which the four state machines share. A common configuration is for each state machine to run the same program, but work with different GPIO lines. If the programs are small then it is also possible for each state machine to have its own program stored in the PIO.

Although MicroPython doesn't really distinguish between the state machines, it is worth keeping in mind that state machines 0 to 3 are part of PIO0 and state machines 4 to 7 are part of PIO1.

State Machines And GPIO

The first and most important thing to understand is that each state machine doesn't have instructions that work with particular GPIO lines. You don't write a PIO program that sets the output of pin GPIO 2, say. Instead you specify which GPIO lines are to be included in a number of groups. Each state machine has its own set of GPIO lines that it works with and, at the simplest, each state machine can perform the same sort of task on different GPIO pins. So, for example, if you programmed the PIO to be an SPI controller then you could define four different SPI interfaces, each to a different set of pins. It is also possible to run each state machine from a different program, but more of this later.

Each state machine has two straightforward sets of GPIO output lines, OUT and SET that are specified by a base and a count, e.g. base is GPIO 4 and count is 2 gives GPIO 4 and GPIO 5. Lines in the OUT group are controlled by instructions that transfer data from the processor to the state machine. That is, they are lines you set by writing data to the state machine and then using instructions to transfer it to the outside world. Typically the lines in the OUT group are what you would think of as data lines.

Those in the SET group are controlled by instructions running on the state machine. That is, they are lines you set within the PIO program and typically are used as clock lines.

A third group of output lines, SIDESET, is also available. While it turns out to be very useful it is slightly more difficult to understand. We will return to it later.

The important point is that these groups of lines are not set in your program but as part of the initialization of the PIO. This means that your program can be reused with different GPIO lines on different state machines.

To work with the PIO there are two new elements in MicroPython, both in the rp2 module. The first is the rp2.asm_pio function which is intended to be used as a decorator applied to a function that defines the PIO program, i.e. the PIO assembly language. The second is the StateMachine class which configures the state machine you are going to use. The key idea is that the PIO program should be specified so that it can be run on any state machine with a specific set of GPIO lines. In other words, there are configuration options that are specific to the program, e.g. the number of GPIO lines used, and there are options which are specific to the state machine, e.g. exactly which lines are used.

The program-specific options are parameters within the `rp2.asm_pio` decorator. It is worth making a list of these here because currently they are mostly undocumented, even though they will be explained as we go along:

`set_init`	Set the initial states and hence number of the SET group
`sideset_init`	Set the initial states and hence number of the SETSIDE group
`out_init`	Set the initial states and hence number of the OUT group
`autopull`	Enable or disable autopull
`autopush`	Enable or disable autopush

The state machine-specific options are set in the `StateMachine` constructor:

`freq`	Clock frequency in Hz
`in_base`	Start GPIO pin of IN Group
`out_base`	Start GPIO pin of OUT Group
`set_base`	Start GPIO pin of SET Group
`sideset_base`	Start GPIO pin of SIDESET Group
`jmp_pin`	GPIO pin used for `jmp` instruction
`in_shiftdir`	ISR shift direction using `rp2.PIO.SHIFT_RIGHT/LEFT`
`out_shiftdir`	OSR shift direction using `rp2.PIO.SHIFT_RIGHT/LEFT`
`push_thresh`	Autopush threshold
`pull_thresh`	Autopull threshold

All of this will make sense by the end of the chapter.

PIO Blinky

Now it is time to write and run our first PIO program and, in the grand tradition, we will eventually, write a Blinky program – the Hello World of hardware.

The PIO is programmed using a special assembly language and we will return to its main features later, but for now you can most probably understand the meaning of our first simple program, `blink.py`:

```
.program blink
again:
    set pins, 1      ; Drive pin high
    set pins, 0      ; Drive pin low
    jmp again        ; Set PC to label `again`
```

The first instruction sets pin 1 in the SET group of pins to be an active output, i.e. it changes from a high impedance state to an output. This is more complicated than it seems. More of exactly how this works is in the section on output to the GPIO.

Note: Ignore errors flagged by VS Code in PIO programs. Its Intellisense fails to parse PIO assembly code.

The loop that follows this repeatedly changes the SET group of pins from high to low. Notice that from this program you cannot tell which pins are actually being used – this is set externally to the PIO program.

If you were working with C then the next step would be to use the PIO assembler to convert the program to PIO machine code. With MicroPython, however, you can enter the assembly language as a function and use a decorator to convert it into machine code:

```
@rp2.asm_pio(set_init=rp2.PIO.OUT_LOW)
def blink():
    label("again")
    set(pins, 1)
    set(pins, 0)
    jmp("again")
```

You can see that each of the assembly language instructions is written as a function call and the parameters of the function are the parameters of the assembly language instruction. Notice that we have a `label` function to mark a location in the program. In most cases you can write your PIO assembler using the assembly language and then convert it into function calls, but after a little practice you should find it easy to work directly in function calls. This is the approach used in the rest of this book. Notice that the PIO program's name is the name of the MicroPython function.

The `set_init` parameter in the decorator defines the SET group to have a single GPIO line which is initially set low. In general this would be a tuple of pins and initial states. This is how you determine the number of lines in each of the groups and their initial states.

Now we have the code as a function, the next job is to pick one of the eight possible state machines to execute and configure it. As already mentioned, the first four state machines, 0 to 3, belong to PIO0 and the second four, 4 to 7 belong to PIO1. This is important because all of the state machines in a given PIO share a limited 32-instruction program memory and which PIO is used to host the program depends on the state machine you choose.

To setup a state machine to run the program we use:

```
sm = rp2.StateMachine(0, blink, freq=2300, set_base=Pin(16))
```

This selects state machine zero, which is hosted by PIO0. It loads the `blink` program into PIO0 and sets state machine 0 to start running it using a clock frequency of 2300Hz and the start of the SET group as GPIO 16. This combined with the program decorator:

```
@rp2.asm_pio(set_init=rp2.PIO.OUT_LOW)
```

makes the SET group just the single GPIO line, i.e. GPIO 16.

To set the state machine running the program all we have to do is:

```
sm.active(1)
```

and to stop it running:

```
sm.active(0)
```

If you now look at the output of GPIO 16 you will see a square wave.

The complete program is, `blinky1.py`:

```python
import rp2
from machine import Pin

@rp2.asm_pio(set_init=rp2.PIO.OUT_LOW, )
def blink():
    label("again")
    set(pins, 1)
    set(pins, 0)
    jmp("again")


sm = rp2.StateMachine(0, blink, freq=2300, set_base=Pin(16))
sm.active(1)
while(True):
    pass
```

We do have a square wave-producing program but it isn't suitable as a Blinky example. At the moment the clock rate is set to produce a square wave at around 766Hz and we need to bring down the frequency to something more reasonable so that we can see an LED blink on and off.

Clock Division And Timing

There are a number of ways of controlling the speed with which things happen, the most direct and preferable is to change the clock frequency by specifying a divider. The PIO clock can be divided down using a 16-bit divider – 8-bit integer/8-bit fractional. In most cases, you should avoid using a fractional divider as it introduces extra periods to make the frequency average out to the fractional part. This can make the PIO subject to jitter, which decreases the reliability.

Using MicroPython you don't set the clock divider but its frequency and the system attempts to work out a clock divider that gets as close to the desired frequency as possible. The lowest clock frequency using the default clock, is about 2kHz on a Pico and 2.3kHz on a Pico 2 which is too fast for some things. This brings us to another important idea. Most of the timing in PIO programs is linked to the time an instruction takes to complete and most instructions take one clock cycle. This can cause difficulties in that execution paths may not be equal in time when you want them to be. For example, consider our simple `blink` PIO program:

```
.program blink
again:
    set pins, 1     ; Drive pin high
    set pins, 0     ; Drive pin low
    jmp again       ; Set PC to label `again`
```

The first set pins takes one clock cycle, the second takes one clock cycle, but the `jmp` instruction also takes one clock cycle, meaning that the GPIO line is high for one clock cycle and low for two clock cycles.

There are a number of ways of changing timings. For example, you could include a `nop` instruction which wastes a single clock cycle, but also uses one memory slot. Alternatively you could specify a delay as part of the instruction – all PIO instructions can have a delay in clock cycles specified as [n] at the end of the instruction. So our new program:

```
.program blink
again:
    set pins, 1 [1]   ; Drive pin high
    set pins, 0       ; Drive pin low
    jmp again         ; Set PC to label `again`
```

Holds the line high for two clock cycles and low for two clock cycles.

With the maximum clock divider this gives a square wave output at around 120kHz which is still too fast for flashing an LED. The maximum delay you can specify in any instruction is 31 clock cycles, so even:

```
.program blink
again:
 set pins, 1 [31]   ; Drive pin high
 set pins, 0 [30]   ; Drive pin low
 jmp again          ; Set PC to label `again`
```

or, in function form, `blinky2.py`:

```
@rp2.asm_pio(set_init=rp2.PIO.OUT_LOW, )
def blink():
    label("again")
    set(pins, 1) [31]
    set(pins, 0) [30]
    jmp("again")
```

only brings the clock down to 35Hz.

In general, you should try to choose a clock frequency that makes timing of pulses using just per-instruction delays to adjust the relative timings. Each instruction and delay takes one clock cycle, so this is the natural unit of measurement to use.

In our case we need a much longer delay than can be produced by 32 clock cycles – we need a spin wait loop.

Writing Loops

One of the things you will most likely have to do is write the equivalent of a for or while loop in PIO assembler and it might not be obvious how to do this because it doesn't have control structures like MicroPython. To write a loop you need to know that each state machine has two scratch 32-bit storage registers called x and y. You can store values and use values in these registers from various sources using the in, out, set or mov instructions. If you want to set a register, x say, to a constant value then you need to use:

```
set x,31
```

where 31 is the maximum value you can set because the instruction is limited to a 5-bit immediate value.

You can use the registers to implement a for loop with up to 32 repeats. The jmp instruction can test the value of a register for zero and auto-decrement it after the test. This means an n-repeat for loop can be constructed as:

```
set x,n
loop:
    nop
jmp x--, loop
```

Using this you can slow the rate at which the GPIO line is toggled by repeating the nop 32 times. However, even if you use:

```
set x,n
loop:
    nop [31]
jmp x--, loop
```

the effective rate of toggling the GPIO line is still too great to see an LED flash. To slow it down even more you need two nested loops in the PIO program:

```
.program blink
    again:
     set pins, 1
     set x,31
     loop1:
       nop [31]
     jmp x--,loop1
     pins, 0
     set(x,31)
     loop2:
       nop [31]
       jmp x--,loop2
    jmp again
```

You can see that there are two delay loops. If you try it you will find it runs at about 1.1Hz.

The complete `blinky3.py` program is:

```python
import rp2
from machine import Pin

@rp2.asm_pio(set_init=rp2.PIO.OUT_LOW, )
def blink():
    label("again")
    set(pins, 1)
    set(x,31)
    label("loop1")
    nop() [31]
    jmp(x_dec,"loop1")
    set(pins, 0)
    set(x,31)
    label("loop2")
    nop() [31]
    jmp(x_dec,"loop2")
    jmp("again")

sm = rp2.StateMachine(0, blink, freq=2300, set_base=Pin(16))
sm.active(1)
while(True):
    pass
```

Notice that x-- is entered as x_dec and other conditionals are entered in similar ways.

Also notice that we can only set the x or y register to a maximum of 31 because the PIO assembly instructions only have space for a 5-bit literal field. There is another way to set the x and y register using data transferred into the PIO program from the MicroPython program and this brings us to the subject of data input.

Data To The PIO

Just like any of the I/O subsystems in the Pico, you can send data to the PIO from your MicroPython program. The Pico provides a 3-element, 32-bit FIFO buffer, the TX FIFO, for input to the state machine and, usually, output to the GPIO lines. You can write data to the TX FIFO using:

`sm.put(data)`

It stores data in the TX FIFO and return immediately, unless there is no space when it waits for the PIO to read some data and free some space.

The PIO program can read data from the TX FIFO using the `pull` instruction which moves the first item of data from the FIFO into the Output Shift Register, OSR. Usually the OSR is then used to drive the OUT group of lines, more of this later. However, the `mov` instruction can be used to move the

OSR to a range of destinations including the x and y registers. This means we can use the TX FIFO buffer to set the x or y register to a full 32-bit value.

Using this we can create a Blinky program that just uses one loop and can create time delays in excess of 30 minutes. The PIO program is:

```
.program blink
    pull block
again:
    set pins, 1
    mov x, osr
 loop1:
    jmp x--,loop1
    set pins, 0
    mov x, osr
loop2:
 jmp x--,loop2
jmp again
```

Notice the way the OSR is used as a way of storing the loop count so that it can be used to reset the x register each time. If you needed to use the OSR for something else this wouldn't be possible and you would have to use the y register or some other method. Also notice that the pull block instruction causes the PIO program to wait until there is some data in the TX FIFO to start things off.

The complete blinky4.py program is:

```
import rp2
from machine import Pin

@rp2.asm_pio(set_init=rp2.PIO.OUT_LOW, )
def squarewave():
    pull(block)
    label("again")
    set(pins, 1)
    mov(x,osr)
    label("loop1")
    jmp(x_dec,"loop1")
    set(pins, 0)
    mov(x,osr)
    label("loop2")
    jmp(x_dec,"loop2")
    jmp("again")

sm = rp2.StateMachine(0, squarewave, freq=2300, set_base=Pin(16))
sm.active(1)
sm.put(0xFFF)
while(True):
    pass
```

The only real difference is the `put` function at the end which stores `0xFFF` in the TX FIFO to start the PIO program running. If you run this program you will find that the frequency is 0.3Hz.

This is a way of passing a single parameter to a PIO program. If you want to pass two or more parameters then it can be done, but things become more complicated.

Output To GPIO

The use of the Output Shift Register, OSR, to store a value that is moved to the x register is reasonable, but it isn't the usual role for the OSR, which is normally used as the link between values passed to the state machine and the state of the GPIO lines. We have already seen that the SET group of GPIO lines can be controlled using the `set` command, now we move on to consider how the OUT group of GPIO lines can be controlled using the `out` command. Recall that the OUT group is a set of GPIO lines specified by a starting number and number of lines.

The data in the OSR can be moved to the OUT group of pins using the `out` instruction:

```
out pins, n
```

where n is the number of bits shifted to the OUT group. The bits that are shifted out are used to set the first n GPIO lines in the OUT group and any remaining lines are set to zero. Notice that while we use the term "shift" this applies only to what happens to the contents of the OSR register. The n bits are presented to the n GPIO lines in one operation – i.e. all of the GPIO lines change their state at the same time. The "shift" simply means that the data in the OSR register is moved to remove the n bits used. You can set the direction of the shift when you create the state machine so as to make either the most significant or least significant bits the ones that are used in the OSR register first:

```
out_shiftdir= rp2.PIO.SHIFT_RIGHT/LEFT
```

In general, 32 bits are sent to the destination of the `out` command, the lower n bits coming from the OSR and the remaining bits being zero. Of course, usually only the lower n bits are actually useful. If you repeat the `out` instruction the next n bits are used and so on until the shift register is empty when all 32 bits have been shifted out.

A simple PIO program example will help clarify. In this case we will send the bits from a 32-bit value to two GPIO pins just to show how things work:

```
.program output
    pull block
again:
    out pins,2
    jmp again
```

You can see that all the program does is to pull a single 32-bit value from the TX FIFO into the OSR and then uses the out instruction to send pairs of bits to the first two pins in the OUT group of pins. Of course, we need to set the number and start GPIO pin of the OUT group. The complete program is, output.py:

```
import rp2
from machine import Pin

@rp2.asm_pio(out_init=(rp2.PIO.OUT_LOW,rp2.PIO.OUT_LOW))
def output():
    pull(block)
    label("again")
    out(pins,2)
    jmp("again")

sm = rp2.StateMachine(0, output, freq=2300, out_base=Pin(16),
out_shiftdir=rp2.PIO.SHIFT_RIGHT)
sm.active(1)
sm.put(0xFEDCBA98)
while(True):
    pass
```

You can see that we set the size and initial state of the OUT group to two pins set to low in the decorator and the start pin GPIO 16. These two settings make the OUT group consist of GPIO 16 and GPIO 17. The final instruction sends some arbitrary data to the TX FIFO and this is output two bits at a time to the two GPIO lines, GPIO 16 and GPIO 17:

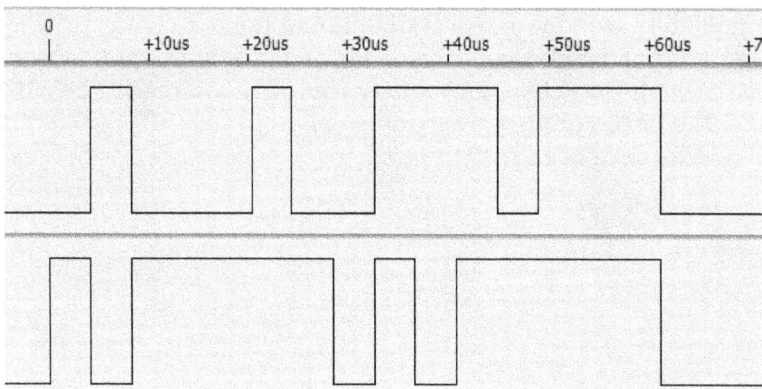

The output stops when the OSR is empty but the `out` instruction keeps sending zeros to the GPIO lines. Also notice the use of:

```
out_shiftdir=rp2.PIO.SHIFT_RIGHT
```

to set the direction of the shift. Try changing it to `rp2.PIO.SHIFT_LEFT`.

If you want to keep the data flowing, you have to keep refilling the OSR. For example, you could change the program to send data to the buffer whenever there was a free space:

```
while True:
    sm.put(0xFEDCBA98)
```

Now the PIO program can read new data from the TX FIFO whenever it wants to:

```
.program output
    pull block

again:
    out pins,2
    out pins,2
    out pins,2
    pull block
    jmp again
```

In this case we send the first three pairs of bits to the output pins and then read the TX FIFO into the OSR to get new data.

Of course, usually you would use all of the data in the OSR before reloading it. This standard task can be done automatically with the `autopull` which reloads the OSR whenever its contents fall below a threshold. You set `autopull` in the `@rp2.asm_pio` decorator:

```
autopull=True
```

If you set `autopull` to true then the OSR will be reloaded from the TX FIFO when it contents fall below the pull threshold which is set in the state machine constructor using:

```
pull_thresh=pt
```

Using this, the PIO program becomes:

```
.program output
again:
    out pins,2
    jmp again
```

The complete program, `output2.py`, is:

```python
import rp2
from machine import Pin

@rp2.asm_pio(out_init=(rp2.PIO.OUT_LOW,rp2.PIO.OUT_LOW),autopull=True)
def output():
    label("again")
    out(pins,2)
    jmp("again")

sm = rp2.StateMachine(0, output, freq=2300, out_base=Pin(16),
out_shiftdir=rp2.PIO.SHIFT_RIGHT)
sm.active(1)
while True:
    sm.put(0xFEDCBA98)
```

There are some minor points of how `autopull` works that we've not covered, but you now have the general principles. Notice that we are using the default pull threshold of 32 bits.

Side Effects

Now we have encountered most of the ideas behind PIO output to the GPIO lines, but there is one additional feature – lines in the SETSIDE group acting as a side effect. As well as being able to explicitly set GPIO lines using `set` or `out`, we can also arrange for any instruction to set GPIO lines as part of its execution. In this sense, the setting of the GPIO lines is a "side effect" of the instruction. Side effects are usually thought of as something to avoid in a standard program – you want an instruction to do what it appears to do and nothing more. In the case of PIO programming, however, side effects are very useful because they allow you to set GPIO lines according to where the program is in its execution. That is, they can be used to signal to the outside world the state of the program. At a more utilitarian level, being able to set a GPIO line as a side effect of another instruction can save both time and instructions.

The only downside of side effects is that they are coded using the space in the PIO instruction that is normally used to specify a delay. There is a 5-bit field used to code the delay and the side effect and you can trade bits for each purpose. The default is that all five bits are used to specify a delay and this makes it possible to specify up to 31 clock cycles of delay.

You can allocate bits to be used to SETSIDES using the PIO instruction:

```
.side_set count opt pindirs
```

where `count` is the number of bits to allocate, `opt` means that the setting is optional on an instruction and `pindirs` is the option to set the pin directions as a side effect. Setting `pindirs` as a side effect is useful if you need to change a line from `out` to `in` as the program progresses.

In MicroPython you configure the program using the decorator's parameter:

```
pio(sideset_init=rp2.PIO.OUT_LOW)
```

which gives the number of pins in the SETSIDE group and in the state machine using the:

```
setsideset_base=Pin(16)
```

parameter which sets the starting pin for the group.

Obviously you should choose to use as few bits as possible if you want to make use of a delay, but in MicroPython you can mostly ignore this and allow the system to determine it for you.

Finally to include a GPIO line to be set as a side effect you can add:

```
side value
```

after any PIO instruction and the value will be used to set the SETSIDE pins (or their directions).

To show how all this works the simplest thing to do is write the square wave generator again, but this time using nothing but `side_set` options:

```
.program blink
.side_set 1 opt
again:
  nop side 1
  jmp  again side 0
```

The `side_set` directive specifies a single bit, which means that the SETSIDE group of GPIO lines is effectively a single line. The `nop` has a side effect of setting the side effect line to 1 and the `jmp` sets it back to 0.

When you translate this into MicroPython you need to know that the `side n` addition is converted into `.side(n)` and you determine the SETSIDE group using the state machine constructor and decorator.

The complete program, `blinky5.py`, is:

```
import rp2
from machine import Pin

@rp2.asm_pio(sideset_init=rp2.PIO.OUT_LOW)
def squarewave():
    label("again")
    nop().side(1)
    jmp("again").side(0)

sm = rp2.StateMachine(0, squarewave,
freq=2300,sideset_base=Pin(16))
sm.active(1)
while(True):
    pass
```

If you run this program you will find that pin GPIO 16 is toggled in a 50% square wave at around 1kHz, without a single `out` or `set` instruction in sight. Notice that the rising edge occurs when the loop starts and the falling edge when the loop ends.

As an example of using more than one GPIO line as a side effect consider, blinky6.py:

```
import rp2
from machine import Pin

@rp2.asm_pio(sideset_init=(rp2.PIO.OUT_LOW,rp2.PIO.OUT_LOW))
def squarewave():
    label("again")
    nop().side(2)
    jmp("again").side(1)

sm = rp2.StateMachine(0, squarewave,
                      freq=2300,sideset_base=Pin(16))
sm.active(1)
while(True):
    pass
```

Now we have set aside two bits to control SETSIDE GPIO lines, which means we can control two of them. First we write 2, 10 in binary, to the pair of lines and then 1, or 01, which switches the lines in anti-phase – when one is high the other is low. Notice that the value written is a mask used to set the SETSIDE group of lines.

SETSIDE lines can overlap with OUT and SET lines and if such instructions set the same GPIO line, the sideset instruction has precedent.

Input

Now that we have described most of the general ideas of PIO output to GPIO lines, it is time to consider input from GPIO lines and using the IN group. The good news is that this is easy to understand as long as you have followed the ideas involved in output. The only problem is that, in practice, input is always harder than output and, in the case of PIO programming, you have to re-think how things work. The reason is that you don't have any edge-triggered events or timers. Everything you do has to be conditioned on the state of the system and raw timings based on how long instructions take to execute.

The basic mechanisms of input are the same as output. There is a 4-element, 32-bit RX FIFO buffer that you can read from your MicroPython program using:

```
data=sm.get()
```

Obviously the function blocks until there is some data to read.

Data gets into the RX FIFO from the PIO via the Input Shift Register, ISR, which is the input equivalent of the OSR. To transfer data from the GPIO lines you use the in instruction,

```
in pins,n
```

The in instruction moves n bits from the IN GPIO group into the ISR shifting up any data that is already present. You can also use it to transfer n bits from the x or y registers and a few other sources. Notice that in MicroPython in has to become in_ to avoid the clash with the Python keyword in. The IN group of GPIO lines is defined in the state machine constructor using:

```
in_base=Pin(n)
```

The IN group is treated differently from the rest. You only have to specify a base number as you can read from any GPIO line, even if it is an output. What this means is that an in instruction can read all of the 32 GPIO lines and only the numbering of the lines changes. For example, after:

```
sm = rp2.StateMachine(0, light, freq=2300,in_base=Pin(16))
```

which sets the base to GPIO 16, the instruction:

```
in pins,3
```

will transfer the state of GPIO 16, GPIO 17 and GPIO 18 to the ISR. The pin states are transferred irrespective of whether the pins are set to input or output. Another difference between the IN group and the others is that you have to initialize the GPIO lines used for input as a separate task as there is no in_init parameter.

Once you have sufficient bits in the ISR, you can transfer the entire 32-bit value to the RX FIFO using the `push` instruction:

```
push block
```

This waits for a free space in the RX FIFO and clears the ISR ready for further use. You can also use `autopush` to transfer data to the RX FIFO automatically when a bit count threshold is reached. You can set the direction in which the ISR is shifted and control the use of auto-push and its threshold using:

```
autopush=True
```

in the decorator and:

```
in_shiftdir
push_thresh=pt
```

in the state machine constructor.

As the simplest example, let's read GPIO 2 and use its state to control the on-board LED. This isn't a useful program, but it is a good illustration of the basics. The PIO program is simply:

```
.program light
again:
  in pins,1
  push block
  jmp  again
```

You can see that this simply reads the state of the first INPUT pin and pushes it to the RX FIFO. Of course, after four reads and pushes, the RX FIFO will be full and the program will stall unless the FIFO is read by the main program.

The complete program simply has to set things up, read the data and set the LED accordingly, `input.py`:

```
import rp2
from machine import Pin
@rp2.asm_pio()
def light():
    label("again")
    in_(pins,1)
    push(block)
    jmp("again")
LED=Pin(17,mode=Pin.OUT)
in1=Pin(16,mode=Pin.IN)
sm = rp2.StateMachine(0, light, freq=2300,in_base=Pin(16))
sm.active(1)
while True:
    flag = sm.get()
    if (flag == 0):
        LED.value(0)
    else:
        LED.value(1)
```

Notice the use of `in_base=Pin(16)` to set GPIO 16 to be the start of the IN group, but it still has to be set to input using:

```
in1=Pin(16,mode=Pin.IN)
```

If you set GPIO 16 to high and low you will see the LED turn on and off. The problem with the program is that you have no idea when it reads the input line. All you can say is that the speed of reading is controlled by how fast the program makes room for new data in the RX FIFO.

Edges

This is all there is to using input, but the big problem is when do you read the state of the GPIO lines? When you are implementing a data transfer protocol, it is usual that you output something and then wait a given time before reading. Alternatively, data is read in response to a clock state transition, often an edge, but we have no direct way of responding to an input edge.

The solution to the problem takes us a little way beyond the simple `in` instruction. The PIO supports a conditional wait and a conditional jump, based on the state of a GPIO line. The instruction:

```
wait state pin n
```

will wait until the pin indexed by n in the INPUT group is in the specified state. Notice that n=0 is the first pin in the group.

You can also select the pin by absolute GPIO number:

```
wait state gpio n
```

This will wait until GP*n* is in the specified state. You can also wait on an IRQ, but this is beyond the scope of this first look at the PIO system.

The conditional jump:

```
jmp pin target
```

jumps to the target if the pin specified by *n* in the state machine constructor

```
jmp_pin=n
```

is a 1 and `pin` is a raw GPIO number and not specified by the INPUT group.

The `wait` instruction is about synchronizing the program to the outside world and the `jmp` is about determining what processing should occur according to the state of the outside world. For example, if you need to start a process based on the start of a rising edge you could use:

```
wait 0 pin 0
wait 1 pin 0
```

This works by waiting for the GPIO line to go to zero and hence, when the second wait ends, you know that a rising edge has just occurred. For this to be accurate the clock rate should be high compared to the pulses being input. Notice that if you read the line after the second wait, the state will be one clock cycle after the rising edge. In general, whatever you do as a result of the edge, will occur some number of clock cycles after the edge. This need for a high clock rate to localize the edge can make other aspects of timing difficult.

For example, we can generate a pulse that is close to the rising edge of an input pulse train. The PIO program is:

```
.program blink
again:
    wait 0 pin 0
    wait 1 pin 0
    set pins, 1
    set pins, 0
jmp   again
```

This waits on the first pin in the INPUT group to change from 0 to 1, i.e. a rising edge, and then toggles the first pin in the SET group.

The complete program is, edge.py:

```
import rp2
from machine import Pin

@rp2.asm_pio(set_init=rp2.PIO.OUT_LOW)
def blink():
    label("again")
    wait(0,pin, 0)
    wait(1,pin, 0)
    set(pins, 1)
    set(pins, 0)
    jmp("again")

in1=Pin(16,mode=Pin.IN)
sm = rp2.StateMachine(0, blink,
            freq=2300,in_base=Pin(16),set_base=Pin(17))
sm.active(1)
while(True):
    pass
```

Notice we have to set the in_base and set_base for the IN and SET groups.

With the clock set to a low rate, you can see that the marker pulse isn't very close to the rising edge:

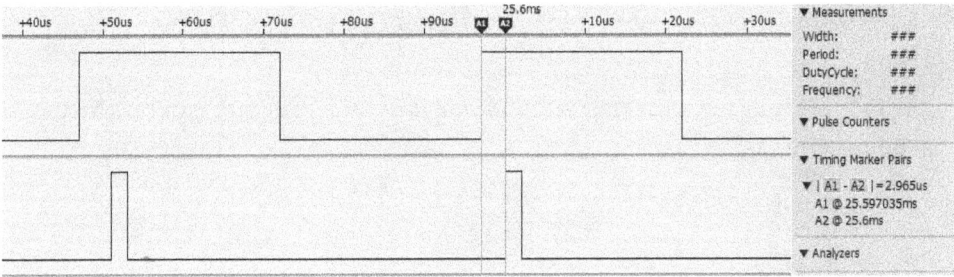

```
+40us    +50us    +60us    +70us    +80us    +90us  A1 A2      +10us    +20us    +30us
                                                25.6ms

▼ Measurements
  Width:        ###
  Period:       ###
  DutyCycle:    ###
  Frequency:    ###
▼ Pulse Counters
▼ Timing Marker Pairs
  ▼ | A1 - A2 | = 2.965us
    A1 @ 25.597035ms
    A2 @ 25.6ms
▼ Analyzers
```

If you increase the clock rate to its maximum, the displacement becomes very small – 45n:

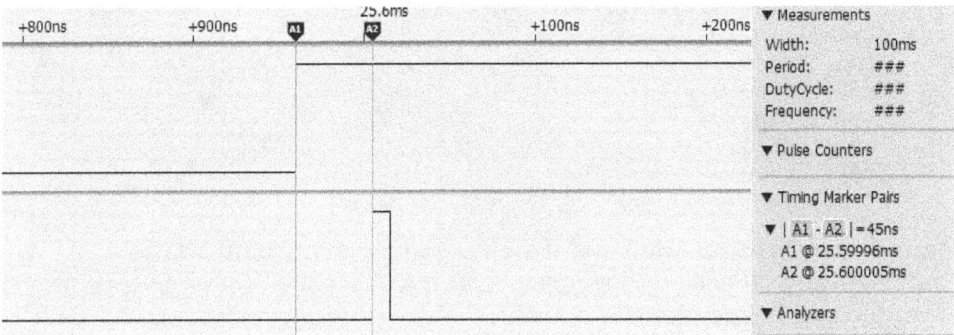

```
+800ns         +900ns      A1     A2          +100ns         +200ns
                            25.6ms

▼ Measurements
  Width:        100ms
  Period:       ###
  DutyCycle:    ###
  Frequency:    ###
▼ Pulse Counters
▼ Timing Marker Pairs
  ▼ | A1 - A2 | = 45ns
    A1 @ 25.59996ms
    A2 @ 25.600005ms
▼ Analyzers
```

To see the problem, consider the task of moving the marker to the middle of the pulse where you might want to sample the line's state. At maximum clock rate this might be too many cycles to use a simple delay. A slower clock rate is easier, but less accurate in its alignment with the edge.

Advanced PIO

This first look at the PIO and its use has covered the main topics to make it possible for you to write PIO programs and use them in your projects. It isn't complete and there are many additional features that you still have to discover. Most of these features are about optimization. For example, nearly all PIO programs take the form of an infinite loop and this is a waste of one of the scarce 32 instruction locations and introduces a clock cycle delay.

As an alternative you can place:

```
.wrap_target
```

before the instruction that you want to restart the program at and:

```
.wrap
```

after the last instruction. For example, our previous program can be written

```
.program blink
.wrap_target
 wait 0 pin 0
 wait 1 pin 0
 set pins, 1
 set pins, 0
.wrap
```

The corresponding MicroPython function is:

```
@rp2.asm_pio(set_init=rp2.PIO.OUT_LOW)
def blink():
    wrap_target()
    wait(0,pin, 0)
    wait(1,pin, 0)
    set(pins, 1)
    set(pins, 0)
    wrap()
```

In this case there is no jmp instruction as the program counter is automatically set back to the target when it reaches the wrap. It is as if the program's address space was circular.

Other topics not discussed are the use of DMA, interrupts and the interaction between multiple PIOs. This is all very straightforward and logical, once you have mastered the basics.

Now we move on to discover how the PIO can do useful work for us.

Summary

- The PIO and the state machine are special processors designed to interact with the outside world.
- You can use a PIO attempt to implement any otherwise unsupported protocol.
- The Pico has two PIOs, each with four state machines.
- The GPIO lines associated with the PIO are determined by a set of groups – OUT, SET and SETSIDE for output and IN for input. GPIO lines also have to be set to PIO mode before they will work in any of the groups.
- You can set the clock frequency that the PIO uses to execute instructions one per clock cycle.
- The clock should be set to a frequency that is suitable for the sort of pulses the PIO is working with.
- It is easy to toggle a GPIO line, but slightly harder to make it slow enough to flash an LED. To do this you need to implement a spin wait loop.
- The OSR and ISR are used to send data to and receive data from the GPIO lines.
- There are two FIFO stacks which can be used to send data to the OSR and ISR from the processor.
- Every instruction can change the state of GPIO lines in the SETSIDE group as a side effect of its execution.
- Working with edges isn't natural for the state machine, but it can be achieved using wait instructions.

## Chapter 14

The DHT22 Sensor
Implementing A Custom Protocol

In this chapter we make use of all the ideas introduced in earlier chapters to create a raw interface with the low-cost DHT11/22 temperature and humidity sensor. It is an exercise in implementing a custom protocol directly in MicroPython using bit banging and then using the PIO. Given the documentation advises against using it, you might be wondering why we start with bit banging? The answer is that bit banging is easier to debug and it is usually a good idea to implement it first if possible, if only to prove that the device in question works and you know how it works.

The DHT22

The DHT22 is a more accurate version of the DHT11 and it is used in this project. The software will work with both versions and also with the AM2302, which is equivalent to the DHT22.

Model AM2302/DHT22
Power supply 3.3-5.5V DC
Output signal digital signal via 1-wire bus
Sensing element Polymer humidity capacitor
Operating range
 humidity 0-100%RH;
 temperature -40~80Celsius
Accuracy
 humidity +-2%RH(Max +-5%RH);
 temperature +-0.5Celsius
Resolution or sensitivity
 humidity 0.1%RH;
 temperature 0.1Celsius
Repeatability
 humidity +-1%RH;
 temperature +-0.2Celsius

The device will work at 3.3V and it makes use of a 1-wire open collector-style bus, which makes it very easy to make the physical connection to the Pico.

The "1-wire bus" used isn't standard and is only used by this family of devices.

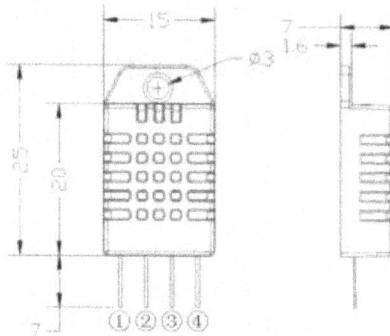

The pinouts are:

1. VDD
2. SDA serial data
3. Not used
4. GND

and the standard way of connecting the device is:

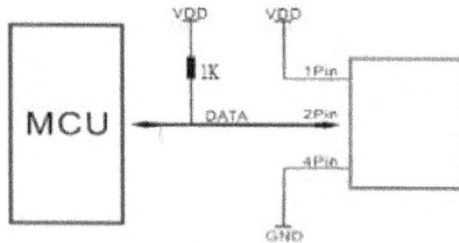

Although the recommended pull-up resistor is 1K, a higher value works better with the Pico - typically 4.7K, but larger will work.

The serial protocol is also fairly simple:

1. The host pulls the line low for between 0.8ms and 29ms, usually 1ms.

2. It then releases the bus which is pulled high.

3. After between 20μs and 200μs, usually 30μs, the device starts to send data by pulling the line down for around 80μs and then lets it float high for another 80μs.

4. Next 40 bits of data are sent using a 70μs high for a 1 and a 26μs high for a 0 with the high pulses separated by around 50μs low periods.

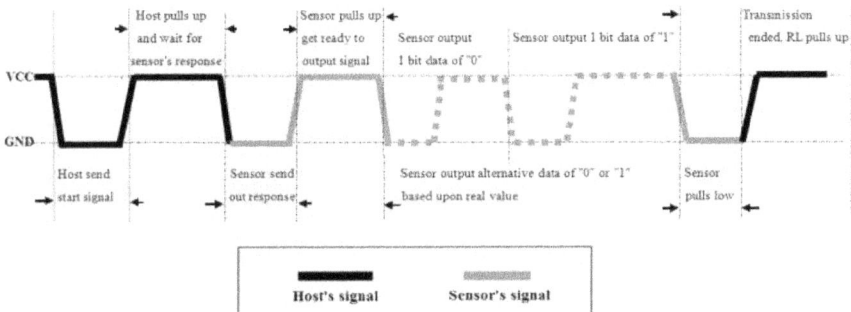

What we have to do is pull the line low for 1ms or so to start the device sending data and this is very easy. Then we have to wait for the device to pull the line down and let it pull up again for about 160μs and then read the time that the line is high or low 40 times.

A 1 corresponds to 70μs and a 0 corresponds to 26 to 28μs. This is within the range of pulse measurements that can be achieved using standard library functions. There is also a 50μs low period between each data bit and this can be used to do some limited processing. The time between falling edge transitions is therefore 120μs for a 1 and 76μs for a 0.

When trying to work out how to decode a new protocol it often helps to try to answer the question, "how can I tell the difference between a 0 and a 1?"

If you have a logic analyzer it can help to look at the waveform and see how you work it out manually. In this case, despite the complex-looking timing diagram, the difference comes down to a short versus a long pulse!

The Electronics

Exactly how you build the circuit is a matter of preference. The basic layout can be seen below.

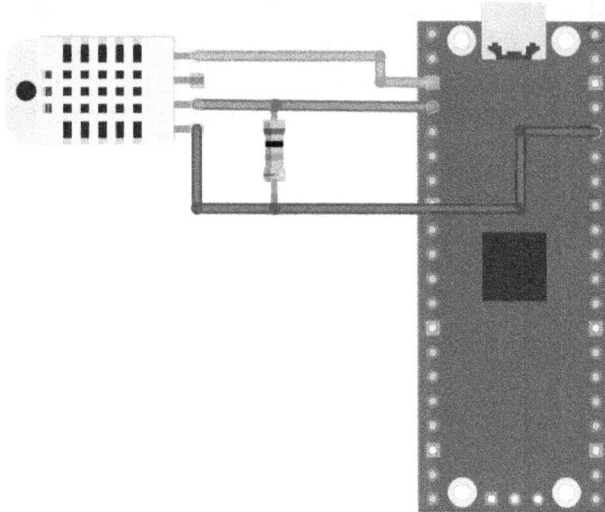

Pico	DHT22
3.5V OUT pin 36	VDD pin 1
GPIO 2 pin 4	SDA serial data pin 2
GND pin 3	GND pin 4

It is very easy to create this circuit using a prototyping board and some jumper wires. You can also put the resistor close to the DHT22 to make a sensor package connected to the Pico using three cables.

The DHT Driver

There is an under-documented and mostly ignored driver for the DHT11 and DHT 22. If you only want to use a temperature and humidity sensor without worrying about how it works then use the driver – it is simple and the only risk is that it fails to be maintained in the future. You use the driver by creating either a DHT11 or DHT22 object connected to a specified pin – any general GPIO line will work. Once you have the object initialized you can use the measure() method to take a reading. This doesn't return any results and to get the temperature and humidity you have to use temperature() to return the temperature in C and humidity() to return the humidity as a percentage.

If you have a DHT22 wired up to GPIO 2 then you can display the temperature and humidity readings using dht22.py:

```
import dht
from machine import Pin
import time

dht = dht.DHT22(Pin(2))
while True:
    dht.measure()
    temp = dht.temperature()
    print(temp)
    hum = dht.humidity()
    print(hum)
    time.sleep(1)
```

The Protocol

Before implementing a program to read the DHT22 using the PIO we need to see how the device communicates, i.e. we need to examine its protocol.

With the hardware shown on the previous page connected to the Pico, the first thing that we need to do is establish that the system is working. The simplest way to do this is to pull the line down for 1ms and see if the device responds with a stream of pulses. These can be seen on a logic analyzer or an oscilloscope, both are indispensable tools. If you don't have access to either tool then you will just have to skip to the next stage and see if you can read in some data. The simplest code that will do the job is:

```
from machine import Pin
from utime import sleep_ms

DHT=Pin(2,mode=Pin.OUT,value=1)
sleep_ms(1)
DHT.low()
sleep_ms(1)
DHT.init(mode=Pin.IN)
```

Setting the line initially high, to ensure that it is configured as an output, we then set it low, wait for around 1ms and then change its direction to input and so allow the line to be pulled high. There is no need to set the line's pull-up mode because the Pico is the only device driving the line until it releases the line by changing direction to input. When a line is in input mode it is high impedance and this is why we need an external pull-up resistor in the circuit.

As long as the circuit has been correctly assembled and you have a working device, you should see something like:

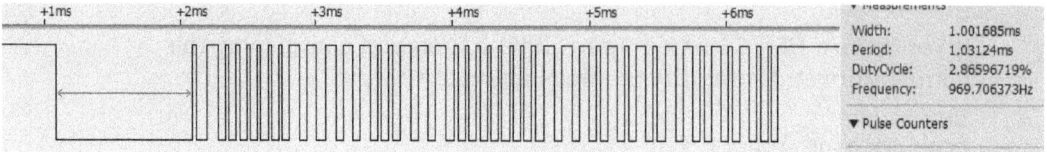

Width:	1.001685ms
Period:	1.03124ms
DutyCycle:	2.86596719%
Frequency:	969.706373Hz

▼ Pulse Counters

Reading The Data

With preliminary flight checks complete, it is time to read the 40-bit data stream. The first thing to do is wait for the low that the device sends before the start bit and then wait for the start bit:

```
from machine import Pin,time_pulse_us
t=time_pulse_us(DHT, 1, 1000)
t=time_pulse_us(DHT, 1, 1000)
```

The first time_pulse_us measures the duration of the high pause before the device pulls the line low, the second measures the duration of the next high, i.e. the pause before the data is sent. Notice that we don't actually need the time of each of these pulses, but the timeout of 1000μs can be used to detect if the device is present.

Next we can start to read in the data. A total of 40 bits, i.e. 5 bytes, is difficult to work with. A good compromise is to read in the first 32 bits into a 32-bit integer and then read the final byte into a separate variable. The reason is that the fifth byte is a checksum, so we have separated out the data and the checksum, but there are many different ways to organize this task. First we read the 32 data bits:

```
data = 0
for i in range(32):
    t=time_pulse_us(DHT, 1, 1000)
    data = data << 1
    data = data | (t > 50)
```

You can see the general idea is to simply find the time that the line is high and then treat anything bigger than 50μs as a 1. In practice, the measured times the pulses are measured as high for 25μs for a 0 and 75μs for a 1 and 50μs is a threshold halfway between the two. The bits are shifted into the variable data so that the first byte transmitted is the high-order byte.

Next we need to read the checksum byte:

```
checksum=0
for i in range(8):
    t=time_pulse_us(DHT, 1, 1000)
    checksum = checksum << 1
    checksum = checksum |(t > 50)
```

232

This works in the same way. At the end of this we have 32 data bits in `data` and eight checksum bits in `checksum` and all we have to do is process the data to get the temperature and humidity.

Extracting The Data

You can process the data without unpacking it into individual bytes, but it is easier to see what is happening if we do:

```
byte1 = (data >> 24 & 0xFF)
byte2 = (data >> 16 & 0xFF)
byte3 = (data >> 8 & 0xFF)
byte4 = (data & 0xFF)
```

The first two bytes are the humidity measurement and the second two the temperature.

The checksum is just the sum of the first four bytes reduced to eight bits and we can test it using:

```
print("Checksum",checksum,(byte1+byte2+byte3+byte4)&0xFF)
```

If the two values are different, there has been a transmission error. The addition of the bytes is done as a full integer and then it is reduced back to a single byte by the AND operation. If there is a checksum error, the simplest thing to do is get another reading from the device. Notice, however, that you shouldn't read the device more than once every two seconds.

The humidity and temperature data are also easy to reconstruct as they are transmitted high byte first and 10 times the actual value.

Extracting the humidity data is easy:

```
humidity = ((byte1 <<8)| byte2) / 10.0
print("Humidity= ", humidity)
```

The temperature data is slightly more difficult in that the topmost bit is used to indicate a negative temperature. This means we have to test for the most significant bit and flip the sign of the temperature if it is set:

```
neg = byte3 & 0x80
byte3 = byte3 & 0x7F
temperature =(byte3 << 8 | byte4) / 10.0
if neg > 0:
    temperature = -temperature
print("Temperature=", temperature)
```

This completes the data processing.

The program as presented works, but it would benefit from refactoring into an object with suitable methods. A complete, refactored, listing including a main program can be seen below. This is just one way to break the program down into functions and exactly how best to do it depends on many factors.

```python
from machine import Pin,time_pulse_us
from utime import sleep_ms,sleep_us

class DHT22():
    def __init__(self,gpio):
        self.pin = Pin(gpio, mode=Pin.IN)
        self.checksum=0
        self.temperature=0
        self.humidity=0
        sleep_ms(1)

    def getReading(self):
        DHT=self.pin
        DHT.init(mode=Pin.OUT,value=0)
        sleep_ms(1)
        DHT.init(mode=Pin.IN)

        t=time_pulse_us(DHT, 1, 1000)
        t=time_pulse_us(DHT, 1, 1000)

        data = 0
        for i in range(32):
            t=time_pulse_us(DHT, 1, 1000)
            data = data << 1
            data = data | (t > 50)

        checksum=0
        for i in range(8):
            t=time_pulse_us(DHT, 1, 1000)
            checksum = checksum << 1
            checksum = checksum |(t > 50)

        byte1 = (data >> 24 & 0xFF)
        byte2 = (data >> 16 & 0xFF)
        byte3 = (data >> 8 & 0xFF)
        byte4 = (data & 0xFF)
        self.checksum=(checksum ==(byte1+byte2+byte3+byte4)&0xFF)
        self.humidity = ((byte1 <<8)| byte2) / 10.0
        neg = byte3 & 0x80
        byte3 = byte3 & 0x7F
        self.temperature =(byte3 << 8 | byte4) / 10.0
        if neg > 0:
            self.temperature = -self.temperature
```

Once you have the class you can write simple programs like `dht22bit.py`:

```
dht = DHT22(2)
dht.getReading()
print("Checksum",dht.checksum)
print("Humidity= ", dht.humidity)
print("Temperature=", dht.temperature)
```

For real use, the program needs to check for a device being present and a check for timeout errors.

DHT22 Using the PIO – Counting

The DHT22 is not well suited to working with the PIO. The reason is that its protocol doesn't use fixed time slots for each bit or synchronization via a separate clock, two situations where it is usually possible to write compact PIO programs to send and receive data. The DHT22 relies on the length of the slot used to transmit a single bit to code zero or one and this means that decoding is a matter of measuring the time between edges. The PIO doesn't have access to a timer and implementing an instruction clock counter isn't straightforward – but it can be done. The following PIO program does exactly this, but it is a long program and it only just satisfies the constraints placed on it to work. After presenting the obvious algorithm with a slightly difficult implementation, a simpler and more direct but less obvious method is implemented.

Before going into details, it is worth explaining what the constraints are and what makes PIO access worth the effort. The bit-banging solution given earlier works and is perfectly good. However, it demands the full attention of the processor while the data is being read in. If an interrupt occurs during reading, the data will be corrupt. On the other hand, if you can implement a PIO program that reads in the data the processor is free to do something else until it wants to use the data and interrupts have no effect. This all depends on the PIO being able to read the data from the device and keep it stored ready for when the processor wants to read it. If you consider this for a few moments, it means that you can hold data in the 4-word FIFO buffer and an additional word in the ISR, making a total of 160 bits of temporary storage, which seems to be more than enough for the 40 bits that the DHT22 produces. However, for a timing-based protocol, things are more complicated.

We can write a loop that counts instruction cycles when the input line is high and this count can be up to 32 bits in resolution. However, there is no easy way to convert the 32-bit count into single bits by applying a threshold as in the bit-banging example. What this means is that we are forced to send the bit counts, rather than the decoded bits back to the processor. A little arithmetic reveals that we can store the counts for all 40 bits, as long as the

235

count is represented as a 4-bit number. We can store the first 32-bits, the data in the 4-word FIFO buffer with the counts for each byte, in a single element. The final byte can be stored in the ISR until the processor reads the FIFO register and frees up space. A count of 4 bits is enough to tell the difference between the times for a zero and a one and this makes the whole scheme possible, as long as we adjust the clock frequency correctly.

What all this means is that we can write a PIO program that can be set to read the data from the DHT22 and store the result in the FIFO and the ISR until the processor is ready to read it. The downside is that the processor has to convert the timing counts to bits and pack the results into bytes before processing the humidity, temperature and checksum – a small price to pay.

With all this worked out we can write the PIO program. The first problem is that we have to send a 1ms initialization pulse:

```
.program dht
        set pins, 1
again:
        pull block
        set pins, 0
        mov x, osr
loop1:
        jmp x--,loop1
        set pindirs, 0
```

This uses a data value written to the state machine by a MicroPython program to execute a delay loop that takes 1ms. It also serves to start the conversion. Also notice that the low pulse is terminated by setting the pin to input using set pindirs.

Next we have to wait for two rising edges to pass before we get to the data pulses:

```
        wait 1 pin 0
        wait 0 pin 0
        wait 1 pin 0
        wait 0 pin 0
```

Finally we can start reading in the four bytes of data:

```
        set y,31
bits:
        wait 1 pin 0
        set x, 0
loop2:
        jmp x--,continue
continue: jmp pin,loop2
        in x,4
        jmp y--,bits
```

The bits loop processes all 32 bits. The inner loop2 processes each bit in turn. The x register is set to zero and then decremented using a forward jump to the end of the loop. Notice that it doesn't matter if the jump is taken, the next instruction is always continue. Decrementing the x register when it is already at zero seems to increment it, but as this is not part of the PIO specification there is a small danger that this behavior might change. Once the loop has completed, the 4-bit count is transferred to the ISR and the next bit starts. Notice that it is assumed that auto-push is set so that the FIFO is automatically added to when the ISR is full.

We have to repeat the process for the checksum:

```
        set y,7
check:
        wait 1 pin 0
        set x, 0
loop3:
        jmp x--,continue2
continue2: jmp pin,loop3
        in x,4
        jmp y--,check
jmp again
```

Notice that if the MicroPython program hasn't read the FIFO then this blocks and waits for free space. Finally, we jump back to the start of the PIO program to wait for the MicroPython program to write to the FIFO.

The MicroPython program to make all this work is fairly straightforward, but it involves a lot of bit manipulation to convert the counts into bits:

```
    def getByte(self):
        count = self.sm.get()
        byte = 0
        for i in range(8):
            byte = byte << 1
            if ((count >> i * 4) & 0x0F) > 8:
                byte = byte | 1
        return byte
```

This reads a word from the PIO and converts it into a byte by comparing each 4-bit count with a threshold, i.e. 8. We also need to set the shift direction to a right shift to keep the bits the correct order.

Using this function we can obtain the five bytes needed to compute the humidity, temperature and checksum as per the previous program. This makes it very easy to convert the DHT22 class to use the PIO program.

The complete program, dht22pio.py, to read a DHT22 is:

```python
import rp2
from machine import Pin

@rp2.asm_pio(set_init=rp2.PIO.OUT_LOW, autopush=True,
                        in_shiftdir=rp2.PIO.SHIFT_RIGHT)
def dht22():
    wrap_target()
    label("again")
    pull(block)
    set(pins, 0)
    mov(x, osr)
    label("loop1")
    jmp(x_dec, "loop1")
    set(pindirs, 0)

    wait(1, pin, 0)
    wait(0, pin, 0)
    wait(1, pin, 0)
    wait(0, pin, 0)

    set(y, 31)
    label("bits")
    wait(1, pin, 0)
    set(x, 0)
    label("loop2")
    jmp(x_dec, "continue")
    label("continue")
    jmp(pin, "loop2")
    in_(x, 4)
    jmp(y_dec, "bits")

    set(y, 7)
    label("check")
    wait(1, pin, 0)
    set(x, 0)
    label("loop3")
    jmp(x_dec, "continue2")
    label("continue2")
    jmp(pin, "loop3")
    in_(x, 4)
    jmp(y_dec, "check")
    wrap()
```

```
class DHT22():
    def __init__(self, gpio):
        self.sm = rp2.StateMachine(0, dht22,
                        freq=976562, in_base=Pin(gpio),
                        set_base=Pin(gpio), jmp_pin=Pin(gpio))
        self.sm.active(1)

    def getByte(self):
        count = self.sm.get()
        byte = 0
        for i in range(8):
            byte = byte << 1
            if ((count >> i * 4) & 0x0F) > 8:
                byte = byte | 1
        return byte

    def getReading(self):
        self.sm.put(1000)
        byte1 = self.getByte()
        byte2 = self.getByte()
        byte3 = self.getByte()
        byte4 = self.getByte()
        checksum = self.getByte()
        self.checksum =
                    (checksum == (byte1+byte2+byte3+byte4) & 0xFF)
        self.humidity = ((byte1 << 8) | byte2) / 10.0
        neg = byte3 & 0x80
        byte3 = byte3 & 0x7F
        self.temperature = (byte3 << 8 | byte4) / 10.0
        if neg > 0:
            self.temperature = -self.temperature


dht = DHT22(2)
dht.getReading()
print("Checksum", dht.checksum)
print("Humidity= ", dht.humidity)
print("Temperature=", dht.temperature)
```

The initialization is the only function of additional interest as most of the
rest of the program follows the previous example. It sets the clock
frequency so that instructions take $1\mu s$. This gives a count in the region of 4
to 13 and the threshold is set accordingly. At this clock speed, you also need
to set the x register to 1000 to get the 1ms initialization pulse. It also sets the
auto-push to 32 bits and a right shift. Notice that, as well as the SET and IN
groups, you have to set the jump pin to the GPIO line being used or the
counting loop doesn't work.

DHT22 Using the PIO – Sampling

A simpler alternative way for decoding the data is to ignore the fact that it is the width of each bit's frame that defines a zero, a short frame, or a one a long frame, and notice that if you sample at a suitable fixed time from the rising edge of a pulse then you will get a zero in a zero frame and a one in a one frame:

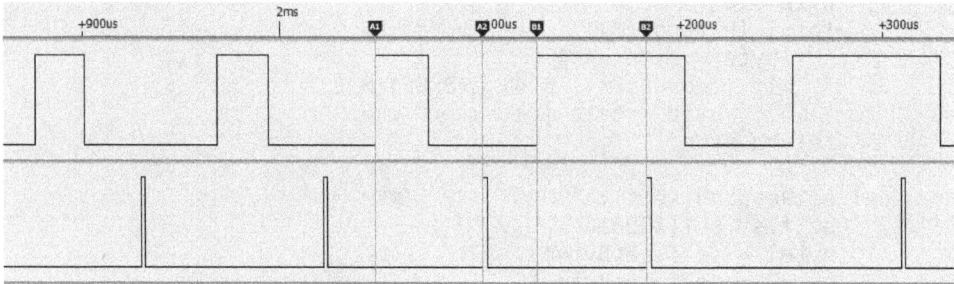

You can see the sampling times from the pulses on the lower trace of the logic analyzer and the fact that you do indeed get a 0 in a zero frame and a 1 in a one frame. You can also see that the time to sample from the rising edge is constant, even if the sampling period varies.

Surprisingly, the PIO program to implement this sampling isn't significantly simpler than the previous program, but the entire four data bytes can now be packed into a single FIFO entry and the checksum byte can occupy a second entry.

The PIO program starts off in the same way:

```
.program dht
    set pins, 1
    set pindirs, 1
again:
  pull block
  set pins, 0
mov x, osr
loop1:
    jmp x--,loop1
set pindirs, 0
wait 1 pin 0
wait 0 pin 0
wait 1 pin 0
wait 0 pin 0
```

The waits' position is at the state of the data and now we can wait for a rising edge and then delay until the sample time:

```
set y,31
bits:
   wait 1 pin 0 [25]
    in pins,1
    wait 0 pin 0
 jmp y--,bits
```

This too is very similar, only now we don't keep a count but simply add the single bit sampled from the input line to the ISR. When all 32 bits have been added, the autopush moves the data to the FIFO.

The eight checksum bits are just as easy to process and the complete PIO program is:

```
.program dht
 set pins, 1
 set pindirs, 1
again:
 pull block
 set pins, 0
mov x, osr
loop1:
 jmp x--,loop1
set pindirs, 0
wait 1 pin 0
wait 0 pin 0
wait 1 pin 0
wait 0 pin 0

set y,31
bits:
 wait 1 pin 0 [25]
 in pins,1
 wait 0 pin 0
 jmp y--,bits

 set y,7
check:
wait 1 pin 0 [25]
 in pins,1
 wait 0 pin 0
 jmp y--,check
push block
jmp again
```

Notice that we have to manually push the ISR because it doesn't fill up with just the eight bytes of the checksum.

The MicroPython program is also very like the previous program, but we have to change the clock frequency and the shift direction to make decoding the bytes from the 32-bit word easier.

We need a slower clock speed to make the delay position the sample point about $50\mu s$ from the rising edge – recall that the delay is limited to 32 clock cycles.

The getReading method now might as well read the FIFO and decode the data directly as it is a much simpler task:

```
def getReading(self):
    self.sm.put(500)
    data=0
    data = self.sm.get()
    byte1 = (data >> 24 & 0xFF)
    byte2 = (data >> 16 & 0xFF)
    byte3 = (data >> 8 & 0xFF)
    byte4 = (data & 0xFF)
    checksum = self.sm.get() & 0xFF
```

Notice the need to change the value sent to the input to account for the slower clock rate – 500 now produces a 1ms initialization pulse. The rest of the program is unchanged as we now have the four data bytes and the checksum as before. The revised program. dht22pio2.py, is simpler to implement and can be extended to a protocol that needs to read in more than 40 bits at a time.

Complete Listing

dht22pio2.py

```
import rp2
from machine import Pin

@rp2.asm_pio(set_init=(rp2.PIO.OUT_LOW,rp2.PIO.OUT_LOW),
             autopush=True, in_shiftdir=rp2.PIO.SHIFT_LEFT)
def dht22():
    wrap_target()
    label("again")
    pull(block)
    set(pins, 0)
    mov(x, osr)
    label("loop1")
    jmp(x_dec, "loop1")
    set(pindirs, 0)
    wait(1, pin, 0)
    wait(0, pin, 0)
    wait(1, pin, 0)
    wait(0, pin, 0)
```

```
    set(y, 31)
      label("bits")
      wait(1, pin, 0) [25]
      in_(pins, 1)
      wait(0, pin, 0)
      jmp(y_dec, "bits")

      set(y, 7)
      label("check")
      wait(1, pin, 0)[25]
      set(pins,2)
      set(pins,0)
      in_(pins, 1)
      wait(0, pin, 0)
      jmp(y_dec, "check")
      push(block)
      wrap()


class DHT22():
    def __init__(self, gpio):
        self.sm = rp2.StateMachine(0, dht22, freq=490196,
                in_base=Pin(gpio), set_base=Pin(gpio),
                                        jmp_pin=Pin(gpio))
        self.sm.active(1)

    def getReading(self):
        self.sm.put(500)
        data=0
        data = self.sm.get()
        byte1 = (data >> 24 & 0xFF)
        byte2 = (data >> 16 & 0xFF)
        byte3 = (data >> 8 & 0xFF)
        byte4 = (data & 0xFF)
        checksum = self.sm.get() & 0xFF
        self.checksum =
            (checksum == (byte1+byte2+byte3+byte4) & 0xFF)
        self.humidity = ((byte1 << 8) | byte2) / 10.0
        neg = byte3 & 0x80
        byte3 = byte3 & 0x7F
        self.temperature = (byte3 << 8 | byte4) / 10.0
        if neg > 0:
            self.temperature = -self.temperature


dht = DHT22(2)
dht.getReading()
print("Checksum", dht.checksum)
print("Humidity= ", dht.humidity)
print("Temperature=", dht.temperature)
```

Summary

- The DHT22 is a low-cost temperature and humidity sensor.

- It uses a custom single wire bus which is not compatible with the 1-Wire bus.

- Its asynchronous protocol is easy to implement directly in user space.

- A very simple checksum is used to detect errors.

- It is possible to implement the protocol as defined in the datasheet using a PIO by using counting loops to time each pulse.

- A better use of the PIO is to notice that the protocol can be decoded by testing the state of the line a fixed time after the rising edge.

Chapter 15
The 1-Wire Bus And The DS1820

The 1-Wire bus is a proprietary bus that is very easy to use and has a lot of useful devices you can connect to it, including the iButton security devices, memory, data loggers, fuel gauges and more. However, probably the most popular of all 1-Wire devices is the DS18B20 temperature sensor - it is small, cheap and very easy to use. This chapter shows you how to work with it, but first let's deal with the general techniques needed to work with the 1-Wire bus.

Programming in MicroPython on the Pico only just has enough speed to implement a bit-banging driver, which, even so, is enough for many purposes. There is a standard One Wire Driver which uses bit banging to make communicating with any 1-Wire device easy. As it is a very popular 1-Wire device, there is also a specific DS12S20 driver. Using the drivers, working with the 1-Wire bus is made easy, but it is still worth knowing how it works in case you need to work with a device that doesn't work well with the driver. Here we will look at how to implement the 1-Wire protocol from scratch and show how the driver does the same job. Armed with the knowledge of how the 1-Wire bus protocol works we next implement a PIO-based program which has the advantage of not making use of the CPU.

The Hardware

One-wire devices are very simple and only use a single wire to transmit data:

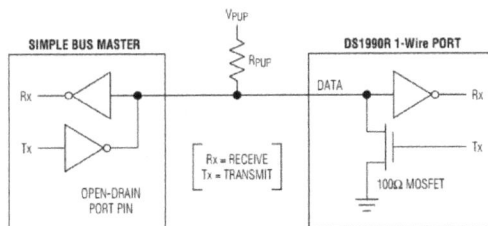

The 1-Wire device can pull the bus low using its Tx line and can read the line using its Rx line. The reason for the pull-up resistor is that both the bus master and the slave can pull the bus low and it will stay low until they both release the bus.

The device can even be powered from the bus line by drawing sufficient current through the pull-up resistor - so called parasitic mode. Low power devices work well in parasitic mode, but some devices have such a heavy current draw that the master has to provide a way to connect them to the power line - so called strong pull-up. In practice, parasitic mode can be difficult to make work reliably for high-power devices.

In normal-powered mode there are just three connections – V usually 3.3V for the Pico, Ground and Data:

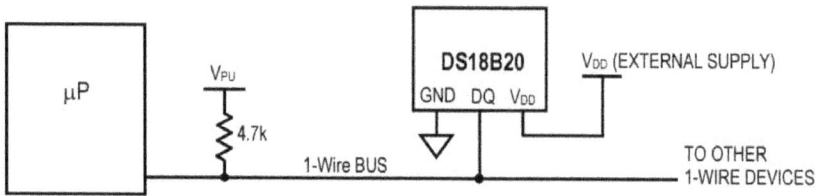

The pull-up resistor varies according to the device, but anything from 2.2K to $4.7k\Omega$ works. The longer the bus, the lower the pull-up resistor has to be to reduce "ringing". There can be multiple devices on the bus and each one has a unique 64-bit lasered ROM code, which can be used as an address to select the active devices.

For simplicity, it is better to start off with a single device and avoid the problem of enumerating the devices on the bus, although once you know how everything works this isn't difficult to implement. To get started, select a 1-wire device that you want to work with and set it up ready to talk to the Pico, in this case the DS18B20 is explained. The functions described in this chapter should work with any 1-wire device.

Initialization

Every transaction with a 1-wire device starts with an initialization handshake. First we have to work out how to configure the GPIO line. This example assumes that the 1-wire device is connected to GPIO 22.

You might think that we have to initialize the GPIO line so that it works in pull-up mode. This isn't necessary and the default push-pull mode will do. The reason is that, in the case of the 1-wire bus, the master controls when other devices send their data. Typically the master sends a pulse and then the slaves respond by pulling the line low. As long as the master doesn't drive the line during the period when the slaves are responding, everything is fine.

What we do in practice is to configure the GPIO line for output only when the master needs to drive the line. Once the master is finished the GPIO line is set back to input and the pull-up resistor is allowed to pull the line back up. After this, any slave wanting to send data is free to pull the line low.

The first transaction we need is the initialization pulse. This is simply a low pulse that lasts at least 480μs, a pause of 15μs to 60μs follows and then any and all of the devices on the bus pull the line low for 60μs to 240μs.

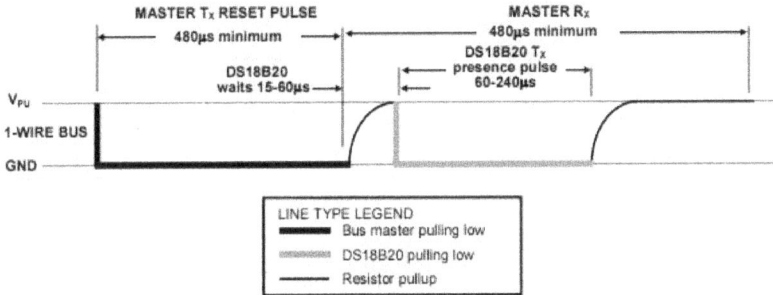

The suggested timings are: set the line low for 480μs and read the line after 70μs followed by a pause of 410μs.

This is fairly easy to implement as a function:

```
def presence(pin):
    pin.init(mode=Pin.OUT)
    pin.high()
    sleep_ms(1)
    pin.low()
    sleep_us(480)
    pin.init(mode=Pin.IN)
    sleep_us(70)
    b = pin.value()
    sleep_us(410)
    return b
```

We pull the line low for 480μs and then let it be pulled back up by changing the line to input, i.e. high impedance. After a 70μs wait, which is right at the start of the guaranteed period when the line should be low if there is an active device on the bus, we read the input line and then wait another 410μs to complete the data slot.

The timings in this case are not critical as long as the line is read while it is held low by the slaves, which is never less than 60μs and is typically as much as 100μs.

If there is a device, the function should return a 0 and if there are no devices it should return a 1.

```
pin=Pin(2,Pin.OUT)
pin.high()
if presence(pin) == 1:
    print("No device")
else:
    print("Device present")
```

If you try this partial program and have a logic analyzer with a 1-wire protocol analyzer you will see something like:

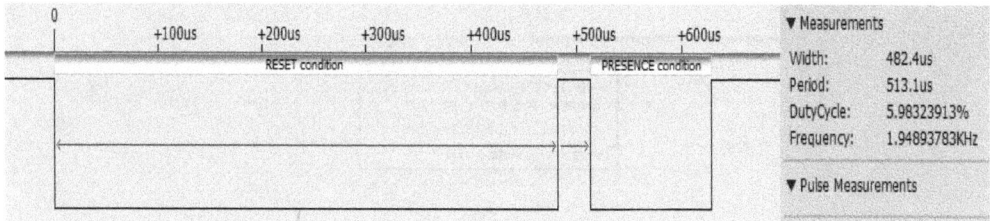

Seeing a presence pulse is the simplest and quickest way to be sure that your hardware is working.

Using The Driver

The One-Wire driver has a reset method which pulls the line low for $520\mu s$ and returns True if there is a device connected to the bus. Using the driver the previous program can be written:

```
from machine import Pin
import onewire
ow = onewire.OneWire(Pin(2))
presence=ow.reset()
if presence:
    print("Device present")
else:
    print("No device")
```

To use the driver all you have to do is create a OneWire instance and you can specify any pin to use. After this you simply call methods to communicate with the device.

Writing Bits

Our next task is to implement the sending of some data bits to the device. The 1-Wire bus has a very simple data protocol. All bits are sent using a minimum of $60\mu s$ for a read/write slot. Each slot must be separated from the next by a minimum of $1\mu s$.

248

The good news is that timing is only critical within each slot. You can send the first bit in a slot and then take your time before you send the next bit as the device will wait for you. This means you only have to worry about timing within the functions that read and write individual bits.

To send a 0 you have to hold the line low for most of the slot. To send a 1 you have to hold the line low for just between 1μs and 15μs and leave the line high for the rest of the slot. The exact timings can be seen below:

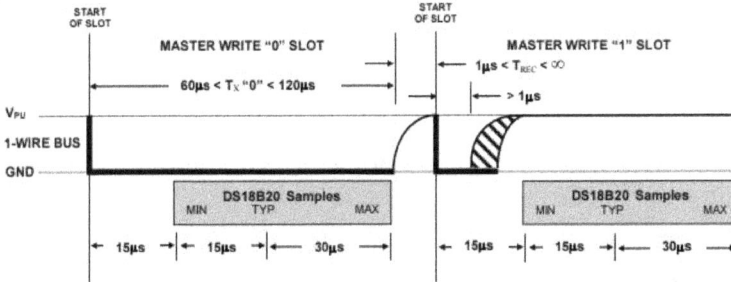

It seems reasonable to use the typical timings given in the datasheets. So for a 0 we hold the line low for 60μs then let it go high for the remainder of the slot, 10μs. To send a 1 we hold the line for 6μs and then let it go high for the remainder of the slot, 64μs. As the only time critical operations are the actual setting of the line low and then back to high, there is no need to worry too much about the speed of operation of the entire function so we might as well combine writing 0 and 1 into a single writeBit function. The problem is that these timings are very close to what is possible using MicroPython. To get the necessary speed and accuracy we need to use busy wait for loops for the timing and, while the function does just work without, it benefits from using native compilation:

```
@micropython.native
def writeBit(pin,b):
    if b == 1:
        delay1 = 1
        delay2 = 30
    else:
        delay1 = 30
        delay2 = 0
    pin.low()
    for i in range(delay1):
        pass
    pin.high()
    for i in range(delay2):
        pass
```

The code at the start of the function simply increases the time between slots slightly. To avoid having to set the line's output mode between each bit, it is assumed that any function that uses writeBit sets the line to OUT before calling it and to IN after calling it. This allows the line to be pulled high, ready for any response from the slave after a set of bits has been sent.

You can see two zeros followed by two ones in the following logic analyzer trace:

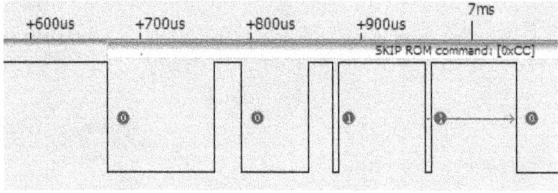

The pulse for a 1 at 6μs is just short enough to work. If the function is not compiled to native code then it is closer to 12μs and, while it tends to work, it is more prone to error.

Writing With The Driver

The One-Wire driver has a `writebit` method which does the same job as our function but using 12μs for a 1 and 61μs for a 0 with a slot time of just over 100μs. For example:

```
from machine import Pin
import onewire
ow = onewire.OneWire(Pin(2))
presence=ow.reset()
if presence:
    print("Device present")
else:
    print("No device")
ow.writebit(1)
ow.writebit(0)
ow.writebit(1)
ow.writebit(1)
```

This writes 1011:

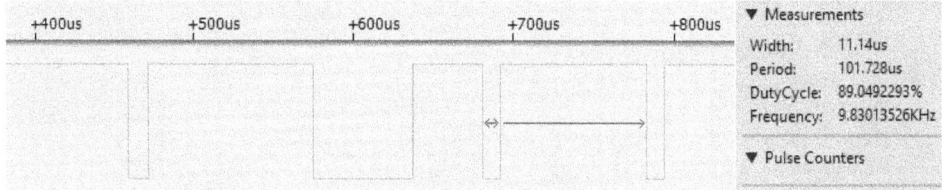

A First Command - Writing Bytes

After discovering that there is at least one device connected to the bus, the master has to issue a ROM command. In many cases the ROM command used first will be the Search ROM command, which enumerates the 64-bit codes of all of the devices on the bus. After collecting all of these codes, the master can use Match ROM commands with a specific 64-bit code to select the device the master wants to talk to.

While it is perfectly possible to implement the Search ROM procedure, it is simpler to work with the single device by using commands which ignore the 64-bit code and address all of the devices on the bus at the same time. Of course, this only works as long as there is only one device on the bus. If there is only one device then we can use the Skip ROM command 0xCC to tell all the devices on the bus to be active.

We now need a function that can send a byte. As we have a writeBit function this is easy:

```
def sendskip(pin):
        writeBit(pin, 0)
        writeBit(pin, 0)
        writeBit(pin, 1)
        writeBit(pin, 1)
        writeBit(pin, 0)
        writeBit(pin, 0)
        writeBit(pin, 1)
        writeBit(pin, 1)
```

Notice that 0xCC is 1100 1100 in binary and the 1-Wire bus sends the least significant bit first. If you try this out you should find it works, but the device doesn't respond because it is waiting for another command. Again, as the time between writing bits isn't critical, we can take this first implementation of the function and write something more general, if slightly slower.

The writeByte function will write the low eight bits of an int to the device:

```
def writeByte(pin, byte):
    pin.init(mode=Pin.OUT)
    for i in range(8):
        writeBit(pin, byte & 1)
        byte = byte >> 1
    pin.init(mode=Pin.IN)
```

Using this we can send a Skip ROM command using:

```
writeByte(2, 0xCC)
```

You can see the pattern of bits sent on a logic analyzer:

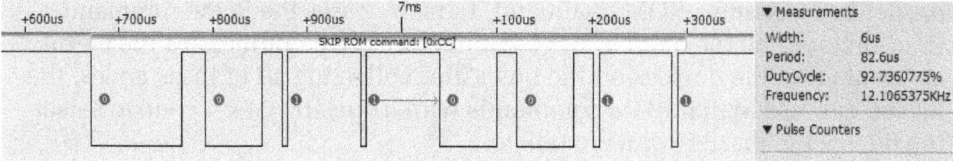

Writing Bytes With the Driver

The driver has two write byte methods:

```
def writebyte(value)
def write(buf)
```

The first will write a single byte to the device. The second will write a sequence of bytes in buf which is a bytes object.

For example, to write the Skip ROM command, 0xCC, we can use:

```
from machine import Pin
import onewire

ow = onewire.OneWire(Pin(2))
presence=ow.reset()
if presence:
    print("Device present")
else:
    print("No device")
ow.writebyte(0xCC)
```

You can send a set of bytes using write. For example to send two Skip ROM commands:

```
b=bytearray([0xCC,0xCC])
ow.write(b)
```

252

Reading Bits

We already know how the master sends a 1 and a 0. The protocol for the slave device is exactly the same except that the master still provides the slot's starting pulse. That is, the master starts a 60μs slot by pulling the bus down for at least 1μs. Then the slave device either holds the line down for a further 15μs minimum or it simply allows the line to float high. See below for the exact timings:

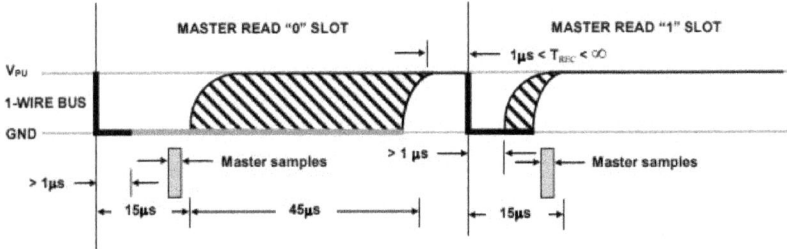

So all we have to do to read bits is to pull the line down for more than 1μs and then sample the bus after pausing long enough for the line to be pulled up or held low. The datasheet gives 6μs for the master's pulse and a 9μs pause. In practice, even native code is only just fast enough as the time to change from output to input is quite high and we need to read the input line at once to avoid missing the data:

```python
@micropython.native
def readBit(pin):
    pin.init(mode=Pin.OUT)
    pin.low()
    pin.high()
    pin.init(mode=Pin.IN)
    b = pin.value()
    sleep_us(60)
    return b
```

A logic analyzer shows the typical pattern of bits from the device:

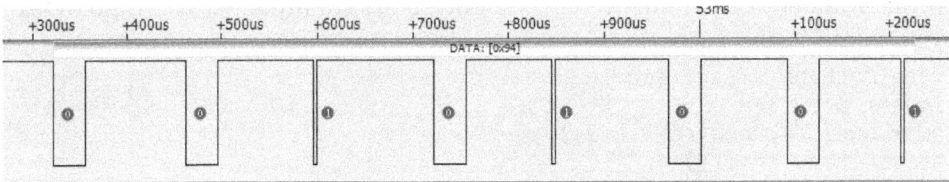

By adding some commands to toggle a line after the sample is taken, we can see how the timing works:

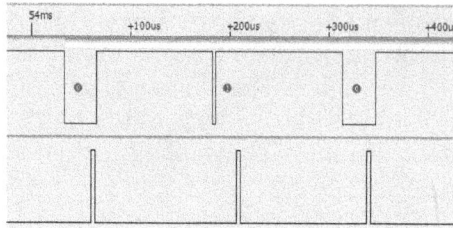

The reading is taken just before the indicator pulse on the lower trace. You can see that it is within the timing window to read a zero or a one correctly, but it would benefit from being closer to the down going edge.

Finally, we need a function that will read a byte. As in the case of writing a byte, there is no time criticality in the time between reading bits, so we don't need to take extra special care in constructing the function:

```
def readByte(pin):
    byte = 0
    for i in range(8):
        byte = byte | readBit(pin) << i
    return byte
```

The only difficult part is to remember that the 1-Wire bus sends the least significant bit first and so this has to be shifted into the result from the right.

Reading Using The Driver

The One-Wire Driver supports three read methods:

- readbit()
- readbyte()
- readinto(buf)

The first two return an integer corresponding to the bit or byte read. The third method reads bytes into a byte object buffer. The number of bytes read is the number of elements in the byte object. For example, to read nine bytes you would use:

```
from machine import Pin
import onewire
ow = onewire.OneWire(Pin(2))
presence=ow.reset()
if presence:
    print("Device present")
else:
    print("No device")
buf = bytearray(9)
ow.readinto(buf)
```

Working With 1-Wire Devices

So far the discussion has been about how to implement the 1-wire protocol without any particular device in mind. In practice 1-wire devices follow a fairly standard sequence of instructions.

The sequence is:

- Test to see if a device is present:
    `presence(uint8_t pin)`
- Write a byte command:
    `writeByte(pin, byte)`
- Read a given number of bytes:
    `readByte(pin)`

These functions and their driver equivalents will be used in the rest of the chapter to work with real 1-wire devices.

These are not the only functions we need to work with the 1-Wire bus. We need to be able to compute the CRC error checks that are commonly used to confirm that data has been transmitted correctly and we need to perform a ROM search to discover what devices are connected to the bus, but this is beyond the scope of this introduction. For details of a C implementation, see *Raspberry Pi IOT in C, 3rd Ed*, ISBN:9781871962840.

Computing the CRC

We have already encountered the idea and implementation of a CRC (Cyclic Redundancy Checksum) in Chapter 12. The 1-Wire bus uses the same CRC for all its devices and therefore we need to implement it just once. This is perhaps not in the most efficient way, but it will work. For low data rate applications high efficiency isn't needed and you can make use of a direct implementation. The 1-Wire datasheet specifies the CRC used in 1-wire devices as a shift register rather than as a polynomial equation:

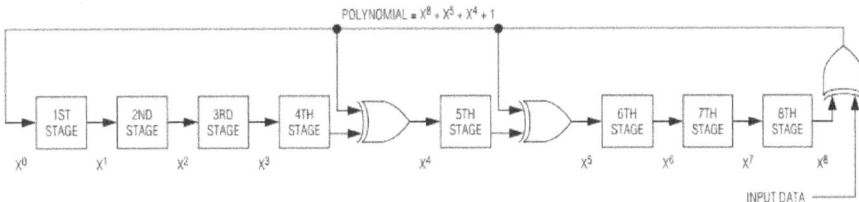

POLYNOMIAL = $X^8 + X^5 + X^4 + 1$

| 1ST STAGE | 2ND STAGE | 3RD STAGE | 4TH STAGE | | 5TH STAGE | | 6TH STAGE | 7TH STAGE | 8TH STAGE |

X^0 X^1 X^2 X^3 X^4 X^5 X^6 X^7 X^8

INPUT DATA

However, this is equivalent to a generator polynomial that defines the CRC as it is simply the hardware implementation of the calculation.

In this case it is:

$X^8 + X^5 + X^4 + 1$

The first question to answer is, what is the connection between binary values, polynomials and shift-registers? The answer is that you can treat a binary number as the coefficients of a polynomial, for example 101 is $1*X^2+0*X+1$. Each bit position corresponds to a power of X. Using this notation creates a very simple relationship between multiplying by X and a left-shift.

For example:

$(1*X^2 + 0*X + 1)*X = 1*X^3 + 0*X^2 + 1X + 0$

corresponds to:

101 <<1 == 1010

You can see that this extends to multiplying one polynomial by another and even polynomial division, all accomplished by shifting and XOR (eXclusive OR).

The CRC is the remainder when you divide the polynomial that represents the data by the generator polynomial. The computation of the remainder is what the shift register specified on the datasheet does. The fact that the division can be implemented so simply in hardware is what makes this sort of CRC computation so common. All the hardware has to do is zero the shift register and feed the data into it. When all the data has been shifted in, what is left in the shift register is the CRC, i.e. the remainder.

To check the data you have received, all you have to do is run it through the shift register again and compare the computed CRC with the one received. A better trick is also to run the received CRC through the shift register. If there have been no errors, this will result in 0.

You can look into the theory of CRCs, bit sequences and polynomials further, it is interesting and practically useful, but we now know everything we need to if we want to implement the CRC used by1-Wire devices. All we have to do is implement the shift register in software.

From the diagram, what we have to do is take each bit of the input data and XOR it with the least significant bit of the current shift register. If the input bit is 0, the XORs in the shift register don't have any effect and the CRC just has to be moved one bit to the right. If the input bit is 1, we have to XOR the bits at positions 3 and 4 with 1 and put a 1 in at position 7 to simulate shifting a 1 into the register, i.e. XOR the shift register with 10001100.
So the algorithm for a single byte is:

```
for j in range(8):
    temp = (crc ^ databyte) & 0x01
    crc >>= 1
    if temp:
        crc ^= 0x8C
    databyte >>= 1
return crc
```

First we XOR the data with the current CRC and extract the low-order bit into `temp`. Then we right-shift the CRC by one place. If the low-order result stored in temp was a 1, we have to XOR the CRC with `0x8C` to simulate the XORs in the shift register and shift in a 1 at the most significant bit. Then shift the data one place right and repeat for the next data bit.

With this worked out, we can now write a `crc8` function that computes the CRC for the entire eight bytes of data:

```
def crc8(data,len):
    crc = 0
    for i in range(len):
        databyte = data[i]
        for j in range(8):
            temp = (crc ^ databyte) & 0x01
            crc >>= 1
            if temp:
                crc ^= 0x8C
            databyte >>= 1
    return crc
```

With this in place we can now check the CRC of any data a 1-Wire bus device sends us.

There is also a CRC method in the One-Wire Driver. It isn't often used, but it is flexible. If you call it with a buffer of bytes it will compute the CRC for those bytes and return it as the result. For example:

```
print(ow.crc8(buf))
```

displays the CRC for the bytes in the buffer.

Notice that if you compute the CRC for a set of bytes with the correct CRC appended the result is always zero. You can use this as an easy test for an error.

The DS18B20 Hardware

Now let's put all of this to work with the most popular 1-Wire device, the DS18B20. It is available in a number of formats, but the most common makes it look just like a standard BJT (Bipolar Junction Transistor) which can sometimes be a problem when you are trying to find one. You can also get them made up into waterproof sensors complete with cable.

No matter how packaged, they will work at 3.3V or 5V.

The basic specification of the DS18B20 is:

- Measures temperatures from -55°C to +125°C (-67°F to +257°F)
- ±0.5°C accuracy from -10°C to +85°C
- Thermometer resolution is user-selectable from 9 to 12 bits
- Converts temperature to 12-bit digital word in 750ms (max)

It can also be powered from the data line, allowing the bus to operate with only two wires - data and ground. However, this "parasitic power" mode is difficult to make work reliably and best avoided in an initial design.

There are also the original DS1820 and the DS18S20, which are best avoided in new applications.

To supply it with enough power during a conversion, the host has to connect it directly to the data line by providing a "strong pull-up" - essentially a transistor. In normal-powered mode there are just three connections:

Ground needs to be connected to the system ground, VDD to 3.3V and DQ to the pull-up resistor of an open collector bus.

While you can have multiple devices on the same bus, for simplicity it is better to start off with a single device until you know that everything is working.

You can build the circuit in a variety of ways. You can solder the resistor to the temperature sensor and then use some longer wires with clips to connect to the Pico. You could also solder directly to the Pico or use a prototyping board. The diagram below shows it connected to GPIO 2.

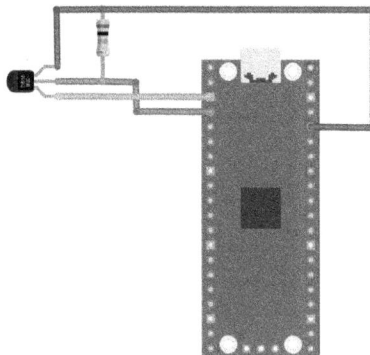

The DS18B20 Driver

MicroPython supports a driver specifically for this 1-wire device and if you simply want to read the temperature this is by far the easiest way to do the job. The only complication is that the driver assumes that you could have multiple devices connected to the bus. To use the driver you have to first create a OneWire driver object which sets the pin that the devices are connected to.

Next you have to create a ds18x20 object which works with any DS18B20 or DS18S20 devices connected to the bus. To find out what devices are connected you first have to use the scan method which returns a roms object for each of the devices as a list. To make a temperature measurement you have to issue a convert_temp command which causes all of the connected devices to perform the measurement. Finally you use the roms object to read the temperature from each of the devices, for example, ds18b20.py:

```
from machine import Pin
import onewire,ds18x20
ow = onewire.OneWire(Pin(2))
presence = ow.reset()
if presence:
    print("Device present")
else:
    print("No device")

DS = ds18x20.DS18X20(ow)
roms = DS.scan()
DS.convert_temp()

print(DS.read_temp(roms[0]))
```

You can see how this program works. After setting up the 1-wire bus, the DS18X20 object is created. The scan of the bus returns a list of devices and then we initiate a conversion and read the temperature of the first, and often only, device. Notice that you only take a new temperature reading when you use the convert_temp method.

There are some additional methods that provide access to more advanced functions of the DS18B20 and these are discussed at the end of the chapter.

As already said, if you just want to read the temperature the driver is all you need. However, if you want to know how the 1-wire bus works and use other 1-wire devices read on.

Reading the DS18X20 Directly

As already described, every transaction with a 1-wire device starts with an initialization handshake. The master holds the bus low for at least $480\mu s$, a pause of $15\mu s$ to $60\mu s$ follows, and then any and all of the devices on the bus pull the line low for $60\mu s$ to $240\mu s$.

For this we need the `presence` function given earlier:

```
if presence(2) == 1:
    print("No device \n")
read temperature
    ...
```

After discovering that there is at least one device connected to the bus, the master has to issue a ROM command. In many cases the ROM command used first will be the Search ROM command, which enumerates the 64-bit codes of all of the devices on the bus. After collecting all of these codes, the master can use Match ROM commands with a specific 64-bit code to select the device the master wants to talk to.

Having to find and use the ROM codes is often a nuisance and is unnecessary if you only have a single device of a known type connected to the bus. If there is only one device then we can use the Skip ROM command, `0xCC`, to tell all the devices, i.e. the only device, on the bus to be active. The only problem is that the DS18X20 driver doesn't support the Skip ROM command and always needs the ROM code to read the temperature. However, it is a worthwhile exercise to create another class that will read a single device and it also demonstrates how to read the temperature.

The steps to read the temperature from the only DS18B20 connected to the bus are:

1. Send a Reset
2. Send a Skip ROM, `0xCC`, command
3. Send a Convert, `0x44`, command
4. Wait for the temperature to be ready to read
5. Send a Read Scratchpad, `0xBE`, command and then read the nine bytes that the device returns

The Convert command, `0x44`, starts the DS18B20 making a temperature measurement. Depending on the resolution selected, this can take as long as 750ms. How the device tells the master that the measurement has completed depends on the mode in which it is operating, but using an external power line, i.e. not using parasitic mode, the device sends a `0` bit in response to a bit read until it is completed, when it sends a `1`.

This is how 1-Wire devices that need time to get data ready slow down the master until they are ready. The master can read a single bit as often as it likes and the slave will respond with a 0 until it is ready with the data.

As we already have a `readBit` function this is easy. The software polls for the completion by reading the bus until it gets a 1 bit:

```
def convert(pin):
    writeByte(pin, 0x44)
    for i in range(500):
        sleep_ms(10)
        if readBit(pin) == 1:
            j=i
            break
```

You can of course test the return value to check that the result has been obtained. If `convert` returns 500 then the loop has timed out. When the function returns normally, the new temperature measurement is stored in the device's scratchpad memory and all we have to do is read it.

The scratchpad memory has nine bytes of storage in total and does things like control the accuracy of conversion and provide status information.

SCRATCHPAD

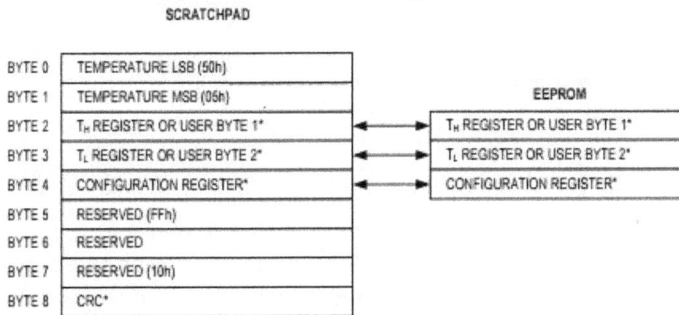

In our simple example the only two bytes of any great interest are the first two, which hold the result of a temperature conversion. However, as we are going to check the CRC for error detection, we need to read all nine bytes.

All we have to do is issue a Read Scratchpad, 0xBE, command and then read the nine bytes that the device returns. To send the new command we have to issue a new initialization pulse and a Skip ROM, 0xCC, command followed by a Read Scratchpad command, 0xBE:

```
presence(pin)
writeByte(pin, 0xCC)
writeByte(pin, 0xBE)
```

Now the data is ready to read. We can read all nine bytes of it or just the first two that we are interested in. The device will keep track of which bytes have been read. If you come back later and read more bytes you will continue the read from where you left off. If you issue another initialization pulse then the device aborts the data transmission.

As we do want to check the CRC for errors, we will read all nine bytes:

```
data = []
for i in range(9):
    data.append(readByte(pin))
```

Now we have all of the data stored in the scratchpad and the CRC byte, we can check for errors:

```
print(crc8(data,9))
```

As before, the value returned will be 0 if there are no transmission errors. The crc8 function was given earlier, see Computing the CRC.

To obtain the temperature measurement we need to work with the first two bytes, which are the least and most significant bytes of the 12-bit temperature reading:

```
t1 = data[0]
t2 = data[1]
```

t1 holds the low-order bits and t2 the high-order bits.

All we now have to do is to put the two bytes together as a 16-bit two's complement integer. We can do this very easily:

```
temp1 = (t2 << 8 | t1)
```

As this is a 32-bit integer, you will have to propagate the sign bit manually into the high order bits to get a negative number:

```
if t2 & 0x80:
    temp1=temp1 | 0xFFFF0000
```

Finally, we have to convert the temperature to a scaled value. As the returned data gives the temperature in centigrade with the low-order four bits giving the fractional part, it has to be scaled by a factor of 1/16:

```
temp=temp1/16
print(temp)
```

Complete Program

The complete program, ds18b20bit.py, to read and display the temperature making use of the previous functions to implement a DS18D20 class, is:

```
from utime import sleep_ms, sleep_us
from machine import Pin
from time import sleep

class DS18B20:

    def __init__(self,pin):
        self.pin=Pin(pin,mode = Pin.IN)
        self.pin.high()
```

```python
def presence(self):
    self.pin.init(mode=Pin.OUT)
    self.pin.high()
    sleep_ms(1)
    self.pin.low()
    sleep_us(480)
    self.pin.init(mode = Pin.IN)
    sleep_us(70)
    b = self.pin.value()
    sleep_us(410)
    return b

@micropython.native
def writeBit(self,b):
    if b == 1:
        delay1 = 1
        delay2 = 30
    else:
        delay1 = 30
        delay2 = 0
    self.pin.low()
    for i in range(delay1):
        pass
    self.pin.high()
    for i in range(delay2):
        pass

def writeByte(self,byte):
    self.pin.init(mode = Pin.OUT)
    for i in range(8):
        self.writeBit(byte & 1)
        byte = byte >> 1
    self.pin.init(mode = Pin.IN)

@micropython.native
def readBit(self):
    self.pin.init(mode=Pin.OUT)
    self.pin.low()
    self.pin.high()
    self.pin.init(mode=Pin.IN)
    b = self.pin.value()
    sleep_us(60)
    return b

def readByte(self):
    byte = 0
    for i in range(8):
        byte = byte | self.readBit() << i
    return byte
```

```python
    def convert(self):
        self.writeByte(0x44)
        for i in range(500):
            sleep_ms(10)
            if self.readBit() == 1:
                j=i
                break
        return j

    def crc8(self,data,len):
        crc = 0
        for i in range(len):
            databyte = data[i]
            for j in range(8):
                temp = (crc ^ databyte) & 0x01
                crc >>= 1
                if temp:
                    crc ^= 0x8C
                databyte >>= 1
        return crc

    def getTemp(self):
        if self.presence()==1:
            return -1000
        self.writeByte(0xCC)
        if self.convert()==500:
            return -3000
        self.presence()
        self.writeByte( 0xCC)
        self.writeByte( 0xBE)
        data=[]
        for i in range(9):
            data.append(self.readByte())
        if self.crc8(data,9)!=0:
            return -2000
        t1 = data[0]
        t2 = data[1]
        temp1 = (t2 << 8 | t1)
        if t2 & 0x80:
            temp1=temp1 | 0xFFFF0000
        return temp1/16

dS18B20=DS18B20(2)
if dS18B20.presence() == 1:
    print("No device")
else:
    print("Device present")

print(dS18B20.getTemp())
```

Notice that the `getTemp` method returns -1000 if there is no device, -2000 if there is a CRC error and -3000 if the device fails to provide data. These values are outside the range of temperatures that can be measured.

Driver Version

It is trivial to use the general One-Wire driver to implement a DS18B20 program using the Skip Rom command which the DS18B20 driver doesn't support:

```
from utime import sleep_ms
from machine import Pin
import onewire

class DS18B20:
    def __init__(self,pin):
        self.ow = onewire.OneWire(Pin(pin))

    def convert(self):
        self.ow.writebyte(0x44)
        for i in range(500):
            sleep_ms(10)
            if self.ow.readbit() == 1:
                j = i
                break
        return j

    def getTemp(self):
        if not self.ow.reset:
            return -1000
        self.ow.writebyte(0xCC)
        if self.convert() == 500:
            return -3000
        self.ow.reset()
        self.ow.writebyte(0xCC)
        self.ow.writebyte(0xBE)
        data=bytearray(9)
        self.ow.readinto(data)
        if self.ow.crc8(data)!=0:
            return -2000
        t1 = data[0]
        t2 = data[1]
        temp1 = (t2 << 8 | t1)
        if t2 & 0x80:
            temp1=temp1 | 0xFFFF0000
        return temp1/16

dS18B20=DS18B20(2)
print(dS18B20.getTemp())
```

265

A PIO DS18B20 Program

Implementing the 1-Wire protocol using a PIO is one of the most difficult tasks we tackle. It needs to both send and receive data and the master has to provide the start pulse for the slave to send data. The specification also makes it seem that we have to use a conditional to vary the timing of the data part of the pulse depending on sending a one or a zero. This is a lot of logic to fit into 32 instructions. In addition a 1-Wire device can send far more data than the FIFO can hold. At first appraisal the idea of implementing the 1-Wire protocol in a PIO program seems hopeless, but with a shift in emphasis it can be made easier. Given the fact that the big-banging interface to the 1-Wire bus is operating on the edge of what is possible, this makes it all the more worthwhile to implement a fast PIO-based program.

The main operations that you need to work with a 1-Wire device is to send a set of bytes and receive a set of bytes. In general, the timing requirements of the 1-Wire bus are at the bit level. That is, when you read data the device will generally store the data until you are ready for it. This means that if you can implement a byte read/write in the PIO then the main program can get on with something else while the 1-Wire device processes data. If the main program is interrupted then no harm is done as it can expect the PIO to continue to process the next byte ready for when it returns.

What all of this implies is that all we really have to do is implement a bit send and bit receive facility. Using the way that 1-Wire protocol is usually described, this would be very difficult. In other words, trying to implement the simple-minded bit-banging protocol as a PIO program isn't going to work. A slightly different interpretation of the protocol, however, makes it very possible. If you think of each bit frame as starting with a short low pulse which signals the start of the frame, then a zero sends a low after the initial pulse and a one sends a high. In other words, we can implement the write protocol as:

1) Send short "start bit" of about $6\mu s$

2) Send the data bit for the rest of the frame – about $60\mu s$

3) Set the line high for $10\mu s$ as a spacer between bit frames

The read protocol is much the same:

1) Send short "start bit" of about $6\mu s$

2) After about $9\mu s$ sample the line and use this as the read bit

3) Do nothing for about $55\mu s$ as a spacer between bit frames

In this form the protocol doesn't need conditionals as the sending of a zero or a one and the receiving of a zero or a one follows the same steps.

Using this version you could simplify the logic of the bit-banging example given earlier, but there is no real need to as there is plenty of space and computational power – using a PIO is a very different matter and regularity in the implementation of a protocol is important.

There is also the problem of how to implement the PIO program so that the MicroPython program can make use of it. One possibility is to use one state machine for send and another to receive, but it is possible to create a single program to do both jobs.

The PIO program starts off with a presence pulse and, as this is long compared to the clock time, we use a loop set by the MicroPython program. As you generally don't need a presence pulse when reading data from a device, we can use a zero value to indicate that the operation is a read, not a write. That is, you use the program by pushing data onto the FIFO – the first byte starts the program off and if it is zero it starts a read operation and otherwise starts a write operation with its value setting the length of the initialization pulse:

```
.program DS1820
.wrap_target
again:
        pull block
        mov x, osr
        jmp !x, read
write: set pindirs, 1
        set pins, 0
loop1:
        jmp x--,loop1
        set pindirs, 0 [31]
        wait 1 pin 0 [31]
```

Once the write part of the code gets started, the non-zero value passed in via the FIFO is used to create a long, 500μs, low pulse which the slave responds to with a 120μs low presence plus. The final instruction waits for the end of the pulse so that we can start to send some data.

The second byte pushed onto the FIFO gives the number of bytes to send and these are pushed onto the stack to follow.

Notice that if there are more than four or five then the program might stall until the FIFO has space.

```
        pull block
        mov x, osr
bytes1:
        pull block
        set y, 7
        set pindirs, 1
bit1:
                set pins, 0 [1]
                out pins,1 [31]
                set pins, 1 [20]
                jmp y--,bit1
        jmp x--,bytes1

        set pindirs, 0 [31]
        jmp again
```

You can see that the inner loop starting at bit1 takes the data byte in the OSR and sends it out to the GPIO line, a bit at a time. The first instruction in the loop generates the short start pulse and the second instruction sets the line high or low for 32 clock cycles. The final instruction in the loop provides the space between the bit frames. The loop repeats until all eight bits have been sent when the outer loop gets another byte to send, if there is one. If not, the program restarts and waits for the next set of data.

The read part of the program is very similar to the write:

```
read:
        pull block
        mov x, osr
bytes2:
        set y, 7
        bit2:
                set pindirs, 1
                set pins, 0 [1]
                set pindirs, 0 [5]
                in pins,1 [10]
        jmp y--,bit2
jmp x--,bytes2
.wrap
```

In this case the only data we need from the FIFO is the number of bytes to read. This is stored in the X register and controls the number of bytes processed. The inner loop, starting at bit2, reads each bit in turn. The first three instructions change the line to output, send the short start pulse and sets the line back to input. The in instruction samples the line after a short delay and gets the data which is auto-pushed onto the FIFO ready for the MicroPython program to read. Notice that if the MicroPython program fails to read the data then the loop stalls, which is fine as long as the 1-Wire device can live with a pause which the DS18B20 can.

The entire program is 29 instructions, which does leave space for instructions to toggle another GPIO line for debugging purposes. It is very probable that it can be made shorter by the use of setside operations.

Next we move on to the MicroPython program. We first need an initialize things using the state machine constructor:

```
sm = rp2.StateMachine(0,DS1820,freq = 490196, set_base = Pin(2),
                          out_base = Pin(2),in_base = Pin(2),
                          out_shiftdir = rp2.PIO.SHIFT_RIGHT,
                              in_shiftdir = rp2.PIO.SHIFT_RIGHT)
sm.active(1)
```

The frequency is selected to allow the pulse times to be implemented using delays from 1 to 31.

The PIO program is fairly general in that you could use it to talk to almost any 1-Wire device, but we are interested in the DS18B20 and it is easy enough to implement a function to read the temperature along the lines of the previous function:

```
def getTemperature(sm):
```

First we send an initialization pulse, followed by a Skip ROM and a Convert command. The first item sets a write operation with an initialization pulse:

```
    sm.put(250)
    sm.put(1)
    sm.put(0xCC)
    sm.put(0x44)
```

Next we should wait until the conversion is complete, but for simplicity we wait for 1 second, after which time the conversion is either complete or the device is broken. Then we send another initialization pulse, a Skip ROM and a Read ScratchPad command:

```
    sleep_ms(1000)
    sm.put(250)
    sm.put(1)
    sm.put(0xCC)
    sm.put(0xBE)
```

Finally we send a read command for nine bytes of data:

```
    sm.put( 0)
    sm.put( 8)
```

and read the nine bytes from the FIFO:

```
    data=[]
    for i in range(9):
        data.append(sm.get() >> 24)
    return data
```

Now we have the same nine bytes of data as in the bit-banging example, ds18b20bit.py, and the rest of the program is identical.

A better idea is to create two functions which read and write an array of bytes to the device:

```
def writeBytes(sm, bytes, len):
    sm.put(250)
    sm.put(len-1)
    for i in range(len):
        sm.put(bytes[i])

def readBytes(sm,len):
    sm.put(0)
    sm.put(len-1)
    bytes=[]
    for i in range(len):
        bytes.append(sm.get() >> 24)
    return bytes
```

Using these two functions, the interaction with the 1-Wire device starts to look a lot like using the SPI or I2C bus. For example, the readTemperature function becomes:

```
def getTemperature(sm):
    writeBytes(sm,[0xCC,0x44],2)
    sleep_ms(1000)
    writeBytes(sm,[0xCC,0xBE],2)
    data =  readBytes(sm,9)
    return data
```

As you can see this is now just a set of calls to general read/write functions. Notice that, rather than test for the data to be ready, we simply wait for 1000ms.

This is about as complex a PIO program as you can implement. This raises the question of what to do if you need something more complex? You might think that using additional state machines would help, but you are still limited to 32 instructions in total. There are two possible practical solutions. You can use immediately executed instructions put directly into the state machine from the MicroPython program. This works for small tasks such as initialization. The second solution is more generally useful. If you can split your program into two small modules, each no more than 32 instructions, then you can load one into one PIO and another into the second PIO. This, of course, occupies both PIOs and you can't use a PIO for another task. For example, you could use one PIO to send data to a 1-Wire bus device and the other to receive data. This approach is limited to just two modules, so a total of 64 instructions. You can extend this idea to any number of modules if they can be reloaded into the same PIO. For example, by splitting the 1-Wire code into a receive and a send module you could easily afford the time to load each module and set it up in the same PIO.

The current program can only work with a single device on the 1-Wire bus. If you want to support more, you could implement the search algorithm outlined in Chapter 15 of *Raspberry Pi IOT in C, Third Edition,* though this is complex. A simpler solution is to use one state machine and one GPIO line per device. This can support up to eight different 1-Wire devices.

Complete Program

Of course, things are much easier to use when packaged as a class. The complete program listed below, ds18b20pio.py, is a version of ds18b20bit.py, the program that used bit-banging to implement a DS18B20, but now using the PIO:

```
import rp2
from machine import Pin
from utime import sleep_ms

@rp2.asm_pio(set_init=rp2.PIO.OUT_HIGH,
    out_init = rp2.PIO.OUT_HIGH, autopush = True, push_thresh = 8)
def DS1820():
    wrap_target()
    label("again")
    pull(block)
    mov(x, osr)
    jmp(not_x, "read")
    label("write")
    set(pindirs, 1)
    set(pins,0)
    label("loop1")
    jmp(x_dec,"loop1")
    set(pindirs, 2) [31]
    wait(1, pin, 0) [31]

    pull(block)
    mov(x, osr)
    label("bytes1")
    pull(block)
    set(y, 7)
    set(pindirs, 3)
    label("bit1")
    set(pins, 0) [1]
    out(pins,1) [31]
    set(pins, 1) [20]
    jmp(y_dec,"bit1")
    jmp(x_dec,"bytes1")
    set(pindirs, 0) [31]
    jmp("again")
```

```
        label("read")
        pull(block)
        mov(x, osr)
        label("bytes2")
        set(y, 7)
        label("bit2")
        set(pindirs, 1)
        set(pins, 0) [1]
        set(pindirs, 0) [5]
        in_(pins,1) [10]
        jmp(y_dec,"bit2")
        jmp(x_dec,"bytes2")
        wrap()

class DS18B20:
    def __init__(self,pin):
        self.sm = rp2.StateMachine(0,DS1820,freq = 490196,
            set_base = Pin(2),out_base = Pin(2),
             in_base = Pin(2),out_shiftdir = rp2.PIO.SHIFT_RIGHT,
                               in_shiftdir = rp2.PIO.SHIFT_RIGHT)
        self.sm.active(1)

    def writeBytes(self, bytes, len):
        self.sm.put(250)
        self.sm.put(len-1)
        for i in range(len):
            self.sm.put(bytes[i])

    def readBytes(self,len):
        self.sm.put(0)
        self.sm.put(len-1)
        bytes = []
        for i in range(len):
            bytes.append(self.sm.get() >> 24)
        return bytes

    def getTemp(self):
        self.writeBytes([0xCC,0x44],2)
        sleep_ms(1000)
        self.writeBytes([0xCC,0xBE],2)
        data = self.readBytes(9)
        t1 = data[0]
        t2 = data[1]
        temp1 = (t2 << 8 | t1)
        if t2 & 0x80:
            temp1=temp1 | 0xFFFF0000
        return temp1/16
dS18B20=DS18B20(2)
print(dS18B20.getTemp())
```

Other Commands

As well as the commands that we have used to read the temperature, the DS18B20 supports a range of other commands. There are two commands concerned with when there are more devices on the bus. Search ROM, 0xF0, is used to scan the bus to discover what devices are connected and Match ROM, 0x55, is used to select a particular device.

You can also read the unique 64-bit code of a device using the Read ROM command, 0x33. In this case, the slave transmits eight bytes, comprised of a single-byte device family code, 0x28 for the DS18B20, six bytes of serial number and a single CRC byte.

The One-Wire driver supports a scan method which performs a Search ROM and returns a list with one byte array for each ROM found containing its unique id code.

```
ow = onewire.OneWire(Pin(22))
print(ow.scan())
```

Notice that the first byte of the id identifies the type of the device. For example, a DS18B20 starts with 0x10.

There is also a select_rom method which will select a device according to its id. This uses a Match ROM command to select the device and following this all data transfer is between the selected device and the controller until the next reset. For example:

```
ow = onewire.OneWire(Pin(22))
ids = ow.scan()
ow.select_rom(ids[0])
```

selects the first device returned by the scan.

The DS18X20 driver has a specific scan method which only returns the ids of DS18X20 devices.

As well as the Read ScratchPad command that we used to read the temperature, there is also a Write ScratchPad command, 0x4E.

The format of the scratchpad is:

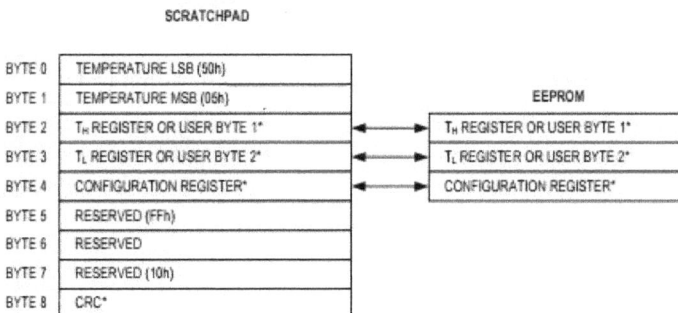

SCRATCHPAD

		EEPROM
BYTE 0	TEMPERATURE LSB (50h)	
BYTE 1	TEMPERATURE MSB (05h)	
BYTE 2	T_H REGISTER OR USER BYTE 1*	T_H REGISTER OR USER BYTE 1*
BYTE 3	T_L REGISTER OR USER BYTE 2*	T_L REGISTER OR USER BYTE 2*
BYTE 4	CONFIGURATION REGISTER*	CONFIGURATION REGISTER*
BYTE 5	RESERVED (FFh)	
BYTE 6	RESERVED	
BYTE 7	RESERVED (10h)	
BYTE 8	CRC*	

The first two bytes are the temperature that we have already used. The only writable entries are bytes 2, 3 and 4. The Write ScratchPad command transfers three bytes to these locations. Notice that there is no CRC and no error response if there is a transmission error. The datasheet suggests that you read the scratchpad after writing it to check that you have been successful in setting the three bytes.

The third byte written to the scratchpad is to the configuration register:

BIT 7	BIT 6	BIT 5	BIT 4	BIT 3	BIT 2	BIT 1	BIT 0
0	R1	R0	1	1	1	1	1

Essentially the only thing you can change is the resolution of the temperature measurement.

Configuration Register	Resolution	Time
0x1F	9 bits	93ms
0x3F	10 bits	175ms
0x5F	11 bits	375ms
0x7F	12 bits	750ms

The time quoted is the maximum for a conversion at the given precision. You can see that the only real advantage of decreasing precision is to make conversion faster. The default is 0x7F and 12 bits of precision.

The DS18X20 has a read_scratch method which returns a byte array of the scratchpad data of the specified device. For example:

```
from machine import Pin
import onewire,ds18x20
ow = onewire.OneWire(Pin(22))
presence = ow.reset()
DS = ds18x20.DS18X20(ow)
roms = DS.scan()
print(DS.read_scratch(roms[0]))
```

This prints the scratchpad for the first device returned by the scan. For example:

```
bytearray(b'\xe9\x00\x7f\x80\x7f\xff\x07\x10~')
```

in which the third byte gives the resolution as 12 bits.

You can use the write_scratch(id) to write three bytes to the scratchpad.

The first two bytes of the write scratchpad set a high and low temperature alarm. This feature isn't much used, but you can set two temperatures that will trigger the device into alarm mode. Notice you only set the top eight bits of the threshold temperatures. This is easy enough, but the alarm status is set with every read so if the temperature goes outside the set bounds and then back in the alarm is cleared.

274

The second problem is that, to discover which devices are in alarm mode, you have to use the Alarm Search command, 0xEC. This works like the Search ROM command, but the only devices that respond are the ones with an alarm state. The alarm feature might be useful if you have a lot of devices and simply want to detect an out-of-band temperature. You could set up multiple devices with appropriate temperature limits and then simply repeatedly scan the bus for devices with alarms set.

You may notice that the scratchpad also has an EEPROM memory connected. You can transfer the three bytes of the scratchpad to the EEPROM using Copy Scratchpad, 0x48, and transfer them back using the Recall EEPROM command, 0xB8. You can use this to make the settings non-volatile.

Finally there is the Read Power Supply command, 0xB4. If the master reads the bus after issuing this command a 0 indicates that there are parasitic powered devices on the bus. If there are such devices the master has to run the bus in such a way that they are powered correctly.

The drivers don't support any of these extended commands but they are easy enough to implement yourself using the basic read/write methods.

If you want to know how the scan function is implemented, and it is very clever, the description of the algorithm in Chapter 15 of *Raspberry Pi IoT in C, 3rd Ed*, ISBN:978-1871962840, will allow you to implement your own version.

Summary

- The 1-Wire bus is a proprietary but widely-used bus. It is simple and very capable.

- As its name suggests, it makes use of a single data wire and usually a power supply and ground. It is possible to dispense with the power line and the connected device will draw power from the data line.

- MicroPython provides a One-Wire driver which works with all 1-Wire devices.

- Implementing the 1-Wire protocol is mostly a matter of getting the timing right.

- There are three types of interaction: presence pulse, read and write. The presence pulse simply asks any connected devices to reply and make themselves known.

- The 1-Wire protocol is easier to implement than you might think because each bit is sent as a "slot" and, while timing is critical within the slot, how fast slots are sent isn't and the master is in control of when this happens.

- The DS18B20 temperature sensor is one of the most commonly encountered 1-Wire bus devices. It is small, low-cost and you can use multiple devices on a single bus.

- MicroPython provides a simple DS18X20 driver, but it is also easy to implement your own driver.

- After a convert command is sent to the device, it can take 750ms before a reading is ready.

- To test for data ready you have to poll on a single bit. Reading a zero means data not ready and reading a one means data ready.

- When the data is ready, you can read the scratchpad memory where the data is stored.

- The DS18B20 has other commands that can be used to set temperature alarms etc, but these are rarely used.

- With a shift in viewpoint, it is just possible to squeeze a 1-Wire bus protocol into a 32-instruction PIO program.

Chapter 16

The Serial Port

The serial port is one of the oldest of ways of connecting devices together, but it is still very useful as it provides a reasonably fast communication channel that can be used over a longer distance than most other connections such as USB. Today, however, its most common and important use is in making connections with small computers and simple peripherals. It can also be used as a custom signal decoder, see later.

Serial Protocol

The serial protocol is very simple. It has to be because it was invented in the days when it was generated using electro-mechanical components, motors and the like. It was invented to make early teletype machines work and hence you will often find abbreviations such as TTY used in connection with it. As the electronic device used to work with serial is called a Universal Asynchronous Receiver/Transmitter, the term UART is also often used.

The earliest standards are V24 and RS232. Notice, however, that early serial communications worked between plus and minus 24V and later ones ±12V. Today's serial communications work at logic, or TTL, levels of 0V to 5V or 0V to 3.3V. This voltage difference is a problem we will return to later. What matters is that, irrespective of the voltage, the protocol is always the same.

For the moment let's concentrate on the protocol. As already mentioned, the protocol is simple. The line rests high and represents a zero. When the device starts to transmit it first pulls the line low to generate a start bit. The width of this start bit sets the transmission speed - all bits are the same width as the start bit. After the start bit there are a variable number, usually seven or eight, data bits, an optional single parity bit, and finally one or two stop bits.

Originally the purpose of the start bit was to allow the motors etc to get started and allow the receiving end to perform any timing corrections. The stop bits were similarly there to give time for the motors to come back to their rest position. In the early days the protocol was used at very slow speeds; 300 baud, i.e. roughly 300 bits per second, was considered fast enough.

Today the protocol is much the same, but there is little need for multiple stop bits and communication is often so reliable that parity bits are dispensed with. Transmission speeds are also higher, typically 9600 or 115200 baud.

To specify what exact protocol is in use, you will often encounter a short form notation. For example, 9600 baud, 8 data bits, no parity, one stop bit, will be written as 9600 8n1. Here you can see the letter 0 (01101111 or 0x6F) transmitted using 8n1:

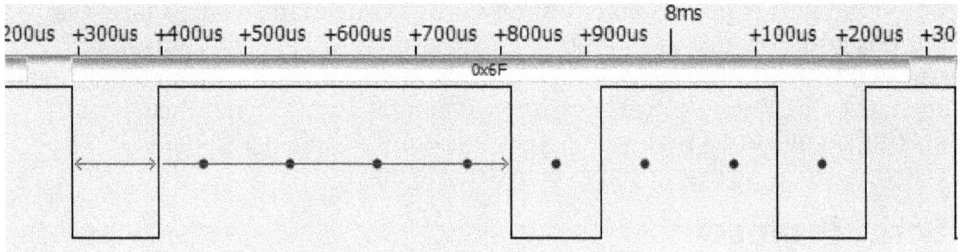

Notice that the signal is sent least significant bit first. The first low is the start bit, then the eight dots show the ideal sampling positions for the receiver. The basic decoding algorithm for receiving serial data is to detect the start of the start bit and then sample the line at the center of each bit time. Notice that the final high on the right is the stop bit.

Notice also that the sampling points can be put to use on custom protocols. As long as the data is transmitted in fixed time "cells" indicated by a start bit, you can use a serial port to read individual bits.

For a serial connection to work, it is essential that the transmitter and the receiver are set to the same speed, data bits and parity. Serial interfaces most often fail because they are not working with the same settings.

A logic analyzer with a serial decoder option is an essential piece of equipment if you are going to do anything complicated with serial interfacing.

What is a baud? Baud rate refers to the basic bit time. That is, 300 baud has a start bit that is 1/300s wide. This means that for 9600 baud a bit is 1/9600 wide or roughly $104\mu s$ and at 115200 baud a bit is 1/115200 or roughly $8.6\mu s$. Notice that baud rate doesn't equate to speed of sending data because of the overhead in stop, start and perhaps parity bits to include in the calculation.

UART Hardware

A simple serial interface has a transmit pin, TX, and a receive pin, RX. That is, a full serial interface uses two wires for two-way communications. Typically you connect the TX pin on one device to the RX pin on the other and vice versa. The only problem is that some manufacturers label the pins by what they should be connected to not what they are and then you have to connect RX to RX and TX to TX. You generally need to check with a scope, logic probe or meter which pin is which if you are in any doubt.

In addition to the TX and RX pins, a full serial interface also has a lot of control lines. Most of these were designed to help with old fashioned teleprinters and they are not often used. For example, RTS - Request To Send is a line that is used to ask permission to send data from the device at the other end of the connection, CTS - Clear To Send is a line that indicates that it is okay to send data and so on. Usually these are set by the hardware automatically when the receive buffer is full or empty.

You can use RTS and CTS as a hardware flow control. There is also a standard software flow control involving sending XON and XOFF characters to start and stop the transmission of data. For most connections between modern devices you can ignore these additional lines and just send and receive data. If you need to interface to something that implements a complex serial interface you are going to have to look up the details and hand-craft a program to interact with it.

The Pico has two UARTs which can be used in addition to the USB interface. Both UARTs support buffered (32-character) and unbuffered modes and RTS/CTS hardware flow control. The UARTs can be connected to a group of four GPIO pins:

UART0			
TX	GPIO 0	GPIO 12	GPIO 16	GPIO 28
RX	GPIO 1	GPIO 13	GPIO 17	GPIO 29
CTS	GPIO 2	GPIO 14	GPIO 18	
RTS	GPIO 3	GPIO 15	GPIO 19	

UART1			
TX	GPIO 4	GPIO 8	GPIO 20	GPIO 24
RX	GPIO 5	GPIO 9	GPIO 21	GPIO 25
CTS	GPIO 6	GPIO 10	GPIO 22	GPIO 26
RTS	GPIO 7	GPIO 11	GPIO 23	GPIO 27

You can select any combination of pins and if you don't want to use the RTS/CTS lines they can be used for some other purpose. At the moment MicroPython doesn't support the use of RTS/CTS.

There is a problem with making the connection to the Pico's RX and TX pins in that devices work at different voltages. PC-based serial ports usually use +13V to -13V and all RS232-compliant ports use a + to - voltage swing, which is completely incompatible with most microprocessors which work at 5V or 3.3V.

If you want to connect the Pico to a PC or other standard device then you need to use a TTL-to-RS232 level converter. In this case it is easier to use the PC's USB port as a serial interface with a USB-to-TTL level converter. All you have to do is plug the USB port into the PC, install a driver and start to transmit data.

Remember when you connect the Pico to another device that TX goes to the other device's RX and RX goes to the other device's TX pin. Also remember that the signaling voltage is 0V to 3.3V.

Setting Up the UART

To create a UART object you use its constructor which at its most basic is:

```
uart = UART(id=, baudrate=, bits=, parity=, stop=,
                                tx=, rx=, timeout= )
```

There are some more advanced parameters which are described in detail later.

The id has to be 0, 1 or 2 depending on the UART you want to use.

bits specifies the number of bits per character - 7, 8 or 9.

parity can be any of:

    None   = none
    0   = even
    1   = odd

stop can be 1 or 2 depending on the number of stop bits to be used.

The tx and rx pins are specified as numbers not as Pin objects.

The timeout specifies, in milliseconds, how long read methods will wait for data.

There is also an init method which takes the same parameters as the constructor and can be used to modify how the existing UART instance is configured.

When you have finished with the UART you can release it using

```
UART.deinit()
```

Data Transfer

After you have set up the UART you can start sending and receiving data using methods. There are three general-purpose read functions:

```
read(nbytes)
readinto(buf,nbytes)
readline()
```

In the first two methods data is stored in a byte array. In `readline` bytes are read in until a newline character is encountered and a string is returned.

The `readinto` method is slightly more flexible. If you don't specify the number of bytes to read then the number read is determined by the size of the buffer, i.e. a buffer's worth of data is read in. If you specify the number of bytes less than the size of the buffer then only that number of bytes are read. The function also returns the number of bytes read.

There is a single write method:

```
write(buf)
```

this writes the number of bytes in the bytearray `buf` and returns the number of bytes written.

These methods are more difficult to use than you might expect. The problem is that they don't allow a timeout to be specified and this is often essential in a UART-based protocol. In addition, the functions work with the FIFO and will block if there is no data to read or space to write in the FIFO buffer. If there is no external device to send or read data, this means that any of the read or write functions could hang the machine indefinitely.

Also notice that in practice the `nbytes` parameter in `read` and `readinto` is optional, but if you don't specify the number of bytes then the method will hang forever trying to gather data.

If you connect GPIO 4 to GPIO 5 we can use these pins to perform some loopback tests that demonstrate some of the problems, `loopback.py`:

```
from machine import UART,Pin
from utime import sleep_ms

uart = UART(1,baudrate=9600,bits=8,parity=2,rx=Pin(5),tx=Pin(4))
SendData = bytearray("Hello World \n","utf-8")
uart.write(SendData)
RecData = uart.read()
print(RecData)
```

Notice that we are using UART1 because UART0 is the alternative REPL port for MicroPython. However it isn't used very often so feel free to use it if UART1 isn't suitable for some reason.

If you try this out you will find that it doesn't work – it displays None rather than the message. The reason is that the write method stores the data in a buffer and returns almost at once and the data is sent by the UART later which at 9600 baud takes around 13.5ms. The problem is that the read tries to read the data even before the first character has arrived.

This is another example of input being harder than output. To send data via a serial port you simply write the data to the buffer and wait while it is sent. To read data from a serial port you need to know when to read it.

There are a number of ways around this problem and which one you use depends on the agreed protocol between the transmitter and the receiver. As the UART has buffers it is ready to receive data at any time without the intervention of a MicroPython program and as long as the buffer doesn't fill up you can delay reading until you are ready to process the data. You might think that given the transmitted data only takes 13.5ms, we only need a delay that long to get the data. Adding time.sleep_ms(12) between the write and the read and the program works and you will see the message.

Instead of inserting an estimated delay we can arrange to poll for the data.

Serial Polling

The key method in implementing UART polling is any(), which returns 0 if there are no characters in the RX buffer and the number of characters that are waiting in the buffer otherwise.

It is easy to see that you can use this function to write polling loops which test to see if there is anything to read. For example, to create a blocking read:

```
def uart_read(uart):
    while uart.any() == 0:
        pass
    return uart.read()
```

The advantage this offers is that you can do other work within the while loop and check that reading hasn't been waiting too long. That is, you can easily extend it to include a timeout. However, there are still problems with this blocking function. It waits for data to be ready to read, but how can you know that all of the data that you are expecting has been read?

There are three general solutions to this problem:

1. Work in fixed sized blocks – that is, everything that is exchanged between transmitter and receiver has the same number of bytes. If you want to send something smaller then you need to pad the block with null bytes. Of course, this only works if you can identify a code to use as a null byte.

2. Use a terminator such as a line feed or a carriage return – this is what the readline method is for. Again you have to have a suitable code to use as a terminator.

3. Rely on timing to tell you when a transmission is complete. This is typically how interactions with users take place if they are not line-oriented. The algorithm is – wait till the first character arrives, keep waiting for additional characters until an inter-byte timeout is up. The idea is that a transmission is a continuous flow of bytes separated by a maximum time interval.

Buffers

If you read the specifications for the Pico's UART you will discover that it has a 32-byte FIFO hardware buffer. MicroPython then adds a variable sized software buffer which feeds the hardware buffer with data as required.

The write method is effectively non-blocking if there is space in the software buffer for it to write its data and return. If the buffer is full the write method blocks and waits for space to become free.

Notice that data written is transmitted out at a steady rate determined by the baud rate, irrespective of whether there is anything receiving that data – i.e. by default there is no flow control. What this means is that the TX buffer is filled at the rate that the program can submit data and the TX FIFO buffer empties at the baud rate, which is much slower.

For the RX buffers things are the other way round – the FIFO buffer fills at the baud rate and is transferred to the buffer at a much higher rate.

Clearly in any given situation the size of the buffers matters. The UART constructor and init method both allow rxbuf= and txbuf= parameters to set the size of the software buffer.

This all sounds complicated, but it is easier to understand after a few extreme examples.

First consider what happens in buffer.py when the TX buffer is too small for the amount of data being sent, but the RX buffer is more than big enough:

```
from machine import UART,Pin, Timer
from utime import sleep_ms,sleep, time_ns
uart = UART(1,baudrate=1200,bits=8,parity=None,rx=Pin(5),tx=Pin(4),
                                      txbuf=256,rxbuf=16*1024)
test="A"*(257+32)
s = time_ns()
uart.write(test)
print((time_ns()-s)/1000000)
```

Notice that, to make the effect greater the baud rate is set low so that each character takes 8.33ms to transmit. If you send only 257+32 characters, one in the UART TX register, 256 in the software buffer and 32 in the hardware buffer, then the buffer just copes and the write takes less than 1ms, if you increase this to 258+32 characters then the `write` has to wait for the buffer to be free and takes around 11ms. Notice that the RX buffer is large enough to store all of the data sent and, as long as you leave a long enough delay before reading the data or arranging polling, then no data is lost. For example, if you send 1000 bytes:

```
test="A"*1000
```

the time to write goes up to 5928.ms and the time to send the data at 1200 baud is around 8 seconds. This is because the write returns as soon as it has written its last byte to the buffer, but the buffer still has around 250 bytes to send at this point. So if we wait around 8333ms all of the data should be in the receive buffer:

```
sleep_ms(8333)
RecData = uart.read()
print(RecData)
print(len(RecData))
```

and you will see all of the data printed.

Now consider what happens if the receive buffer is too small. If we arrange to send 1000 bytes with a large enough TX buffer then the write returns in about 0.68 ms and the data then takes just over a second to be transmitted. With an RX buffer of 512 bytes only 544 bytes are ever received:

```
from machine import UART,Pin, Timer
from utime import sleep_ms,sleep, time_ns
uart = UART(1,baudrate=1200,bits=8,parity=None,rx=Pin(5),tx=Pin(4),
                                    txbuf=16*1024,rxbuf=512)
test="A"*(1000)
s = time_ns()
uart.write(test)
print((time_ns()-s)/1000000)
sleep_ms(8333)
RecData = uart.read()
print(RecData)
print(len(RecData))
```

The extra 32 bytes are due to the hardware-provided 32-byte FIFO buffer.

This raises the question of which bytes are missing? A simple test program reveals that, once the RX buffers are full, incoming characters are silently ignored. That is, you lose all data received while the buffers are full.

If you want to avoid problems with serial data make sure that the RX buffer is large enough not to fill up, and read data from it often. The size of the TX buffer is less critical, but it can slow your program down.

Timeouts

From the previous section you should be able to see that the usual way that a transmitter and receiver interact is that the transmitter, after perhaps a longish silence, "decides" to send some data. This is usually sent as a block and, as long as the transmitter isn't overloaded, each character follows the next with minimum delay. This means that, from the receiver's point of view, there might be a long wait before being able to start reading data, but after that there should be only a short interval between each character. If the receiver finds itself waiting for a long time for the next character then the chances are the transmitter has finished sending a block of data.

Thus there are two sorts of "timeout" we need to specify. An initial timeout, which is how long to wait before the first character is received, and an inter-character timeout, which is the maximum time the receiver should wait between characters before concluding that in all probability the transmitter has finished.

You can specify the two types of timeout in the constructor and the init method using the timeout and timeout_char parameters, both specified in milliseconds. For example:

```
uart = UART(1,baudrate=9600,bits=8,parity=None,
                    rx=Pin(12),tx=Pin(13),
                              timeout=1,timeout_char=10)
```

waits 1ms for the first character to arrive and then 10ms for each subsequent character to arrive. The time to wait for the first character is usually set by a combination of how much time the receiver can devote to waiting in a polling loop and how often the transmitter sends data. The inter-character time is usually low if the transmitter manages to keep the RX FIFO topped up. It should be set to less than the characteristic time between data blocks from the transmitter.

Polling On Write

Writing data to the UART is much simpler than reading it. Data is written to the TX buffer as fast as it can be and the only thing that can go wrong is having to wait because the buffer is full. If the buffer is full then the call to the write method will block until there is space to accept all of the data. If your program has nothing else to do while the transmission is underway, there is no problem. If, however, your program has to service a polling loop doing a range of other things then it can be a big problem.

There is no MicroPython method to check on the status of the buffer. The best you can do is check to see if a transmission is in progress using the txdone method. This returns True if there is no data to be transmitted and

`False` otherwise. For example, you can use it to block until all of the data has been sent:

```
while(not uart.txdone()):
    pass
```

Notice that this waits for the buffer to be emptied after the write method. This isn't ideal as it returns `False` even when there is space in the buffer, but it is the best you can do. You can use it to test if the buffer is completely empty before trying to send data.

There is also the `flush` method which simply waits for all of the data to be sent, i.e. it blocks until the buffer is empty. This is usually far less useful.

Reading and Writing Characters and Strings

In the previous examples we have used a `bytearray` to read and write data. A more basic method of working is to read and write a single character at a time. While there are no easy-to-use UART methods to read and write a character, the functions:

```
def uart_putc(uart,char):
    uart.write(char[0])

def uart_getc(uart):
    char=uart.read(1)
    return char.decode("utf-8")
```

do the job. They are both blocking, but it is easy to convert them to non-blocking using the techniques in the previous section.

You can use the provided UART methods to send and receive simple strings. For example:

```
uart.write("Hello World \n")
print(uart.readline())
```

Notice that we need the newline character at the end of the string so that the `readline` method will return.

Flow Control

The problem of buffers filling up is usually dealt with by flow control, i.e. signaling whether or not it is okay to send more data. Hardware flow control is based on two control lines, Request To Sent (RTS) and Clear To Send (CTS). For the Pico RTS is an output and CTS is an input. Exactly how the RTS and CTS lines are actually used depends on what you are connecting to and what control lines it has. As already mentioned, a lot of the jargon and procedures involved have their origins back in the days of the mechanical teletype and the non-digital phone system. What matters today is to know that the RTS line is low when there is space in the Pico's RX FIFO buffer and high when it is full to a specified level – usually 80% or 90% of the buffer capacity. What this means is that the transmitter can use this to determine if it is "clear to send" data to the receiver. That is, if RTS is low, send data, if RTS is high, stop sending data. This is exactly what happens if you connect the RTS line to the CTS line. That is, if the CTS line is low the Pico will send any data in its TX FIFO buffer. If the CTS line is high, it will hold the data in the TX FIFO buffer.

What this means is if you have two Pico-like devices, traditionally referred to as DTE (Data Terminal Equipment), then you can connect them together to implement flow control on TX and RX using:

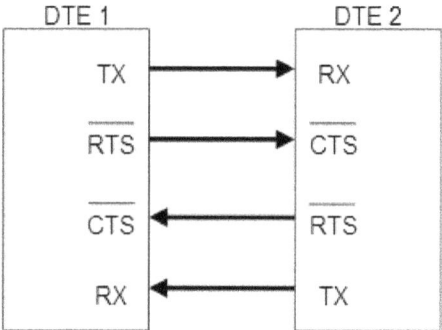

```
     DTE 1                    DTE 2
   ┌─────────┐             ┌─────────┐
   │   TX    │───────────▶ │   RX    │
   │         │             │         │
   │   RTS   │───────────▶ │   CTS   │
   │         │             │         │
   │   CTS   │◀─────────── │   RTS   │
   │         │             │         │
   │   RX    │◀─────────── │   TX    │
   └─────────┘             └─────────┘
```

The only complication is that some devices are regarded as DCE, Data Communication Equipment, which are always connected to a DTE and these have their RTS and CTS line labels swapped over. This allows the connections to be specified as "connect RTS to RTS and CTS to CTS". In practice, you need to make sure that RTS is an output connected to CTS, which is an input on the other device, or to RTS, which is an input on the other device.

To test flow control we can simply connect the RTS line on the Pico to the CTS line as the Pico is acting as DCE1 and DCE2. In the examples given below, it is assumed that GPIO 7 is RTS and GPIO 6 is CTS and they are connected together in loopback mode.

You can see that this is the case in the following example, `flow.py`:

```
from machine import UART,Pin, Timer
from utime import sleep_ms,sleep, time_ns
uart = UART(1,baudrate=9600,bits=8,parity=None,rx=Pin(5),tx=Pin(4)
            ,rts=Pin(7),cts=Pin(6), timeout=0,timeout_char=0,
                 txbuf=2000,rxbuf=128,flow=UART.RTS|UART.CTS)
test = "A"*1000
s = time_ns()
uart.write(test)
print((time_ns()-s)/1000000)
RecData = bytes()
while len(RecData)<1000:
    sleep_ms(500)
    if uart.any():
            RecData = RecData + uart.read()
            print(RecData)
            print(len(RecData))
```

This program sets up the UART to use flow control on GPIO 5 and GPIO 7. It then sends 1000 bytes and attempts to read them back in. The `while` loop reads new data until 1000 bytes have been received. It also contains a delay of 500ms which represents some data processing. Notice that we have set a TX buffer large enough to take all of the data to be transmitted. This is important because, in a loopback configuration, if the data could not be sent at once the program would stall at the write method, waiting forever for the Pico to read data.

You can see the pattern of start/stop transmission on the logic analyzer:

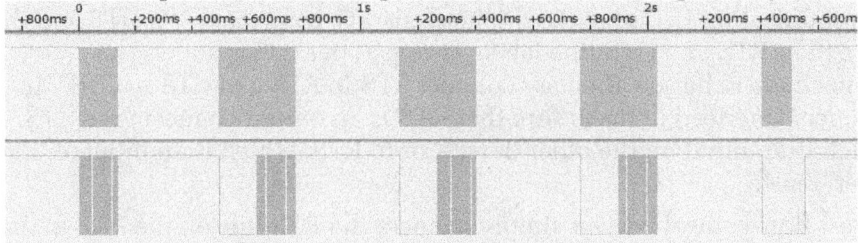

The top trace is the TX line and the bottom trace is the RTS line. You can see what happens.

If you set the `flow=0` parameter from the constructor and run the program again you will discover that the transmission occurs in one block and you do lose data as the RX buffer isn't large enough.

Finally, it is worth mentioning that there is a function, `sendbreak()`, that will send a break signal which corresponds to holding the TX line low for more than the time to transmit a single character. It isn't often used today, but there are serial-based protocols that use it to synchronize data transfer often along with flow control.

Using a UART to Decode Data

As an exercise in using a UART to decode a general serial protocol, we can implement the temperature-reading function given in Chapter 15 to read the DS18B20 one-wire device. This is worthwhile as it provides access to the device using hardware.

The first thing we have to do is deal with the electronics. The default configuration of the UART TX pin seems to work reliably with a pull-up. If you are unhappy about this you can use a transistor buffer to act as an open drain output.

The basic idea is that we can use the UART to send an initial stop pulse which pulls the line down. After this we can send data on the line for a write or just allow the DS18B20 to pull the line low. Of course, we have to get the timing right. Let's start with the presence/reset pulse.

If we use a speed of 9600 baud, the start bit pulls the line down for 104.2μs, the next four zero bits holds the line low for 502μs and then the final four 1 bits allow it to be pulled up. If there is a device connected to the line, it will pull the line down for a few microseconds. The serial port will read the line at the same time it is being written as the RX is connected to the TX. The TX sends 0xF0, and you might expect this to be what is received. If there is no device connected then RX will receive 0xF0, but if there is an active device connected the line will be pulled down for some part of the last four bits. As the low-order bits are sent first, this causes the RX to receive something like 0xE0, 0xD0, and so on, i.e. some of the four high order bits are zeroed by the device pulling the line low. You can use this to detect the device.

Assuming that the serial line is set to 9600 baud, the presence/reset pulse can be implemented as a function:

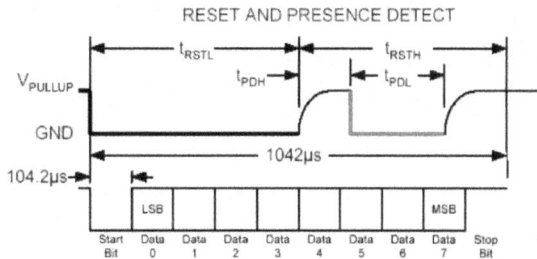

RESET AND PRESENCE DETECT

```
def presence(uart):
    uart.init(baudrate=9600)
    uart.write(bytes([0xF0]))
    sleep_ms(20)
    buf = uart.read(1)
    uart.init(baudrate=115200)
    if buf[0] == 0xF0:
        return -1
    return 0
```

To read and write a single bit we need to increase the baud rate to 115200. In this case the start bit lasts 8.7μs, which acts as the initial pulse to read or write a single bit.

To write a zero we simply write 0x00 which holds the line low for eight bits, about 78μs. To write a one we let the line be pulled up after the start bit, which leaves it high for 78μs. To make things slightly faster, we can deal with a single byte at a time:

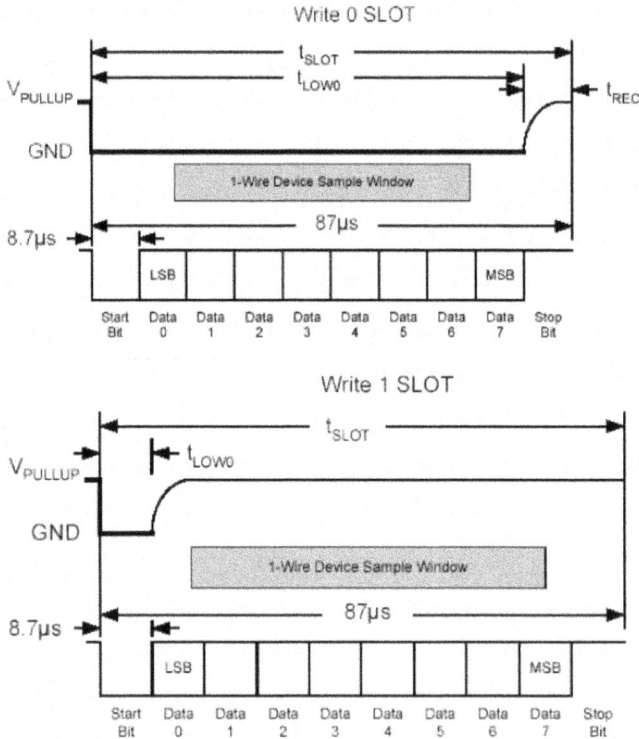

Write 0 SLOT

t_{SLOT}
t_{LOW0}
V_{PULLUP}
t_{REC}
GND
1-Wire Device Sample Window
87μs
8.7μs
LSB   MSB
Start Bit | Data 0 | Data 1 | Data 2 | Data 3 | Data 4 | Data 5 | Data 6 | Data 7 | Stop Bit

Write 1 SLOT

t_{SLOT}
t_{LOW0}
V_{PULLUP}
GND
1-Wire Device Sample Window
87μs
8.7μs
LSB   MSB
Start Bit | Data 0 | Data 1 | Data 2 | Data 3 | Data 4 | Data 5 | Data 6 | Data 7 | Stop Bit

```python
def writeByte(uart,byte):
    buf=[]
    for i in range(8):
        if byte & 1 == 1:
            buf.append(0xFF)
        else:
            buf.append(0x00)
        byte = byte >> 1
    uart.write(bytes(buf))
    sleep_ms(10)
    byte=uart.read(8)
```

We have to remember to read the bytes back in otherwise they would still be in the RX buffer. It is also necessary to wait for the data to be sent.

Reading a bit works in the same way. If you write `0xFF` then the line is allowed to be pulled high and the remote device can pull it low for a zero or let it remain high to signal a one. That is, if you write `0xFF` and read back `0xFF` then you have read a one:

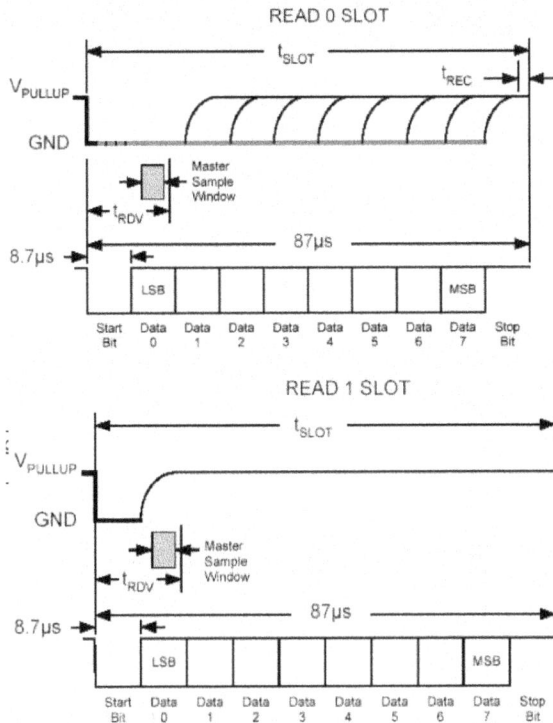

```
def readByte(uart):
    byte = bytes([0xFF]*8)
    uart.write(byte)
    sleep_ms(10)
    byte = uart.read(8)
    result=0
    for b in byte:
        result=result>>1
        if b==0xFF:
            result=result|0x80
    return result
```

Again we can read in a whole byte rather than a bit at a time. With these modified `readByte` and `writeByte` functions we can use the program developed in Chapter 13 to read the device. The only modifications are to change the parameter that specifies the GPIO line to be used to one that specifies the UART being used and the need to open and set the line's baud rate.

291

The complete program is, ds18b20.py:

```python
from machine import UART,Pin, mem32
from utime import sleep_ms, time_ns

def presence(uart):
    uart.init(baudrate=9600)
    uart.write(bytes([0xF0]))
    sleep_ms(20)
    buf = uart.read(1)
    uart.init(baudrate=115200)
    if buf[0] == 0xF0:
        return -1
    return 0

def writeByte(uart,byte):
    buf=[]
    for i in range(8):
        if byte & 1 == 1:
            buf.append(0xFF)
        else:
            buf.append(0x00)
        byte = byte >> 1
    uart.write(bytes(buf))
    sleep_ms(10)
    byte=uart.read(8)

def readByte(uart):
    byte = bytes([0xFF]*8)
    uart.write(byte)
    sleep_ms(10)
    byte = uart.read(8)
    result=0
    for b in byte:
        result=result>>1
        if b==0xFF:
            result=result|0x80
    return result
```

```
uart = UART(1,baudrate=115200,bits=8,parity=None,
                                rx=Pin(5),tx=Pin(4) )

print(presence(uart))

presence(uart)
writeByte(uart, 0xCC)
writeByte(uart, 0x44)
sleep_ms(1000)
presence(uart)
writeByte(uart, 0xCC)
writeByte(uart, 0xBE)

data=[]
for i in range(9):
    data.append(readByte(uart))

t1 = data[0]
t2 = data[1]
temp1 = (t2 << 8 | t1)
if t2 & 0x80:
    temp1=temp1 | 0xFFFF0000
temp=temp1/16
print(temp)
```

Of course, you can use the `readByte` and `writeByte` functions within other one-wire functions with minor modifications.

You can use the UART approach whenever a signaling protocol uses an initial start bit to signal that the data bits that follow use a fixed size "cell". However, you cannot use the UART approach with the DHT22 temperature and humidity sensor because, although it sends each bit with a start bit, the time to the next start bit varies.

Summary

- The serial port is one of the oldest ways of connecting devices together, but it is still very much in use.

- The serial protocol is asynchronous, but simple. A start bit gives the timing for the entire exchange.

- There are many control lines once used with telephone equipment that are mostly ignored in computer use. Similarly, the original ±12V signaling has been mostly replaced by 5V, and even 3.3V, signaling.

- The standard hardware that implements a serial connection is usually called a UART.

- The Pico contains two UARTs in addition to the USB serial connection.

- MicroPython provides functions for initializing and sending and receiving data.

- Each UART has a 32-element FIFO send and receive buffer which can be disabled.

- You can use the read and write blocking functions to send and receive byte buffers of data.

- The built-in methods are all blocking and while they don't have facilities for timeouts, you can construct functions to implement them using the basic methods.

- The write method is blocking but as it writes to the buffer it returns at once as long as there is free space.

- With the help of a custom function you can also test to see if the TX FIFO has space and so create a non-blocking write function also create functions to work with single characters and strings.

- As the UART buffers are small, all transactions should be in terms of amounts of data that do not fill the buffers.

- You can specify timeouts for the time the read methods will wait for the first character and for subsequent characters.

- The Pico supports simple flow control using the RTS and CTS lines but exactly how these work is complicated by the use of the FIFO and buffers.

Chapter 17

Using The Pico W - WiFi

In most respects the basic Pico and its WiFi-enabled counterpart, the Pico W are very similar and so far in this book any differences we have been pointing out have been between the original Pico and the Pico 2. Now, however, the focus is on the important difference between the Pico and the Pico W - the additional hardware that enables the latter to use WiFi. In this chapter all references to the Pico W encompass the Pico 2W. From the programming point of view, however, the task is to learn how to use the new WiFi driver and the LwIP library that provides higher-level networking. This is made more difficult than need be by the inadequate documentation currently provided for both. This may improve over time.

The Pico W

The Pico W adds WiFi to the original Pico design using an Infineon CYW43439 which has a pair of ARM processors and is connected to the Pico via a simple 3-wire SPI bus. You can see the configuration from the official schematics:

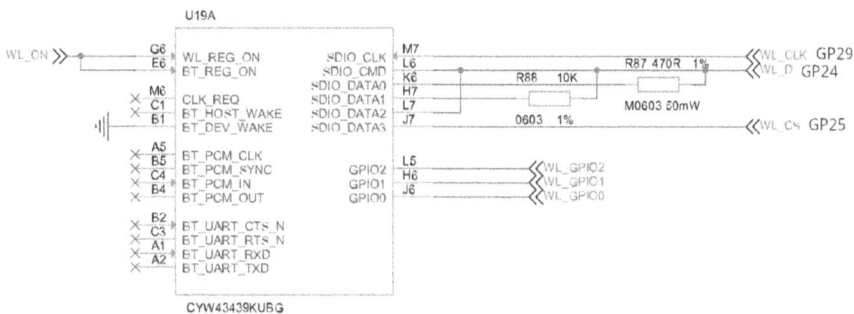

The CYW43439 has a 4-bit Secure Digital Input Output bus which originated with SD cards. The SDIO bus is an extension of the SPI protocol to use additional data lines. Typically a Quad or 4-bit mode is used with SD cards, usually called QSPI Quad SPI, but there are also 2-bit and 1-bit modes and a 2-line SPI mode. These modes are not true SPI as the data lines are bidirectional. The CYW43439 does support a true SPI interface, but the mode used with the Pico is SD 1-bit which uses a single bidirectional data line.

As you can see, the SPI bus is connected to the internal GPIO line's GPIO 29, GPIO 24 and GPIO 25. This causes some problems because in the original Pico they were already used for other things. We have already encountered the problem with using the onboard LED caused by it being driven by GPIO 25. In the case of the Pico W it is driven by one of the WiFi chip's GPIO lines, WL_GPIO0.

When the SPI bus is not active some of the other pins revert to their use in the Pico and some have their original use shifted to the WiFi chip's GPIO lines:

GPIO29	ADC mode (ADC3) to measure VSYS/3
GPIO25	When high enables GPIO29 ADC pin to read VSYS
GPIO24	IRQ to CYW43439 in the Pico it is VBUS sense.
GPIO23	Wireless power on signal

The CYW43439 GPIO lines are:

WL_GPIO2	VBUS sense - high if VBUS is present
WL_GPIO1	Controls the onboard SMPS power save
WL_GPIO0	Connected to user LED

The WLAN Class

Networking in MicroPython is taken care of in the network module which contains specific classes to work with different implementations according to the hardware in use. The custom WiFi class for the Pico W is WLAN. All you have to do is create an instance of the class, set the WiFi to active and then use the connect method. For example:

```
import network
wifi = network.WLAN(network.STA_IF)
wifi.active(True)
wifi.connect("ssid","key")
```

You have to supply the *ssid* and the *key* used to connect to the access point. You can set things up in two modes STA_IF which makes the Pico W a client or AP_IF which makes the Pico W an access point. In most cases you want the Pico W to be a client of another access point.

It is also a good idea to set the country of operation because different WiFi frequencies are used in different countries and if you don't specify a location not all of the available channels will be used. To set the country you simply call rp2.country("*XX*") with *XX* replaced by a two-character country code. You can find a full list of supported codes in the SDK documentation for the `cyw43_driver`. For example, to set the country to USA you would use:

```
import network
import rp2
rp2.country("US")
wifi=network.WLAN(network.STA_IF)
wifi.active(True)
wifi.connect("ssid","key")
```

MicroPython also supports connecting to a specific access point using its `bssid` which is the same as the access point's MAC address, but at the time of writing the Pico W doesn't support this.

To disconnect from an access point you can use the `disconnect` method.

A Practical Connect

In practice, you need to check that the attempted connection has worked. The `connect` method returns at once and usually before the connection has been made. Ideally you would select a connection method that informed you of progress and reported any errors. You can find out the status of the current connection using the status method which returns an integer status code:

STAT_IDLE	0	No connection and no activity
STAT_CONNECTING	1	Connection in progress
STAT_GOT_IP	3	Connection successful
STAT_WRONG_PASSWORD	-3	Failed due to incorrect password
STAT_NO_AP_FOUND	-2	Failed because no access point replied
STAT_CONNECT_FAIL	-1	Failed due to other problems

The problem is how to communicate this state to the user? The simplest solution is to flash the on-board LED. For example:

```
def setup(country, ssid, key):
    rp2.country(country)
    wifi = network.WLAN(network.STA_IF)
    wifi.active(True)
    wifi.disconnect()
    LED = Pin("LED", Pin.OUT)
    LED.high()
    timeout = 20000
    wifi.connect(ssid,key)
    timer = Timer()
    timer.init(period = 200, mode = Timer.PERIODIC,
                        callback = lambda t:LED.toggle())
    s=0
    while timeout>0:
        s = wifi.status()
        if s==3 or s<0:
            break
        sleep_ms(100)
        timeout = timeout-100

    if(s<2):
        timer.init(period = 1000, mode = Timer.PERIODIC,
                            callback = lambda t:LED.toggle())
    else:
        timer.deinit()
        LED.high()
    return wifi
```

This function accepts the country code, the SSID (Service Set Identifier), i.e. your network's name and the key for the connection. It then creates a WLAN object and activates the hardware. The Pico W tends to keep its connections even after the current program has ended so a call to disconnect ensures that the connection is a fresh one. If you don't want to do this you can sometimes speed up the function if the connection is already made. After the attempt to connect, a while loop checks the status every 100ms. While the connection is being made, s=1, the LED is flashed every 200ms. If the loop ends with a connection, the LED is switched on, but if there is an error it is reset to flash every second. You can see this in use in example.py on the book's webpage.

You can expand the LED feedback to indicate to the user different error conditions using different flashing patterns.

In you can get the signal strength of the current connection using:

```
wifi.status('rssi')
```

You can test for a connection using:

```
wifi.isconnected()
```

You can also find out about the current configuration of the connection using:

```
wifi.ifconfig()
```

which returns a tuple of:

```
(ip address, subnet mask, gateway ip, dns ip)
```

You can also set these parameters by calling `ifconfig` with an appropriate tuple. For example:

```
wifi.ifconfig(("192.168.253.120","255.255.255.0",
                   "192.168.253.1","8.8.8.8"))
```

You can also read and set some general configuration parameters and `wifi.config("parameter")` will return the value of the named parameter. In theory you can request any of the following:

`mac *`	MAC address (bytes)
`ssid *`	WiFi access point name (string)
`channel *`	WiFi channel (integer)
`hidden`	Whether SSID is hidden (boolean)
`security *`	Security protocol supported (enumeration, see module constants)
`key *`	Access key (string)
`hostname`	The hostname that will be sent to DHCP (STA interfaces) and mDNS (if supported, both STA and AP)
`reconnects`	Number of reconnect attempts to make (`0`=none, `-1`=unlimited)
`txpower *`	Maximum transmit power in dBm (integer or float)

*At the time of writing only the parameters with an asterisk are supported on the Pico W. You can also use the parameter names as named parameters in a call to `config` to set the corresponding parameter. At the time of writing the majority are not supported and those that are seem to have no effect. The most important, `hostname`, currently isn't supported but it will be in the future.

By default the WiFi chip will place the Pico W in power-saving mode if nothing is happening. This can cause the connection to disconnect and will slow things down. If you don't want automatic power-saving use:

```
wifi.active(True)
wifi.config(pm = 0xa11140)
```

WiFi Scan

The scan method can be used to survey what access points are available. It returns a list of tuples, each tuple of which has the format:

```
(ssid, bssid, channel, RSSI, security, hidden)
```

where ssid is the usual name of the network, bssid is the mac address of the access point, channel is the channel number of the access point. RSSI is a relative measure of the strength of the received signal. If your app needs to choose an access point then picking the one with the highest RSSI is reasonable. The security item is one of:

```
0 - open
1 - WEP
2 - WPA-PSK
3 - WPA2-PSK
4 - WPA/WPA2-PSK
```

Finally, hidden is 0 if the access point is broadcasting its SSID and 1 if not.

To display the WiFi access points in range you could use scan.py:

```
import network
wifi = network.WLAN(network.STA_IF)
wifi.active(True)
wifi.disconnect()
aps = wifi.scan()
for ap in aps:
    print(ap)
```

A Simple HTTP Client

The simplest way to make use of a WiFi connection is to work with an HTTP server. This is simple because the difficult parts of the transaction are handled by the server making the client much easier to implement. MicroPython makes this even easier by providing urequests which is a port of the Python requests module. This has methods that implement the standard HTTP transactions and a request object which wraps the data involved in the transaction.

The urequests module should work on any MicroPython implementation and it is built on top of the sockets module which is discussed later. The sockets module provides a lower-level interface to the network and urequests uses this to implement the HTTP protocol. While HTTP was invented to allow the transport of HTML pages, it can be used to transfer any data between the client and the server.

It is important to understand what the distinction is between the client and the server. In this case the client initiates the connection and the server accepts the connection. The connection once established is two-way – the client can send data to the server and vice versa. This said, HTTP is most commonly used to send data from the server to the client in the form of web pages.

300

Request Methods

HTTP supports a number of request methods which transfer data. Usually these are described in terms of what they do to resources hosted by a web server, but from our point of view what matters is what happens to the data.

The HTTP request methods available are:

GET	Transfers data from server to client
HEAD	Transfers HTTP headers for the equivalent GET request
PUT	Transfers data from the client to the server
POST	Transfers data from the client to the server
PATCH	Transfers data from the client to the server
DELETE	Specifies that the data on the server should be deleted
OPTIONS	Transfers data from the client to the server

If you know about HTTP request methods you will find the above list disconcerting. If you don't know about HTTP requests then you will be wondering why there are so many requests that transfer data from the client to the server? The answer is that in the HTTP model the server stores the master copy of the resource – usually a file or a database entry. The client can request a copy of the resource using GET and then ask the server to modify the resource using the other requests. For example, the PUT request sends a new copy of the resource for the server to use, i.e. it replaces the old copy. POST does the same thing, but PUT should be idempotent, which means if you repeat it the result is as if you had done it just once. With POST you are allowed side effects. For example, PUT 1 might just store 1 but POST 1 might increment a count.

Another example is where you send some text to the server to save under a supplied file name. For this you should use a PUT as repeating the request with the same text changes nothing. If, on the other hand, you supply text to the server and allow it to assign a name and store it then you should use a POST as you get a new file each time you send the data, even if it is the same.

Similarly the PATCH request should be used by the client to request that that server makes a change to part of an existing resource. Exactly how the change is specified depends on the server. Usually a key value scheme is used, but this isn't part of the specification.

Notice that all of these interpretations of the HTTP request methods are "optional" in the sense that it is up to you and the server you are using to interpret them and implement them. If you write your own server, or server application, then you can treat POST as if it was PUT and vice versa.

A Custom Server

The problem with writing HTTP examples is that how they are handled depends on the server in use. Not all HTTP servers implement the same range of requests. A simple solution to this problem is to write a custom server and Python makes this very easy. Before you try any of the following examples, create the following Python program on a suitable machine on your local network.

Notice that this code is in Python, not MicroPython, server.py:

```python
from http.server import HTTPServer, BaseHTTPRequestHandler
from io import BytesIO

class SimpleHTTPRequestHandler(BaseHTTPRequestHandler):
    def sendResponse(self, cmd):
        content_length = int(self.headers['Content-Length'])
        body = self.rfile.read(content_length)
        self.send_response(200)
        self.end_headers()
        response = BytesIO()
        response.write(b'This is a '+bytes(cmd, 'utf-8')+
                                            b' request. ')
        response.write(b'Received: ')
        response.write(body)
        self.wfile.write(response.getvalue())

    def do_GET(self):
        self.send_response(200)
        self.end_headers()
        self.wfile.write(b'Hello, world!')

    def do_HEAD(self):
        self.send_response(200)
        self.end_headers()

    def do_POST(self):
        self.sendResponse("POST")

    def do_PUT(self):
        self.sendResponse("PUT")

    def do_DELETE(self):
        self.sendResponse("DELETE")

    def do_PATCH(self):
        self.sendResponse("PATCH")

httpd = HTTPServer(('', 8080), SimpleHTTPRequestHandler)
httpd.serve_forever()
```

This server implements simple methods to respond to GET, HEAD, PUT, POST, DELETE and PATCH requests. If you want to support a custom request simply include a method that is called do_request where request is the command you want to use. Notice that this custom request is unlikely to be serviced by a standard server, but there is nothing stopping you from implementing your own. In the case of GET, the server sends fixed data – "Hello World" - and for the others it sends back whatever was sent to it by the client, with the exception of HEAD that sends nothing at all except for the headers.

If you install this program on a remote machine on the same network as the Pico then you can use it to test HTTP request programs. With a little work you can also turn it into a server that supports your Pico app in the real world. You can even convert it into an SSL server for HTTPS connections using the Python SSL module.

The urequests Module

The urequests module implements the GET, PUT, POST, PATCH, HEAD and DELETE requests. The most commonly used is GET to retrieve data from a server. All of the methods return a Response object which contains details of the server's response. This supports a subset of the Python Response object's properties/methods:

status_code	Integer HTTP status code
reason	Text from of HTTP status code
headers	Dictionary of headers sent by server
content	Data returned by server as bytes
text	Data returned by server as a string
raw	Data returned by server as a file-like object
json	Data returned by server as a JSON object
encoding	Encoding to be used to convert raw to text utf-8 by default
close	Release Response object

It also has a set of methods – one for each type of request:

```
head(url)
get(url)
post(url,data=data)
put(url,data=data)
patch(url,data=data)
delete(url)
```

There is also a single general-purpose method which implements any type of request, including custom requests. It is used by the earlier `request` methods:

```
request(
    method,
    url,
    data = None,
    json = None,
    headers ={},
    stream = None,
    auth = None,
    timeout = None,
    parse_headers = True,
)
```

So for example, a call to `get(url)` is translated into:

```
request(url,"GET")
```

The request method will supply the basic HTTP/HTTPS header and the Host header if these are not already provided in the headers dictionary. You can include a user name and password as a tuple for the `auth` parameter and these are passed to the server in an Authorization header. You can also set `json=object` as an alternative to using data and have the `urequests` module send a JSON encoded string, see later. All of the specific request methods will pass on any keyword parameters you include to the general request method.

Notice that the `urequests` module works with both HTTP and HTTPS and you don't have to do anything to make HTTPS work. However at the time of writing the support only extends to encrypting the data transfer, the server's certificate is not checked for validity.

For example, to download a web page using HTTPS you might use `client.py`:

```
import network
from machine import Pin, Timer
from time import sleep_ms
import urequests
import rp2
def setup(country, ssid, key):
    . . .
wifi = setup("country", "ssid", "password")
print("Connected")
r = urequests.get("https://www.example.com")
print(r.content.decode("utf-8"))
r.close()
```

This listing omits the setup function. The site `www.example.com` provides a test server which works with HTTP and HTTPS. If you run this program you will see the HTML that makes up its standard web page.

If you target the Python custom server, `server.py,` listed earlier then you can see all of the request methods in action using `request.py`:

```python
import urequests
url = "http://192.168.253.45:8080"
r = urequests.get(url)
print(r.content)
r.close()
buf = b'Hello World'
r = urequests.post(url,data = buf)
print(r.content)
r.close()
r = urequests.put(url,data = buf)
print(r.content)
r.close()
r = urequests.patch(url,data = buf)
print(r.content)
r.close()
r=urequests.head(url)
print(r.content)
print(r.headers)
r.close()
r=urequests.delete(url,data = buf)
print(r.content)
r.close()
```

Of course, to make this work you have to substitute the IP address of the machine running the Python custom server. Notice that the custom server only supports HTTP, but it is relatively easy to convert it to HTTPS.

If you run `request.py` you expect to see something like:

```
b'Hello, world!'
b'This is a POST request. Received: Hello World'
b'This is a PUT request. Received: Hello World'
b'This is a PATCH request. Received: Hello World'
b''
{'Server': 'BaseHTTP/0.6 Python/3.9.2',
                'Date': 'Fri, 4 Jul 2025 18:20:42 GMT'}
b'This is a DELETE request. Received: Hello World'
```

If you run it with a standard web server it is unlikely you will see anything other than error messages. The response of a standard web server has to be configured to respond to anything but a simple GET. Usually you have to install a CGI script to deal with anything that sends data to the server.

You should be able to see now that the only difference between an HTTP client and server is that the client initiates the connection and the request. The server simply responds to the client, but it can send data to and receive data from the client. Using this it is possible to implement a simple sensor feeding data to a central server.

A Temperature Sensor Client

The standard approach to implementing a sensor device that makes its readings available to other devices is to implement a web server or a custom protocol that allows other devices to connect. A simpler solution is to implement an HTTP client and allow the sensor device to send data to a server which other devices can then connect to as required.

As we have already seen in Chapter 15, it is very easy to use the DS18B20 to collect data about ambient temperature. All we have to do is take a reading every so often, convert the floating-point value to a byte object and send it to the server using a PUT, ds18b20.py:

```
from machine import Pin, Timer
import network
import rp2
import onewire
import ds18x20
from time import sleep_ms
import urequests

wifi = setup("country", "ssid", "key")
url = "http://192.168.253.45:8080"

ow = onewire.OneWire(Pin(2))
presence = ow.reset()
if presence:
    print("Device present")
else:
    print("No device")

DS = ds18x20.DS18X20(ow)
roms = DS.scan()

while True:
    DS.convert_temp()
    temp = DS.read_temp(roms[0])
    buf = str(temp).encode("utf-8")
    try:
        r = urequests.put(url, data=buf)
        r.close()
    except:
        print("Server Not Online")
    sleep_ms(500)
```

The setup function given earlier, which makes the WiFi connection, has been omitted.

The server, `server2.py`, simply has to respond to the PUT request and convert the bytes to a string and then a float:

```
from http.server import HTTPServer, BaseHTTPRequestHandler
from io import BytesIO

class SimpleHTTPRequestHandler(BaseHTTPRequestHandler):

    def log_message(self,*args, **kwargs):
        pass

    def do_PUT(self):
        content_length = int(self.headers['Content-Length'])
        body = self.rfile.read(content_length)
        bodyString = body.decode(encoding="utf-8")
        temp = float(bodyString)
        print(temp)
        self.send_response(200)
        self.end_headers()

httpd = HTTPServer(('', 8080), SimpleHTTPRequestHandler)
httpd.serve_forever()
```

As before, it is simple enough to convert the server to HTTPS. The overriding of the `log_message` method is to suppress the regular printing of status messages. The `do_PUT` handler method simply prints the temperature. It could, of course, do much more.

You can appreciate that this architecture works well if you can allocate a simple device to act as a server. If the sensor supplies more data than a single measurement then using a JSON encoding makes things easier. For example, if you want to send a timestamp along with the temperature you could change the `while` loop to read:

```
while True:
    DS.convert_temp()
    temp = DS.read_temp(roms[0])
    jsonData={"temp":temp,"time":time()}

    try:
        r = urequests.put(url,json=jsonData)
        r.close()
    except:
        print("Server Not Online")
    sleep_ms(500)
```

You can see that the only difference is that now we make up a dictionary with key/value pairs corresponding to the data we want to send to the server. The only other difference is that we now set `json` to `jsonData` rather than setting it to `data` and the `urequests` module converts the dictionary into a JSON string.

To process the JSON string the do_PUT method now has to use the json module to convert the received JSON string back into a dictionary object:

```
def do_PUT(self):
    content_length = int(self.headers['Content-Length'])
    body = self.rfile.read(content_length)
    bodyString= body.decode(encoding="utf-8")
    jsonData=json.loads(bodyString)
    print(jsonData)
    self.send_response(200)
    self.end_headers()
```

If you run the client and the server with these changes you will see something like:

```
{'time': 1609459985, 'temp': 14.4375}
{'time': 1609459986, 'temp': 14.5}
{'time': 1609459987, 'temp': 14.4375}
```

You can unpack the data from the dictionary and use it as you would any other data.

Summary

- Connecting to a WiFi network is a matter of using the WLAN class.

- Implementing error handling for a WiFi connection can be challenging.

- The simplest way of implementing an HTTP client is to use `urequests`.

- An HTTP client can both send and receive data to the server depending on the request it makes.

- The most common request is GET which accepts data from the server.

- Both POST and PUT can be used to send data to the server.

- The only difference between a client and server is that a client can only make a connection, a server can accept a connection.

- It is possible to avoid having to implement a server on the ESP32 by allowing a client to connect to a server running on another machine and send its data using a PUT or POST request.

Chapter 18

Sockets

If you want to go beyond a simple client you need to make use of a more general network connection method. The usual way of doing this is to make use of "sockets". This is a widely supported internet standard and most servers support socket connections.

MicroPython supports a limited version of the full Python Sockets module. The parts of the module that are not supported are mostly those concerned with making connections using non-IP networks and hence are generally minor.

The most important thing to understand about sockets is that they are a very general way of making a two-way connection between a client and a server. A client can create a socket to transfer data between itself and a server and a server can use a socket to accept a connection from a client. The only difference between the two situations is that the server has to either poll or use interrupts to detect a new connection attempt.

Socket Objects

Before you can start to send and receive data you have to create a socket object:

```
import socket
s = socket.socket()
```

This default constructor creates a socket suitable for IPv4 connections. If you want to specify the type of socket being created you have to use:

```
socket(af=AF_INET, type=SOCK_STREAM, proto=IPPROTO_TCP)¶
```

The af parameter gives the address family and it is either AF_INET for IPv4 or AF_INET6 for IPv6 – at the time of writing only IPv4 is supported. The type parameter indicates either SOCK_STREAM or SOCK_DGRAM, the stream option. The default, SOCK_STREAM, corresponds to the usual TCP/IP connection used to transfer web pages and files in general. It is a persisted and error-corrected connection whereas SOCK_DGRAM sends individual packets without error checking or confirmation that the data was received.

The final parameter, proto, sets the exact type of protocol, but as the only two supported are IPPROTO_TCP and IPPROTO_UDP this is set according to the type parameter:

type	proto
SOCK_STREAM	IPPROTO_TCP
SOCK_DGRAM	IPPROTO_UDP

In a more general setting there could be more types of proto supported for each type.

Socket Address

After defining the type of connection you need to specify the addresses involved in the connection. As sockets can be used to connect to a wide range of different types of network the address format could vary a lot and not just be a simple URL or an IP address. For this reason sockets are used with their own internal address representation and you have to use the getaddrinfo method:

```
socket.getaddrinfo(host, port, af=0, type=0, proto=0, flags=0)
```

The first two parameters are familiar and simple. The host has to be specified using a URL or an IP address. The second is the numeric port to use with the socket. The next three parameters are the same as used in creating the socket. In general you use the same parameter values for an address intended to be used with a socket as used to create the socket. If you don't specify a parameter then getaddrinfo will return a list of tuples for each possible address type. Each tuple has the following format:

```
(af, type, proto, canonname, sockaddr)
```

where af, type and proto are as before and canonname is the cannonical name for the address type and sockaddr is the actual address, which may also be a tuple. In the case of an IP address, the sockaddr is a tuple with the format:

```
(IP, port)
```

At the time of writing, the Pico only supports IPv4 and it only returns a list with a single tuple. The only really useful part of this tuple is the final element which is an IP tuple that most of the socket methods actually use. You could short circuit everything by simply creating the IP tuple without using getaddrinfo. It is however, advisable to use getaddrinfo to allow for compatibility with the full sockets module and for future development.

So, for example:

```
ai = socket.getaddrinfo("www.example.com",
                    80,socket.AF_INET,socket.SOCK_DGRAM)
```

returns the list:

```
[(2, 1, 0, '', ('93.184.216.34', 80))]
```

and is it the final tuple

```
('93.184.216.34', 80)
```

which we actually use in calls to socket methods. To extract this final tuple we use:

```
addr=ai[0][-1]
```

While on the subject of addresses, there are two functions which can be used to convert an IP address in "dotted" form to a byte value and vice versa:

```
socket.inet_ntop(socket.AF_INET,bytes)
```

gives the dotted text form and:

```
socket.inet_pton(socket.AF_INET,string)
```

gives the binary form of the IP address.

Client Sockets

Once we have a socket object and the ability to specify an address we have to connect it to another socket to make a two-way communication channel. Data can be written and read at both sockets that form the connection. Exactly how sockets are connected depends on which is the client and which the server. In this section we look at how to connect to a server. By default all socket methods are blocking. See later for non-blocking operation.

If you want to connect a socket to a server socket than all you have to do is use:

```
socket.connect(address)
```

where `address` is the address of the server socket you are trying to connect to and has to be specified as an IP tuple:

```
(ip,port)
```

For example:

```
socket.connect(('93.184.216.34',80))
```

While you can use an IP tuple, it is more usual to use `socket.getaddrinfo` to generate it.

You should always close a socket when you are finished using it with a call to the close method.

Once you have a connected socket you can send and receive data using a range of methods.

The methods used to send data are:

send(bytes)	Returns the number of bytes actually sent.
sendall(bytes)	Sends all of the data even if it takes multiple chunks of data. Doesn't work well with non-blocking sockets and write is preferred.
write(buf)	Tries to write all of the buffer but this may not be possible with a non-blocking socket and it returns the number of bytes actually sent.

The receive methods are:

recv(len)	Returns no more than len bytes as a bytes object.
recvfrom(len)	Returns no more than len bytes as a tuple *(bytes,address)where address* is the address of the device sending the database.
read(len)	Returns no more than len bytes as a bytes object. If len is not specified it reads as much data is sent until the socket is closed.
readinto(buf, len)	Reads no more than len bytes into the buf. If len is not specified len(buf) is used. Returns the number of bytes actually read.
readline()	Read a line, ending in a newline character.

There are also:

sendto(bytes, address)	Sends data to the address specified – the socket used has to be unconnected for this to work.
makefile(mode = 'rb', buffering = 0)	Available for compatibility with Python which needs the socket to be converted to a file before reading or writing. In MicroPython this can be used but it does nothing.

A Socket Web Client

Using what we know so far about sockets, we can easily connect to a server and send and receive data. What data we actually send and receive depends on the protocol in use. Web servers use HTTP, which is a very simple text-based protocol. Using the urequests module we could ignore the nature of the protocol as it implemented most of it for us. When it comes to using sockets we have to work out what to send in detail.

The HTTP protocol is essentially a set of text headers of the form:

headername: *headerdata* \r\n

that tell the server what to do, and a set of headers that the server sends back to tell you what it has done. You can look up the details of HTTP headers in the documentation – there are a lot of them.

The most basic transaction the client can have with the server is to send a GET request for the server to send back a particular file. Thus the simplest header is:

```
"GET /index.html HTTP/1.1\r\n\r\n"
```

which is a request for the server to send index.html. In most cases we need one more header, HOST, which gives the domain name of the server. Why do we need it? Simply because HTTP says you should and many websites are hosted by a single server at the same IP address. Which website the server retrieves the file from is governed by the domain name you specify in the HOST header.

This means that the simplest set of headers we can send the server is:

```
"GET /index.htm HTTP/1.1\r\nHOST:example.org\r\n\r\n";
```

which corresponds to the headers:

```
GET /index.html HTTP/1.1
HOST:example.org
```

An HTTP request always ends with a blank line. If you don't send the blank line then you will get no response from most servers. In addition, the HOST header has to have the domain name with no additional syntax - no slashes and no http: or similar.

```
request = b"GET /index.html HTTP/1.1\r\nHost:example.org\r\n\r\n"
```

Now we are ready to send our request to the server but first we need its address and we need to connect the socket:

```
ai = socket.getaddrinfo("www.example.com", 80,socket.AF_INET)
addr = ai[0][-1]
s = socket.socket(socket.AF_INET)
s.connect(addr)
```

Now we can send the headers which constitute the GET request:

```
request = b"GET /index.html HTTP/1.1\r\nHost:example.org\r\n\r\n"
s.send(request)
```

Finally we can wait for the response from the server and display it:

```
print(s.recv(512))
```

Notice that all of the methods are blocking in the sense that they don't return until the operation is complete.

The complete `client.py` program, with the `setup` function, given earlier, omitted is:

```
import network
import socket
import rp2
from machine import Pin, Timer
from time import sleep_ms
def setup(country, ssid, key):
    . . .

wifi = setup("country", "ssid", "key")
ai = socket.getaddrinfo("www.example.com", 80,socket.AF_INET)
addr = ai[0][-1]
s = socket.socket(socket.AF_INET)
s.connect(addr)
request = b"GET /index.html HTTP/1.1\r\nHost:example.org\r\n\r\n"
s.send(request)
print(s.recv(512).decode("utf-8"))
```

You can see that the `urequests` module is much easier to use. Of course, it makes use of sockets to do its job.

SSL Socket Based HTTPS Client

Many websites now refuse to serve unencrypted data and insist on HTTPS. Fortunately it is very easy to create an HTTPS client as you don't need to create a digital certificate. If you need to prove to a server that it is indeed you trying to connect then you should install a new certificate and use it. This is exactly the same procedure as installing a new server certificate, see later.

MicroPython has a very minimal implementation of the Python `ssl` module. It only has a single function `wrap_socket` but it is enough to do what you need to make an HTTPS client or server. What this does is to add encryption and in some cases authentication to an existing socket. At the time of writing MicroPython for the Pico doesn't support authentication.

The `wrap_socket` function is:

```
ssl.wrap_socket(sock, keyfile=None, certfile=None,
            server_side=False, cert_reqs=CERT_NONE,
            ca_certs=None,
            do_handshake_on_connect=True,
            )
```

This takes an existing socket specified by `sock` and turns it into an encrypted SSL socket. Apart from `sock` all of the other parameters, including `keyfile` and `certfile` which specify files which contain the certificate and/or key, are optional.

All certificates have to be in PEM format. If the key is stored in the certificate then you only need to use certfile. If the key is stored separately from the certificate you need both certfile and keyfile.

server_side sets the behavior appropriate to a client (False) or server (True)

cert_reqs determines the level of certificate checking, from CERT_NONE, CERT_OPTIONAL to CERT_REQUIRED. The validity of the certificate is only checked if you select CERT_REQUIRED and currently the Pico never checks the certificate for validity.

ca_certs is a bytes object containin the certificate chain to be used to validate the client's certificate.

server_hostname is used to set the server's hostname so that the certificate can be checked to ascertain that it does belong to the web site and to allow the server to present the appropriate certificate if it is hosting multiple sites.

do_handshake should be used with non-blocking sockets and if True defers the handshake . If False, wrap_socket doesn't return until the handshake is complete.

Notice that not all of the full Python wrap_socket parameters are supported and not all TLS and encryption levels work. What this means is that you will discover that connecting to some websites is difficult, if not impossible, at the moment. However, in many cases it should simply work, as long as the website concerned is not using a cutting edge implementation.

The only modification that the previous HTTP client needs to work with an HTTPS web site is, sslclient.py:

```
import network
import socket
import rp2
from machine import Pin, Timer
from time import sleep_ms

def setup(country, ssid, key):
    .  .  .

wifi = setup("country", "ssid", "key")
ai = socket.getaddrinfo("example.com", 443,socket.AF_INET)
addr = ai[0][-1]
s = socket.socket(socket.AF_INET)
s.connect(addr)
sslSock=ssl.wrap_socket(s)
request = b"GET / HTTP/1.1\r\nHost:example.com\r\n\r\n"
sslSock.write(request)
print(sslSock.read(1024))
```

where the setup function has been omitted.

Notice that all we need to do is perform a default `wrap_socket` after making the connection. The downloaded HTML is now fetched using HTTPS. The `sslSock` returned by the `wrap_socket` function only has stream `read` and `write` methods.

Socket Server

The problem of connecting a socket when you are the server is more complicated than when you are a client. In this case the socket has to be read and listening for a client to make a connection. It then sets up a completely new socket which is used to communicate with the client. This new socket is destroyed when the communication with the client is over. The original socket continues listening for new client connections.

In principle the listening socket can create multiple new sockets, one for each client that wants to connect to the server. In this way, in theory, the server is capable of handling multiple clients at the same time.. The problem is that to handle more than one client implies that the program is organized to process multiple clients and, as always, there are various ways of doing this. You can simply implement a polling loop that cycles round the set of active clients, you can implement a multithreaded program, one thread per client, or you can adopt an asynchronous task approach where a single thread services all of the clients using an event queue. If you would like to know more about asynchronous programming in Python, see *Programmer's Python: Async,* ISBN:9781871962765.

The problem with implementing a server for the Pico and in MicroPython is that neither makes use of an operating system that manages threads and processes. As a result we can either opt to handle clients using polling or using a single-threaded asynchronous event queue. If you want to use an event queue then there is the MicroPython implementation of the `asyncio` module, which is the topic of the next chapter.

To use a socket as a server you first have to bind it to the external network ports that you want it to respond to. A machine might well have more than one internet adapter and hence more than one IP address. In the case of the Pico the only thing that might vary is the port in use. For example:

```
addr = socket.getaddrinfo('0.0.0.0', 8080)[0][-1]
```

creates an IP tuple with the current IP address and port 8080. The IP address '0.0.0.0' means any IP address you have available. Once you have the address, the socket can be made to use it with the `bind` method:

```
s = socket.socket(socket.AF_INET)
s.bind(addr)
```

Now the socket will use the specified address, but to make it listen out for connecting clients you have to use the `listen` method:

```
s.listen(backlog)
```

The `backlog` parameter specifies the number of unaccepted clients allowed before the socket responds by refusing the connection. To actually work with the client you have to accept the connection using the `accept` method.

```
s.accept()
```

This blocks until a client tries to connect and then returns a tuple of the form:

```
(socket,address)
```

The socket can be used to communicate with the client at the specified address. You can use all of the standard socket methods with this new socket and you should close it when you have finished communicating with the client.

A Socket Temperature Server

With all of this in place we can now use sockets to build a server.

First we need to create a socket and bind it to the local IP address:

```
addr = socket.getaddrinfo('192.168.253.58', 8080)[0][-1]
s = socket.socket()
s.setsockopt(socket.SOL_SOCKET, socket.SO_REUSEADDR, 1)
s.bind(addr)
s.listen(0)
```

Of course, you need to change the IP address to that of the Pico that the program is running on. The only new element is that we have used the `setsockopt` method to allow the socket to reuse the address – without this you would get an error that the address was in use after each restart.

Now we have a socket listening on port 8080 and we can wait until a client attempts to connect:

```
cl, addr = s.accept()
```

This waits until a client connects and returns the socket `cl` and its IP address. We can now use the socket to read the request from the client:

```
print('client connected from', addr)
print(cl.recv(512))
```

In this case we aren't particularly interested in the content of the request because we are going to serve the same content no matter what. However, this does mean that we will probably serve the same content twice to any client as even the simplest web page request generates an additional file download request for the site's icon which is used in the browser's tab.

If the client used the url:

```
http://192.168.253.58:8080/temperature
```

the request would start with:

```
b'GET /temperature HTTP/1.1\r\n
Host: 192.168.253.58\r\n
Connection: keep-alive\r\n
```

and so on.

You can use the string following GET to determine what the client wants in return. In this case you would test for temperature before returning a value.

Now all we have to do is send a web page with the current temperature in it. Logically we first need to create the headers, but one of the headers, Content-Length, needs to contain the number of bytes in the content. This means we first have to create the content so we can obtain its size. A simple HTML page is:

```
template = """<!DOCTYPE html>
<html>
<head> <title>Temperature</title> </head>
<body> <h1>Current Temperature</h1>
Hello Pico W Server World <br/>
The Temperature is: <!--#temp--><br/>
</body>
</html>
"""
```

The idea is that we will use this as a template and replace <!--#temp-> by the measured temperature each time the page is served:

```
html=template.replace("<!--#temp->",str(temp))
```

assuming temp has the current temperature. Now we can create the headers:

```
headers = ("HTTP/1.1 200 OK\r\n"
           "Content-Type: text/html; charset=UTF-8\r\n"
           "Server:Pico\r\n"
           f"Content-Length:{len(html)}\r\n\r\n"
           )
```

Notice the way that we use a formatted string, an f string, to add the length of the html into the Content-Length header.

Now we can send the response to the client:

```
buf = headers.encode("utf-8")+html.encode("utf-8")
cl.send(buf)
cl.close()
```

The client now has the web page that displays the current temperature and so we can close the client socket.

Of course, this only serves a single request from a single client. To keep on serving as clients try to connect, we need to put the accept and what we do to send the data into an infinite loop.

The complete program, minus the setup function given earlier, but including reading a DS18B20 temperature sensor, server.py, is:

```
import network
import socket
import rp2
from time import sleep_ms
from machine import Pin, Timer
import onewire
import ds18x20

def setup(country, ssid, key):
    ...

wifi = setup("country", "ssid", "key")

ow = onewire.OneWire(Pin(2))
presence = ow.reset()
if presence:
    print("Device present")
else:
    print("No device")

DS = ds18x20.DS18X20(ow)
roms = DS.scan()

template = """<!DOCTYPE html>
<html>
<head> <title>Temperature</title> </head>
<body> <h1>Current Temperature</h1>
Hello Pico W Server World <br/>
The Temperature is: <!--#temp--><br/>
</body>
</html>
"""

addr = socket.getaddrinfo('192.168.253.58', 80)[0][-1]

s = socket.socket()
s.setsockopt(socket.SOL_SOCKET, socket.SO_REUSEADDR, 1)
s.bind(addr)
s.listen(0)
```

```
while True:
    cl, addr = s.accept()
    print('client connected from', addr)
    print(cl.recv(512))

    DS.convert_temp()
    temp = DS.read_temp(roms[0])

    html=template.replace("<!--#temp-->",str(temp))
    headers = ("HTTP/1.1 200 OK\r\n"
               "Content-Type: text/html; charset=UTF-8\r\n"
               "Server:Pico\r\n"
               f"Content-Length:{len(html)}\r\n\r\n"
               )
    buf = headers.encode("utf-8")+html.encode("utf-8")

    cl.send(buf)

    cl.close()
s.close()
```

If you try this out and connect a browser you will see:

Current Temperature

Hello Pico W Server World
The Temperature is: 13.0

You can modify this program to send as much data as you like and you can make it machine readable by using JSON or another similar format.

An SSL HTTPS Server

If you want to implement an SSL server then things are slightly more complicated because you need to provide a certificate. Getting a certificate can be an involved process. Even popular free certificate-issuing sites like Let's Encrypt require proof that you own the domain that the certificate applies to. To do this you have to write code which generates a new key pair and then either create a specific DNS record or store a file on the website. This is easy enough for production purposes, but not so easy when you are in the process of creating a program.

The usual solution is to create a self-signed certificate. If the operating system has OpenSSL installed, and Windows and most versions of Linux do, then you can create a key and certificate pair using:

```
openssl req -newkey rsa:2048 -nodes -keyout iopress.key -x509
                        -days 365 -out iopress.crt
```

changing *iopress* to the name of your server. You will be asked a set of questions for information that is included in the certificate. How you answer these questions only modifies what the user sees if they ask to inspect the certificate so you can simply accept the defaults.

The openssl command creates two files, a .key file and a .crt file, which need to be processed to create strings that can be used in the Pico program. Normally the files would be loaded into the server, but the Pico doesn't support a standard filing system and so the binary in the files needs to be loaded into a pair of strings. The certificate and key are saved on disk using an encoding called Base64 with a line of unencoded ASCII text at the start and end. To make use of this data we have to remove the first and last line of the file and unencode the Base64 to a standard byte or ASCII string. This can be done using standard operating system command line programs, but it is also very easy to write a standard Python program, decode.py, to do the job:

```
import binascii

with open("iopress.key", 'rb') as f:
    lines = f.readlines()
lines = b"".join(lines[1:-1])
key = binascii.a2b_base64(lines)
print("key=", key)

with open("iopress.crt", 'rb') as f:
    lines = f.readlines()
lines = b"".join(lines[1:-1])
cert = binascii.a2b_base64(lines)
print()
print("cert=", cert)
```

If you run this program, with the names of the .key and .crt files corrected to apply to the certificate you have generated, then it will read in each file, remove the first and last line, remove the Base64 encoding and print the MicroPython line needed to load the file's contents into a string:

```
key= b'0\x82\x04\xbf\x02\x01\x000\r\x06\t*\x86H\ ...
cert= b'0\x82\x03k0\x82\x02S\xa0\x03\x02\x01\x02\...
```

where the long list of hex codes has been truncated to save space.

You can simply copy and paste these two lines to get the certificate you have generated into the program. Once we have the certificates in the program the rest is fairly straightforward. The listening socket is the same as before, but it now listens on 443 which is the standard HTTPS port:

```
addr = socket.getaddrinfo('0.0.0.0', 443)[0][-1]
s = socket.socket()
s.setsockopt(socket.SOL_SOCKET, socket.SO_REUSEADDR, 1)
s.bind(addr)
s.listen(5)
```

The socket that you accept from the client has to be wrapped in an SSL socket before you try to transfer any data:

```
    cl, addr = s.accept()
    print('client connected from', addr)
    client_s =None

    try:
        client_s = ssl.wrap_socket(cl, server_side=True,
                                      key=key, cert=cert)
```

The wrap_socket function has to be in a try clause because with a self-signed certificate the client will abort the connection unless the site is added as a security exception. Notice that the key and the certificate are specified as the strings that we created earlier.

Once the client socket is wrapped we can start reading data, but the SSL handshaking procedure is messy and we need to allow the client to send some null packets and some packets containing a blank line when it encounters a problem with the connection. When you detect that a connection has gone wrong, the correct thing to do is abandon the transaction and wait for a new one. The client generally gets it right eventually. If we don't handle broken connections correctly then the server will block, waiting for more headers to be sent:

```
        while True:
            h = client_s.readline()
            if h == b"" or h == b"\r\n":
                    break
            print(h.decode(), end="")
```

In a more complicated program you might well have to gather and process the headers that the client sends. In this case we simply display them.

With these changes everything should work and here is the complete listing of the DS18x20 temperature sensor program given earlier now converted to SSL and renamed sslserver.py:

```
import network
import socket
import rp2
from time import sleep_ms
from machine import Pin, Timer
import onewire
import ds18x20

import ssl

def setup(country, ssid, key):
. . .

key=b'0\x82\x04\xbf\x02\x01\x000\r\x06\c6\xe7\xa2\xf4?w\xa4\x0c\n\
. . . x89\xfd\x00S4\xabp\xd1'
cert=b'0\x82\x03k0\x82\x02S\xa0\x03\x02\x01\\xa1N\x00f\x85!\x0e\
 . . .xddt*\x98\x8a'

wifi = setup("country", "ssid", "key")
print(wifi.ifconfig())

ow = onewire.OneWire(Pin(2))
presence = ow.reset()
if presence:
 print("Device present")
else:
 print("No device")

DS = ds18x20.DS18X20(ow)
roms = DS.scan()

template = """<!DOCTYPE html>
<html>
<head> <title>Temperature</title> </head>
<body> <h1>Current Temperature</h1>
Hello Pico W Server World <br/>
The Temperature is: <!--#temp--><br/>
</body>
</html>
"""
addr = socket.getaddrinfo('0.0.0.0', 443)[0][-1]

s = socket.socket()
s.setsockopt(socket.SOL_SOCKET, socket.SO_REUSEADDR, 1)
s.bind(addr)
s.listen(5)
```

```
while True:
    cl, addr = s.accept()
    print('client connected from', addr)
    client_s =None

    try:
        client_s = ssl.wrap_socket(cl, server_side=True,
                                            key=key, cert=cert)

        while True:
            h = client_s.readline()
            if h == b"" or h == b"\r\n":
                    break
            print(h.decode(), end="")

        temp = DS.read_temp(roms[0])

        html=template.replace("<!--#temp-->",str(temp))
        headers = ("HTTP/1.1 200 OK\r\n"
                "Content-Type: text/html; charset=UTF-8\r\n"
                "Server:Pico\r\n"
                f"Content-Length:{len(html)}\r\n\r\n"
                )
        buf = headers.encode("utf-8")+html.encode("utf-8")

        client_s.write(buf)

        client_s.close()
    except Exception as e:
        print("exception ",e)

s.close()
```

As usual the `setup` function has been omitted from the listing and the certificate strings have been truncated to save space. If you want to see what the full `sslserver.py` program looks like, see this book's page at www.iopress.info.

If you try this out you will find that connecting with a browser using

`https:// ip of server`

causes a security warning to pop-up due to the use of a self-signed certificate.

This is what you will see if you use Chrome.

⚠

Your connection is not private

Attackers might be trying to steal your information from **192.168.1.32**for example, passwords, messages, or credit cards). Learn more

NET::ERR_CERT_AUTHORITY_INVALID

💡   To get Chrome's highest level of security, turn on enhanced protection

Advanced   Back to safety

Messages like this are because browsers don't trust self-signed certificates. However, if you allow the page to download it will use SSL encryption. To do this click on Advanced and then confirm that you want to proceed. You can force a browser to accept the certificate by adding it to its trusted root certification authorities tab. However, for most testing purposes this isn't necessary. If you have a valid certificate and key for a particular web server you can substitute it for the self-signed certificates.

It is worth saying that making an SSL connection is not fast. The Pico is being asked to do significant computation to implement the cryptography and the handshake process is involved and hence time-consuming. You will also see a number of exceptions caused by the client aborting the connection due to the self-signed certificate, which is perfectly normal. Firefox is a much more friendly browser to use when testing SSL connections. Chrome tends to want to lock things down as soon as it detects a problem with the certificate.

If you are seeing error messages about running out of memory then perform a hard reset on the Pico. The problem is that any SSL sockets that are unclosed when the program ends due to an exception survive a soft reset and so slowly use up memory. A hard reset solves the problem.

Non-Blocking Sockets

The problem with the approach we have been using is that it is synchronous and you have to poll to see if there is a client wanting data. This has the unfortunate effect of stalling the pooling loop while it waits for `accept` to return. This is fine if you only have to do something when a request from a client comes in, but if you need to do other things like flash an LED or adjust a heater then stalling the polling loop isn't a good idea. There are a number of solutions to this, but the simplest is to make the socket non-blocking.

The MicroPython implementation of sockets allows you to set a timeout in milliseconds for all socket operations:

```
s.settimeout(time)
```

After you have set a non-zero timeout any operation will raise an `OSError` if it isn't complete in the specified time. If you set it to `None`, which is the default, all operations are blocking and will wait until the operation is complete or a timeout occurs due to the client or the server. Setting a timeout of zero makes the socket non-blocking and setting a positive value provides a behavior that is somewhere between blocking and non-blocking.

You can use:

```
s.setblocking(True/False)
```

as a shorthand for:

```
True = s.settimeout(None)
False = s.settimeout(0)
```

In the first case operations are blocking; in the second they are non-blocking in the sense that they return with a result immediately or raise an `OSError`.

To see how to make use of this in `servernonblock.py` change the polling loop to:

```
addr = socket.getaddrinfo('0.0.0.0', 80)[0][-1]

s = socket.socket()
s.setsockopt(socket.SOL_SOCKET, socket.SO_REUSEADDR, 1)
s.setblocking(False)
s.bind(addr)
s.listen(0)
```

```
while True:
    print("doing something")
    try:
        cl, addr = s.accept()
    except(OSError):
        continue
    cl.setblocking(True)
    print('client connected from', addr)
    print(cl.recv(512))
    DS.convert_temp()
    temp = DS.read_temp(roms[0])

    html = template.replace("<!--#temp-->",str(temp))
    headers = ("HTTP/1.1 200 OK\r\n"
               "Content-Type: text/html; charset = UTF-8\r\n"
               "Server:Pico\r\n"
               f"Content-Length:{len(html)}\r\n\r\n\r\n"
               )
    buf = headers.encode("utf-8")+html.encode("utf-8")

    cl.send(buf)

    cl.close()
```

Notice that now the listening socket is set to non-blocking, which means that the accept returns at once. If there is no client waiting it raises an OSError and the loop continues skipping the processing of the client's request. If there is a client waiting then its request is processed as before. Notice that the client's socket inherits the timeout value of the listening socket and in this case we change it to blocking to make processing the request simpler. If the request takes too long to process it can be converted to non-blocking.

If you run this modified server, servernonblock.py, you will see doing something repeatedly displayed as the polling loop waits for a client. If you take out the setblocking call then you will see doing something displayed twice per client connect – once for the temperature request and once for the web page's icon request.

The Connection Queue

Using non-blocking sockets usually provides sufficient responsiveness to serve clients and get other jobs done at the same time. There are generally sufficient timeouts and retries built into browsers to allow clients to connect even if the server is busy. If, however, the clients are not browsers but applications making direct use of sockets then they might not be so forgiving. In this case you can use the connection queue to avoid losing clients.

When you start a socket listening you can specify the size of the connection queue:

```
s.listen(n)
```

starts the socket listening with a queue of size n. When the first client connects it is processed. When subsequent clients try to connect while the first one is still being processed they are added to the queue until it is full at which point the client connection is reset.

If you try this out, with a long delay in processing a client, what you see will be complicated by the way the client tries to connect. For example, if you try to connect using Chrome it uses a long timeout with a retry algorithm that effectively makes the connect queue irrelevant. If you try the same thing with Firefox you will see that, with a queue of zero, two requests succeed and the rest return a "The connection was reset" error. Why two and not one isn't clear, but you also have to remember that each web page request generates at least two requests – one for the page and one for the page icon. If you set the queue size to one you will still see two requests succeed. Setting the queue to two and you will see three pages or more succeed in loading. The reason for more than three pages is that the page requested will be cached. Things get confusing after this because of additional requests for the page icon and the effect of caching it.

What all this means is that the connect queue's effect on a client trying to connect is real, but complicated. It all depends on the connection algorithm the client uses. In most cases a browser will manage to connect unless the server is extremely overloaded.

Summary

- If you want to do anything beyond HTTP, or you want to implement an HTTP server, then you need to make use of sockets.

- Sockets are completely general and you can use them to implement an HTTP client or a server.

- To allow for different types of connection, sockets can be used with a range of different types of addresses. In the case of the ESP32, however, we only need to use IP addresses.

- A socket client has to handle the details of the data transferred. In particular, you have to handle the details of HTTP headers.

- Implementing a socket server is easy, but it can be difficult to ensure that both clients and internal services are both attended to.

- The simplest solution to the server problem is to implement a polling loop and to do this you need to make use of non-blocking sockets.

- Simple sockets work with unencrypted data. If you want to use encryption you have to "wrap" the socket using the ssl module.

- HTTPS clients don't need a certificate to implement encryption, but servers do.

- For testing you can generate your own "self-signed" certificates although most browsers will complain that this isn't secure.

- The connection queue allows you to handle more than one client connection at a time.

Chapter 19

Asyncio and Servers

MicroPython has a basic implementation of the Python `asyncio` module. The `asyncio` module is very useful in providing asynchronous programming in Python and you might think that it would be exceptionally useful in low-level hardware applications as an alternative to polling or event driven approaches. In fact it isn't quite as useful as you might expect as there are few existing asynchronous subsystems. In full Python we have a complete filing system and network connections and this means that asynchronous programming can improve efficiency by putting the processor to work while waiting for I/O operations to complete. As the Pico doesn't have either an operating system or a filing system, there isn't much opportunity to make use of idle processor time. However, now that the Pico has a network connection via WiFi the `asyncio` module is suddenly much more useful.

In this chapter we first look at the basic idea of asynchronous programming as implemented by `uasyncio`, the MicroPython version of `asyncio`, and then at how to use it to implement a server asynchronously. If you want to know more about asynchronous programming in general and `asyncio` in particular see *Programmer's Python: Async*, ISBN:9781871962765.

Coroutines and Tasks

Asyncio is all about sharing a single thread of execution between different tasks. A key ability of a task is that it can be suspended and resumed and this is what a coroutine is all about. In a single-threaded environment the thread has to save its current state, start or resume work on another function and restore the state when it returns to the previous function. A function that can be suspended and restarted in this way is generally called a "coroutine".

A modern Python coroutine is created using the `async` keyword:

```
async def myCo():
    print("Hello Coroutine World")
    return 42
```

When you call `myCo` it doesn't execute its code, instead it returns a coroutine object which can execute the code. The only problem is that a coroutine isn't a runnable. You have to use features provided by `usasync` to run a coroutine. The simplest is the `asyncio.run` method which creates and manages the task loop without you having to know anything about it:

```
import uasyncio
async def myCo():
    print("Hello Coroutine World")
    return 42

myCoObject=myCo()
result= uasyncio.run(myCoObject)
print(result)
```

This runs the coroutine object and displays:

```
Hello Coroutine World
42
```

Instead of passing the coroutine object, the `asyncio.run` call is usually written as a single action:

```
result= uasyncio.run(myCo())
```

It is also important to realize that `asyncio.run` runs `myCo` at once and the thread doesn't return until `myCo` is completed. While running `myCo` a task loop is started and if the thread is freed it starts running any tasks queued before returning to `myCo`. In this sense the call to `asyncio.run` is where the asynchronous part of your program starts and you can think of it as starting the asynchronous main program.

Await

As it stands our coroutine might as well be a standard function as it doesn't suspend and resume its operation. To suspend a coroutine you have to use the `await` keyword to pause the coroutine while an awaitable completes.

An `await` suspends the awaiting program and this means it can only be used within a coroutine, i.e. the only code in Python that can be suspended and resumed. Once you have a coroutine running you can use `await` within it and within any coroutines it awaits.

What this means is that you have to use `uasyncio.run` to get a first coroutine running, but after this you can use `await` to run other coroutines as `Tasks`.

Most asyncio programs are organized so that there is a single `asyncio.run` instruction at the top level of the program and this starts a coroutine, often called `main`, which then runs the rest of the asynchronous program by awaiting other coroutines.

That is, a typical `asyncio` program is:

```
async def main():
    call other coroutines using await

uasyncio.run(main())
```

The call to `uasyncio.run` sets up the event loop as well as starting `main` running. You can call ordinary, i.e. non-coroutine, functions from within coroutines, but these cannot use `await`. Only a coroutine can use `await`, for example:

```
import uasyncio

async def test1(msg):
    print(msg)

async def main():
    await test1("Hello Coroutine World")

uasyncio.run(main())
```

Notice that even though `main` now awaits the `test1` coroutine there is no new behavior. The program would work in exactly the same way with functions replacing coroutines. The reason is that none of our coroutines actually release the main thread, they simply keep running.

There are two distinct things that can occur when you `await` another coroutine. Some coroutines hold onto the main thread and continue to execute instructions until they finish – they are essentially synchronous coroutines. Some release the main thread while they wait for some operation to complete and only these are truly asynchronous coroutines. At the moment we only know about synchronous coroutines.

Awaiting Sleep

Until the Pico had a network connection the `uasyncio.sleep` method was the only coroutine you could run that actually released the main thread so that other tasks in the queue got a chance to execute. With the Pico W there are also network connection methods that work in this way.

The simplest asynchronous coroutine is `uasyncio.sleep` is:

`uasyncio.sleep(delay)`

which returns after *delay* seconds.

There is also a MicroPython extension:

`uasyncio.sleep_ms(delay)`

which returns after *delay* milli-seconds.

Notice that these are not the same as the corresponding sleep function in the time module and it is important to understand the difference. The time.sleep function suspends the current thread for the specified amount of time. That is, the one thread that you were depending on to do the work would be frozen and if used in an asynchronous program so would the task loop. In fact time.sleep is a very good way to keep the thread busy and so simulate a coroutine that doesn't give up the thread.

Compare this to uasyncio.sleep which doesn't suspend the thread at all - it suspends the coroutine. The main thread stops running the coroutine and returns to the event loop to find another coroutine to run. When the time delay is up and the main thread next visits the task loop for more work, the suspended coroutine is restarted. Of course, this means that the coroutine might be suspended for longer than the specified time and this is usually the case. The coroutine is restarted when the main thread is free to run it and the time delay is up.

The uasyncio.sleep function suspends the current coroutine and not the thread.

A standard idiom is to call sleep with a value of zero seconds:

```
await uasyncio.sleep(0)
```

or

```
await usasyncio.sleep_ms(0)
```

This gives up the thread to the task loop with the minimum delay if there is nothing to be done in the event loop queue. That is, all that happens is that the main thread is freed and, if there is nothing waiting to be executed in the task loop, it returns at once to running the coroutine. This gives the event loop a chance to run other coroutines and it is a good idea to include any coroutine that runs for a long time. The call sleep(0) is equivalent to DoEvents in other languages, i.e. an instruction to process the event loop's queue.

We can easily add an await for 10 seconds to our example:

```
import asyncio

async def main(myValue):
    print("Hello Coroutine World")
    await asyncio.sleep(10)
    return myValue

result= asyncio.run(main(42))
print(result)
```

There is now a ten-second delay between displaying Hello Coroutine World and the result, i.e. 42. In this case the main thread is freed when the await starts and has 10 seconds in which to run any other coroutines waiting in the task loop. In this case there aren't any and so it just waits for the time to be up. We next need to know how to add coroutines to the task loop so that they can be run when the main thread is free.

Tasks

A Task is a coroutine that you have added to the task loop for execution by the thread when the opportunity arises. A Task has some additional methods added to the basic coroutine and in Python it inherits from a Future, but in MicroPython things are simpler.

To add a Task to the task loop you need to use:

```
uasyncio.create_task(coroutine)
```

This adds *coroutine* to the task loop as a Task. It adds the coroutine to the task loop queue ready to be executed. It doesn't actually get to run until the main thread is free to return to the task loop and run the tasks that it finds there. This only happens when the currently executing coroutine awaits an asynchronous coroutine or terminates.

The uasyncio.create_task function returns a Task which behaves like a Future in Python. The only important point for MicroPython is that any result that the task returns is only available after the task has completed, or resolved in the terminology. To get the result we need to use an await to retrieve a result. For example, if we create a coroutine that prints a range of numbers then this can be added to the event loop within main:

```
import uasyncio

async def count(n):
    for i in range(n):
        print(i)
    return n

async def main(myValue):
    t1 = uasyncio.create_task(count(10))
    print("Hello Coroutine World")
    await uasyncio.sleep(5)
    result = await t1
    print("The result of the task =",result)
    return myValue

result= uasyncio.run(main(42))
print(result)
```

The count coroutine is added to the task loop before the print, but it doesn't get to run until main awaits sleep for 5 seconds and so frees the thread. This allows the count function to display 0 to 9 but then the thread continues to wait till the full five seconds are up. At this point it awaits the task so as to get its result. If t1 hadn't completed then the thread would execute it until it was complete. As it is, t1 is complete and so returns its result at once and there is no delay before it is printed.

What you see displayed is;

```
Hello Coroutine World
0
1
2
3
4
5
6
7
8
9
The result of the task = 10
42
```

Make sure that this example makes sense before you move on to more complex things.

At this point you should be wondering why we bothered creating a Task and adding it to the event loops's queue? Why not just use await count? This produces the same result, but for different reasons. In this case the Task isn't added to the task queue until the await and then the Task is run to completion. This means that it isn't in the queue earlier and cannot benefit from any time that the thread might be free.

You will sometimes see instructions like:

```
value = await asyncio.create_task(count(10))
```

This adds the coroutine to the queue as a Task and then immediately awaits it, which of course, starts it running. There is no point in doing this and it is entirely equivalent to:

```
value = await count(10)
```

To summarize:

- create_task(*coroutine*) runs the *coroutine* at a later time. It adds it as a Task to the task loop's queue for execution when the thread is free
- await *coroutine* runs the *coroutine* immediately
- await *Task* runs the Task to completion taking into account any process it might have already made by being on the task queue.

Another way of thinking about this is to use `create_task` when you want the coroutine to run when the thread is free and use `await` when you need the coroutine to run now.

There is also a way to `await` a coroutine with a timeout:

`uasyncio.wait_for(aw, timeout)`

which waits for *aw*, an awaitable, to complete or until the *timeout* in seconds is up.

MicroPython also adds

`uasyncio.wait_for_ms(aw, timeout)`

which of course specifies the timeout in milliseconds. If the timeout happens the task raises a `uasyncio.TimeoutError` in the waiting code and a `uasyncio.CancelledError` in the Task. Each of these methods is a coroutine so to use them you write:

`await uasyncio.wait_for(t1,1)`

Sequential and Concurrent

The `gather` function is usually described as being a way of running `Task` coroutines concurrently, but it is better thought of as a way of running and waiting for a set of `Task` coroutines to complete:

`uasyncio.gather(tasks, return_exceptions = False)`

Any coroutine in the `tasks` comma-separated list of Tasks is added to the task queue as a `Task`. All of the tasks are then executed as the queue schedules them with the calling coroutine suspended until all of them complete. The function returns a list of results in the same order as the awaitables were originally listed in `tasks`. If `return_exceptions` is `False` then any exception is propagated to the calling coroutine, but the other coroutines in the `tasks` list are left to complete. If it is `True` then the exceptions are returned as valid results in the list.

If the `gather` is canceled all of the items in `aws` are canceled. If any of the items in `aws` are canceled then it raises a `CancelledError`, which is either passed to the calling coroutine or added to the result list and the `gather` itself is not canceled. Using `gather` is almost the same as adding coroutines to the event loop using `asyncio.create_task` and then waiting for them to complete.

For example:

```
import uasyncio
async def test1(msg):
    print(msg)
    return msg

async def main():
    result = await uasyncio.gather(test1("one"),test1("two"))
    print(result)
    print("Hello Coroutine World")

uasyncio.run(main())
```

This starts two copies of the test1 coroutine running as tasks on the task loop. As we await them immediately the main coroutine pauses until both are complete and then prints the results as a list. As test1 doesn't release the main thread the first task runs to completion and then the second is run. This isn't necessarily the case if either of the tasks releases the thread. The order in which they execute in isn't determined by the order in which they occur in the gather.

It should be obvious by this point, but is worth making clear, that if you want to run coroutines one after another, i.e. sequentially, then you should use:

```
await coroutine1()
await coroutine2()
await coroutine3()
```

and so on. This adds each coroutine to the task loop queue one at a time and the calling coroutine waits for each one to end in turn. If the called coroutine releases the main thread other coroutines, if any, already on the task loop get a chance to run. You can be sure, however, that coroutine1 completes before coroutine2 starts and coroutine2 completes before coroutine3 starts.

Compare this to:

```
await gather(coroutine1(), coroutine2(), coroutine3(), …)
```

which adds all of the coroutines to the event loop and then runs each one in turn. If any of the coroutines releases the main thread the other coroutines listed get a chance to run, along with anything that was on the event loop before the gather. As a result all of the coroutines in the gather make progress to completion at the same time, if this is possible. They are executed concurrently in the sense that you cannot be sure that coroutine1 completes before coroutine2 or coroutine3 starts.

Canceling Tasks

In a single-threaded environment canceling a `Task` cannot mean canceling the thread because it has other work to do. If you use the `task.cancel` method then the `Task` is marked to receive a `CancelledError` exception the next time it runs on the event loop. If you don't handle the exception the `Task` simply dies silently. If you have any resources to close then you have to handle the exception to perform the cleanup. You can even opt to ignore the `CancelledError` exception altogether.

For example:

```
import uasyncio
async def test1(msg):
    try:
        await uasyncio.sleep(0)
    except:
        pass
    print(msg)
    return msg
async def main():
    t1 = uasyncio.create_task(test1("one"))
    await uasyncio.sleep(0)
    t1.cancel()
    print("Hello Coroutine World")
    await uasyncio.sleep(0)
uasyncio.run(main())
```

In this case the `try` suppresses the exception and everything works as if `cancel` had not been called. If you remove the `try/except` then you don't see one displayed as `test1` is canceled.

Dealing With Exceptions

The fact that a `Task` is modeled on a `Future` should immediately tell you how to handle exceptions in asynchronous programs. The `Task` either returns a result or an exception object and by default the `Exception` object is used to raise the exception in the calling coroutine. For example:

```
import uasyncio
async def test(msg):
    print(msg)
    raise Exception("Test exception")
async def main():
    t1=uasyncio.create_task(test("one"))
    try:
        await t1
    except:
        print("an exception has occurred")
    print("Hello Coroutine World")
    await uasyncio.sleep(0)
uasyncio.run(main())
```

In this case `test` raises an exception as soon as it is called. This is returned to the calling coroutine and raised again by the `await` operation.

If you want to access the exception object and handle it manually you will have to use one of the `gather` methods as `await` always consumes the `Task` and hence raises the exception whereas `gather` can return all results including exceptions.

For example:

```
import uasyncio

async def test(msg):
    print(msg)
    raise Exception("Test exception")


async def main():
    t1=uasyncio.create_task(test("one"))
    result=None
    try:
        result=await uasyncio.gather(t1,return_exceptions=True)
    except:
        print("an exception has occurred")
    print("Hello Coroutine World")
    print(result)
    await uasyncio.sleep(0)

uasyncio.run(main())
```

displays:

```
one
Hello Coroutine World
[Exception('Test exception',)]
```

You can see that now you have the `Exception` object and you can choose to do what you like with it or raise it when you are ready.

Finally if you don't `await` a `Task` then any exceptions are ignored, just as any results are ignored. The `Task` fails silently, just as it succeeds silently if it is not awaited.

Shared Variables and Locks

Coroutines share global variables and have their own local variables as is the case for functions. If you are not used to asynchronous programming this can have some surprising consequences. The problem is that access to global resources by more than one task carries the risk of a race condition. For example, if two tasks attempt to update a resource and one is part way through an update when the other starts and begins its own update then the final outcome depends on which task gets to complete its update last. This is a "race condition". Given that uasyncio implements a form of asynchronous programming that only starts another Task if the currently running Task gives up the thread, i.e. it voluntarily allows another Task to start, this is far less of a problem You can avoid it altogether by always making sure that any Task only gives up the thread when any use of a shared resources is complete. However, as hardware-oriented programs of the sort you run on the Pico tend to use shared hardware resources, this is more of a problem than in other situations. The solution is to use a lock of one sort or another so as to restrict access to the shared resource to one task at a time.

The uasyncio module contains asynchronous equivalents for most of the standard threading locks:

◆ Lock

The Lock object has three methods that control the way that tasks interact with it:

lock.locked() Returns True if locked

lock.aquire() Waits for lock to be unlocked and then locks it

lock.release() Unlocks the lock

The basic idea is that all of the tasks that want to access a shared resource follow the protocol that they first have to acquire the Lock object that is protecting it by using acquire(). If another task has already acquired the lock then subsequent attempts to acquire it suspend the task until the lock is released. When the lock is released one of the tasks waiting to acquire it is allowed to run. This means that only one task accesses the shared resource at a time and other tasks queue up to use it.

◆ Event

The Event object has four methods:

is_set() True if the event is set and False otherwise.

set () Sets the event, any waiting tasks can now run

clear() Clears the event

wait() Waits for the event to be set

The Event object is intended to be used to synchronize tasks. Any number of tasks can wait on an event and then any other task can set the event and allow the waiting tasks to be scheduled to run when the thread is free. For example, a set of tasks might process a file that is downloaded by another task. The downloading task can set the event to signal to the processing tasks that the data is ready to process.

◆ ThreadSafeFlag

The ThreadSafeFlag has three methods:

set() Sets the flag

clear Clears the flag

wait Waits for the flag to be set.

ThreadSafeFlag works like the Event object, but it can be used by functions that are not coroutines such as interrupt handlers.

The whole subject of locks and how to use them is a big one and if you want to know more see *Programmer's Python: Async*, ISBN:9781871962765. However, you need to be aware of the two big problems in using locks. The first is that they slow things down. Locks are slow to use and restrict access often unnecessarily. The second is the potential for deadlock – where one task is waiting on a lock that another holds while it is waiting for a lock that the first task is holding. Consider the following example, count1.py based on a simple counter updating a global variable, myCounter:

```
import uasyncio

async def count():
    global myCounter
    for i in range(1000):
        temp = myCounter+1
        await uasyncio.sleep(0)
        myCounter = temp

async def main():
    await uasyncio.gather(count(),count())
    print(myCounter)

myCounter=0
uasyncio.run(main())
```

Each task updates myCounter a thousand times and so the total should be 2000, but if you run the program you will find that it is 1000. Where have the other thousand updates gone?

Both t1 and t2 release the main thread in the middle of the update of the global variable. As a result each task updates myCounter at exactly the same time and as a result there is a perfect race condition on every update and the program displays 1000.

The simplest solution to this problem is not to release the main thread in the middle of an operation. As long as the task doesn't release the main thread it is an atomic operation. This is usually one of the benefits of using single-threaded multi-tasking.

If this approach cannot be used then there is no alternative but to add a lock. The uasyncio module provides its own locks. Rather than having to explicitly call acquire and release we can use "async with". This acquires the lock on entry to the block and automatically releases it on exit. This can only be used in a coroutine and can be suspended during the enter and exit phase, count2.py:

```
import uasyncio

async def count():
    global myCounter
    global myLock
    for i in range(1000):
        async with myLock:
            temp=myCounter+1
            await uasyncio.sleep(0)
            myCounter=temp


async def main():
    await uasyncio.gather(count(),count())
    print(myCounter)

myCounter=0
myLock=uasyncio.Lock()
uasyncio.run(main())
```

Now t2 has to wait until t1 releases the lock before it can continue. Notice the use of async with rather than just with. The program now displays 2000. In this case the problem has been caused deliberately, but when you are using coroutines there are occasions that you cannot modify in which locking is the only option.

Using uasyncio

When you first meet uasyncio, or its full Python equivalent asyncio, it is all too easy to see it as a total solution. The idea that you can structure a program as a collection of tasks which get to run when they are needed seems to be a simplification. However, the Pico implementation of uasyncio provides only two coroutines that free the thread – uasyncio.sleep() and uasyncio.sleep_ms(). The Pico W also has some network classes and methods which make uasyncio much more useful, but it is still worth looking at its more basic use.

345

The only sort of task you can write that actually gives up the thread, and hence take advantage of asynchronous implementation, are of the form:

```
async task1():
     while True:
            do something
            await uasyncio.sleep(t)
            do something
```

The call to sleep releases the thread and allows other tasks to run for at least t seconds. What this means is that all of the tasks you create have to be able to be suspended for a given amount of time to allow other tasks to run. Notice that there is no indication of how often any of the tasks will run. For example, if one of the tasks is designed to read a sensor every few seconds then there is no way that you can use an asynchronous approach to guarantee that this is the case unless you handcraft all of the other tasks to ensure that the sensor task gets its turn at the right time. This is just as difficult, if not more so, than writing a simple polling loop that calls the tasks in a fixed order.

For example, the following program is modeled on the example in the documentation:

```
import uasyncio
from machine import Pin

async def blink(led, period_ms):
    while True:
        led.on()
        await uasyncio.sleep_ms(5)
        led.off()
        await uasyncio.sleep_ms(period_ms)

async def main(led1, led2):
    uasyncio.create_task(blink(led1, 700))
    uasyncio.create_task(blink(led2, 400))
    await uasyncio.sleep_ms(10_000)

uasyncio.run(main(Pin(0,Pin.OUT), Pin(1,Pin.OUT)))
```

This flashes two LEDs connected to GPIO 0 and GPIO 1. The blink coroutine turns the LED on and then sleeps for 5ms, giving other tasks a chance to run. It then switches the LED off and sleeps for a specified period. If you try this out you will find that you do get 5ms pulses spaced at 700ms and 400ms. However, none of the periods are guaranteed. All it takes is another task, or a set of tasks, that take longer to process than 5ms.

For example, we can introduce a task that simply wastes some time:

```
import uasyncio
from machine import Pin
from time import sleep_ms
async def blink(led, period_ms):
    while True:
        led.on()
        await uasyncio.sleep_ms(5)
        led.off()
        await uasyncio.sleep_ms(period_ms)

async def timewaste():
    while True:
        sleep_ms(10)
        await uasyncio.sleep_ms(0)


async def main(led1, led2):
    uasyncio.create_task(blink(led1, 700))
    uasyncio.create_task(blink(led2, 400))
    uasyncio.create_task(timewaste())
    await uasyncio.sleep_ms(10_000)

uasyncio.run(main(Pin(0,Pin.OUT), Pin(1,Pin.OUT)))
```

Now if you run the program you will discover that the pulses are now 10ms in size. The `timewaste` coroutine now hogs the only thread of execution, only giving it up every 10ms, which means that the `blink` coroutine only gets the thread back after at least 10ms whenever it gives it up.

Even if you find this difficult to understand, an additional negative point for the approach is that the timing of blink depends on the timing of the other tasks it finds itself running with.

Asynchronous approaches generally only work well when each task keeps the thread for a time that is much shorter than the time that each task needs to run – and this implies that the thread has to be idle for most of the time.

Async Networking

The `asyncio` module is primarily designed to work with asynchronous network connections. It doesn't provide high-level networking facilities. There is no asynchronous download of an HTML page, for example. However, it provides a class that caters for high-level clients and another for server objects which make working with general TCP connections very easy.

Communication with both client and server objects is via streams which are modeled on files. Both client and server objects return streams to allow the

347

TCP connection to be used. The MicroPython implementation of uasyncio uses a single Stream object as a reader and a writer.

The supported read methods are:

- read(n = -1) Reads up to n bytes as a bytes object
  The default, n = -1, is to read until the end of the file signal (EOF) is received and return all read bytes

- readline() Reads a sequence of bytes ending with \n
  If EOF is received and \n was not found, the method returns partially read data. If EOF is received and the internal buffer is empty, returns an empty bytes object

- readexactly(n) Reads exactly n bytes and raises an EOF error if EOF is reached before n can be read

- readinto(buf) Reads up to len(buf) bytes into buf

Notice that all of the reading methods are coroutines as there may not be enough data ready to satisfy the call. In this case the coroutine is suspended and the main thread is freed. That is, calls to functions that read data are asynchronous coroutines. Also notice that while there are references to using EOF to signal the end of a transaction, in general EOF isn't particularly useful when dealing with sockets. Sockets tend to be left open until they are no longer required and data is usually sent in some sort of format that lets you work out when you have read a useful chunk of data that can be processed. Generally, if you wait for an EOF you will wait a long time until the server times out and closes the socket.

The only write method is:

- write(buf) Attempts to write the buf to the stream
  The data is only written following a call to the drain() method

This is not a coroutine and always returns immediately. However, the drain() coroutine, which waits until it is appropriate to resume writing to the stream, should be called after each write operation, for example:

```
stream.write(data)
await stream.drain()
```

The close() method closes both the stream and the underlying socket used in the TCP connection and should be used along with the wait_closed() coroutine:

```
stream.close()
await stream.wait_closed()
```

The logic is that there is no point in carrying on until the stream has been closed and so you might as well free the main thread. You can also use is_closing() to test whether the stream is closed or is in the process of closing.

Downloading A Web Page

We have already used the urequest module to download a web page and we have used sockets to do the same job asynchronously with non-blocking sockets. An alternative approach is to use uasyncio to do the job as part of an overall asynchronous system.

The coroutine:

uasyncio.open_connection(host,port)

uses sockets to open a connection to the host, specified as an IP address or a URL and a port. If successful this returns a (*reader*, *writer*) tuple which can be used to communicate with the server. The *reader* and *writer* are actually the same stream object, but for clarity we will make use of each one appropriately. For example, to connect to www.example.com, as we did in the previous chapter, you would use client.py:

```
import uasyncio
from time import sleep_ms
from machine import Pin, Timer
import rp2
import network

def setup(country, ssid, key):
    ...
async def main():
    reader,writer = await uasyncio.open_connection(
                                "www.example.com",80)
    request = b"GET /index.html HTTP/1.1\r\n
                        Host:example.org\r\n\r\n"
    writer.write(request)
    await writer.drain()
    print((await reader.read(512)).decode("utf-8"))
    reader.close()
wifi = setup(country, ssid, key)
uasyncio.run(main())
```

What is the advantage of this approach?

The simple answer is that it makes it easier to overlap downloads. For example, if you convert the download actions into a function:

```
async def getPage(url):
    reader,writer = await uasyncio.open_connection(url,80)
    request = b"GET /index.html HTTP/1.1\r\n
                        Host:example.org\r\n\r\n"
    writer.write(request)
    await writer.drain()
    page = await reader.read(512)
    reader.close()
    return page
```

you can now call it sequentially or concurrently.

If you call it sequentially:

```
results = await getPage('www.example.com')
results = await getPage('www.example.com')
```

it takes 800ms to download the page twice. However, if you call it concurrently:

```
results = await uasyncio.gather( getPage('www.example.com'),
                                 getPage('www.example.com'))
```

it takes only 400ms, which is only a little more than the 350ms it takes to download the page once. The improvement is due to the fact that while the getPage coroutine is waiting for the download, it releases the thread and the other coroutine can execute.

Server

As well as making a stream connection to a server, uasyncio also allows you to create a server that will accept incoming connections as streams:

```
asyncio.start_server(callback, host, port, backlog=5)
```

This starts a socket server, with a callback for each client connected. The return value is a Server object. When a client connects the callback is passed two parameters, a reader and a writer, to communicate with the client. As in the case of the TCP client, these refer to the same Stream object. Each client connection is independent and can be continued until the transaction is complete. The callback can be a standard function, but this would block the event loop so it is usual to make it a coroutine.

The Server object has the following methods:

- ◆ close() Stops serving, closes listening sockets and sets the sockets attribute to None. The sockets that represent existing incoming client connections are left open and can continue to be used until they are closed.

- ◆ wait_closed() Waits until the stream has closed.

The Server object also supports use as an async context manager. When the with block is exited the server.close method is called.

350

A Web Server

Implementing a simple web server using the Server object is very easy.

First create the server:

```
async def main():
    await uasyncio.start_server(serve_client,
                                '192.168.253.58', 80,backlog=5)
    while True:
        print("heartbeat")
        await uasyncio.sleep(1)
```

The server will respond to requests on the network connections on port 80. After creating the server the main coroutine simply loops, printing a message and then going to sleep so freeing the thread.

The Server object now monitors incoming TCP packets on the specified address and port. When a client sends a packet, the Server object calls the callback, serve_client in this case. Each client gets its own copy of serve_client which runs asynchronously on the event loop. This means that you could have many requests handled using just a single thread. Our serve_client is going to be simple, it will return the HTML page giving the current temperature as for the server at the end of the previous chapter.

The callback has a reader and writer Stream object passed to it which enables two-way communication with the client:

```
async def serve_client(reader,writer):
    print("client")
    print(await reader.read(512))
    DS.convert_temp()
    temp = DS.read_temp(roms[0])
    html=template.replace("<!--#temp-->",str(temp))
    headers = ("HTTP/1.1 200 OK\r\n"
            "Content-Type: text/html; charset=UTF-8\r\n"
            "Server:Pico\r\n"
            f"Content-Length:{len(html)}\r\n\r\n"
            )
    buf = headers.encode("utf-8")+html.encode("utf-8")

    writer.write(buf)
    await writer.drain()
    writer.close()
    await writer.wait_closed()
```

The callback reads the request that the client has sent and, irrespective of what it is, obtains a temperature reading and sends this as part of the HTML page back to the client.

As before, the `server.py` program ignores the details of the request sent by the client, but this is easy to correct. You can also add additional processing as part of the `main` coroutine or you can add tasks to the task queue.

Leaving out the setup function the rest of the `server.py` program is:

```
import uasyncio
import network
import rp2
from machine import Pin, Timer
from time import sleep_ms
import onewire
import ds18x20

def setup(country, ssid, key):
    . . .
wifi = setup("country", "ssid", "key")

ow = onewire.OneWire(Pin(2))
presence = ow.reset()
if presence:
    print("Device present")
else:
    print("No device")

DS = ds18x20.DS18X20(ow)
roms = DS.scan()

template = """<!DOCTYPE html>
<html>
<head> <title>Temperature</title> </head>
<body> <h1>Current Temperature</h1>
Hello Pico W Server World <br/>
The Temperature is: <!--#temp--><br/>
</body>
</html>
"""
async def serve_client(reader,writer):
    print("client")
    print(await reader.read(512))
    DS.convert_temp()
    temp = DS.read_temp(roms[0])
    html=template.replace("<!--#temp-->",str(temp))
    headers = ("HTTP/1.1 200 OK\r\n"
                "Content-Type: text/html; charset=UTF-8\r\n"
                "Server:Pico\r\n"
                f"Content-Length:{len(html)}\r\n\r\n"
            )
    buf = headers.encode("utf-8")+html.encode("utf-8")
```

```
    writer.write(buf)
    await writer.drain()
    writer.close()
    await writer.wait_closed()

async def main():
    await uasyncio.start_server(serve_client, '192.168.253.58',
                                                80,backlog=5)

    while True:
        print("heartbeat")
        await uasyncio.sleep(1)

uasyncio.run(main())
```

Best Practice

How best to implement a server?

Although the uasyncio approach is attractive from a theoretical point of view, it is built using non-blocking sockets. If you really need to serve multiple clients at the same time then directly using non-blocking sockets is probably the best way to do the job from the point of not having additional overhead and having more control over timing in a polling loop.

Notice that uasyncio doesn't include any support for events and this is true of the full asyncio module. If the task loop could be modified to include event handlers then it might be more useful in an IoT context. The Pico has the hardware to work with events and it should be easy to add this to uasyncio by adding an event handling Task when an event occurs.

There is also a lot to be said for using a client to deliver data to a server via a PUT or POST request. This would save a lot of effort in implementing an asynchronous system and makes timing easier to deal with.

Summary

- The `asyncio` module provides single-threaded multi-tasking.

- A coroutine is a function that can be suspended and resumed by the use of the `await` instruction.

- A coroutine has to be run in conjunction with an event loop. `asyncio.run` creates an event loop and runs a coroutine as a task using it.

- A `Task` is a coroutine with some additional methods and it is what is added to the event loop's queue using `asyncio.create_task`. The `Task` is run when the thread becomes free.

- When you `await` a coroutine it starts running to completion.

- When you `await` a `Task`, i.e. a coroutine already on the task loop, it only starts running if it isn't already completed.

- The `await` always returns the result of the `Task`, including any exceptions that might have occurred.

- You can use `wait_for` as a version of `await` with a timeout.

- Task coroutines can be executed in sequential order by awaiting each one in turn. They can be run concurrently by adding them to the queue or by using the `gather` coroutine.

- A `Task` can be canceled, but is up to you to handle the exception.

- A `Task` returns any exceptions to the awaiting coroutine – these can be raised or processed.

- Locks are less useful for coroutines because unless the thread is released they are atomic. If a race condition can occur there are asynchronous equivalents of some of the standard synchronization objects.

- The `asyncio` module makes network connections easy and asynchronous.

- Implementing a web client is easy, but there is no high-level function which downloads an HTML page. You have to work with the HTTP protocol.

- Creating a web server is only slightly more difficult in that you have to support multiple potential clients.

Chapter 20

Advanced Hardware

In this chapter we take a look at some of the more advanced features of the Pico. They are advanced in the sense not that they are difficult but they are less often required and mostly poorly documented and sometimes with incomplete implementations.

Two Processors

The Pico has two cores processors and it is very tempting to consider making use of the one that sits idle most of the time. But this isn't as easy as it sounds. While MicroPython has a _thread module which implements some of the facilities in the full Python _thread module, at the time of writing this module isn't even in beta, it is marked as "experimental". Additionally, of course, without an operating system this module isn't going to be as capable when it comes to the Pico. Despite these warnings the basic facilities seem to work reasonably well.

The Pico port of MicroPython does make use of threads to run programs on the second, usually idle, core and if you really want to, all you have to do is create a new thread and it runs on the second core. Creating a thread is just a matter of using:

```
thread.start_new_thread(task,args,keys)
```

where task is the function you want to run and args is a tuple passed to the task as its arguments. The final parameter, keys, a dict of keyword args, is optional. This isn't a general creation of a new thread and you can only use it once to create a thread of execution running on the second core. If you try to start a second thread you will see the error message that the core is already in use.

As long as you don't want the two parts of your program to share resources, this is easy and workable, but most applications need some sort of communication between the two threads which makes things more difficult. The two threads have separate local variables, but they both have access to the same global variables.

For example, suppose you want to use both cores to update a count as in thread1.py:

```
import _thread
counter=0

def task():
    global counter
    print("thread started")
    for i in range(1000):
        counter=counter+1

_thread.start_new_thread(task,())
for i in range(1000):
        counter=counter+1
time.sleep(0.5)
print(counter)
```

The task updates the shared counter a thousand times and the main program does the same. If you run the program you will discover that the result is around 1400 rather than the correct 2000. The reason is that we have a race condition. Imagine what happens if both cores read the contents of counter and add one to it at the same time and then store the result back in counter. Instead of incrementing by two, counter increments by one.

The solution is to use a lock to restrict access to any shared resources. While the _thread module does provide a lock class, it doesn't actually work very well. The idea is that a thread has to acquire the lock before using the resource and if it tries to acquire the lock and it is already locked then the thread has to wait. When the other thread releases the lock, the waiting thread can proceed. To know more about locking, and multiprocessing in general, see **Programmer's Python: Async**, ISBN:9781871962765.

To avoid the race condition we need to lock the access to the counter variable, thread1.py with comments removed:

```
import time, _thread, machine
counter=0
myLock=_thread.allocate_lock()
def task():

    global counter, myLock
    print("thread started")
    print(myLock.locked())
    for i in range(1000):
        myLock.acquire()
        counter=counter+1
        myLock.release()

_thread.start_new_thread(task,())
```

```
for i in range(1000):
        myLock.acquire()
        counter=counter+1
        myLock.release()
time.sleep(0.5)
print(counter)
```

If you try out the modified version of thread1.py you should find that the count is 2000 as the locks ensure that only one core can access the shared variable at the same time.

Watchdog and FlashNuke

One piece of hardware that we haven't yet considered is the Pico's watchdog timer. This is a very simple idea and once you have encountered it there are few problems in using it. A standard problem for any IoT device is how to cope with a system crash – caused by software or hardware. Clearly you need to protect your system from crashes as much as possible, but despite precautions bad things still happen.

What should your system do if it crashes? The usual, but not universal, answer is that it should restart and try to pick up where it left off. This is what a watchdog timer is all about. It has to be a very reliable piece of hardware, preferably implemented separately from the main system and, if possible, powered separately. In practice, most processors have a watchdog timer built in, which makes them easy to implement but not as robust as you might like. The watchdog timer simply counts down at a steady rate and when it reaches zero it applies a hardware reset signal to the main processor. The application software sets the countdown time and before this interval is up it resets the timer. Resetting the timer is an "I'm alive and well" signal that stops the system from being restarted. If the application has crashed then the timer will not be reset and the system will restart.

Start the watchdog timer using:

```
from machine import WDT
wdt = WDT(timeout=2000)
```

where timeout sets the countdown in milliseconds with a minimum of one second. Once set you cannot stop or modify the watchdog timer, but you can feed it:

```
wdt.feed()
```

which restarts the countdown.

If the watchdog does timeout it restarts the Pico and this restarts the MicroPython interpreter. It doesn't automatically restart the program that started the watchdog timer. So how do you keep an application running? The answer is that if your MicroPython program is called main.py then it will be automatically loaded and run when the system is powered on or reset by the watchdog timer.

Putting a program called `main.py` onto your Pico runs the risk that you will lose control of it. If `main.py` runs in a loop and occupies the hardware by, say, toggling a GPIO line very fast, then any IDE will not be able to gain control of the program and the Ctrl-C break will not work. Even if you reinstall MicroPython it will still run the original `main.py` because your programs live in flash memory, independent of the MicroPython `.uf2` file. The solution is to use a FlashNuke utility to wipe all of the flash memory on the Pico. You can find this at:

```
pico-examples/flash/nuke.c
```

in:

```
https://github.com/raspberrypi/pico-examples
```

and you can download a compiled UF2 file from:

```
https://datasheets.raspberrypi.com/soft/flash_nuke.uf2
```

All you have to do is power the Pico on with the BOOTSEL button held down and drag-and-drop the file `flash_nuke.uf2` onto the directory. This resets the Pico back to factory state and you will have to repeat installation of the Python interpreter by powering on while holding down the BOOTSEL button and dragging-and-dropping its `.uf2` file.

If you are exploring the watchdog timer you will almost certainly need FlashNuke as it is very easy to create a program that never stops running and that you cannot break into.

The following program has the potential to lock the Pico. Don't run it unless you understand how to remove it from memory:

```
from machine import WDT
import time

print("starting")
wdt = WDT(timeout=4000)
wdt.feed()
while True:
    time.sleep(0.1)
    print("still running")
    pass
```

If you run this using, say, VS Code then it will behave like a standard program, but if you name it `main.py` and use the Upload Current File command then it will start running every time the Pico starts. The watchdog timer will restart the MicroPython interpreter every four seconds and this in turn will load and run `main.py`. It doesn't matter what you do to gain control of the program - the watchdog timer will restart it after four seconds. To stop it you need to download and use FlashNuke and reinstall MicroPython.

Using the RTC

The Pico has a built-in RTC (Real Time Clock) which, while not having a battery backup, can be kept accurate using the `ntptime` module to retrieve the time from the Internet. The Pico 2 doesn't have the same hardware, but MicroPython covers up this difference so that you can simply work with date and time in the same way.

You can set the system time using the `ntptime` module. This allows you to look up the time from an NTP (Network Time Protocol) server and to use it to set the RTC. The `ntptime` object has two properties and one method:

```
ntptime.host = ntpserver
ntptime.timeout = timeinmilliseconds
ntptime.settime()
```

The host that you set should be one of the many NTP pool servers. A pool server has a list of time servers that it issues in response to a DNS request so as to spread the load. For example, if you query `pool.ntp.org` or `time.nist.gov` then a different SNTP server is returned each time on a round robin basis so that the load is spread between the servers in the pool. The `settime` method sets the RTC to the current time in UTC (Coordinated Universal Time). Currently time zones are not supported.

For example, to set the RTC you can use, `rtc.py`:

```
import ntptime
from machine import RTC
import network
from machine import Pin, Timer
from time import sleep_ms

def setup(country, ssid, key):
        .   .   .
wifi = setup(country, ssid, key)
print("Connected")
print(wifi.ifconfig())

ntptime.host = "pool.ntp.org"
ntptime.timeout = 1000
try:
    ntptime.settime()
except Exception:
    print("NTP server not available")
    pass
rtc = RTC()
print(rtc.datetime())
```

The RTC constructor also allows you to set the date and time:

```
RTC((year, month, day, weekday, hours, minutes,
                            seconds, microseconds))¶
```

The *weekday* value is Monday to Sunday corresponding to 0 to 6 and the *seconds* value has a fractional part accurate to the millisecond.

The RTC object has two methods:

- RTC.datetime(*datetimetuple*)¶

  Gets or sets the date and time of the RTC where *datetimetuple* is the same as for the constructor. With no arguments it returns a date, time tuple.

- RTC.init(*datetimetuple*)¶

  Initializes the RTC.

There is also a low-power memory associated with the RTC which can be used to store data while the processor is in deepsleep mode, as explained in the next section.

Light and Deep Sleep

The Pico has the ability to enter power saving states, but at the time of writing this hasn't been fully implemented in MicroPython.

There are two standard functions which put the Pico to sleep:

- machine.lightsleep(*wakeuptime*)
- machine.deepsleep(*wakeuptime*)

The *wakeuptime* is the maximum number of milliseconds the machine will sleep for. That is, if it isn't woken up by some other event, it will wake up after *wakeuptime* milliseconds. The difference between the two is that in deepsleep the contents of main memory is lost and this has a big effect on the way MicroPython behaves.

After a light sleep the program will continue on from where it left off. After a deep sleep the entire MicroPython system is rebooted and the system doesn't continue from where it went to sleep. This means that lightsleep is easier to use but it doesn't save as much power as deepsleep. To make use of deepsleep you have to name your program main.py as the system will load and run the Python program with this name on restart.

There are also systems that can supposedly be configured to wake the machine up from either form of sleep, but at the time of writing none of them work.

Flash Memory

The Raspberry Pi Pico doesn't have any removable storage, but you can use its internal flash memory to read and write files and it is easy to add an SD card reader.

The Pico has 2MB of flash memory which is used to store the MicroPython interpreter. The rest of the memory is converted into a file system that you can make use of from within your own MicroPython programs.

The flash memory is divided into a number of partitions that hold the system and data. Unlike some other implementations of MicroPython, only the data partition,1.6MB, is available and it is automatically mounted as the root when the system boots up. You can gain access to this partition using the rp2.Flash() function which returns a `Partition` object representing the data partition.

Once you have an instance of `Partition` you can use any of the following methods:

- `part.readblocks(block_num, buf, offset)`
- `part.writeblocks(block_num, buf, offset)`
- `part.ioctl(cmd, arg)`

These methods implement both the simple and extended block protocols defined by `os.AbstractBlockDev`.

Only a subset of ioctl commands are implemented for the Pico:

- 4 – Gets a count of the number of blocks and return an integer (`arg` is unused)

- 5 – Get the number of bytes in a block and returns an integer, or `None` in which case the default value of 512 is used

- 6 – Erases a block where `arg` is the block number to erase

Generally these commands are at too low a level to work with a partition and instead you need to install a file system so that you can work in terms of files. But if you really want to reinvent the wheel, then you can work directly in terms of raw blocks.

The `Flash` object is set up to ensure isolation from other partitions and its block numbers start at 0. So to write some data to the first block and read it back we can use `flash1.py`:

```
from rp2 import Flash
import os
flash=Flash()
os.umount("/")
print(flash.ioctl(4,0))
print(flash.ioctl(5,0))
flash.ioctl(6,0)
flash.writeblocks(0,b"Hello World")
buf=bytearray(25)
flash.readblocks(0,buf)
print(buf)
```

First we umount the file system so that it can't be used. If the partition was left mounted, the file system could use the block we are about to use and overwrite it. Next we get the number of blocks and the block size. Before we can write new data to a block we have to erase it using ioctl command 6. After this we can write any number of bytes up to the block size. Reading the data back is just a matter of setting the length of the buffer to specify the number of bytes to read in. If you try this out you will find that we have stored "Hello World":

```
bytearray(b'Hello World\x00\x00\x00\x00\x008\x01\x00\x00
                                       \xa0\x00 \x0b')
```

The bytes beyond "Hello World" are whatever was already stored in the block.

File Systems

Working at the block level is fairly tedious and something you can generally avoid. As already mentioned, when MicroPython is first started it ensures that there is a file system installed in the partition and mounts it on the root ready for you to use.

The Pico supports two general file systems – VfsFat, a traditional FAT system, and VfsLfs2, MicroPython's own littlefs v2. You can create either type of file system on the data partition. The advantage of FAT is that it is a standard file system that can be read by other devices, but as we are using the internal Flash memory this isn't relevant. FAT is more prone to errors than the alternative littlefs v2, which has the advantage of supporting wear-leveling. For these reasons the Pico creates a littlefs v2 file system for you to use.

To work with a file system you first have to create it in a suitable partition – usually indicated by block_dev:

```
os.VfsFat.mkfs(block_dev)
```

creates a FAT file system and:

```
os.VfsLfs2.mkfs(block_dev, readsize=32, progsize=32,
                          lookahead=32, mtime=True)
```

creates a littlefs v2 file system. Creating a file system on a partition is essentially formatting it and hence all existing data is lost.

Once you have created a file system it can be mounted either as the root file system or on any existing subdirectory:

```
os.mount(fsobj, mount_point, *, readonly)
```

To make modifications to the file system you have to unmount it:

```
os.umount(mount_point)
```

You can install an alternative file system or just reformat the partition to remove all of the data, as for example in flash2.py:

```
from rp2 import Flash
import os
flash = Flash()
os.umount('/')
os.VfsLfs2.mkfs(flash)
os.mount(flash, '/')
```

Most of the time you simply use a file system via the standard MicroPython os functions:

- os.chdir(path) Change current directory
- os.getcwd() Get the current directory
- os.ilistdir(dir) Iterate through directories returning:
                    (name, type, inode[, size])
- os.listdir(dir) List the given directory
- os.mkdir(path) Create a new directory
- os.remove(path) Remove a file
- os.rmdir(path) Remove a directory
- os.rename(old_path, new_path) Rename a file
- os.stat(path) Get the status of a file or directory
- os.sync() Sync all file systems

There is also:

- os.statvfs(path) Get the status of a file system

which returns a tuple with the file system information in the following order:

- f_bsize – block size
- f_frsize – fragment size
- f_blocks – size in f_frsize units
- f_bfree – number of free blocks
- f_bavail – number of free blocks for unprivileged users
- f_files – number of inodes
- f_ffree – number of free inodes
- f_favail – number of free inodes for unprivileged users
- f_flag – mount flags
- f_namemax – maximum filename length

363

Not all values are returned for a `littlefs` v2 file system.

You can also open a file and work with it using the standard stream functions:

```
read(), write(), readinto(), seek(), flush(), close()
```

For example, `flash3.py`:

```python
from rp2 import Flash
import os

print(os.listdir("/"))
f = open("Hello.txt","wt")
f.write("Hello World")
f.close
f.flush()
print(os.listdir("/"))
f = open("Hello.txt","rt")
s = f.read()
f.close
print(s)
```

If you try this out you will discover that there is a new file called `Hello.txt` and you should see its contents displayed. Notice that you do need the flush as the system is buffered and if you simply open the file after closing it you will find that it is empty.

As this is non-volatile storage, you can use it to save state between boots.

Adding an External SD Card Reader

Although the Pico doesn't have an SD card reader it is fairly easy to add one. Add-on SD card readers are available to order at very reasonable prices ($1.50):

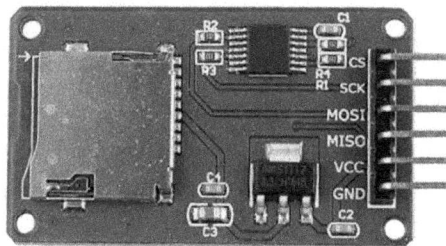

The problem is that most have no documentation or specifications. In addition they tend to lack a card-detect and a write-protect pin.

Connection to the Pico is fairly easy via one of the SPI buses. The only complication is that most of the devices need a 5V supply. They work at 3.3V logic levels and so can be directly connected to the Pico and have an onboard voltage regulator to reduce the supply to 3.3V. Most claim to work if powered from 3.3V, but this depends on the regulator used and some fail or become unreliable. The Pico has a suitable 5V supply pin in the form of VBUS but notice that this only works if it is being powered from the USB connection. In most cases this is the VCC connection to use.

Notice that you don't actually need an SD card reader as the pins on an SD card are nothing more than an SPI bus. The problem is you have to find a way to connect to them!

You can use any GPIO lines for the SPI connection and in this example the following are used:

SCK GPIO 10

CS GPIO 9

MISO GPIO 11

MOSI GPIO 8

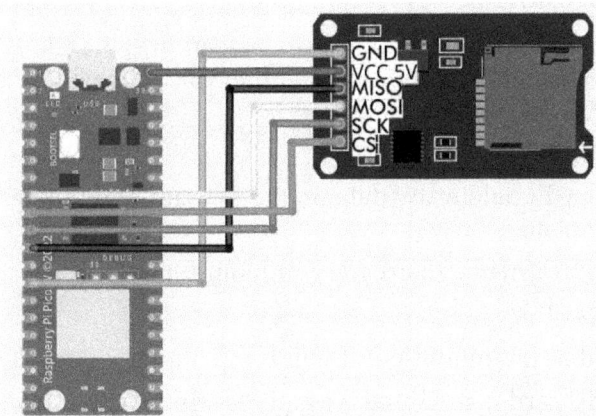

Once you have this wired up you need an SD card freshly formatted using FAT and a single partition – which is what you get if you use a new SD card. Make sure the card is correctly inserted before moving on to the software.

The SD Card driver isn't currently a default module in MicroPython. The simplest thing to do is to go to:

```
https://github.com/micropython/micropython-lib/blob/master/
                    micropython/drivers/storage/sdcard/sdcard.py
```

and copy and paste the Python code into a file called `sdcard.py`. Upload this to the Pico and you should be able to include it in your program.

To make use of it you first have to define the SPI interface:

```
spi = machine.SPI(1,
                    baudrate=100000,
                    polarity=0,
                    phase=0,
                    bits=8,
                    firstbit=machine.SPI.MSB,
                    sck=machine.Pin(10),
                    mosi=machine.Pin(11),
                    miso=machine.Pin(8))
```

and a GPIO line to use as CS:

```
cs = machine.Pin(9, machine.Pin.OUT)
```

You then use these to create an instance of `sdCard`:

```
sd = sdcard.SDCard(spi, cs)
```

The instance is a block device to which you can install a file system and then mount. For example, assuming that the SD card isn't formatted, you can format it to a FAT file system using:

```
os.VfsFat.mkfs(sd)
```

Notice that this will delete any data on the SD card and it takes a few minutes to complete.

Once you have a formatted card you can mount it:

```
os.mount(sd,"/sd")
```

The folder used as the mount point will be created if it doesn't exist.

Now that the SD card is mounted we can read and write it using the standard file operations.

A complete test program, sd.py, that erases the SD card, writes some data and reads it back is:

```
import machine
import os
import sdcard
cs = machine.Pin(9, machine.Pin.OUT)
spi = machine.SPI(1,
                  baudrate=100000,
                  polarity=0,
                  phase=0,
                  bits=8,
                  firstbit=machine.SPI.MSB,
                  sck=machine.Pin(10),
                  mosi=machine.Pin(11),
                  miso=machine.Pin(8))
sd = sdcard.SDCard(spi, cs)
os.VfsFat.mkfs(sd)
os.mount(sd,"/sd")
f=open("/sd/Hello.txt", "w")
f.write("Hello World!\r\n")
f.write("Some more data\r\n")
f.close()
f=open("/sd/Hello.txt", "r")
data = f.read()
print(data)
```

If you don't want to format the card first, comment out the line:

```
os.VfsFat.mkfs(sd)
```

As the SD card is FAT formatted it can be read in any machine that has an SD card slot.

If you find you have an SD card that doesn't work with this program try a lower clock speed. You can subsequently try increasing the clock speed to see if the SD card reader will cope. Some SD cards will fail to work at any speed as they don't implement the SPI bus in the correct way.

Summary

- Although the Pico has two cores, making use of the second processor is full of subtle traps and is best avoided unless you have the time and confidence to test your program.

- The watchdog timer can be used to make your program unstoppable. When you want to stop it you need to use a flash memory-wiping program such as FlashNuke.

- There is a Real Time Clock, RTC, that you can set using the `ntptime` object.

- You can work with the internal flash memory as a partition and you can install file systems onto the partition and then work with files.

- If you add an external SD card reader you can work with an SD card using the same techniques as used for the internal flash memory.

Chapter 21

Direct To The Hardware

MicroPython provides classes and methods to let you access most of the major hardware features of the Pico. They are very simple wrappers around the basic mechanism of working with the hardware – memory-mapped registers. Unfortunately at the time of writing there are many hardware features which are simply not exposed via MicroPython. In most cases it is possible to extend what you access using lower-level interactions with the hardware. This way you can stay in MicroPython while writing and reading the low-level, register-based hardware.

The obvious reason for knowing how to use memory-mapped registers is that if MicroPython doesn't provide a function that does just what you want, you simply create it! Perhaps a better reason is just to know how things work. In this chapter we take a look at how the Pico presents its hardware for you to use and how to access it via basic software.

Registers

Some processors have special ways of connecting devices, but the Pico's processor uses the more common memory-mapping approach. In this, each external device is represented by a set of memory locations or "registers" that control it. Each bit in the register controls some aspect of the way the device behaves. Groups of bits also can be interpreted as short integers which set operating values or modes.

How do you access a register? MicroPython provides a number of ways of doing this but the simplest is to make use of the mem functions in the machine module:

```
machine.mem32[address]      Returns or sets a 32-bit value at the address
machine.mem16[address]      Returns or sets a 16-bit value at the address
machine.mem8[address]       Returns or sets an 8-bit value at the address
```

The only difficult part is in working out the address you need to use and the value that sets or resets the bits you need to modify.

If you look in the documentation you will find that the GPIO registers for the Pico using the RP2040 start at address 0x40014000, but for the Pico 2 using the RP2350, the start address is 0x40028000. The registers are defined by their offset from this starting address and these are mostly the same for both the Pico and Pico 2, but the Pico 2 sometimes has additional registers to provide secure access functions.

What this means is that, if you write code that directly accesses registers, the program has to be customized for the Pico or the Pico 2. Fortunately there is an easy way to do this. More difficult is coping with any extra registers that the Pico 2 is using. In such cases the program is specific to the Pico 2.

As already mentioned, most of the register offsets are the same for the Pico 2 as the Pico. So, for example, the table of GPIO registers in both cases starts:

Offset	Register Name	Description
0x000	GPIO0_STATUS	GPIO status
0x004	GPIO0_CTRL	GPIO control including function select and overrides
0X008	GPIO1_STATUS	GPIO status
0x00c	GPIO1_CTRL	GPIO control including function select and overrides
... and so on down to		
0x0ec	GPIO29_CTRL	GPIO control including function select and overrides

You can see that there are two registers for each GPIO line from GPIO 0 to GPIO 29, one control register and one status register.

Each register has the same format for each GPIO line. For example, the status register is:

Bits	Name	Description	Type	Reset
31:27	Reserved		-	-
26	IRQTOPROC	Interrupt to processors, after override applied	RO	0x0
25	Reserved		-	-
24	IRQFROMPAD	Interrupt from pad, before override applied	RO	0x0
23:20	Reserved		-	-
19	INTOPERI	Input signal to peripheral, after override applied	RO	0x0
18	Reserved		-	-
17	INFROMPAD	Input signal from pad, before override applied	RO	0x0
16:14	Reserved		-	-
13	OETOPAD	Output enable to pad, after override applied	RO	0x0
12	OEFROMPERI	Output enable from peripheral, before override	RO	0x0
11:10	Reserved		-	-
9	OUTTOPAD	Output signal to pad after override applied	RO	0x0
8	OUTFROMPERI	Output signal from peripheral, before override	RO	0x0
7: 0	Reserved		-	-

Even here there is a slight difference - in the RP2350 bit 8 isn't used for OUTFROMPERI but is reserved.

You can read the current value of the register using:

```
from machine import mem32
#addrGPIO = 0x40014000   #pico
addrGPIO = 0x40028000    #pico 2
value=mem32[addrGPIO]
print(bin(value))
```

This prints the current status of GPIO 0 in binary. If you want to find the status of GP*n* you need to use address addrGPIO+2*n*. Usually addresses are specified as a base address, i.e. where things start, and an offset that has to be added to the base to get the address of a specific device.

This is the general way you work with peripheral devices such as the PWM units or I2C hardware, but the GPIO is special in that it has another set of registers that control it.

Single-Cycle IO Block

At this point you might think that we are ready to access the state of the GPIO lines for general input and output. This isn't quite the whole story. To accommodate the fact that the processor has two cores, and to make access faster to important devices, there is a special connection, the SIO or Single-cycle IO Block, between the cores and, among other things, the GPIO. The SIO connects directly to the two cores and they can perform single-cycle 32-bit reads and writes to any register in the SIO. Notice that the SIO is not connected via the general address bus.

You can see the general structure of the SIO in the diagram below. You can find out about the other devices it connects to from the documentation - our focus is on the GPIO lines.

The original Pico with the RP2040 has a simple design:

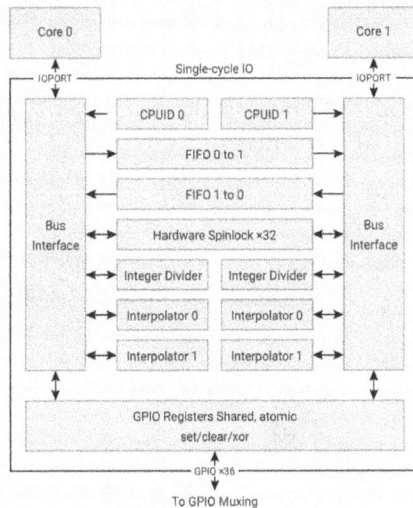

The Pico 2's RP2350 is more complicated due to the need to implement a secure version and a non-secure version:

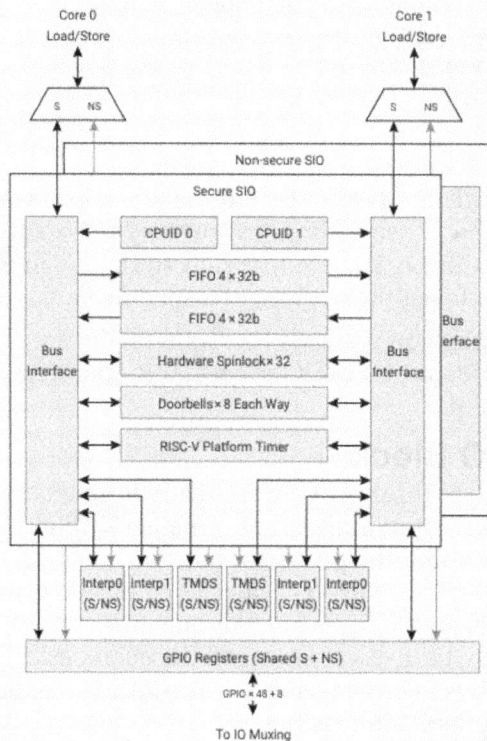

Core 0
Load/Store

Core 1
Load/Store

S   NS

S   NS

Non-secure SIO

Secure SIO

| CPUID 0 | CPUID 1 |

FIFO 4 × 32b

FIFO 4 × 32b

Bus Interface

Bus Interface

Bus Interface

Hardware Spinlock × 32

Doorbells × 8 Each Way

RISC-V Platform Timer

| Interp0 (S/NS) | Interp1 (S/NS) | TMDS (S/NS) | TMDS (S/NS) | Interp1 (S/NS) | Interp0 (S/NS) |

GPIO Registers (Shared S + NS)

GPIO × 48 + 8

To IO Muxing

Notice that the GPIO lines are multipurpose and the SIO only has control when they are being used as GPIO lines. In this sense the SIO is just another peripheral that can take control of a GPIO line.

The SIO provides a set of registers that makes using the GPIO much faster and much easier. The basic registers are:

GPIO_OUT	Sets all GPIO lines to high or low
GPIO_IN	Reads all GPIO lines
GPIO_OE	Sets any GPIO line to output driver or high impedance

There are also three registers, SET, CLR and XOR, that make working with GPIO_OUT and GPIO_OE easier. Each of these can be thought of as a mask that sets, clears or XORs bits in the corresponding register. For example, GPIO_OUT_SET can be used to set just those bits in GPIO_OUT that correspond to the positions that are set high.

The locations of these registers are as offsets from 0xd0000000 in both the Pico and Pico 2:

Offset Pico 2	Offset Pico	Name	Description
0x004	0x004	GPIO_IN	GPIO input value
0x010	0x010	GPIO_OUT	GPIO output value
0x018	0x014	GPIO_OUT_SET	GPIO output value set
0x020	0x018	GPIO_OUT_CLR	GPIO output value clear
0x028	0x01c	GPIO_OUT_XOR	GPIO output value XOR
0x030	0x020	GPIO_OE	GPIO output enable
0x038	0x024	GPIO_OE_SET	GPIO output enable set
0x040	0x028	GPIO_OE_CLR	GPIO output enable clear
0x048	0x02c	GPIO_OE_XOR	GPIO output enable XOR

Blinky Revisited

Now we can re-write Blinky yet again, but this time using direct access to the SIO GPIO registers, blinky.py.

```
from machine import mem32,Pin
from time import sleep_ms
led=Pin(2,mode=Pin.OUT)
addrSIO = 0xd0000000
while True:
    mem32[addrSIO + 0x018] = 1 << 2   #0x014 for Pico
    sleep_ms(500)
    mem32[addrSIO + 0x020] = 1 << 2   #0x18 for Pico
    sleep_ms(500)
```

This program uses the standard MicroPython class to set the GPIO line to SIO control and output. If you think that this is cheating, it is an exercise in setting the line correctly using the GPIO control register and the SIO.

This example is a demonstration rather than being useful, but there are some very useful functions we can now write using our knowledge of how the GPIO lines are controlled. MicroPython is limited to controlling a single GPIO line at a time, but the hardware can change or read multiple GPIO lines in a single register operation. For example:

```
def gpio_get():
    return mem32[0xd0000000+0x010]
```

Here the get function simply reads the GPIO_OUT register which has a single bit for the output state of each GPIO line. Notice that GPIO lines set to output reflect their last written-to state.

373

A set function to simply write the mask to the GPIO_OUT_SET register is:

```
def gpio_set(mask):
    mem32[0xd0000000+0x018] = mask # 0x014 for Pico
```

A clear function is just as easy and this just writes to the GPIO_OUT_CLR register:

```
def gpio_clear(mask):
    mem32[0xd0000000+0x20] = mask # 0x018 for Pico
```

Example I - Simultaneous Setting of GPIO Lines

You can use these two functions to set or clear any GPIO lines, but you often want to select a set of bits and set or clear them in one operation. For example, if you want to change two or more GPIO lines in phase, i.e. all high or all low, then you can use set and clear one after the other. For example;

```
gpio_set(0x3)
gpio_clear(0x3)
```

sets the bottom 2 bits and toggles GPIO0 and GPIO1 together. Both turn on and off at exactly the same time.

Now consider how you set GPIO0 high when GPIO1 is low?

The best you can do is:

```
gpio_set(0x1)
gpio_clear(0x2)
gpio_set(0x2)
gpio_clear(0x1)
```

While this does set the GPIO lines correctly, the changes don't happen at the same time.

What we need is a function that will set any group of GPIO lines to 0 or 1 at the same time:

```
def gpio_set(value, mask):
```

The mask gives the GPIO lines that need to be changed, i.e. it determines the group and the value gives the state they are to be set to. For example, if mask is 0111 and value is 0100 and the low four bits of the register are 1010 then reg & ~mask is 1000, value & mask is 0100 and finally reg | value is 1100. You can see that bits 0 to 3 have been set to 100 and bit 4 has been unchanged.

The trick to working out how to do this is to construct one mask to set the bits that need to be set and another to unset the bits that need to be unset.

If a bit is to be set, it needs a 1 in the mask and a 1 in the data and the mask to set bits is:

```
setmask = mask & data
```

If a bit is to be unset it needs a 1 in the mask and 0 in the data, so the mask to reset bits is:

```
resetmask = mask & ~data
```

Applying both gives the required result:

```
(value | setmask) & ~(resetmask) =
```
$$(value \mid (mask \& data)) \& \sim(mask \& \sim data)$$

which, after simplification, is:

```
value & ~mask | mask & data
```

As demonstrated in Chapter 4, in phase2.py the value,mask function can be used to set GPIO lines simultaneously:

```
from machine import Pin
import machine

def gpio_get():
    return machine.mem32[0xd0000000+0x010]
def gpio_set(value,mask):
    machine.mem32[0xd0000000+0x010] =
machine.mem32[0xd0000000+0x010] & ~mask | value & mask
pin=Pin(2,Pin.OUT)
pin=Pin(3,Pin.OUT)
value1=1<<2 | 0<<3
value2=0<<2 | 1<<3
mask=1<<2 | 1<<3
while True:
    gpio_set(value1,mask)
    gpio_set(value2,mask)
```

This sets lines GPIO 2 and GPIO 3 to 01 and 10 on each pass through the loop:

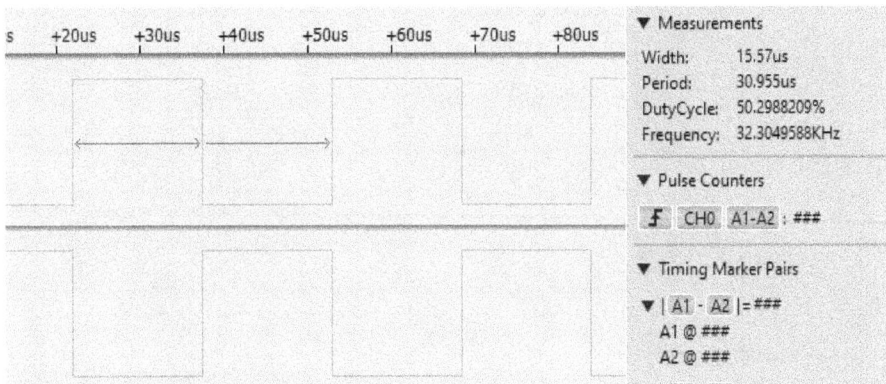

Example II - Events

In Chapter 7 the idea of events was introduced, but MicroPython doesn't provide any access to events. The solution is to add our own function that accesses the GPIO register that records interrupts. This is a register in the GPIO set of registers rather than in the SIO as GPIO interrupts aren't specific to what is controlling the GPIO line.

The base address of the GPIO registers is `0x40014000`. After the end of the set of status and control registers, starting at offset `0x0f0`, there is a block of four interrupt registers that record the status of the GPIO lines. Each group of four bits gives the status of the various level and edge events:

Bits	Name	Type	Reset
31	GPIO7_EDGE_HIGH	WC	0x0
30	GPIO7_EDGE_LOW	WC	0x0
29	GPIO7_LEVEL_HIGH	RO	0x0
28	GPIO7_LEVEL_LOW	RO	0x0
27	GPIO6_EDGE_HIGH	WC	0x0
26	GPIO6_EDGE_LOW	WC	0x0
25	GPIO6_LEVEL_HIGH	RO	0x0
24	GPIO6_LEVEL_LOW	RO	0x0
	. . .		
8	GPIO2_LEVEL_LOW	RW	0x0
7	GPIO1_EDGE_HIGH	RW	0x0
6	GPIO1_EDGE_LOW	RW	0x0
5	GPIO1_LEVEL_HIGH	RW	0x0
4	GPIO1_LEVEL_LOW	RW	0x0
3	GPIO0_EDGE_HIGH	RW	0x0
2	GPIO0_EDGE_LOW	RW	0x0
1	GPIO0_LEVEL_HIGH	RW	0x0
0	GPIO0_LEVEL_LOW	RW	0x0

The format of the raw interrupt registers is more complicated than the one-bit-to-one-GPIO-line arrangement we have encountered before. In this case there are four bits per GPIO line and they record different interrupt types. The first four bits of the first register record interrupts on GPIO 0:

3	GPIO0_EDGE_HIGH	WC	0x0
2	GPIO0_EDGE_LOW	WC	0x0
1	GPIO0_LEVEL_HIGH	RO	0x0
0	GPIO0_LEVEL_LOW	RO	0x0

This pattern is repeated for each of the GPIO lines and, when all of the bits in the first register have been used, the pattern continues in the second register with GPIO 8 and so on. Each register records the event data for eight GPIO lines. Notice that each of the bits is set if the event that would cause the interrupt occurs – the interrupt itself only occurs if it is enabled. What this means is that the level bits track the current level of the GPIO line and the edge bits are set if an edge of that type has occurred. The WC in the third column indicates that the bit is cleared if you write to it and this is how the event is cleared.

The new problem here is that we have to work out which register is concerned with which GPIO line – each register looks after eight GPIO lines – and which group of four bits in the register gives the events for that GPIO line. The following function accepts the GPIO number and works out which register and group of bits it corresponds to:

```
def gpio_get_events(pinNo):
    IO_BANK0_BASE=0x40028000  #Pico 2
    INTR0=0x230 #Pico 2
  # IO_BANK0_BASE=0x40014000 #Pico
  # INTR0=0xF0 #Pico
    mask = 0xF << 4 * (pinNo % 8)
    intrAddr = IO_BANK0_BASE + INTR0 + (pinNo // 8)*4
    return (machine.mem32[intrAddr] & mask) >> (4 * (pinNo % 8))
```

The calculation for the address of the register needed is just the base address plus the offset of the first interrupt register which is then subjected to the operation +(pinNo//8)*4. As each register deals with a group of 8, the integer division pinNo//8 gives the number of the register needed and, as each register is four bytes, *4 converts this to a byte address. The mask is constructed using a similar technique. The first GPIO line uses four bits starting at 0, the second uses four bits starting at 4 the third at 8 and so on, i.e. (4*(pinNo % 8), and this is used to create a mask.

Once you have the basic way of accessing the bits you need, you can reuse it to create a clear events function:

```
def gpio_clear_events(pinNo, events):
    IO_BANK0_BASE=0x40028000   #Pico 2
    INTR0=0x230 #Pico 2
  # IO_BANK0_BASE=0x40014000 #Pico
  # INTR0=0xF0 #Pico
    intrAddr = IO_BANK0_BASE + INTR0 + (pinNo // 8)*4
    machine.mem32[intrAddr] = events << (4 * (pinNo % 8))
```

To clear the raw interrupt bit you simply have to write a zero to it.

Example III – PAD, Pull, Drive and Schmitt

Each GPIO line has an identical input output stage, called a PAD, which is the connection to the outside world, no matter what mode the GPIO line is being used in. This is fundamental to the workings of the GPIO line and you might be wondering why it is being introduced so late? The answer is that MicroPython doesn't fully support it and the aspects of the PAD that it does support, Pull Up and Pull Down, are simple enough. If you are interested in the finer details then you are going to have to implement functions that work with them.

The structure of the PAD can be seen below:

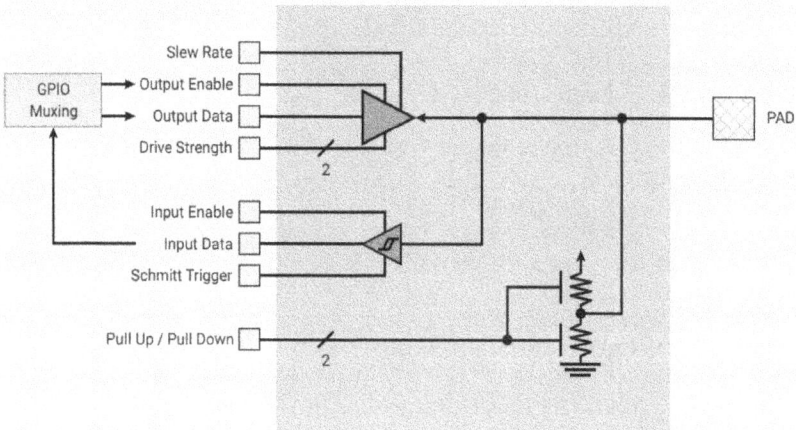

You can see that under program control you can set the pull up/pull down configuration and enable the input/output. The input also has a Schmitt trigger that can be enabled to clean up noisy inputs. The output can be customized by slew rate, how fast it changes and drive strength.

Before moving on to the software, it is worth explaining the basic ideas of the options. The Schmitt trigger adds hysteresis to the input line. This means that before the state changes from high to low it has to cross a threshold, but to change back to a low state it has to cross a lower threshold. This acts like a limited debounce mechanism in that it stops the line from going low because the input drops a little after going high. The Pico's Schmitt trigger uses thresholds of a 0.2V difference if the processor supply voltage is 2.5V to 3.3V and 0.18V if the voltage is 1.8V. What this means is that at 3.3V the input has to be greater than 2V to be a one, but after this the voltage has to fall to 1.8V before it changes back to a zero. For a zero, the thresholds are 0.8V to change a zero and 2V to change back to a one.

The output drive strength isn't to do with how much current the GPIO line can source, it is about the voltage output at different currents. It is the effective output resistance. Each time the drive current is increased by 2mA another transistor is used in the drive, so lowering the output resistance. This has the effect of increasing or decreasing the voltage at the pin. For example, if you set the drive to 1 then, if you want to keep the output voltage at or above 2.62V, i.e. a logic 1, you can't draw more than 2mA. Put more simply, if you want the output to maintain voltages that are within the threshold for a logic 1 or 0 then you can only draw 2, 4, 8 or 12mA from the GPIO line depending on the setting of the drive strength. If you draw more current, this is fine, but the voltage will fall below the standards for 3.3V logic.

The final option is to change the slew rate. There is no information on this in the datasheet, but slowing the rate of change of the GPIO line can be useful when driving long lines or reactive loads. How useful this is in practice is a matter of experimentation.

If you want to work with the PAD directly then you need to know the location and format of the PAD control registers. These start at 0x4001c000, Pico and 0x40038000 Pico 2 and the first, controlling the GPIO 0 PAD is at offset 0x04 and in general the register for GPIO n PAD is at offset 4(n+1).

The format of the PAD register is:

Bits	Name	Description	Type	Reset
31:8	Reserved	Pico 2 31:9 are reserved	-	-
8		Pico 2 only ISO: Pad isolation control. Remove this once the pad is configured by software.	RW	0x1
7	OD	Output disable. Has priority over output enable from peripherals	RW	0x0
6	IE	Input enable	RW	0x1
5:4	DRIVE	Drive strength. 0x0 → 2mA 0x1 → 4mA 0x2 → 8mA 0x3 → 12mA	RW	0x1
3	PUE	Pull up enable	RW	0x0
2	PDE	Pull down enable	RW	0x1
1	SCHMITT	Enable Schmitt trigger	RW	0x1
0	SLEWFAST	Slew rate control. 1 = Fast, 0 = Slow	RW	0x0

Using this information it is fairly easy to write functions to set each of the characteristics of the PAD. For example, to read the slew rate:

```
PADS_BANK0_BASE = 0x4001c000   #Pico
PADS_BANK0_BASE = 0x40038000   #Pico 2

def pad_get_slew(gpio):
    return mem32[PADS_BANK0_BASE+(gpio+1)*4] & 0x01
```

To set the skew rate:

```
def pad_set_slew(gpio,value):
    if value:
        mem32[PADS_BANK0_BASE+(gpio+1)*4]=
                mem32[PADS_BANK0_BASE+(gpio+1)*4] | 0x1
    else:
        mem32[PADS_BANK0_BASE+(gpio+1)*4]=
                mem32[PADS_BANK0_BASE+(gpio+1)*4] & 0xFFFFFFFE
```

Getting and setting the Schmitt trigger is just as easy, but now we set or clear the second bit, not the first:

```
def pad_set_schmitt(gpio,value):
    if value:
        mem32[PADS_BANK0_BASE+(gpio+1)*4]=
                mem32[PADS_BANK0_BASE+(gpio+1)*4] | 0x2
    else:
        mem32[PADS_BANK0_BASE+(gpio+1)*4]=
                mem32[PADS_BANK0_BASE+(gpio+1)*4] & 0xFFFFFFFD
```

Setting the drive is slightly more complicated as it is a three-bit value:

```
def pad_get_drive(gpio):
    return (mem32[PADS_BANK0_BASE+(gpio+1)*4] & 0xE0) >> 5


def pad_set_drive(gpio, value):
    mem32[PADS_BANK0_BASE+(gpio+1)*4]=
        mem32[PADS_BANK0_BASE+(gpio+1)*4] ^ (0xE0 & (value<< 5))
```

The set function uses the same logic as the value mask function given earlier to only change the bits we are interested in changing. Of course, we don't need to deal with the pull-ups or pull-downs as there are methods that do the job.

Digging Deeper

There is so much more to explore about the Pico and Pico W hardware, but you now should have the confidence to read their datasheets to find out how the registers control things and implement MicroPython functions to extend what you can do. The biggest difficulty is finding the register that contains the bits that reflect the status or control whatever it is you are interested in. Once you have found this out, the only remaining difficulty is in working out how to set or clear the bits you need to work with without changing other bits. It also has to be said that hardware documentation at this level is often incomplete due to assumptions the writer makes about what you should already know. In such a circumstance your best approach is the experimental method. Work out the simplest program you can think of to verify that you understand what the hardware does – and if you are wrong always check the addresses and bits you are changing before concluding that things work differently to the manual.

Summary

- All of the Pico peripherals, including the GPIO lines, are controlled by registers – special memory locations that you write and read to configure and use the hardware. Exactly where the registers are positioned in address space is given in the documentation as a base address used for all of the similar registers and an offset that has to be added to the base to get the address of a particular register.

- Unfortunately some of the base addresses and offsets are different for the Pico and the Pico 2.

- The SIO block provides a more convenient way to access the GPIO lines and it has a different set of addresses and registers to the GPIO lines.

- With knowledge of how things work, you can add functions that are missing from MicroPython such as events and PAD control.

- Each GPIO line connects to the outside world via a PAD which has a number of configurable elements such as pull-up, slew rate and so on.

Index

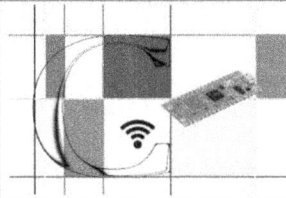

Master the Raspberry Pi Pico
ISBN: 978-1871962819

Having introduced the Pico WiFi Stack and basic network connections, this book looks at how to use TCP to create the all-important Protocol Control Block and then tackle implementing an HTTP client. As well as covering the basic mechanics of using lwIP, we also concentrate on how to organize the use of an asynchronous library based on callbacks, implementing encryption using mbedtls to create an HTTPS client. The later chapters are devoted to specific protocols, making use of both lwIP and mbedtls. We look at UDP; SNTP to set the Pico W's real time clock; SMTP to allow email notifications and MQTT.

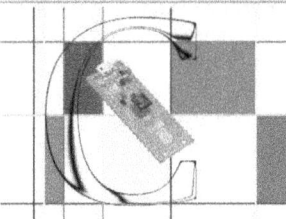

Programming The Raspberry Pi Pico/W In C, Third Edition
ISBN: 978-1871962963

This updated and expanded edition was prompted by the launch of the Pico 2 and Pico 2W which use a new chip, the RP2350, which offers significant improvements but also requires changes. After covering the GPIO, outputs and inputs, events and interrupts, it gives you hands-on experience of PWM, the SPI bus, the I2C bus and the 1-Wire bus. One of the key advantages of the Pico is its PIO (Programmable I/O) and while this is an advanced feature it is introduced in this book. New in this edition is coverage of FreeRTOS – a realtime operating system that provides a way of organizing your program into asynchronous tasks. FreeRTOS also provides arguably the best way of utilizing both cores of the Pico2.

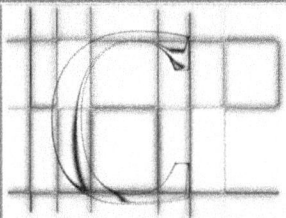

Fundamental C: Getting Closer To The Machine
ISBN: 978-1871962604

For beginners, the book covers installing an IDE and GCC before writing a Hello World program and then presents the fundamental building blocks of any program - variables, assignment and expressions, flow of control using conditionals and loops.

When programming in C you need to think about the way data is represented, and this book emphasizes the idea of modifying how a bit pattern is treated using type punning and unions and tackles the topic of undefined behavior, which is ignored in many books on C.

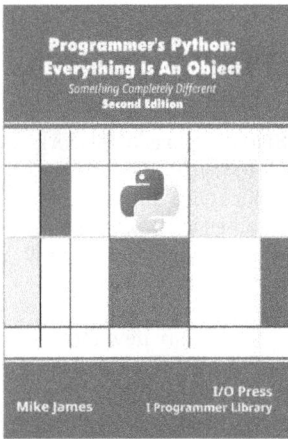

Programmer's Python: Everything is an Object, Second Edition
ISBN: 978-1871962741

This is the first in the *Something Completely Different* series of book that look at what makes Python special and sets it apart from other programming languages. It explains the deeper logic in the approach that Python 3 takes to classes and objects. The subject is roughly speaking everything to do with the way Python implements objects - metaclass; class; object; attribute; and all of the other facilities such as functions, methods and the many "magic methods" that Python uses to make it all work.

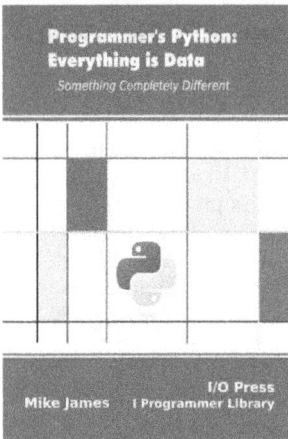

Programmer's Python: Everything is Data
ISBN: 978-1871962595

Following the same philosophy, this book shows how Python treats data in a distinctly Pythonic way. Python's data objects are both very usable and very extensible. From the unlimited precision integers, referred to as bignums, through the choice of a list to play the role of the array, to the availability of the dictionary as a built-in data type, This book is what you need to help you make the most of these special features.

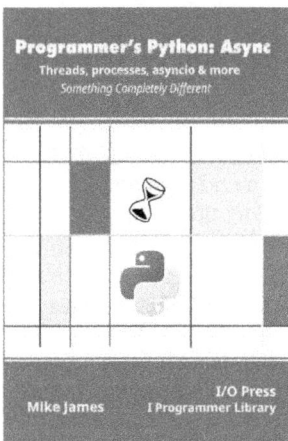

Programmer's Python: Async
ISBN: 978-1871962595

An application that doesn't make use of async code is wasting a huge amount of the machine's potential. Subtitled "Threads, processes, asyncio & more, this volume is about asynchronous programming, something that is hard to get right, but well worth the trouble and reveals how Python tackles the problems in its own unique way.

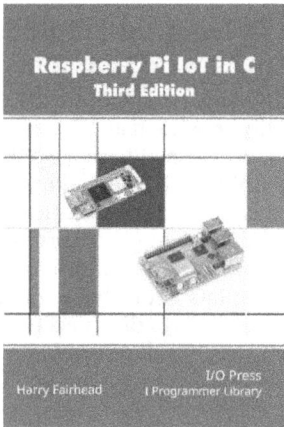

Raspberry Pi IoT in C, Third Edition
ISBN: 978-1871962840 (Paperback)
ISBN: 978-1871962154 (Hardback)

In this book you will find a practical approach to understanding electronic circuits and datasheets and translating this to code, specifically using the C programming language. The main reason for choosing C is speed, a crucial factor when you are writing programs to communicate with the outside world. If you are familiar with another programming language, C shouldn't be hard to pick up. This third edition has been brought up-to-date and includes the Pi Zero 2W and the latest OS. An entire chapter is devoted to the Pi 5 and it is covered elsewhere in the book wherever possible.

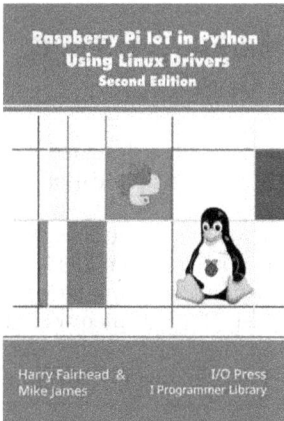

Raspberry Pi IoT in Python With Linux Drivers, 2nd Edition
ISBN: 9781871962864 (Paperback)
ISBN: 9781871962178 (Hardback)

This is the Python version of this book and covers much of the same ground. It explains how to use Python to connect to and control external devices with the full current range of Raspberry Pis, including the Pi 5 and the Raspberry Pi Zero 2W using the standard Linux drivers.

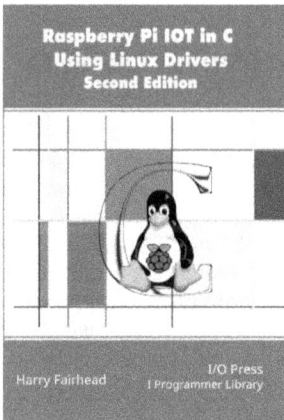

Raspberry Pi IoT in C With Linux Drivers, 2nd Edition
ISBN: 978-1871962857(Paperback)
ISBN: 9781871962161 (Hardback)

This second edition has been updated and expanded to cover the Raspberry Pi 5 and the Raspberry Pi Zero W/2W. There are Linux drivers for many off-the-shelf IoT devices and they provide a very easy-to-use, high-level way of working. The big problem is that there is very little documentation to help you get started. This book explains the principles so that you can tackle new devices.

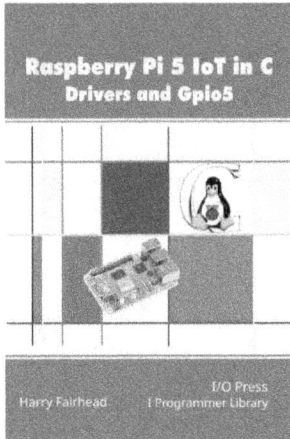

Raspberry Pi 5 IoT In C: Drivers and Gpio5
ISBN: 978-1871962949

As the Pi 5 uses the RP1 chip to implement its peripherals, it does not work with the usual IoT libraries such as Wiring Pi, bcm2835, pigpio and so on. Gpio5, is designed to replace them and provide direct access to GPIO, PWM, I2C, SPI and more. This makes the Pi 5 much more capable of IoT applications. With Linux, the accepted way to access the outside world and other devices is to use drivers. Discovering, installing and using drivers is the topic of early chapters of this book. Having seen how to work with drivers we move on to direct access to the hardware via the Gpio5 library, which is developed and enhanced throughout the book.

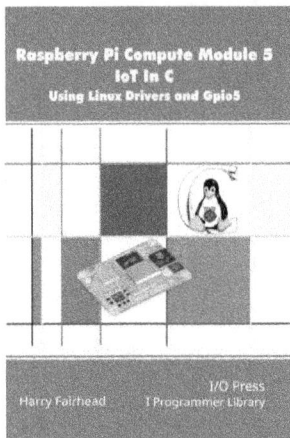

Raspberry Pi Compute Module 5 IoT In C: Using Linux Drivers and Gpio5
ISBN: 978-1871962956

The Raspberry Pi Compute Module 5, CM5, is designed specifically to be used in IoT and embedded applications. The problems are exacerbated by the use of the RP1 chip to implement the CM5's peripherals which means it doesn't work with the usual IoT libraries such as Wiring Pi, bcm2835, pigpio and so on. This book demonstrates how to interact with the hardware both using Linux drivers, the accepted way of accessing external devices, and via Gpio5, a new open source IoT library specifically for the Raspberry Pi 5 and CM5, that provides direct access to the CM5's hardware, with functions for working with GPIO, PWM, I2C, SPI and more.

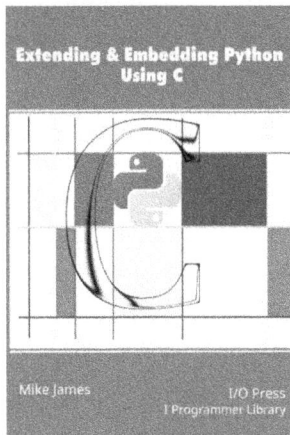

Extending & Embedding Python Using C
ISBN: 978-1871962833

Writing a C extension for Python is good for fun and profit! The fun part is that adding Python to C gives you so much more power and a deeper understanding of how Python works. The internals of Python are worth knowing about because they suggest new approaches to other problems. As well as being interesting, it is also a valuable skill. Extending & Embedding Python Using C tells you everything you need to know about the C API, which is what you use to create an extension. It is essentially the Python runtime and so exploring it tells you a lot about Python. You don't need to be an expert Python programmer to create an extension, but it helps.